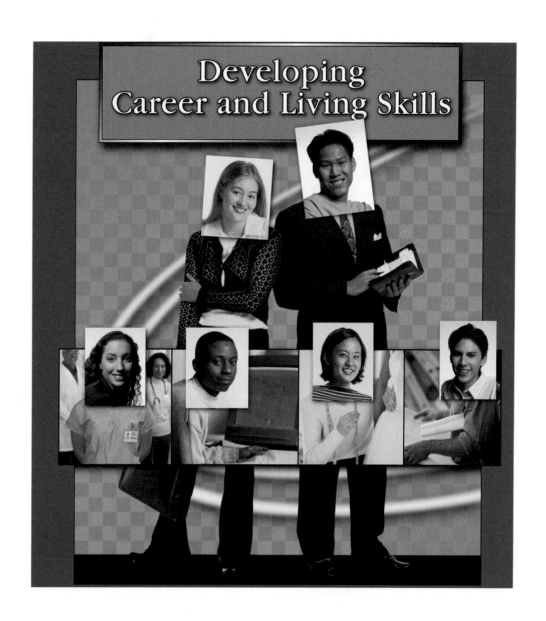

# Developing
# Career and Living Skills

**Mary Sue Burkhardt, CFCS**

with

**Barb Terry Howe, Contributing Editor**

America's Career Publisher®

# Developing Career and Living Skills
© 2009 by Mary Sue Burkhardt and JIST Publishing

Published by JIST Publishing and EMC Publishing, LLC
E-mails: info@jist.com and educate@emcp.com
Web sites: www.jist.com and www.emcp.com

## Note to Instructors

Support materials are available for *Developing Career and Living Skills*. *Developing Career and Living Skills* (978-1-59357-543-4) is the student textbook. *Developing Career and Living Skills Annotated Teacher's Edition* (978-1-59357-544-1) contains teaching tips, answers to review questions, and more. *Developing Career and Living Skills Interactive Lesson Planner Plus Instructor's Resources on CD-ROM* (978-1-59357-578-6) provides resource materials for teachers. *Developing Career and Living Skills Student Interest Inventory* (978-1-59357-123-8) is an assessment that helps students correlate their interests with career clusters. *Developing Career and Living Skills Student Activity Book* (978-1-59357-124-5) contains study guides, key term reviews, and activities for each chapter. *Developing Career and Living Skills ExamView® Test Generator* (978-1-59357-206-8) provides instructors with a variety of types of test questions for assessing student performance. *Developing Career and Living Skills Student Portfolio* (978-1-59357-581-6) provides a place for students to keep track of their career plans and portfolio documents. *Developing Career and Living Skills Career Cluster Discovery Guide* (978-1-59357-586-1) provides information on occupations in each of the career clusters. *Developing Career and Living Skills Video Tour on DVD* (978-1-59357-579-3) includes a short, engaging video introduction for each chapter in the textbook. *Developing Career and Living Skills Finding Your Career Direction* (978-1-59357-580-9) is a DVD that inspires young people to explore careers by showing them everyday, hands-on ideas that they can use to learn more about their career interests.

**Visit www.jist.com** for information on JIST, free job search information, tables of contents and sample pages, and ordering information on our many products!

**Quantity discounts are available for JIST books.** Have future editions of JIST books automatically delivered to you on publication through our convenient standing order program. Please call our Sales Department at 800-648-5478 for a free catalog and more information.

**Acquisitions Editor:** Randy Haubner
**Contributing Editor:** Barb Terry Howe
**Development Editor:** Heather Stith
**Researcher:** Laurence Shatkin, Ph.D.
**Copy Editors:** Nancy Sixsmith, Stephanie Koutek
**Cover Designer:** Honeymoon Image & Design Inc.
**Interior Designer:** Marie Kristine Parial-Leonardo
**Photographer:** Trudy Coler
**Illustrator:** Katherine Knutson
**Proofreaders:** Linda Seifert, Jeanne Clark
**Indexers:** Cheryl Lenser, Jeanne Clark

Printed in the United States of America

1 2 3 4 5 6 7 8 9 10   12 11 10 09 08

ISBN 978-1-59357-543-4   Hardcover Student Edition
ISBN 978-1-59357-544-1   Annotated Teacher's Edition

# Dedication

*Be true to your work, your word,*
*and your friend.*
*—Henry David Thoreau*

To my husband, Ron, for believing in me and supporting me every step of the way;
To John and Krissie, for assuming Mom can do anything;
To Barb Terry Howe, for becoming an editor in the first place, and more importantly being my editor
and friend, at exactly the right time;
To my friends, for cheering me on;
To my thousands of students, for making me believe in myself;
This book is dedicated to you.

Love,
Mary Sue Burkhardt

# About the Author

**M**ary Sue Burkhardt has been Department Chair of the Family and Consumer Sciences Department and Career Education Educator at Twin Lakes High School and the Indian Trails Career Cooperative in Monticello, IN, since 1972. Mary Sue serves as lead teacher for Orientation to Life and Careers course, overseeing the curriculum development and training of other teachers. At Twin Lakes High School, she coordinates the Interdisciplinary Cooperative Education (I.C.E.) program. She develops and maintains relations with extensive local business and industrial contacts for more than 100 students each semester.

Mary Sue is also an adjunct faculty member at Ivy Tech State College in Lafayette and Logansport, IN. She was an instructor at Purdue University in West Lafayette, IN, from 1998 through 2001. Mary Sue has been a Career Specialist since 1993, leading workshops for the Indiana Department of Education Family and Consumer Science Department and serving on the Leadership Development Programs Advisory Committee in Career Education and on the Consumer and Family Sciences Advisory Committee at Purdue University.

Mary Sue earned a Bachelor of Science in Vocational Home Economics Education and a Master of Science in Education degree with an emphasis in Child Development and Family Studies and Career Education. She received the following recognitions: *Who's Who of American Women, Who's Who In American Education,* Indian Trails Teacher of the Year Award in 2002, INAFCS Honor Award in 2001, AAFCS National Top Ten Teacher of the Year Award in 2000; INAFCS Teacher of the Year Award in 1999; Indian Trails Leader Award in 1997; and Shining Star Award in 1992. She maintains the following affiliations: AAFCS, INAFCS (District C Past President and Advisor), ACTE, INACTE, INDFACS, IICCA, NEA, ISTA, Psi Iota Xi Sorority, St. James Lutheran Church, and Purdue Alumni Association.

Mary Sue's husband Ronald is a counselor at Purdue University in West Lafayette, IN. Their son John is a Music Director and Youth Leader. Their daughter Kristine is a fashion designer in New York City.

# Acknowledgments

*"I know, indeed, of nothing more subtly satisfying and cheering than a knowledge of the real good will and appreciation of others. Such happiness does not come with money, nor does it flow from fine physical state. It cannot be brought. But it is the keenest job, after all; and the toiler's truest and best reward."*
—*William Dean Howells*

To my colleagues, JIST Publishing and I sincerely thank you for all your professional efforts in reviewing this textbook. Your feedback has been most helpful in turning my words and practices into a viable textbook. Without you, this project never would have moved from concept to reality. I believe *Developing Career and Living Skills* will be a successful venture, thanks to your efforts.

Sincerely,
Mary Sue Burkhardt, CFCS

## Contributing Editor

Barb Terry Howe, JIST Publishing
Substantial contributions to the ideas, research, and content in this book.

## Interior Designer and Page Layout Technician

Marie Kristine Parial-Leonardo, JIST Publishing
Overall art direction, page design, and page layout.

## Photographer

Trudy Coler, JIST Publishing
Photographic work throughout this book.

## Technical Reviewers

Dr. Shirl Barker, Purdue University
Checked facts and provided content suggestions.

Andrew Broere, Mathematics Teacher, Connersville High School
Technical review of content.

Mary Olson, Human Resources, JIST Publishing
Technical review of content.

## Reviewers

Linda Bennett, Teacher
Shoals Junior Senior High School

Danette Blackwell, Curriculum,
Textbooks, and Instruction
Hattiesburg School District

Sharon Collins, Vice-President of
Professional Development
Kentucky Association of Family
and Consumer Sciences
Morton Middle School

Myrt Collins, Teacher
North White High School

Sandy Cortez-Rucker, Teacher
NW Arctic Borough School
District

Kimberly Embry, Teacher
Butler County High School

Cathy Ewald, Teacher
Lawrence Central High School

Jutta Gebauer, School-to-Career
Specialist
Garza High School

Cathy Grams, Teacher
Walker Career Center
Warren Central High School

Suzie Huber, Teacher
Noblesville High School

Becky Kaylor, Teacher
Center Grove High School

Linda Pranger, President
Illinois Association of Family and
Consumer Sciences
Lincoln-Way Central High School

Teri Roscka, Teacher
Twin Lakes High School

Jennifer Thomas, Teacher
J. Everett Light Career Center

Iris Villoch, Teacher
Michigan City High School

Peggy Wild, State Advisory Council
Counselor, Indiana Family, Career
and Community Leaders of America

## Photography Credits

Trudy Coler, Janet Banks, Troy Barnes, Marlene Bateman, Felicia Batman, Ron Burkhardt, Richard Del Castillo, Lori Cates Hand, Dennis Leonardo, Jim Londeree, Carolyn Newland, Judy Pierson, Robin Reuter, John Taylor, and Barb Terry with special thanks to Angola High School, The Children's Museum of Indianapolis, Indianapolis Executive Airport, Lawrence Central High School, Lawrence Central High School Honor Society, McKenzie Career Center, Tom Wood Lexus, and Twin Lakes High School. Contributions also from Getty Images®, iStockphoto® Images and Comstock Images®.

# Table of Contents

# Unit 3: Accepting Responsibility for Your Life. . . . . . . . . . . . . . . . . . . . . . . 236

# Chapter 14: Successfully Handling Adult Roles and Responsibilities . . . . . . . . . . . . . . . . . . . . **321**

# Chapter 15: Designing Your Tomorrow Today . . . . . . **347**

# Introduction

"What do you want to do with your life?" "What do you want to be when you grow up?" How many times have you already heard these questions? Do you have an answer yet? Do you know there really is no right answer? The only person who can answer those questions is YOU! Who are you? Where are you going? What's important to you? When will something happen? Your answers to these questions will determine much of your life's direction. This textbook, *Developing Career and Living Skills*, gives you an opportunity to look into yourself and answer those questions in ways that will enable you to achieve your highest dreams.

## Unit 1: Exploring Career Options

*Two roads diverged in a wood, and I—I took the one less traveled by,*
*And that has made all the difference.*
*—Robert Frost*
*"The Road Not Taken"*

How will you know which road is best for you? How can a road map help you? In this unit, you define who you are, what is important to you, where you are going, and the tools to help you along your chosen path.

## Unit 2: Becoming Familiar with the Workplace

*"What's really important in life? Sitting on a beach? Looking at television eight hours a day? I think we have to appreciate that we're alive for only a limited period of time, and we'll spend most of our lives working. That being the case, I believe one of the most important priorities is to do whatever we do as well as we can. We should take pride in that."*
*—Victor Kiam*

Do you understand what "work" is? What is a workplace? What does it take to be successful in today's workplace? When pursuing your interests and careers, you achieve more when you are familiar with the workplace, you know what is expected of you, and you know what to expect. The chapters in this unit guide you in taking your place in the world of work.

## Unit 3: Accepting Responsibility for Your Life

*"I've come to believe that each of us has a personal calling that's as unique as a fingerprint—and that the best way to succeed is to discover what you love and then find a way to offer it to others in the form of service, working hard, and also allowing the energy of the universe to lead you."*
*—Oprah Winfrey*

What are your responsibilities now? What will your responsibilities be in the future? How can you successfully handle all those different roles? Your careers and workplaces are only part of your life. Your role in community and family life also makes up a major part of who you become. Your attitude toward all these responsibilities quite often determines the quality of your life. Use the chapters in this unit to think about your life in the future. It may seem far away right now, but you are preparing for it today.

# Unit 1

# Exploring Career Options

## Chapter 1:
## Mapping Your Path to Success

*Chapter 1 focuses on Arts, Entertainment, and Media careers.*

## Chapter 2:
## Discovering Who You Are

*Chapter 2 focuses on Science, Math, and Engineering careers.*

# Chapter 3: Developing Strategies for Solving Problems

*Chapter 3 focuses on Plants and Animals careers.*

# Chapter 4: Exploring Careers

*Chapter 4 focuses on Law, Law Enforcement, and Public Safety careers.*

# Chapter 5: Creating a Career Plan

*Chapter 5 focuses on Mechanics, Installers, and Repairers careers.*

1

# Chapter 1

# Mapping Your Path to Success

## What You'll Learn

▶ Developing self-management skills

▶ Getting oriented to new settings

▶ Getting a world-wise view of life

▶ Developing a plan for success

▶ Strengthening your study skills

When was the last time someone asked you what you want to "be?" Probably not too long ago. If you are like most students, you probably replied, "I don't know—maybe a physical therapist, a professional baseball player, or a rock star." This reply lists three **careers** (people's life-work) that might interest you, but have you really answered the question, "What do you want to 'be'?"

*Dare to begin! He who postpones living rightly is like the man who waits for the river to run out before he crosses.*

—Horace

## Key Terms

| | | |
|---|---|---|
| careers | oriented | responsibility |
| consequences | personal transition | roles |
| deadline | policies | self-management |
| destination | prioritizing | skills |
| evaluating | procedures | strategies |
| feedback | punctuality | world-wise view |
| global | quality | |
| observe | quantity | |

# Section 1-1: Mapping Your Success N.O.W.

There is a lot more to "being" than selecting a career. Right now, you are developing your high school career. Yes, right now school is your job—and a very important one! Your high school **roles** (the behavior others expect of you because of your position) are student and perhaps team, club, or choir member. Throughout high school, you will have many opportunities to discover more about yourself, such as who you are and what you enjoy doing. You can begin NOW to map your path to success in high school and life.

The place and time to begin is right here, right *N.O.W.* The letters N-O-W can help you remember the three key points that are important to planning your future:

N—New skills

O—Orientation to new settings

W—World-wise view

*Where are you going? How will you get there?*

**CAREER FACT**

Careers in arts, entertainment, and media include acting, all types of art, camera work, editing, journalism, modeling, photography, public relations, sports, and writing.

**New Skills.** For most of your life, you might have been accustomed to having parents, teachers, or even friends tell you what to do. Now you are becoming more independent; you are making more decisions for yourself. At this point, you may not feel very comfortable thinking about who you are and where you're going, but that is an important part of life—one that will require you to develop new **skills** (abilities to successfully complete tasks). This chapter focuses on the skill of **self-management**: taking good care of yourself. How do you think people act if they lack self-management skills?

**Orientation.** When you walk into most malls, you see a map showing the locations of the stores, restaurants, restrooms, and mall offices. However, the You Are Here is the most helpful information on the map. It helps you get **oriented** (knowing where you are in relation to everything else) so that you can decide which direction to go. Every time you enter a new classroom, school, workplace, or community, you must get oriented to your new surroundings and then decide where you are and in what direction you want to go. You may be given a map to help you, but you also are given a list of **policies** (rules) and **procedures** (ways of doing things) that can help you get oriented. Have you ever been lost? How did you feel? How did you find your way?

**World-wise View.** Some students attend small schools and live in small communities; others come from large schools in large communities. However, both small and large schools have students from different cultures. Whether you live in a small town or a large city, people from other countries probably live near you. No matter the size of your immediate world, changes in technology, such as the Internet, can bring you information quickly from places very far away. E-mail messages can be sent and received in seconds. Advances in telecommunication allow you to easily and cheaply talk to friends and family in England; Japan; or Kalamazoo, Michigan. Your television shows news events in Iraq, Australia, and Spain. This easy access to people and events around the world has probably given you a **world-wise view**, helping you understand that you live in a *very* big world. That world will have a huge influence on your career and life. How do events in other parts of the world affect your life?

---

### Section 1-1: Review

**Understanding Key Concepts**

1. What is an important skill that people need as they grow up?
2. Why do you need to know where you are when you look at a map?
3. What technologies have brought information about the world into homes today?

**Thinking Creatively**

What is a new skill you developed recently? How did you feel when you realized that you mastered it?

Do you know anyone who lives in or has visited another country? How is life in that country different from life in your neighborhood?

What are some new technologies that were not available a few years ago? How have they changed the world?

**Taking It a Step Further**

A representative from your favorite radio station just walked into the school library and told you that you have won a trip, and you now have two minutes to decide between two destinations. Would you rather go to Kelowna or Ruiru? How can you quickly find out more about these two locations? What one would you choose? What would you take with you on the trip?

---

# Section 1-2: Developing Skills in Self-Management

What do you think of when someone mentions skills? Do you immediately think of the basketball court, race track, or soccer field? Do you think of learning a difficult dance step, playing a musical instrument, or designing a one-of-a-kind gown? What about solving a tough mathematical problem or writing a persuasive letter to the school board? Although all these skills are important, none is as important as being able to manage yourself.

Self-management means that you take the **responsibility** (accepting the blame or praise) for what you do. Part of taking responsibility is **evaluating** (judging) two factors: the **quality** (how good it is) and the **quantity** of your performance (how much you do or how hard you try). You can then adjust your behavior accordingly. Self-management is very important wherever you go. To successfully manage yourself, you must understand the role of evaluations and then respond the right way to evaluations.

**CAREER FACT**

One-third of all salaried musicians or singers are employed by religious organizations.

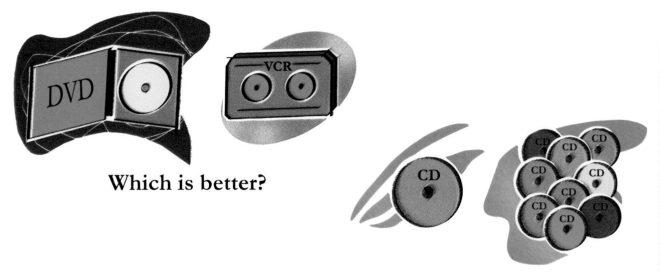

**Which is better?**

**How many CDs?**

*How are the terms quality and quantity similar? How are they different?*

## Understand the Role of Evaluations

You make evaluations every day. For example, you buy the latest recording of your favorite music group. Then you evaluate it by deciding whether the music is good or bad. If you think it's good, you may buy the group's next recording, too. Or you decide that you do not like the group's music and never buy the music again. What are some examples of products you have decided are good? Why? What are some examples of products you think are not worth buying? Why?

You are evaluated on a daily basis in school. Graded assignments and projects, tests, and grade reports are **feedback** (performance evaluations) from your teachers. You will also be evaluated in the workplace. These types of feedback—grade reports or written evaluations of work performance—are formal.

Sometimes the feedback is informal, such as a "good job" note from a teacher at the top of your paper or a "thank-you" from a co-worker. You probably even give yourself feedback, such as "Wow! I really like the way I sang today," or "That speech was the best I have ever given."

## Respond Appropriately to Evaluations

If you get a low grade on an assignment, what do you think? How do you feel? What do you do? If your employer criticizes the way you treat a customer, how do you respond? Your response to an evaluation, whether it is a self-evaluation or an evaluation from someone else, is a critical part of the self-management process.

*How do you feel when you know your performance will be evaluated?*

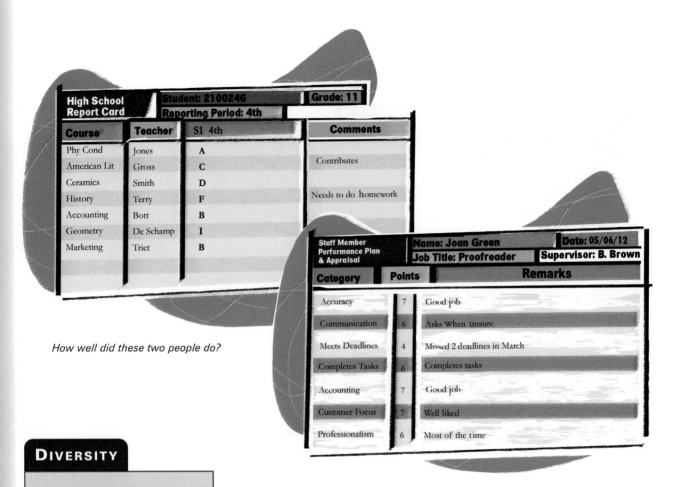

| High School Report Card | Student: 2100246 | | Grade: 11 |
| | Reporting Period: 4th | | |

| Course | Teacher | S1 4th | Comments |
|--------|---------|--------|----------|
| Phy Cond | Jones | A | |
| American Lit | Gross | C | Contributes |
| Ceramics | Smith | D | |
| History | Terry | F | Needs to do homework |
| Accounting | Bott | B | |
| Geometry | De Schamp | I | |
| Marketing | Triet | B | |

| Staff Member Performance Plan & Appraisal | Name: Joan Green | | Date: 05/06/12 |
| | Job Title: Proofreader | | Supervisor: B. Brown |

| Category | Points | Remarks |
|----------|--------|---------|
| Accuracy | 7 | Good job |
| Communication | 6 | Asks when unsure |
| Meets Deadlines | 4 | Missed 2 deadlines in March |
| Completes Tasks | 6 | Completes tasks |
| Accounting | 7 | Good job |
| Customer Focus | 7 | Well liked |
| Professionalism | 6 | Most of the time |

*How well did these two people do?*

Michael Farr and Susan Christophersen (authors of *Identify Your Skills for School, Work, and Life,* published by JIST Publishing) created this checklist you can use to decide whether you are skillful in managing yourself:

▶ You do not blame anyone else for what happens to you.

▶ You do not try to control anyone else.

▶ You take credit for what you do right.

▶ You admit it when you make mistakes.

▶ You promise to learn from every mistake.

▶ You think about the results of your actions *before* you act.

Can you think of other behaviors that a person who practices self-management does?

When you use evaluations to improve your performance, you are demonstrating skill in managing yourself. You also are developing a skill that will improve the way you work and enable you to reach many of the other goals in life you set for yourself. Having skill in self-management not only helps you; it also helps other people, too, as you will see in the next section.

## Self-Management Skills

| At School | On the Job |
|---|---|
| Attendance | Attendance |
| *Come to school every day* | *Come to work every day* |
| **Punctuality** | Punctuality |
| *Be on time* | *Be on time* |
| Good attitude | Good attitude |
| *Work cooperatively with others* | *Work cooperatively with others* |
| Basic Skills | Basic Skills |
| *Be able to read, write, talk, listen, and compute well* | *Be able to read, write, talk, listen, and compute well* |
| Problem solve | Problem solve |
| *Be able to choose good solutions to resolve issues* | *Be able to choose good solutions to resolve issues* |
| Responsibility | Responsibility |
| *Set goals and be organized* | *Set goals and be organized* |
| Honesty | Honesty |
| *Can be trusted* | *Can be trusted* |
| Leadership | Leadership |
| *Motivate others toward goals* | *Motivate others toward goals* |
| Teamwork | Teamwork |
| *Contribute to a group effort* | *Contribute to a group effort* |

*What do you notice about the skills listed in this chart?*

## Section 1-2: Review

### Understanding Key Concepts

1. What are two factors used in making evaluations?
2. What are two steps to self-management?
3. Why is self-management so important?

### Thinking Creatively

Getting a poor evaluation is never easy. What do you do to calm yourself down or make yourself feel better when you are confronted with one?

Describe a time when you responded correctly to a poor evaluation and improved your performance because of your positive response.

### Taking It a Step Further

Type the word "self-management" into an Internet search engine, such as Google or Yahoo, and then read a Web article about self-management. Compare the methods you find with the information in this book.

# Section 1-3: Getting Oriented

Life is filled with changes, whether it is changing from one school to another, graduating from school and beginning a job, or moving from one city to another. Each time you make a **personal transition** (an important change in your personal or work life), you must become oriented. These personal transitions can be exciting, depressing, and frightening. How can you become oriented to any new situation you encounter?

One way to become oriented to new situations is to use your new skills in self-management, which requires you to

▶ Learn the policies and procedures of the new setting

▶ Recognize the consequences of your choices

▶ Be responsible for yourself

## Learn the Policies and Procedures

Every school, workplace, and community has policies and procedures. These policies and procedures are a map that guides people's choices and behaviors. Because you are now your own manager, you are responsible for learning the policies and procedures in all these settings and making sure that you follow them.

Think of your school handbook as your map for your behavior for school. The handbook gives the policies and the procedures for a variety of school situations, such as displays of affection, dress and grooming, riding the school bus, attendance, and reporting an absence. What are other important policies and procedures in your school handbook?

---

**TECHNOLOGY**

Look in your school's handbook to find out what policies and procedures it has for technology. For example, what procedures must you follow when you use school computers? Ask several adults what policies they must follow when they use computers in the workplace.

---

*A strong, positive self-image is the best possible preparation for success.*

—*Dr. Joyce Brothers*

*How do you react to change?*

*How are documents like these similar?
How are they different?*

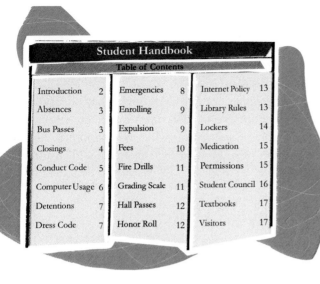

Manuals of policies and procedures in the workplace are very similar. A personnel policy handbook from a food service business, for example, includes information about schedules, being absent, uniforms, and pay days. How are these policies and procedures similar to those in your school handbook? How are they different?

When students choose to **observe** (follow) policies and procedures, they benefit and other students benefit as well. When employees choose to observe workplace policies, they benefit—as do their co-workers, employers, and customers. When citizens observe the laws of their community, everyone benefits. What do students, employees, and citizens gain by following the established policies and procedures? Who suffers when they are not followed?

## Recognize Consequences

As you found in your school handbook, your school has policies and procedures that you must follow. Knowing and understanding the purpose of these policies and procedures is an important part of meeting the requirements that come with being a student. Knowing and understanding the **consequences** (results) of *not* following them is also important. This is also true in the workplace and in society. Understanding what you gain if you follow the requirements (and what you lose by not following them) is critical in today's world.

Whether you are at school or work, for example, you will have deadlines. What does the term *deadline* mean? A **deadline** is a date or time when a project, report, or assignment must be finished. When you have a deadline in the workplace, it means that your work must be finished at a certain time. The customer who is purchasing a product or a service expects you to meet the deadline. Can you think of some examples of deadlines? A person who chooses to ignore deadlines or put things off until a later time is known as a *procrastinator*. This kind of behavior is irresponsible and could lead to more problems later.

### DISCRIMINATION

#### Can an Employer Refuse to Hire You Because of Your Age?

You have been looking for a job for several months now. Yesterday at school, your friend told you that New Threads, a teen clothing store, is hiring. When you pick up an application, the manager tells you that you must be 18 to work there. Is the manager guilty of age discrimination?

Historically, the meaning of the term *deadline* was quite different. It was a point in space, not a point in time. During the Civil War (1861–65), a 'deadline' was the line that surrounded a prison. Prisoners who stepped over the line were liable to be shot. So the term had literal meaning then. If you crossed the deadline, you were dead!

Fortunately, not meeting deadlines does not have such fatal consequences today (although ignoring safety policies and procedures can be disastrous and even deadly). However, not only do you suffer when you choose to ignore workplace policies and procedures, but co-workers, employers, and customers also suffer the consequences.

## Accept Responsibility

What is your school's policy for being in the hallway during class time? Who is affected if you do not have permission? What might be the consequences? How will you respond if you get caught in the hallway when you should be in class? Three keys to self-management and becoming oriented to your surroundings include the following:

▶ Know what is expected of you.

▶ Meet those expectations or ask for help if you cannot meet them.

▶ Change your behavior if necessary.

What will you have to do to make a good grade in each of your classes? What are you willing to do to gain skills in your extracurricular activities? What must you do to get an increase in pay at work? When you are thinking about questions like these, making plans, and following through on the plans, you are demonstrating self-management skills that will produce success throughout your life.

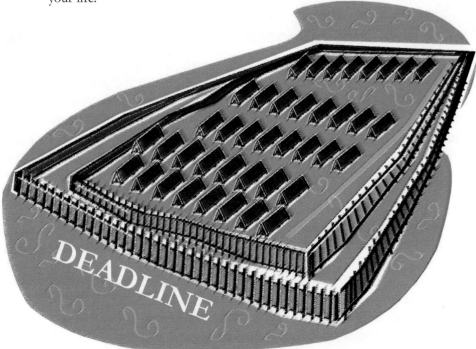

*Historically, if you crossed the deadline, what happened?*

## Case Study: Who Is Affected by Sara's Absence?

The FCCLA club is painting at a preschool, and your group is responsible for bringing refreshments. Your group meets, and everyone agrees on which items each person is to contribute. On the day you are to paint the building, however, Sara, who was supposed to bring the soft drinks, is absent. She did not let anyone know in advance that she was not going to bring the soft drinks.

**Who is affected by Sara's absence?**

**What are the consequences?**

### COMMUNITY

Locate a manual or brochure giving the policies and procedures of your local city or county government, library, or other civic organization. Write a paragraph that compares it to the school handbook.

### CAREER FACT

Of the nearly 120,000 Screen Actors Guild (SAG) members, the average yearly income earned from acting is less than $5,000.

## Section 1-3: Review

### Understanding Key Concepts

1. What is the difference between the terms *policies* and *procedures*?
2. How are student handbooks and employee manuals similar?
3. What are three keys to self-management?

### Thinking Creatively

Talk to your parents, relatives, neighbors, and friends about the policies and procedures they must follow at their workplaces.

See if you can look at a copy of their employee manuals. Compare the manuals to your student handbook.

### Taking It a Step Further

Create a policy and procedure manual for yourself. What are three policies someone needs to follow to be your friend? What are your procedures for a typical school morning? Your manual can be handwritten, typed in a word-processing program and printed, a PowerPoint presentation, or a video presentation. Your audience is your teacher and classmates.

*How many transitions will you experience in your lifetime?*

*Change is good. Call on yourself to make a difference.*

*—Unknown*

# Section 1-4: Getting a World-Wise View of Life

Getting a world-wise view of life means that you gain an awareness of the world and your place in it. Society's expectations of students and workers have changed drastically in the last few years and will continue to change at an ever-increasing rate for several reasons. First, developments in technology have changed the world. Can you think of a technology that has changed what students graduating from high school are expected to know or be able to use?

The changes in technology have made contact between people of different countries and on different continents much easier. With this increased contact has come the second reason for changes in expectations: **global** (relating to the entire world) competition. Now a company in the United States may compete with one in India for business. How can you prepare yourself for this increased competition?

Finally, global competition means that people can be more demanding. They often expect prices to be lower and the quality to be better. What other demands are people making of companies?

Because of developments in technology, global competition, and people's demands, companies must change. Those changes mean that workers have to change jobs and careers more often. Statistics tell us that you will change careers at least four times in your lifetime—and you may change jobs as many as ten times.

## Case Study: Can Helping a Friend Create Problems?

Andrea works as a cashier in a store. The store policy is to add employees during the evening rush hours. The supervisor needs to know ahead of time whether each employee can come to work because it is so difficult to find last-minute replacements. One evening, a friend calls Andrea and desperately needs to be picked up from a volleyball game. Andrea makes a snap decision to go get her. Because Andrea assumes that she will be only a little late to work, she does not call her supervisor. While she is picking up her friend, a group of ten people comes in to the store.

**What policies and procedures did Andrea not meet in this situation?**

**Who is affected?**

**What might be the consequences?**

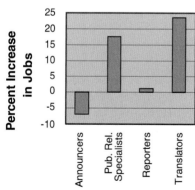

**Projected Outlook for 2016**

*What does this chart tell you about future opportunities in these careers?*

# Section 1-5: Planning for Success

Success probably will not just fall into your lap. You will have to decide what you want (your **destination** or goal) and then create a map for getting there. Two **strategies** (planning tools) that you can use to achieve success, whether you are planning for success in school or on the job, are developing a plan and strengthening your study skills.

## Develop a Plan

How can you tell whether you will be successful in completing a course at school or a project at work? You cannot just wait until the end of the course or until you hand the product over to the customer and hope that your work is good enough. What strategies have you used to keep on track?

These simple procedures can keep you from getting overloaded at the last minute or falling behind:

▶ Use a planner to keep track of your activities and responsibilities.

▶ Make a list of everything you have to do according to each deadline. Then rank each, according to its importance, with 1 as the most important and 3 as the least. Begin each day by doing those tasks that are labeled 1, then 2, and finally 3. When you use this ranking system, you are **prioritizing**.

### On-the-Job Competency

**What Is Wrong with Refusing to Read the Boring Employee Handbook?**

Stephan's employer had a handbook for employees, but Stephan thought that it was too long and boring to read. He threw it in the back seat of his car and ignored it. Why was that a bad idea?

▶ Try to stay a little ahead in all your classes, especially when you have important projects or tests coming up. It's as easy to be consistently a day ahead as consistently a day behind.

▶ Stay healthy and have a balanced life. If you get sick or let your work slip early in the semester, you may have difficulty making up your work or learning unfamiliar material. How can you keep balanced?

Do you have a different system that has worked for you? What do you do if you realize that you are falling behind or are not making the progress you want to make? Do not beat yourself up mentally or give up. Remind yourself of what you really want and then take these actions:

▶ Tell your teacher that you need help. He might not be available for tutoring but probably can tell you where to go for help.

▶ Form a study group with classmates. Sometimes hearing another explanation can suddenly make a confusing subject clear.

## Strengthen Your Study Skills

*How important is it to have a system for studying?*

One of the first steps for success in school or in your career is to know how to study. Some simple strategies can improve your study skills. It may sound strange to you that you actually need to learn how to study, but some students do not succeed in school or careers simply because they do not have good study habits or they do not know how to study. Why should you study?

While you are in high school, establish good study habits. These habits will help you learn more and get better grades right now, and will help you

## Are You Disorganized?

Do you forget homework assignments or lose books, papers, pens, and anything not glued down? How can you overcome disorganization?

▸ Admit that you have a problem.

▸ Use a calendar or planner to record everything you need to do.

▸ Declutter your locker, room, and study area by using baskets, boxes, or drawers to group similar items or all the supplies used for a specific activity in one area; and always return items to their designated spot. Think of the time you'll save by knowing exactly where something is!

▸ Establish routines for getting up in the morning, doing homework, cleaning your room, or completing chores. Routines actually give you more time to do the activities you enjoy by making you more efficient.

▸ Celebrate small successes! Give yourself a treat (even if it's just a "Good job!") when you successfully follow through on anything!

learn new things your entire life. The study habits you form now can help you the rest of your life. How do you study?

Try these tips for studying from the Family, Career and Community Leaders of America:

▸ **Study on purpose.** What do you think this means? The study habit does not come naturally to most people. It takes work and time to develop.

▸ **Start now.** It is never too early or too late to begin good study habits!

▸ **Find the best time.** There are 168 hours in a week. Do you know how you use all those hours? Choose a time of day to study when you can concentrate. Most people find that late afternoon or early evening is the best time for them. What time of day do you choose?

▸ **Commit.** Make a plan and stick to it. Making a plan to commit to studying is no different from practicing music or sports: They all require commitment. Set aside the same time of day to study at least five days per week.

▸ **Do not get distracted.** What distracts you when you are trying to study? Some examples include people moving around or talking, television, telephone calls, and visitors. Try to avoid distractions whenever possible.

▸ **Set the stage.** Many people who conduct research about the best study practices have found that the following are very helpful: a good light, a table or desk, and having school supplies and references available. Some people study better with background music, and others need quiet. Which works best for you?

▸ **Use a system.** One system you can use is the 3 "R's" routine: **R**ead, **R**eact, and **R**emember. However, you can develop your own study systems or formulas. Talk to your teachers or do research on materials about study skills. Each system will be a little different; try several and find the one that works best for you.

## Section 1-5: Review

### Understanding Key Concepts

1. What are two strategies for being successful at school or work?
2. What are five study tips that can produce success in school?
3. How can you avoid falling behind in a class?

### Thinking Creatively

Why do students stop paying attention in class or stop attending school? Who can help students who are falling behind?

### Taking It a Step Further

Develop your own plan for learning a new skill or achieving an academic goal. Arrange your plan as manageable and smaller steps.

## Write SMART Goals

You know that your goal is well-written when it contains this information:

| Quality | Question the Goal Answers | Example |
|---|---|---|
| Specific | How can you tell when you achieve the goal? | "I want to be a good student" is too general.<br>"I want to earn an A in this class this grading period" is specific. |
| Measurable | Can you tell how close or how far away from your goal you are? | I have to earn an A on my homework and all my tests. |
| Achievable | Can you reach the goal? | I'm just beginning the class and don't have any low grades in the class. |
| Realistic | Are you willing to do whatever it takes to reach the goal? | I will study and work hard to earn an A. |
| Timed | Do you have a deadline? | My deadline is this grading period. |

## Spotlight on a Career

### Eileen Waldron, Executive Producer
### Fox 29 Undercover

I am the Executive Producer of the investigative unit for Fox29 News in Philadelphia (not the entire newscast; just the investigative unit). I manage the production of investigative stories that air on the 10 o'clock news. This includes story development and scheduling, supervision of producers and associate producers, and working with reporters and photographers. I also work with our station attorney on legal issues as well as the promotions department on story "promos." In addition to the management responsibilities, I also report and write my own investigative stories, which the investigative reporter presents on air.

In high school, I knew I wanted to be a writer, but I had no idea it would happen through journalism. I graduated from San Francisco State University with a B.A. in Broadcast Communications. During college, I had internships every semester, and they enabled me to get my first entry-level job as an assignment desk messenger in San Francisco. I have also done many other types of jobs, ranging from waitress to being the chief of staff for a state environmental agency.

In my free time I like to run and walk, and spend time with my husband and son. I also like to cook and garden.

I am not always successful at balancing work and life; at times I have spent too much time on the job and not enough with my family. The TV news business is volatile and stressful. However, it can also be extremely rewarding when people are helped, laws are changed, and criminals are arrested as the result of your work.

**Scenario:** A parent and child argue over studying.

**Roles:** Parent: You are the parent of a child who refuses to study. You are concerned about your child's future and want her to see the importance of doing well in school, so you want to set up some policies and procedures for doing homework. You treat your child respectfully at all times.
Child: You do not care about your grades, but you do respect your parent.

**Discussion:** Parents, were you able to convince your child of the importance of school? Why or why not? What policies did you establish? What procedures did you establish? What impact did the information that you respect your child have on your attitude as you discussed this issue?
Children, whose parent was most effective? Why? Whose wasn't effective? Why? What impact did the information that you respect your parent have on your attitude as you discussed this issue?

# Chapter Review and Activities

The following sections can help you review the contents of this chapter and develop your workplace competencies.

## Key Concepts

Following are the key concepts presented in the chapter.

▸ The key to success in school, home, or career is to begin *N.O.W.* by developing new skills, getting oriented, and becoming world-wise.

▸ Self-management is very important. To successfully manage yourself, understand the role of evaluations and then respond appropriately.

▸ Personal and professional growth result from recognizing and responding to personal transitions.

▸ Knowing and understanding the purpose of policies and procedures is an important part of meeting the performance requirements that come with being a student or an employee. Knowing and understanding the consequences of *not* following them is also important.

▸ Getting a world-wise view of life means to gain an increased awareness of the world and your place in it, including understanding changing technologies, growing demands by people, and global competition.

▸ Four simple procedures can keep you from getting overloaded at the last minute or falling behind: using a planner; making a list; staying ahead; and staying healthy, including balancing your life.

▸ Know how to study. Some simple strategies can improve your study skills, help you learn more and get better grades right now, and enable you to learn new things your entire life. The study habits you form now can help you the rest of your life.

▸ Your future success will be determined by the habits you are forming today. You have nearly unlimited opportunities if you carefully explore, plan, and take responsibility for your present and future careers.

▸ *You* are the one who is mapping your path to success.

## Key Term Review

Complete the following activity to review your understanding of the key terms.

| | | |
|---|---|---|
| careers | destination | global |
| consequences | evaluating | observe |
| deadline | feedback | oriented |

| personal transition | quality | skills |
| policies | quantity | strategies |
| prioritizing | responsibility | world-wise view |
| procedures | roles | |
| punctuality | self-management | |

You are a reporter for a school newspaper. Your assignment for this month's paper is to write an article about getting oriented to the new school year. Use at least 10 key terms in your article.

. . . . . . . . . . . . . . . . . . . . . . . . . . . . . . . . . . . . . . . . . . . . . . . . . . . .

## Comprehension Review

Answer the following questions to review the concepts in the chapter.

**1.** What are self-management skills, and how can a person develop them?

**2.** How can someone get oriented to new surroundings?

**3.** What is a world-wise view, and why is it important that people develop one?

**4.** Why is planning for success important?

**5.** How can a person improve studying skills?

. . . . . . . . . . . . . . . . . . . . . . . . . . . . . . . . . . . . . . . . . . . . . . . . . . . .

## School to Work

**Math:** Write down the steps you would take to solve the following mathematical problem and the correct answer.

> If you have scores of 87, 78, 84, 92, and 97 with the possibility of 500 total points, what is your percentage? What letter grade have you earned if the grading system is 95% or higher for an A, 89 to 94 for a B, 83 to 88 for a C, and below 82 for an F? Enter the scores into an Excel spreadsheet and set it up to calculate the percentage for you.

**Social Studies:** You live in Cleveland, Ohio, and want to drive to the largest CMA in Canada. What is a CMA in Canada? Where would you be visiting? Approximately how many miles would you have to drive, and what would you need to take with you to be able to enter the country?

**Writing:** Write a description of a time when you thought you did not have the skills to accomplish something, but you were successful. Be sure to describe how you felt before you began and after you succeeded.

**Science:** Investigate the field of neuroscience. Write a paragraph that defines the word *neuroscience* and draw a diagram of a side view of the brain showing the location of the brain stem, cerebellum, occipital lobe, parietal lobe, temporal lobe, and frontal lobe.

. . . . . . . . . . . . . . . . . . . . . . . . . . . . . . . . . . . . . . . . . . . . . . . . . . . .

## Does This Job Interest You?

The following job is posted on the Internet. What education and experience are required? What requirement does this job have that most jobs do not have? What types of interests and skills should a person working in this position have?

### FIND JOBS  POST RESUMES

### Online Marketing Account Manager

| | | | |
|---|---|---|---|
| **Company:** | MyMusic | **Location:** | Los Angeles-CA |
| **Job Type:** | Full-Time Travel | **Experience:** | 2 Years |
| **Education:** | 4-Year Degree | **Minimum Salary:** | Not Specified |

### Job Description

Here is what we are looking for. Our account managers know and like music. You MUST have a strong knowledge and understanding of current pop culture, lifestyles, and trends. You will be responsible for the day-to-day creation and execution of artist-specific Internet marketing campaigns. Account managers are organized and able to work independently while maintaining a strong sense of team spirit. You understand deadlines and you don't miss them! Our account managers have strong written and oral communication skills and must know the Internet inside and out. We work directly with our clients—labels, artists, and managers—to promote artists in targeted marketing campaigns. Account managers work hard, are passionate about their bands, and have fun.

### Job Requirements

All account managers MUST have active "hands-on" knowledge of HTML and Photoshop and be comfortable working in network environments.

**IF YOU DO NOT KNOW HTML, PLEASE DO NOT APPLY FOR THIS JOB.**

If you are not comfortable with HTML or Photoshop, you cannot succeed in this position! Marketing and entertainment experience is important. You must be organized and detail-oriented. It is also essential that you have strong basic writing skills, especially in punctuation, spelling, and grammar. The skill set we require is inflexible. Please apply only if you possess the necessary skills.

Please contact **MyMusic** via e-mail.

**Please do not attach your resume, but include it in the text of your e-mail. E-mail attachments will NOT be considered. Please put ONLINE ACCOUNT MANAGER in the subject of your e-mail.**

( Apply Online )

# What career appeals to you?

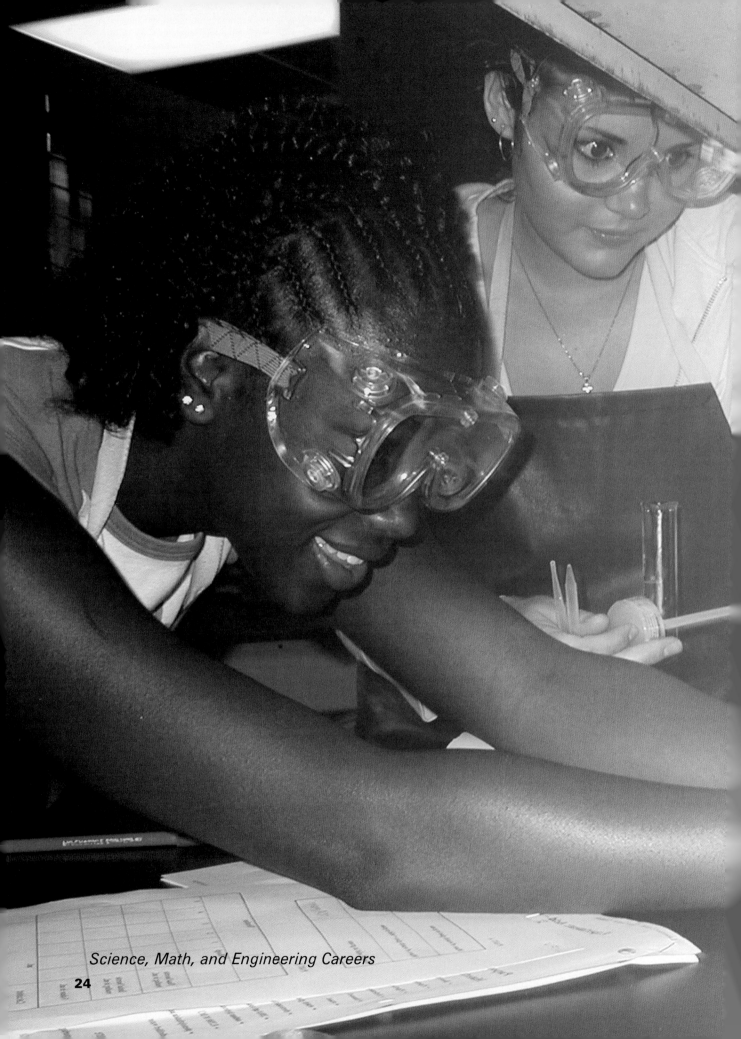

*Science, Math, and Engineering Careers*

# Chapter 2

# Discovering Who You Are

## What You'll Learn

▶ Discovering what makes you who you are

▶ Understanding your personality

▶ Identifying your skills

▶ Recognizing your values

▶ Defining your goals

What do you think William Shakespeare meant when he wrote, "This above all—to thine own self be true"? Who are you? What do you enjoy doing when you have **leisure time** (time free from everyday responsibilities)? Would you rather be in a quiet room or in a noisy one? Would you rather work alone or in a group? What activities do you find easy to do? How can you be true to yourself if you don't know who you are, what you like and dislike, or what you do well?

> *This above all—to thine own self be true; and it must follow, as the night the day. Thou canst not then be false to any man.*
>
> —*William Shakespeare*

# Section 2-1: Discovering What Makes You Who You Are

Getting to know yourself better by thinking about your physical characteristics, **personality** (the psychological and behavioral characteristics that make you unique), skills, **values** (what is important to you), and goals is very important. Why? The only person who can make the best career and **lifestyle** (way of life) choices for you is *you*. Only you can decide how many roles you want to have in life. Will you be a friend, college student, single adult, spouse, parent, soldier, co-worker, employer, or business owner?

Many factors determine who you are. Some include your **heredity** (family traits), **environment** (surroundings), and life experiences. All the physical or mental characteristics passed from your grandparents and parents to you, such as your physical features and intelligence, are called your heredity. What

*Do you pay attention to what interests you and what does not interest you?*

*What influences have made you who you are?*

physical characteristics do you have that are like those of one of your family members?

Your physical characteristics—your **gender** (male or female), the color of your hair and eyes, your height, your weight, and your body type—are a significant part of who you are. Not all of them will affect the decisions you make about your roles in life and your career, however. Which ones have little or no bearing on your future? The body that you inherited, for example, has unique needs. What kinds of food make you feel more energetic, stronger, or healthier? How much sleep do you need each night to be able to function well during the day? Do you feel more comfortable in a quiet surrounding, or do you thrive on activity and excitement?

Your health is another physical characteristic passed down from your family that plays an important part in who you are. How does a person's health play a role in determining his best lifestyle or career choices? What can people do to improve or destroy their health and thereby affect their lifestyles?

Your environment has influenced you from the day you were born, and you have influenced your environment. How has the environment in which you have been raised affected you? How does your school affect your life? How could changing that environment (by moving to a different school district or even to another state, for example) affect your life?

Everything that happens to you and everything you do are your **life experiences**. These experiences, including your **culture** (the way of life in the society in which you live) and your *ethnic* (a group of people that share a common race, religion, and/or language) background, affect how you see the world. Because each culture and ethnic background is different, behaviors that are accepted by people of one culture might not be accepted by people of other cultures and ethnic backgrounds. Your ethnic background may affect how you see other cultures or how you react to certain situations. Can you think of some examples?

*Can you identify people's cultures just by looking at them?*

Life experiences can be positive, negative, or both. Each experience has an impact on your development—physically, socially, emotionally, and intellectually. How have your life experiences affected you? What are some life experiences you have had that have been good for you? What are some of your experiences that were both good and bad?

## Section 2-1: Review

**Understanding Key Concepts**

1. List five physical characteristics that can be passed from generation to generation.
2. Describe the characteristics of an environment.
3. What is a culture?

**Thinking Creatively**

Why is the environment that parents create for their children important? What are some cultural differences you have experienced?

**Taking It a Step Further**

Keep a journal of these details: the day's date, how much sleep you had, what you ate, how much (and what kind of) exercising you did, and how your body felt. Later, look over your descriptions of how you felt and write a summary of whether your sleep, food, and exercise choices are having a positive or negative effect on your body.

# Section 2-2: Understanding Your Personality

What makes you the person you are? How would people describe your personality? Your personality is the sum total of your physical, mental, emotional, and social characteristics. Experts separate personality into categories and say that people have preferred ways of handling each category. One system, the Myers-Briggs Type Indicator, measures these four categories:

- The way a person views the world around her, and whether she is energized by others and her surroundings (**E**xtraverted) or by internal ideas and concepts (**I**ntroverted)

- How a person takes in information: either through the five senses (**S**ensing) or through instincts (i**N**tuitive)

- How a person prefers to make decisions: either logically (**T**hinking) or emotionally (**F**eeling)

- The type of daily lifestyle a person prefers: either structured (**J**udging) or casual (**P**erceiving)

According to the Myers-Briggs Type Indicator, a person with an ISTJ personality may be someone who likes to study alone (I), believes only what he sees (S), decides which college to attend only after careful research (T), and likes to follow a schedule (J). This person would probably enjoy a career as an accountant, lawyer, or computer programmer.

A person with an ENFP personality may be someone who enjoys being in a group (E). She acts on instincts (N). She choose the college that feels most comfortable (F), and lets moods affect her schedule (P). She would probably enjoy careers with unstructured schedules, such as acting, politics, or consulting.

**NETWORKING**

Find a classmate who has (or knows someone who has) a skill that you wish you had.

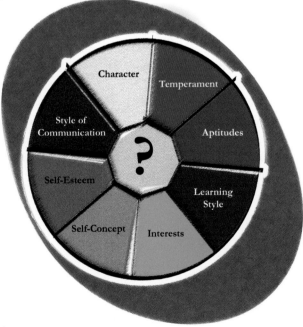

*How would you describe your personality?*

Eight parts of personality include temperament, **aptitudes** (your talents, or how well you *naturally* perform certain tasks), character, learning style, interests, **self-concept** (how you see yourself), **self-esteem** (how you feel about yourself), and style of communication.

# Temperament

Everyone responds to life experiences in different ways. Why is that? Your temperament directs your response to the experiences in your life. **Temperament** (the way a person acts, feels, and thinks) also makes up personality. For example, some people work well under stress, whereas others can actually become physically ill from a stressful job. Can you think of a career that is really stressful? How would you respond to stress on your job?

Following is a list of jobs that are considered to be very stressful:

**COMMUNITY**

Research your community to determine the cultures that have historically been a part of it and how they are unique.

## Ten Stressful Jobs

U.S. President

Firefighter

Senior Corporate Executive

Race Car Driver

Taxi Driver

Surgeon

Astronaut

Police Officer

NFL Football Player

Air Traffic Controller

*Do any of these jobs appeal to you, or would you rather have a less stressful job?*

# Aptitudes

Your aptitudes, or natural abilities, are also part of your personality. These aptitudes can vary widely—from musical to scientific, sports to mechanical, and so on. Although you might share some aptitudes with your friends, no one else has exactly the same combination of aptitudes that you have.

What combination of aptitudes do you have? Do you find it easy to balance a checkbook, fix a computer, or take care of animals, but difficult to learn a new song or write a poem? Those activities that are easy for you are your aptitudes and can form the basis for selecting a specific career.

# Character

**Character** is an important part of who you are. It's your moral sense, your **ethics** or principles (what you believe is acceptable or unacceptable). What behavior do you expect from your friends? Your parents? Your teachers?

*What aptitudes do you have?*

Character is much more than what you *say* you believe; it also includes the choices you make daily. You would not steal money from the cash register where you work, but are you always honest? If you see money fall from the pocket of a person standing in front of you in a line, what do you do? Do you pick up the money and hand it to the person who dropped it? Do you put it in your pocket? With each decision you make, you determine your character.

If you were asked to use one word to describe your character, what word would you choose? Responsible? Reliable? Honest? Having a high standard of ethics will cause others to trust you and can help you succeed in your career.

The following character traits are important to demonstrate to your classmates, teachers, and others in your school. These traits will also help prepare you for life beyond middle and high school:

▶ Be courteous

▶ Be truthful

▶ Be responsible for your actions

▶ Be safe

▶ Be respectful of your environment

▶ Be concerned about your school and classroom community

Can you think of positive or negative examples you have experienced for each of these traits? How could you change the ones that are negative?

## Multiple Intelligences

Howard Gardner identified eight different types of intelligence:

▸ Naturalist: exploring and comparing

▸ Introspective: creating and reflecting

▸ Social: talking and caring

▸ Kinesthetic: experimenting and playing

▸ Musical: listening and timing

▸ Verbal: reading and writing

▸ Logical: organizing and analyzing

▸ Spatial: drawing and visualizing

# Learning Styles

Learning does not take place only at school. You are a student for only a few years; you are a learner for a lifetime. Whether you are studying in school or learning new skills on a job or in your free time, you need to think about your **learning style** or styles: the ways you learn.

Doesn't everybody learn the same way? No. We each have our own style or combination of styles. Howard Gardner is a famous researcher who has found that students use many ways to learn. Gardner believes that some students might learn more easily by relating learning to music, physical movement, or feelings, as well as to reading and writing. He states that students need to know how they learn best and then use their styles to help understand material that is difficult to learn. For example, if you have musical talent, you might write a song about the important points in an assignment to make it easier for you to remember. Here are two styles of learning:

▸ **Traditional learning.** This learning style is also called *classroom learning*. Some people learn best by reading books, listening to lectures, and taking part in activities led by a teacher.

▸ **Experiential learning.** Some people prefer to learn by doing. They like to practice or experiment. As Gardner suggests, they may use their own learning style to understand the material better.

Think about which of these two learning styles describes you. You may find that both apply to you, but you might use one style more than the other. If you know what kind of learner you are, you will have a better chance of being successful. This information helps you take responsibility for your learning.

Even when you know what kind of learner you are, you can experiment with other ways of learning. For example, you might find that you are basically a traditional learner and like to learn by reading books. So try learning something by just doing it or by watching a video. Practicing with other forms of learning will strengthen your ability to learn in any setting.

# Interests

You can use your **interests**, or personal preferences, to identify your career interest areas. When you match your personality to your career, you are more likely to achieve personal and career satisfaction. Which subject in school do you do well in and enjoy the most? Which one is your least favorite?

*In which image is this teen learning through her experience?*

What do you do with your leisure time? What do you and your friends enjoy doing? Which TV programs are your favorites? What do you daydream about doing? Taking the time to list the ways you spend your time will help you identify your interests.

A strong interest can develop into a **hobby** (something you do regularly during leisure time), and hobbies can lead to future careers. Can you think of some examples of hobbies that can become careers? Which hobbies do you enjoy?

What do you talk about with your friends? What do you have in common? Many times we choose friends based on common interests. Think about the activities your friends enjoy. How does identifying your friends' interests help you identify your interests?

What are your favorite TV programs? Do you spend time on the Internet, read books and magazines, or play video games? Ask yourself why you enjoy these activities or why you don't. Your answer can tell you something about yourself.

*How could this hobby become part of a career?*

| If you like to... | Do not select a career in which you... |
|---|---|
| Have lots of change and variety | Do the same thing every day |
| Meet and talk to new people | Work alone in an office |
| Plan your activities | Have constant interruptions |

*Which objects do you find interesting?*

## TECHNOLOGY

Social networking sites, such as Facebook or mySpace, have become a popular way to use the Internet to connect with people who share similar interests. People create pages that link to things they like, show photos, and display comments from other people. How is using this kind of site different than talking to friends in person? What kind of information should a person not share on these sites?

Even daydreams can give you clues about your interests. Do you dream about being a firefighter, a paleontologist, or a famous chef? Thinking about your daydreams can help you learn more about your interests.

You might have realized that sometimes you have to do things that you don't like or that seem boring to reach a future goal. Can you think of an example? Which boring activities are you willing to complete so that you can reach a goal?

## Self-Concept and Self-Esteem

Your self-concept (the picture you have of yourself in your mind) and self-esteem (how you feel about yourself) also contribute to your total personality. If you were making plans to go to the airport to pick up an aunt who had not seen you for several years, how would you describe yourself so that she would recognize you? That description of your physical appearance is part of your self-concept. How would you feel after you described yourself to your aunt? Would you feel embarrassed or proud of the way you look? That feeling is your self-esteem.

How can seeing yourself as a capable person help you do better at school, home, or work? Why is feeling comfortable with yourself important to your success? What can you do to help your family members and friends think more highly of and feel better about themselves? Are you willing to do that for yourself as well?

*How do you see yourself? How do others see you?*

## Communication Styles

Many areas of your life will be affected by how you view yourself. One of the most important is the area of communication. Your **communication style** (the way you give and receive information from others) comes from what your environment has taught you and what you think of yourself. See whether you can find your style of communication in the following chart.

### Three Styles of Communication

|  | **Passive** | **Aggressive** | **Assertive** |
| --- | --- | --- | --- |
| What It Means | You don't stand up for yourself; you give others what is yours | You stand up for yourself, but don't respect the rights of others | You stand up for yourself *and* respect the rights of others |
| What You Think | I am not as important as others | I am more important than everyone else | We are all equal |
| What You Say | "I'm so sorry" | "You are wrong" | "I feel. . ." |

| | Passive | Aggressive | Assertive |
|---|---|---|---|
| How You Speak | Soft, shaky voice | Loud, angry voice | Firm, even voice |
| How You Look at Others | You look down or away | You glare at others with anger in your eyes | You look directly and kindly at others |
| What Your Body Does | You bend your head down | Your body is tense, and your fists are clenched | Your body is relaxed |

## Case Study: What Are John's Aptitudes?

When John was two years old, his parents gave him a toy xylophone (a musical instrument). He started making up little tunes. He began piano lessons when he was five years old and continued until he graduated from high school. He also performed in several plays, musicals, and bands throughout high school and college.

**What type of jobs do you think John would enjoy?**

### Section 2-2: Review

**Understanding Key Concepts**

1. List eight factors that make up personality.
2. What determines a person's character?
3. What are the differences between self-concept and self-esteem?

**Thinking Creatively**

How can knowing your personality type be helpful?
What causes people to have a negative self-concept or low self-esteem?
What can people do to improve their self-concept or self-esteem?

**Taking It a Step Further**

Conduct a survey of five people who know you really well. Ask them to read the "Three Styles of Communication" chart and choose which style they think you use. Write a description of your findings.

# Section 2-3: Identifying Your Skills

Having skills is an important factor in achieving success at school, home, and on the job. You probably already know many of the skills you have. What are some of your skills?

In his work as a career information expert, Michael Farr recommends that you arrange your list of skills in three separate groups: self-management, transferable, and job-related. Self-management skills are those skills that enable you to adjust to a new or changing environment, such as following the rules. Transferable skills are those that you use nearly everywhere, such as being able to read. Job-related skills are skills you use on a specific job, such as using an X-ray machine.

## Self-Management Skills

**Self-management skills** are the skills you use to handle life. These skills include how well and whether you make decisions, take chances, manage your time, deal with stress, stay healthy, and find emotional support.

You may not always like the way you handle your life experiences. If so, you're not alone. The good news is that you can learn self-management skills. Ask people you admire how they manage their lives. Visit a bookstore or library for books with more information. If you learn how to manage your life while you are a student, you will have an easier time managing your career.

*What are the differences between aptitudes and skills?*

Soon you will be totally responsible for your choices. Which self-management skills do you need to make those decisions you will face in your future? If you had to choose between going to a college four hours from your home or attending the local community college, how would you use self-management skills to make your decision?

Taking care of your health and appearance also involves self-management skills. Do you eat a well-balanced diet? Do you hold sadness or anger inside? What can you do to calm down when your mind is racing so fast that you can't think straight? Taking good care of your body and mind is important for your success in school and at work. Looking and feeling your best can make a difference in many areas of your life. What are some things you can do today to improve your wellness?

## Transferable Skills

**Transferable skills** are those you can use in many different jobs. An auto mechanic, for example, needs to be good with his or her hands—and so does a carpenter, artist, or violinist. An administrative assistant, editor, accountant, or librarian, on the other hand, must be well-organized.

As you identify your transferable skills, consider these general areas:

▶ Using your hands

▶ Using words and ideas

▶ Working with people

▶ Working with data

▶ Working with technology

*What skills do you have that you can use in any career?*

## Job-Related Skills

In addition to the self-management and transferable skills needed to succeed on the job, each job requires skills related to that particular job: **job-related skills**. Some job-related skills can be learned quickly, whereas others can take years of training. An auto mechanic, for example, must be able to identify tools and know how to repair cars. A violinist must know how to read music and play a violin.

## SCANS or Necessary Skills

The U.S. Secretary of Labor set up a group called the Secretary's Commission on Achieving Necessary Skills (SCANS) to study workplace skills. The Commission named several foundation skills that everyone needs to succeed in the world of work. It also identified several workplace competencies that are important for career success. Take a look at the list of SCANS skills on the next page. Which skills do you already have? Which skills do you need to improve? Which skills do you still need to learn?

### CAREER FACT

Medical research, infection-control programs, and concerns about bioterrorism are projected to create many new jobs by the year 2018.

*What skills do you have that you can use in a specific career?*

# SCANS Skills

**Foundation skills:** You are developing these skills now in school and in the things you do outside of school. They are the basis for success in the workplace.

**Basic skills:** These skills form the core of basic education.

| | |
|---|---|
| Reading | Speaking |
| Writing | Listening |
| Working with numbers | |

**Thinking skills:** These skills form the process of thinking.

| | |
|---|---|
| Thinking creatively | Visualizing |
| Making decisions | Knowing how to learn |
| Solving problems | Reasoning |

**Personal qualities:** These skills relate to a person's character.

| | |
|---|---|
| Being responsible | Managing yourself |
| Having self-esteem | Being honest |
| Being sociable | |

**Workplace competencies:** These skills are more specific to certain jobs, and you can develop them throughout your life at school and later at work.

**Resources skills**

| | |
|---|---|
| Managing money | Managing materials and facilities |
| Managing time | Managing people |

**Interpersonal skills**

| | |
|---|---|
| Working with a team | Working with diversity |
| Teaching | Negotiating |
| Serving customers | Leading |

**Technology skills**

Selecting tools

Applying technology

Maintaining and troubleshooting equipment

**Systems skills**

Understanding systems

Monitoring and correcting performance

Improving and designing systems

**Information skills**

Finding and evaluating information

Organizing and maintaining information

Interpreting and communicating information

Using computers

**CAREER FACT**

Engineering jobs are shifting from aerospace, chemical, civil, electrical, mechanical, mining, nuclear, and petroleum to biomedical and environmental engineering as our society focuses more on health and the environment.

# Evaluate Your Skills

Be honest with yourself about your skills. What if you desperately want to be a famous singer, but you never made the choir and people cover their ears when you sing (even after you have taken five years of voice lessons)? You probably should consider a career in another area of the music industry. If you earn As in math and bookkeeping, for example, you might consider becoming an accountant for a famous singer.

School grades do reflect how well your skills have developed in certain subjects. Keep in mind, however, that although academic skills are important, they are not equally important for all careers.

As you evaluate your skills, another equally important factor to consider is how skilled you are in comparison with others. Today's world needs highly skilled workers, and those workers need to have a wide range of knowledge. However, the number of factory jobs for workers in the United States is decreasing. When you finish your education, will you be highly skilled and ready to compete for a job? How do your skills compare with those that other people have?

Activities outside the classroom can help you compare your skills with those of other people. Sports teams, extracurricular clubs, and involvement in other organizations can help you learn more about how your skills compare with others' skills.

*When you are competing with others, how well do you perform?*

---

**ROLE-PLAYING**

**Scenario:** One student tries to "buy" something of value from another student.

**Roles:** Student 1 has something on of value: a ring, watch, necklace, or school letter jacket, for example. Student 2 has a wallet filled with money and tries to buy the article.

**Discussion:** How much do you value your possessions? Do you have something that you would not sell for any amount of money?

---

**CAREER FACT**

A person with the title of oceanographer studies the world's oceans, but the field is divided into several categories:

▶ Physical oceanographers study ocean tides, waves, currents, temperatures, and the salt content.

▶ Chemical oceanographers study chemical compounds in the oceans and the inter-actions of various forms of energy, such as light, radar, sound, heat, and wind, with the sea.

▶ Geological oceanographers study the makeup of the ocean floor.

▶ Biological oceanographers are usually referred to as marine biologists.

---

# Section 2-4: Learning More About Yourself

Your personality, your interests, your skills—Is there even more to you as a person? Yes. Your values provide the **motivation**, or reason, for doing what you choose to do. Your goals can give you a plan for living your life. If you have difficulty understanding all these areas of yourself, you are not alone. Many people turn to assessments, which are forms that can help them understand themselves by asking questions.

## Recognize Your Values

What do you have in your possession at this moment that is very important to you? What could you get rid of right now and not care in the least? Those possessions that are important to you (and that you want to keep) are valuable to you. Those that you willingly would give up are not valuable to you.

In addition to possessions that can be seen, people value some things that cannot be seen. Life values (what you believe are important or worthwhile) give direction to your life. In most cases, you learn them automatically from your parents, other family members, teachers, and adults who are important in your life. Knowing and understanding your life values will help you make decisions. Read over the following list of values. Which are important to you? Which one is the most important to you?

| Creativity | Friends | Independence | Loyalty | Religion |
| Family | Honesty | Knowledge | Money | Security and safety |

Career values (those parts of a job that are most important to you) are important to consider when you explore a career. Why do people choose the types of jobs they have? For example, why do some people choose to be electricians and others choose to be nurses? What value does a person gain from being an electrician? What career value does a person gain from being a nurse?

Some people value having a routine: They want to have a specific list of tasks to do on the job and then be able to go home, knowing that they have completed their assigned work. Others find routines boring. They want their work to be challenging and always changing. What are some other career values that people have? What career values are important to you?

Having a job that matches most of your career values can lead to greater happiness with your work and life. If you have a hard time identifying what you value, talk with your friends and family. They may see what you do not see.

## Define Your Goals

**Goals** are plans you want to accomplish or promises to yourself. Some goals are simple and some are difficult. You can reach some goals quickly; others take longer. How willing are you to work toward a difficult goal? How much time are you willing to spend working toward it?

Think of a goal as a target—something to aim for. For example, what's the goal in football? The target is the posts and white line at the end of the field width. Each team is trying to get the football across the opposing team's goal line. Every football game has a *short-term goal* (the quick, simple goal of getting the ball ten yards closer to the goal) and a *long-term goal* (winning the game).

*What career values do these people have?*

*What are the short-term and long-term goals of this game at Twin Lakes High School?*

Now consider the "game of life." Goals are an important part of your game plan. If you are to be successful, you want to have short-term goals: goals that are relatively quick and easy to achieve. You also need long-term goals: goals that take longer to achieve. Above all, make sure that your goals are your own, not someone else's.

Do you know what your long-term goals are? Begin by thinking about the type of lifestyle you want. Do you want to stay where you are, or might you want to move to a different city, state, or even country? Would you prefer to live in a large city, a smaller one, or the country? Do you want to be married? Do you want to have a family? Do you want to work full-time for a large or small company, or own your own company? Would you rather work part-time at a couple of jobs?

Do you want to be physically active? What hobbies and interests do you want to pursue? Do you want to improve your skills? Are you satisfied with your values and ethics, or do you want to change them?

Only you can decide how you want to live and then set the long-term goals that will create the conditions to make your desires a reality. When you know what your long-term goals are, you can then create the short-term ones so that you move in the direction you want to go.

Plan to change your goals when you need to. Their only purpose is to help you, and they might need to be adjusted from time to time.

# Use Assessments to Learn More About Yourself

This chapter has asked you many questions. In answering them, you probably gained a clearer picture of who you really are. For additional information, you may want to take an assessment. An **assessment** is a form, either paper or electronic, with many carefully worded questions that identify and measure factors about you.

Many different types of assessments are available to help you define and identify who you are. For example, an interest inventory is an assessment that measures your interests. Other assessments measure aptitudes, goals, knowledge, skills, or values. During your high school and college career, your teachers and counselors can provide those assessments. Please remember these assessments tell you only what you *might* do, not what you *should* do.

**CAREER FACT**

Because environmental engineers work with water and air-pollution control, recycling, waste disposal, and public health issues, they might work both in offices and outdoors.

**On-the-Job Competency**

**What Transferable Skills Does a Cashier's Position Require?**

Kyle accepted a job as a cashier at the neighborhood food mart. What transferable skills will he need that he has learned in school?

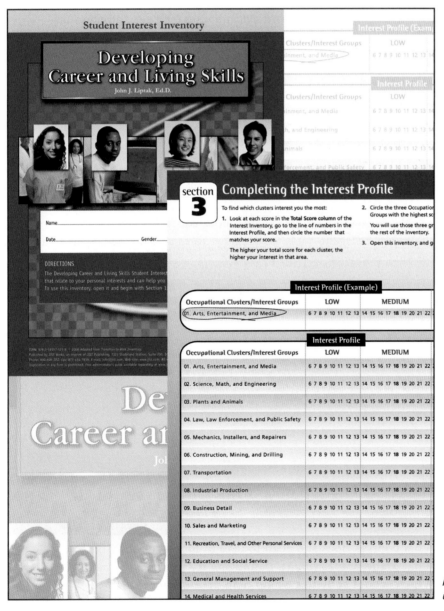

*How can assessments help people understand themselves better?*

**Ron Bateman, Architect**
**Koonce Pfeffer Bettis, Inc.**

I am an architect on the staff of an architectural firm in Anchorage. I oversee the design of government projects, such as schools and community centers, as well as buildings for companies. An architect uses computer programs to draw the plan for a project, creates drawings and builds a model of it, prepares material lists, and works with teams of architects and interior designers to finalize the details. When the client has approved the project, I oversee the construction of it, frequently traveling to the site to make certain that it is being built the way the plans and the client specified. Priorities for me include meeting deadlines; designing safe, efficient, and pleasing buildings; and communicating well with clients, co-workers, and the community.

I have a bachelor's degree in religion from Indiana Wesleyan University, an associate's degree in welding from the University of Alaska in Anchorage, and a master's degree in Architecture from the University of Texas in Austin. As a high school student, I thought that I should become a minister. However, shortly after I graduated from college and accepted a position as a youth pastor, I realized that I did not like the job. I then spent several years working in various fields: booking concerts for a rock group, building houses, and even owning a real estate company. I was never satisfied, though. I knew that I was good at drawing and painting, and I had developed an interest in philosophy and history (which are reflected in architecture), so I went back to school. I then had to work as an apprentice architect before earning my certification.

Balancing work with my life can be difficult. I climb mountains, restore old cars and trucks, work in my yard and on my house (which I designed, of course), and visit with family and friends to relieve the stress.

## Case Study: How Can Natalie Be Prepared to Study Art?

Natalie is a sophomore in high school, and her long-term goal is to attend a four-year college to study art. Help her form an educational plan to achieve her long-term goal.

What courses does she need to take in high school?
What grade point average should she try to earn?
Which school activities would help develop her skills?

## Section 2-4: Review

### Understanding Key Concepts

1. What are two types of values and how are they different?
2. Why are a person's values important when selecting a career?
3. What are goals?
4. What are assessments and how are they used?

### Thinking Creatively

Can you change your values if you know that you have been taught to value the wrong things? If so, how? If you cannot, why not?

Can a person achieve success without having goals?

What are the similarities and differences between assessments and tests?

### Taking It a Step Further

Make a collage or PowerPoint presentation, combining pictures of the things you value and words that describe your life and career values.

# Chapter Review and Activities

The following sections can help you review the contents of this chapter and develop your workplace competencies.

## Key Concepts

Following are the key concepts presented in the chapter.

▶ Many factors determine who you are, including your heredity, environment, and life experiences.

▶ Eight parts of personality include character, temperament, aptitudes, learning style, interests, self-concept, self-esteem, and style of communication.

▶ Identifying your skills is an important factor for achieving success at school, home, and on the job. These skills include self-management skills, transferable skills, and job-related skills.

▶ Evaluate your skills by being honest with yourself.

▶ Knowing and understanding your life values will help you make decisions.

▶ If you are to be successful, you will want to have short- and long-term goals: goals that are your own, not someone else's.

**CAREER FACT**

Biological scientists might be exposed to dangerous organisms or toxic substances in laboratories, and must follow strict safety procedures to avoid contamination.

▸ Assessments will help you define and identify who you are. Remember that assessments tell you only what you *might* do, not what you *should* do.

▸ Most people are more successful at the things they enjoy doing.

▸ A good understanding of yourself will help you set career goals and make a plan for how to achieve them.

▸ It is important that you keep improving your skills in order to be competitive with others.

## Key Term Review

Complete the following activity to review your understanding of the key terms.

| | | |
|---|---|---|
| aptitudes | heredity | personality |
| assessment | hobby | self-concept |
| character | interests | self-esteem |
| communication style | job-related skills | self-management |
| culture | learning style | skills |
| environment | leisure time | temperament |
| ethics | life experiences | transferable skills |
| gender | lifestyle | values |
| goals | motivation | |

You are an engineer who prefers to learn by looking at diagrams. Using at least 15 of the key terms, create a diagram that shows the areas found in a school building and how they are related to each other.

## Comprehension Review

Answer the following questions to review the main concepts in the chapter.

**1.** What factors determine who you are?

**2.** What factors make up a personality?

**3.** What types of skills does each person have?

**4.** Why is character (or ethics) important in determining your future?

**5.** What are the differences between short- and long-term goals and how are they related?

# School-to-Work

**Math:** Sometimes doing the ethical thing can result in a monetary reward. You found a wallet, returned it to its owner, and were given 25 percent of the money in it as your reward. Your reward was $35. How much money was in the wallet originally? Write down the steps you would take to solve this mathematical problem and the correct answer.

**Social Studies:** Conduct your own research to discover whether gender plays a role in a person's future. Individually interview a male/female couple who works full time, lives in the same house, and has at least one child. Prepare a document in which each can list the weekly household chores, who does them, and how long each takes to complete. Compare their answers and write a paragraph summarizing your findings and how the results might affect a person's future.

**Writing:** The application for employment that you are filling out asks you to write a paragraph describing your personality. Write it so that an employer would want to hire you, giving examples of each characteristic or strength you include.

**Science:** Using the Internet, investigate the topic of ethics in genetics. (If you don't know what the term *genetics* means, you will find out as you research the topic.) Write a description of the decisions society must make about the use of genetics to create human life.

## CAREER FACT

If you enjoy chemistry, computer science, drafting, math, physics, or technology classes, you might want to consider one of these careers:

▸ Actuary
▸ Architect
▸ Biomedical Engineer
▸ Computer Programmer
▸ Computer Software Engineer
▸ Environmental Engineer or Scientist
▸ Medical Scientist
▸ Surveyor

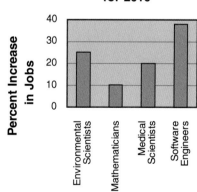

**Projected Outlook for 2016**

*What does this chart tell you about future opportunities in these careers?*

## Does This Job Interest You?

The following job ad was posted on the Internet. What education and experience are required? What requirement does this job have that most jobs do not have? What types of education, interests, and skills should a person working in this position have? How could someone apply for the job?

| FIND JOBS | POST RESUMES |
| --- | --- |

### Mechanical Engineer

**Park:** FrontierTown, Baton Rouge

### Job Description

To redesign all rides and to provide general maintenance on all metal structures and equipment throughout the park. Conduct daily safety inspections for various rides and equipment. Diagnose improper operation of equipment and devices; repair, replace, or notify proper departments of required work. Perform preventative maintenance, repairs, and overhauls on rides, equipment, and facilities. Troubleshoot and/or perform general maintenance of mechanical devices and vehicles to assure proper function and safety. Full time with benefits. Please submit your resume to FrontierTown.

### Job Requirements

Three years minimum experience in mechanical engineering. Basic knowledge of the operational aspects of machinery components. Must have a valid state driver's license and associate degree in mechanical engineering. Must have a basic set of hand tools. Ability to work a variety of shifts, including weekends, nights, and holidays.

### Contact

**Phone:** 000 111 2222 x300
**Fax:** 000 111 2223

**E-mail:** hr@frontiertown.com

**Apply Online**

## What career appeals to you?

*Plants and Animals Careers*

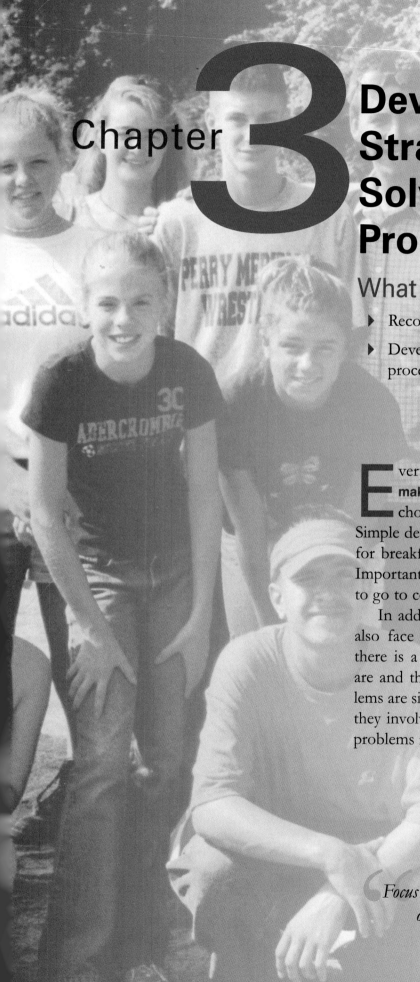

# Chapter 3

# Developing Strategies for Solving Problems

## What You'll Learn

▸ Recognizing five problem-solving styles

▸ Developing a realistic problem-solving process

Every day you make choices. **Decision making** is the process you go through to choose among all the options you have. Simple decisions, such as deciding what to eat for breakfast, don't require a lot of thought. Important decisions, such as deciding where to go to college, are more complicated.

In addition to making decisions daily, you also face problems. A problem exists when there is a difference between the way things are and the way they should be. Some problems are simple, and some are **complex** (that is, they involve more than one factor). Complex problems require a process to resolve them.

*Focus 90% of your time on solutions and only 10% of your time on problems.*

—Anthony J. D'Angelo

# Section 3-1: Recognizing Five Problem-Solving Styles

First things first. Be aware that your personality may determine how you solve problems, or the situation at the time may influence you. When emotions are involved and you have a sensitive temperament, for instance, it is more difficult to look at a problem **objectively**, or without being influenced by personal feelings.

For example, when you are angry with your parents because they say you cannot stay out late two school nights in a row, you may find it difficult to see that two late nights affect your physical health. You may not be getting enough sleep. A lack of sleep can lead to poor performance in school as well as a long list of other problems.

Making decisions is easier when you understand yourself as you face a difficult decision or have to choose among many options. One way of looking at the role of personality in **problem solving**, or finding answers to problems, is to recognize five problem-solving styles.

*What decisions are you making today that will impact your future?*

- **Authoritarian.** You go along with a decision that someone else makes for you without asking any questions.

- **Fatalistic.** You believe that you have no control over your life. What will be will be.

- **Impulsive.** You act quickly to solve problems without thinking about your options or the results of your actions.

- **Intuitive.** You use an inner awareness of the right choice rather than facts or fleeting feelings to make a decision.

- **Realistic.** You consider all the facts before you take action.

Take a closer look at each one of these styles of problem solving.

**Authoritarian.** In an **authoritarian** style of problem solving, someone else makes the decision without asking the people who will be affected by the decision. Those who will be affected by the decision are expected to follow blindly. For example, in some countries, one leader makes the decisions that all the citizens must follow. Saddam Hussein changed laws and made new laws in Iraq without asking the citizens of his country what laws they wanted. How is this system different from the American system of making decisions about laws? What might happen if we let others make decisions for us?

**Fatalistic.** Do you know anyone who believes that things will happen no matter what? People who believe that fate controls their decisions are using a **fatalistic** style of problem solving. When is a fatalistic style of problem solving appropriate? When is it ineffective?

**Impulsive.** Krissie loves to shop. In fact, she has a closet full of clothes and enough shoes to open a shop. Her parents have been telling her that she needs to save the money she earns for a car—not spend it on clothes. When she went to school yesterday, a guy asked her to a dance. Right after school, she didn't even bother to check her closet for an outfit; she just went shopping. Of course, she found an outfit and a pair of shoes she couldn't live without and decided to buy them. Did she need another outfit and pair of shoes? She was **impulsive**—acting on a fleeting feeling that she might regret when she has no money to buy a car or realizes that the shoes hurt her feet because she made a hurried purchase. In Krissie's case, the impulsive decision seems inappropriate. However, many times people must make quick decisions. When is it necessary to make a decision impulsively?

**Intuitive.** When Coach Hay needs to take a player out of a game, he often follows his "gut" feelings and selects the player that he believes will meet the team's immediate needs. The **intuitive** type of problem solving is one in which the person uses an inner guidance based on a calm awareness of the right choice rather than facts or fleeting feelings. When do you think this style of problem solving is effective? When is it ineffective?

**Realistic.** A **realistic** form of problem solving considers the feelings, values, advantages, and disadvantages of a situation. Taking your time to think about the problem by looking at all sides can help you overcome barriers and achieve your goals.

---

**CAREER FACT**

Careers in plants and animals can include agricultural work, animal caretaker, fisher, forester, landscape architect, and rancher.

---

**COMMUNITY**

Investigate plants and animals careers by contacting your local chapter of the National FFA Organization (FFA) or visiting the Web site at http://www.ffa.org. FFA is a career and technical student organization that helps students develop skills in leadership and learn about agriculture and natural resources.

## How Would You Organize Your Tasks?

Your employer asked you to complete several tasks before you leave today: post the sale signs for tomorrow, close the cash register, sweep the floors, restock two shelves, and clean the glass in the front door. She said that she knew that was probably more than you could accomplish but asked you to do your best. How will you decide the order in which you will complete the tasks?

### Change Is Part of Life

Change can be scary, but it also can lead to a better life. Keep these three facts in mind whenever you face change:

▸ You are not helpless.
▸ You have faced change before and have successfully handled it.
▸ You can set new goals and take action.

*What type of leadership is necessary for the Twin Lakes High School football team to be effective?*

Every day, you are faced with decisions to make and problems to solve. You often have to choose between two or more options. The choices you make and the interactions you have with other people will influence your daily activities. These decisions also influence your lifestyle and future career choices. Before you act, stop and choose the problem-solving style that is most appropriate for the problem facing you.

## Section 3-1: Review

### Understanding Key Concepts

1. What are the five problem-solving styles?
2. When is the fatalistic style of problem solving appropriate?
3. What are the differences between the impulsive and intuitive styles?

### Thinking Creatively

From whom did you learn ways to solve problems?
What problem-solving style do you prefer?

### Taking It a Step Further

Interview a family member about his or her problem-solving style. Ask him how he decided on a career, education, marriage, and which car and house to buy. Prepare a timeline that shows when the decisions were made. Beside each problem-solving decision, list the problem-solving style and the positive and negative results of that decision.

# Section 3-2: Developing a Realistic Problem-Solving Process

Most people want to solve a problem as quickly as possible, but most problems can be solved in more than one way. You will probably be happier with the outcome if you develop a realistic problem-solving style. Take time to consider more than one solution. The system of realistic problem solving arranges the process in six steps, discussed in the following sections.

## Step 1: Define the Problem

Recognizing that you have a problem and making a decision to find a solution are critical to defining the problem. Sometimes, you may not want to admit that you have a problem; you avoid facing it. Sometimes, the problem is so complicated that you have a really hard time identifying what it is. If you don't accept the fact that you have a problem, recognize what it is, and decide to find a solution, you have nothing to solve. How can you tell that you have a problem?

You might recognize a problem in one of three ways. First, you might just know or sense that something needs to be changed or is different from the usual. Second, someone might come to you for help. Finally, someone else may assign you the task of solving a problem. The problem solving begins when you identify a **discrepancy** (the difference between the way things are and the way things need to be), when you determine a goal that you want to reach, or when you have to react to a change in your life.

*What problems need to be solved in this situation? How would you organize the cleanup?*

For example, suppose that a tree falls through the roof over your bedroom, making a hole in your ceiling. Do you have a problem? Do you want to solve it? Obviously, the answer is "yes" if you want your bedroom to stay dry the next time it rains or snows. What is the problem? Do you have more than one problem?

## Step 2: Select a Goal

Even when you feel as though you have no control over a problem, you can choose how to respond to the problem. When you know what your goals are, it becomes clearer how you can respond. Follow the rest of the problem-solving steps to resolve the problem.

You may want to consider two factors as you select a goal. First, find the **cause** of the problem, or why it occurred. Then think of the consequence or consequences of the problem. Sometimes you need to understand the cause of a problem to prevent it from happening again. Sometimes you need to know all the consequences of a problem so that you can effectively choose a goal or several goals.

In the case of the hole in the ceiling of your room, you need to know the cause (you probably realized it as soon as you looked up): A tree fell onto the roof. However, the consequences of the falling tree can vary. If a large branch caused the hole, the consequence requires choosing one solution; if the entire tree fell on the entire house, you have a much bigger problem.

Your first goal is probably an immediate or short-term one: How do you keep the rain and snow out of your bedroom right now? The second goal is long term. The roof needs to be fixed. If you continue to use a realistic problem-solving process or system, you have a better chance of finding the best solutions so that you reach your short- and long-term goals.

However, what do you do if you realize that you have a problem, but you do not know the cause of the problem or do not understand all its consequences? Even without that information, you need to deal with the problem. In those circumstances, ask yourself this question: What do I really want? Don't base your answer on your first reaction. Instead, repeat the

### A Quick Way to Solve Problems

If you need to solve a problem quickly, you might want to use outcome-directed thinking. With this system of thinking about problems, you answer these questions:

1. What do I want instead of this problem? (Your answer will be the outcome you strive to achieve.)
2. How will I know when I have achieved this outcome? (What will I see, hear, and feel to know that I've done it?)
3. What will I gain by achieving this outcome? What will I lose? Is it worth it?
4. What resources do I need to achieve this outcome? How will I get them?
5. What is the first step I can take to achieve this outcome?

After you have answered those questions, you are ready to begin to solve your problem.

question several times and over several days, if necessary, until you know that you have found the best goal or goals for you and everyone else involved in the situation.

# Step 3: Analyze Your Possible Solutions

Whenever you face a problem, try to think of as many possible solutions as you can. Coming up with more than one solution will enhance your ability to learn and help you achieve your life goals. Employees who can **generate** (think of) creative solutions to problems are very valuable in today's workplace. **Brainstorming**, thinking of as many ideas as you can, is a very useful tool for generating solutions.

The problem of your bedroom ceiling requires immediate short-term action to keep the rain or snow out. What possible solutions can you see? The problem also requires you to think of possible long-term solutions. What are all your options for fixing the roof? What other details will you have to work out to solve your problem?

Brainstorming is an effective tool to use when creating and developing ideas to solve your problems. But there are certain rules that will make your personal brainstorming session more successful.

Follow these steps when you are brainstorming:

▶ On a piece of paper, quickly list all ideas that come to your mind.

▶ Expect some of your ideas to be wild.

▶ Don't evaluate them.

▶ Remember that it's the quantity, not the quality, of ideas that counts.

*What would you do to take care of this problem?*

After you have listed as many creative solutions to the problem as you can, you need to evaluate each solution and select the best one. How do you evaluate solutions? What questions do you ask yourself when you are analyzing possible solutions to your problem?

Decision making, or problem solving, is becoming increasingly important in a world in which you have so many options. If you search in the library or on the Internet, you can find many different systems for finding possible solutions to a problem. Following are three popular systems. They each have specific purposes and benefits. Keep in mind that sometimes you might need to combine several of the systems to solve a problem.

## Case Study: The Swingset Dilemma

The swingset at the local preschool accommodates only three children at a time. The children are constantly fighting over the swings.

**What is the cause of the problem?**
**What are the consequences of this situation?**
**What is the goal?**

## 80/20 Rule (The Pareto Principle)

The 80/20 Rule, also called the **Pareto Principle**, can help you decide where to begin when you have several tasks or problems. The Pareto Principle is based on the belief that if you concentrate on the most important things, you avoid many smaller problems. To use the 80/20 Rule when analyzing a situation, you make a list of the tasks or problems facing you. Next, you decide which item is creating the greatest immediate problem. Focus all your energy on solving that one problem. Then you are free to solve (or may have already solved) the smaller problems.

In the case of the leaky roof, your list might look like this:

Hole in the roof and ceiling

Rain may come into bedroom

Carpeting and furniture will get wet

When you list the problems like this, you can quickly see that taking care of the hole in the roof will solve the other problems. You know where to focus your attention in coming up with possible solutions.

## Pros and Cons Method

When you are analyzing only one option at a time, you can use the pros and cons method. With the pros and cons method, you create a **grid** (chart). On it, you evaluate what is good about the option (**pros**), what is negative about it (**cons**) and what are the possible outcomes of making the decision (**implications**). The headings on the columns are these three labels: Pros, Cons, and Implications.

If you were trying to decide whether to just move from your house with the hole in the roof to a different part of town, you could create a grid and list all the good and bad things about moving. Then you could look at the implications of each pro and con.

**Concentrating on Schoolwork**

20%

Can Prevent What?

80%

*What happens when you apply the Pareto Principle to schoolwork?*

## Pros and Cons of Moving to a New House

| Pros | Cons | Implications |
|------|------|--------------|
| Closer to school | | Save time and gas money |
| Closer to friends | | Save time and gas money |
| Nicer house | | I want a nicer house |
| | Costs more than old house | Spend more on new house than I saved on gas |
| | Have to fix old house before I can sell it | Twice as much work as just fixing the roof |

*Which solution seems best to you?*

When you are analyzing possible solutions to a problem, the goal is always to improve your situation. If the pros and cons show you that the option will make things harder for you, you need to look for a better solution or do nothing at all.

## Expanded Grid Method

With the expanded grid method, you create a grid to evaluate possible solutions. To create the grid by using paper, skip a couple of lines on a sheet of paper. Then list all your possible solutions in one column down the paper. In the blank lines at the top of the paper, you create a new column for each factor you want to consider, such as Meets Goal, Matches Values/Ethics, Cost, or Time It Takes. You can change those headings, depending on the type of decision you are making. (If you want to use the computer to create the grid, you can use a spreadsheet or the Table feature in your word-processing program.)

For example, you decide to repair the damaged section of your roof and ceiling, and you gather estimates from the contractors. List the contractors that you are considering for the project in the first column (labeled Contractor). You then create column headings for Company Reputation, Cost, and Time. Next you fill in all the information you have gathered on each contractor. With the information laid out as a grid, you can more easily see which contractor option is the best.

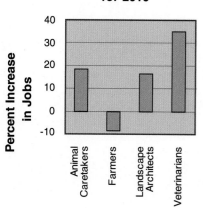

**Projected Outlook for 2016**

*What does this chart tell you about future opportunities in these careers?*

| Contractor | Company Reputation | Cost | Time |
|------------|--------------------|------|------|
| Barters | Excellent | $12,000 | 3 months' wait |
| Renards | One couple had problems | $8,000 | Now |
| Ricks | Three couples had problems | $7,000 | 2 weeks' wait |

*Which factor is most important to you when you decide which company to use: reputation, cost, or time?*

# Risk Taking

Many decisions also have some sort of **risk** (hazard or danger). When you analyze solutions, think about the risks that accompany them. Decide whether you are willing to accept each risk. As you think about the risks involved in any decision, you might

▸ Be tempted to give up what you want just to avoid the risk of failing at it.

▸ Feel upset or even overwhelmed by the risk.

▸ Wish that someone else would make the decision for you.

▸ Postpone taking any action.

▸ See a dangerous risk and ignore it.

*What are the risks associated with these activities?*

When a decision involving risks leaves you feeling confused, fearful, or panicky or if you are tempted to close your eyes to the risk, ask yourself these questions:

▶ Does this seem risky just because I don't have enough information?

▶ Do I know someone who has faced the same risk and would be willing to talk with me?

▶ What is the worst thing that might happen if I take this risk?

▶ What is the worst thing that might happen if I don't take this risk?

▶ What can I do to make my decision less risky?

By asking yourself these questions, you can more effectively and comfortably make a decision.

## Step 4: Make a Plan

### The Plan for Fixing Your Roof

Who...
will do the work?

Why...
are you choosing this approach?

What...
work will be needed to be done to the tree and lawn?

Where...
will you sleep until the repair is finished?

When...
will the work begin?

*What is your plan for fixing your roof?*

After you have analyzed your possible solutions, you can select the best solution and make a plan. Organize your plan around the question words: who, what, where, when, how, and why. These words will help you think of what you need and help you focus on the results you want.

Arrange the sequence: the "when" of your plan. What will you do first, second, and third to solve your problem? Your plan needs to be detailed and must include the tasks, time needed, resources, and responsibilities for reaching your desired outcome.

By now, you're more than ready to take care of that tree lying on your roof. Here is your plan: You decide to hang plastic from the four corners of your ceiling to keep the birds, rain, and who-knows-what-else off your bed. Then you will call the tree-trimming company and schedule the time for them to pull the tree off the house. You will then schedule the contractor to repair the roof. After that, you will be free to sit back and wait for the work to be completed.

## Step 5: Take Action

Until you put your plan into action, it is just a plan. We all know people who talk about doing something but rarely follow through. Taking action is the only way to see whether the problem has been solved. As Nike says, "Just do it!"

To make the roof problem go away, you must take action. You hang the plastic, make the calls, and decide to sleep on the sofa each night until the work is completed.

## Case Study: How Would You Make Decisions About a Family Vacation?

Although your family is most likely very busy these days, you all really need a vacation. Your family assigns you the responsibility of coming up with a vacation plan that will please everyone. How would you organize a family weekend vacation with everyone's busy schedule?

**How can you answer all the "wh-" questions: who, what, when, where, and why, and how?**

## Step 6: Evaluate the Results

How do you evaluate the results of your efforts? Do you have a list of questions that you run through your mind? Do you check with others to see what they think? As you evaluate your results, you may want to keep these questions in mind:

▶ Did your plan work?

▶ Did it solve the problem?

▶ Did the problem become worse?

▶ Did you give the plan enough time to work?

Why do you think you should evaluate your results? What can you gain from looking at the results of your efforts?

Sometimes you will be successful and sometimes you will fail. Remember that you did your best. Also, remember that conditions are always changing, and you may need to modify or change your plan. You are a smart person and can determine whether the plans you make achieve your goals. You can learn from every problem you attempt to solve.

Whether you are making changes in your class schedule, buying a vehicle, or selecting a college or university, use a realistic problem-solving process. It will provide a framework for you to make your choices and reach positive decisions.

## Case Study: What Can You Do About a Disappointing Grade?

Your teacher just returned your first test in the class. You studied really hard for it, but received only an 81 percent (B+ on the class grading scale). You thought that your grade would be higher, and you knew that you really tried to do your best.

How would you evaluate the results?

# Section 3-2: Review

## Understanding Key Concepts

1. What are the six steps this chapter gives for solving problems?
2. What is the Pareto Principle?
3. How are the pros and cons and grid methods of decision making similar?
4. How are the pros and cons and grid methods of decision making different?
5. What are four questions you can ask as you evaluate a result?

## Thinking Creatively

Who is the best problem solver you know?

Can you think of any steps you take to solve problems that are not presented in this chapter?

## Taking It a Step Further

Identify a problem that you have and follow the six steps of problem solving to resolve it. Use Microsoft Word or another word-processing program to prepare a written report, sharing the possible solutions, how you selected the best solution, your plan, the actions you took, and the results of your actions.

## Spotlight on a Career

### Karen Imboden, Waters Area Manager
### Indianapolis Zoo

As the Area Manager of the waters building at the Indianapolis Zoo, my main responsibility is to see that the day-to-day operations of the aquarium run smoothly. I have to make sure that all the animals are healthy and the exhibits look good for the public. I do this with the help of a staff of six aquarists whom I supervise. I find animals to bring in to keep our exhibits new and exciting. Then I monitor the 30-day quarantine period for the new animals. I keep the veterinary staff informed about animal health problems and discuss any diet issues and medical treatments. I am the liaison with the maintenance department.

I graduated from Indiana University in Bloomington with a B.A. in Biology and Environmental Studies. When I was in high school, I enjoyed biology and knew that I eventually wanted to work with animals. I also wanted to be involved in conservation.

I didn't think of working at a zoo as an option until I moved to Indianapolis and answered an ad for an entry-level aquarist position at the Indianapolis Zoo. In that position, I took care of the penguin and puffin area on the weekends. During the rest of the week, I prepared the diets for all the animals in the waters building. When I finished my kitchen duties, I helped others feed their animals so that I could learn about them. I eventually learned about the entire building and all the animals in it, which helped out immensely in my career.

I spend my free time playing volleyball, coaching grade school volleyball, and hanging out with my friends and family. I also read and relax with my three cats, some fish, and a leopard gecko. Balancing my work with my life is fairly easy. I do not like to take any work home with me. I am confident that the staff can handle problems when I'm not there. Of course, sometimes I worry about an animal or drop by on my time off to check on things, but I enjoy my job so much that doing so isn't a problem.

# Chapter Review and Activities

The following sections can help you review the contents of this chapter and develop your workplace competencies.

## Key Concepts

Following are the key concepts presented in the chapter.

▶ Problem solving has many forms and levels, but the process inevitably includes defining the problem, selecting a goal, analyzing possible solutions, making a plan, taking action, and then evaluating the results.

▶ To define the problem, you must recognize that you have a problem and make a decision to find a solution.

▶ When you select a goal, it becomes clearer how you can respond to and follow the problem-solving steps to resolve the problem.

▶ When you face a problem, generate solutions. This ability makes you a very valuable employee in today's workplace. Brainstorming is a very useful tool for generating solutions.

▶ Taking action is the only way to see whether the problem has been solved.

▶ You can learn from every problem that you attempt to solve when you evaluate the results.

▶ Learning to creatively solve problems is a tool you will use in every role you have throughout your career and life.

## Key Term Review

Complete the following activity to review your understanding of the key terms.

| | | |
|---|---|---|
| authoritarian | fatalistic | Pareto Principle |
| brainstorming | generate | problem solving |
| cause | grid | pros |
| complex | implications | realistic |
| cons | impulsive | risk |
| decision making | intuitive | |
| discrepancy | objectively | |

The greenhouse where you work has five employees who use the five problem-solving styles discussed in this chapter. Business has been slow, and the company must do something to cut back on expenses. Using at least 15 of the key terms, write descriptions of how each of your co-workers would solve this problem.

. . . . . . . . . . . . . . . . . . . . . . . . . . . . . . . . . . . . . . . . . . . . . . . . . . . .

## Comprehension Review

Answer the following questions to review the main points in the chapter.

**1.** If the problem were that you needed to buy a house, give examples of how you'd make the decision by using each of the five styles of problem solving.

**2.** What are three ways you can recognize that you have a problem?

**3.** What are two factors you may need to know before you can select a goal?

**4.** How can you analyze the solutions?

**5.** What are the "wh" words you can use in creating a plan?

**6.** Why are the last two steps of the problem-solving process so important?

. . . . . . . . . . . . . . . . . . . . . . . . . . . . . . . . . . . . . . . . . . . . . . . . . . . .

## School-to-Work

**Math:** You want to take a date to see a movie, but you're not certain that you have enough money. **(Defining the problem.)** You really want to see the movie. **(Selecting the goal.)** The matinee price is $2.00 less than the regular one of $8.50. You know that your date will want a small coke for $3.50 and a small popcorn for $3.00. You will want a box of candy that costs $3.75 and a large coke for $4.50. If you have $35.00, do you have enough money to go to the regular show, or will you have to talk your date into seeing a matinee? **(Analyzing the possible solutions.)** How can you quickly analyze your situation to make a decision? Write down the steps you would take to solve this mathematical problem. **(Making a plan.)** Write down the correct answer. Based on your answer, what will you do? **(Taking action.)** Are you happy with your decision? **(Evaluating the results.)**

**Social Studies:** An authoritarian form of government is one in which the people must blindly obey a dictator or ruling party. Can you find three countries on the continent of Asia that have an authoritarian form of government?

**Writing:** Write a short story for a young child that describes a problem that you had when you were younger, the style of problem solving you used when facing it, and the outcome.

**Science:** When your parents pulled out of the garage, you saw a puddle of liquid on the floor. Describe how you could use the scientific method to determine what the liquid was.

. . . . . . . . . . . . . . . . . . . . . . . . . . . . . . . . . . . . . . . . . . . . . . . . . . . .

## Does This Job Interest You?

The following job is posted on the Internet. What education and experience are required? What requirement does this job have that most jobs do not have? What types of interests and skills should a person working in this position have? How could someone apply for the job?

---

**FIND JOBS**    **POST RESUMES**

### Animal Caretaker

**Company:** American Wildlife Rescue and Rehabilitation    **Phone:** (830) 336-2725
**Fax:** (830) 336-3733    **E-mail:** staff@wildlife-rescue.org

### Job Description

Applications are now being accepted for the position of Animal Caretaker. Applicants should possess a combination of experience and education. Animal care positions require substantial physical labor (must be able to lift 30 lbs and work in all types of outdoor conditions), ability to handle a demanding workload and long hours, strong personal work ethic, and a high level of personal integrity and responsibility.

### Job Requirements

This position involves substantial animal husbandry responsibilities, limited basic medical work, and administrative duties (record keeping and telephone work). In addition, the position requires fieldwork involving rescues, releases, and transportation of animals. Rabies pre-exposure vaccinations are required.

### Contact

If you are interested in applying for this position, please send a cover letter and a copy of your resume to Staff Coordinator:
American Wildlife Rescue and Rehabilitation
PO Box 1111
Dallas, TX 78006
staff@wildlife-rescue.org

**Apply Online**

# What career appeals to you?

# Chapter 4

# Exploring Careers

## What You'll Learn

▶ Defining jobs and careers

▶ Beginning to think about a career

▶ Using informal research

▶ Discovering careers through formal research

▶ Using career clusters

▶ Finding information about a specific career

▶ Using the Internet to explore careers

▶ Using other career information sources

▶ Learning about careers through hands-on experiences

▶ Recording information about potential careers

What careers interest you? Do you know how to find out more about careers? Is the process an interesting one to you, or is it too far in the future to matter? In our changing world, planning a career is becoming more important every day.

*We should not let our fears hold us back from pursuing our hopes.*

—*John F. Kennedy*

# Section 4-1: Beginning to Think About a Career

Imagine yourself in the biggest mall in the world! It has stores you probably didn't even know existed! Where would you begin shopping? Now, imagine that you are at The Career Mall, which contains more than 20,000 different stores (or careers), and you don't even know what half of them offer. Who will you take with you as you walk through this mall? Will you travel alone or take a friend, some family members, or your marriage partner? Where will you start? When will you start? Where will you go? What will you choose? When will you stop?

In this chapter, you will "shop" and "browse" your way through The Career Mall as you begin exploring careers and thinking about the type of work you want to do. After you gather information, you will be ready to look for the careers that match your personality, interests, skills, and values.

*When will you begin "shopping" for your career?*

# Recognizing the Difference Between the Terms *Job* and *Career*

What is the difference between a job and a career? A **job** can be defined as work a person does for pay that does not require much training, knowledge, or experience. You might be willing to take a job even if you are not interested in it. A **career** is a person's life work, which requires planning, preparation, interest, and time. Name a job you have right now or might have in the future. Think about two or three careers you want to learn more about.

Sometimes jobs lead to careers. For example, Yolanda started out at age 16 as a crew member (the lowest, or **entry-level**, worker), at a fast-food restaurant. By the time she was a senior in high school, she had a higher-level position as a shift manager, the person in charge of people working during a period of time. She planned to attend a local community college, get a management degree, and eventually have a career in the food service industry. She wanted to be a manager over or owner of several restaurants some day. Can you think of other entry-level jobs that can eventually lead to careers?

Is work something people do just to make money? Realistically, for some people, the answer will be "yes." However, the majority of people work for something more. What do you believe are other reasons to work? Using your skills and abilities, getting a feeling of satisfaction from doing a good job, and helping others might be just a few of the other reasons why you choose to work.

*How many careers can you explore within your own high school setting?*

According to the U.S. Department of Labor, the average person will have at least 7 jobs before age 30! It is projected that many people will change jobs 10 to 12 times—and might change careers as many as 3 times before retirement. Approach these job changes with a positive attitude. Then you can make appropriate decisions about your future. Each job gives you more work experience, better job opportunities, and (in most cases) better pay.

Unless you are a freshman or new to your school campus, you know your way around fairly well. You know many teachers, counselors, and members of the administration. But if you look a little more closely, you will discover that the staff, faculty, and administration have many different occupations.

Let's take a "virtual tour." This tour starts before you come into the building. Many of you arrive at your destination, the school, in a bus. What jobs are required to make this bus available to you? Other than the obvious answer, let's look deeper. Who schedules all the bus routes? Who maintains the buses? What other jobs are related to the buses?

As you continue on your tour before school begins, you will see people working in a variety of offices. Some are administrators, such as the principal and dean of students. Others are guidance counselors and administrative assistants. You might meet the school nurse and a security guard on your tour. All these people help you meet your particular needs at different times during your high school career.

It's time for classes to begin, and you have the opportunity to explore many different careers available through your different classes. For example,

## CAREER FACT

Careers in law, law enforcement, and public safety can include correctional officer, emergency medical technician, firefighter, lawyer, paralegal, police officer, and security guard.

### Projected Outlook for 2016

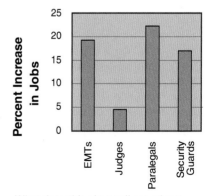

*What does this chart tell you about future opportunities in these careers?*

*Why is it natural for entry-level jobs to lead to higher-level jobs?*

**ETHICS**

### Which Client Was More Important?

You were the only one working in the law office when a thin older man wearing a worn brown coat came in, followed by a younger man in a classy suit. You offered to help the younger man first. He talked about first one problem and then another. When he finally finished, the older man had already slipped out. What does the choice you made about whom to help first say about you?

your Family and Consumer Sciences teacher can help you explore a wide variety of career fields, such as teaching, food sciences, fashion, hotel management, and interior design.

Lunch time! As you go through the lunch line and make your selections, watch the cooks and the other workers. Each one is responsible for a different role to make sure that you receive a nutritious, sanitary, and satisfactory meal at a very low cost. What tasks must they complete each day?

After lunch, your tour continues: You pass classrooms with computers, machinery, instruments, and tools that all look intriguing. You might want to investigate careers involving some type of equipment more thoroughly as you explore career options.

It's the end of the day, and the tour is over. Some days you might return home. Other days you will extend your school day as you go to sports activities, band, play practice, or other extracurricular clubs.

Can you think of any other careers you might discover on the "virtual tour" of your school campus? As you explore careers, think about what is before your eyes! You have a wonderful opportunity to learn about a variety of careers by observing the people around you. You will realize that all the careers represented involve specific interests, skills, and abilities. By researching careers, you will learn whether these match your interests.

# Using Informal Research

Now that you realize that career information is right before your eyes and all around you, can you think of other ways to explore careers? One way to explore careers is through **informal research**, which is learning about careers through a casual and friendly approach. This research can include observing people where you go to school, work, eat, shop, or spend your leisure time. When you observe people working in jobs that interest you, ask them if they would be willing to answer some questions about the work they do. (You may have to set up a separate time for this.) This type of informal research is often called an *informational* or *exploratory interview.* If they agree to answer your questions, listen carefully to what they have to say and make sure you thank them for helping you.

When you are making arrangements for informal research, you are **networking**, or talking to people you know and others in your community to gather and share information. Talking to other people about what they do and observing them in the workplace can give you a more complete picture of their careers.

Your network can include family and friends, people in your community, teachers and counselors, and employers or employees in businesses you use.

*Which experiences in your life are beginning to show you the careers you might want to explore?*

# Discovering Careers Through Formal Research

Through **formal research**, which involves using tools and information to investigate facts, you can discover even more information about jobs and careers. There are many tools you can use to formally research careers. Can you name some of these tools?

As you begin your formal research, it is important for you to know that all careers have been grouped in categories called career clusters. A **career cluster** is a group of occupations having related interests. These groupings include nearly all occupations from **entry level** (low-level jobs) to **professional level** (high-level careers that require earning a particular degree). Career cluster systems can help you explore a range of occupations in a specific area. Although several slightly different career cluster systems are available, the *Guide for*

*Where can you go for additional information about careers?*

*Occupational Exploration,* Third Edition (based on the original work by the U.S. Department of Labor and published by JIST Publishing) groups related occupations into 14 career clusters, shown in the following chart.

## Fourteen Career Interest Areas

| Career Cluster | Jobs Related to the Cluster |
|---|---|
| Arts, Entertainment, and Media | Actor/actress, coach, illustrator, writer |
| Science, Math, and Engineering | Anthropologist, chemist, computer programmer, veterinarian |
| Plants and Animals | Agriculture scientist, forester, landscaper, wildlife biologist |
| Law, Law Enforcement, and Public Safety | Correctional officer, detective, park ranger, special agent |
| Mechanics, Installers, and Repairers | Aircraft mechanic, communication equipment installer, medical equipment repairer |
| Construction, Mining, and Drilling | Bricklayer, electrician, pipe fitter, sheet metal worker |
| Transportation | Airline pilot, freight inspector, traffic technician, transportation manager |
| Industrial Production | Bakery worker, electronics tester, testing-machine operator |
| Business Detail | Administrative assistant, legal secretary, library assistant |
| Sales and Marketing | Advertising agent, public relations specialist, real estate sales agent |
| Recreation, Travel, and Other Personal Services | Convention planner, personal aide, social director |
| Education and Social Service | Caseworker, clergy member, teacher, urban planner |
| General Management and Support | Accountant, financial manager, human resource manager, purchasing agent |
| Medical and Health Services | Audiologist, health educator, medical assistant, recreational therapist |

*Which career clusters interest you the most?*

Information you will want to find about each career cluster includes

▸ Job title and summaries of jobs within each career cluster

▸ General job description

- ▶ Education and/or training required for each career cluster
- ▶ Skills required for the career cluster
- ▶ Average earnings
- ▶ **Projected outlook**, which is the prediction of future jobs and number of job openings expected

## 04.01 Managerial Work in Law, Law Enforcement, and Public Safety

Workers in this group manage fire and police departments. They set goals and policies, oversee financial and human resources, evaluate outcomes, and represent their departments to the public and the governments of the jurisdictions they serve. They work for cities and towns. Supervisors of forest fire fighters mostly work for the federal government.

### What kind of work would you do?

**Your work activities would depend on your job. For example, you might**
- Direct building inspections to ensure compliance with fire and safety regulations
- Discipline staff for violation of department rules and regulations

### What things about you point to this kind of work?

**Is it important for you to**
- Give directions and instructions to others?
- Have a feeling of accomplishment?

**Have you enjoyed any of the following as a hobby or leisure-time activity?**
- Directing traffic at community events
- Reading detective stories; watching television detective shows

**Are you able to**
- Communicate information and ideas in speaking so others will understand?
- Listen and understand information and ideas presented through spoken words and sentences?

**Would you work in places such as**
- Fire stations?
- Police headquarters?

### What skills and knowledge do you need for this kind of work?

- Coordination—adjusting actions in relation to others' actions
- Management of Personnel Resources—motivating, developing, and directing people as they work, identifying the best people for the job

*What information on this page would you use to determine whether you want to pursue a career in law enforcement?*

## Levels of Education

| Education | Examples of Careers |
| --- | --- |
| High School Diploma or G.E.D. | Child care worker |
| Proficiency Certificate | Credentialed or licensed day care provider |
| Associate Degree (AS) | Nursery school teacher |
| Bachelor of Science or Bachelor of Arts (BS/BA) | Kindergarten teacher |
| Master of Science or Master of Arts (MS/MA) | Children's librarian |
| Doctorate (MD or PhD) | Pediatrician |
| Educational Specialist (EdS) | Principal or superintendent of schools |

*Can you think of other careers that require these levels of education?*

### Section 4-1: Review

**Understanding Key Concepts**

1. What is the difference between a job and a career?
2. Give one example of a job and one example of a career.
3. List three reasons why people work.
4. Give one example of informal research and one example of formal research.
5. What information can you find about each career cluster?

**Thinking Creatively**

Who do you know who has a job that you want to know more about?
Can you name two or three jobs that match your current skills and interests?

**Taking It a Step Further**

Given the fact that most people have more than one career, is learning about career clusters still a worthwhile activity? Why or why not?

# Section 4-2: Gathering Information About a Specific Career

Where can you look for information about a specific career? Do you have many ideas about where to look for career information? With today's technologies, you can gather information very easily. You can also gather information through hands-on experiences.

# Using the Internet to Explore Careers

Many resources for exploring careers are available through the Internet. They are sponsored by the U.S. government, state governments, or educational institutions. Two Web sites sponsored by the Department of Labor (DOL) are the Occupational Outlook Handbook and the O*NET database. Check the Internet for the most up-to-date information.

**NETWORKING**

Talk to parents, friends, and neighbors to find someone who is willing to let you shadow them on the job for one day.

## Occupational Outlook Handbook

The terms *occupational outlook, job outlook,* and *employment outlook* all refer to information about opportunities for or changes in a career in the near future. The Occupational Outlook Handbook (OOH) provides information about 250 occupations. The DOL updates it frequently online. If you use only one source, this is the best one because it describes general information about jobs and careers. Using the OOH, you can learn about what workers do, how much they are paid, future job prospects, and working conditions. You can also learn about educational and training requirements, **advancement** (getting more responsibility and authority), and job trends.

http://www.dol.gov

*What types of information does the Bureau of Labor Statistics within the U.S. Department of Labor Web site offer?*

## O*NET Database

The O*NET database is a government-sponsored computer program that collects information from workers about their jobs. People can sort the database to find information about jobs—their titles, descriptions, requirements, and so on. Each entry in the database also lists *related occupations,* which are jobs that require similar knowledge, abilities, or skills. People can compare occupations and find out about skill changes now and in the future.

Look at the traffic technician example that follows. What are some things you can learn about that particular career?

---

### Career Research Checklist

When you are researching a specific career, gather the following information:

- ☑ What is the job description?
- ☑ How much education and training does the job require?
- ☑ What is the job demand?
- ☑ What can you do to prepare for the career?
- ☑ What kind of people will be most satisfied with this career?

---

## Traffic Technician

### Summary

Under the direction of a traffic engineer, traffic technicians conduct field studies to determine traffic volume, speed, effectiveness of signals, adequacy of lighting, and other factors influencing traffic conditions.

### Work Activities

▸ Answer the public's traffic-related questions, respond to complaints and requests, and discuss traffic control issues

▸ Draw traffic signal installations using computer-automated drafting equipment

▸ Plan, design, and improve components of traffic control systems

▸ Analyze data about traffic flow, accident rates, and proposed development to determine how best to improve traffic flow

### Employment

Nationally, about 6,916 traffic technicians work in this very small occupation group. However, most positions are in larger cities that have problems with traffic congestion and accidents.

### Outlook

Nationally, the number of jobs for traffic technicians is expected to grow at an average rate through the year 2016. As cities and suburban areas continue to grow, the need for traffic technicians will increase.

### Getting Hired

Employers prefer to hire traffic technicians who have a high school diploma or GED, and two years of experience or an associate degree. Employers also look for technicians who have good communication skills. Because they interview the public, technicians must be good at asking questions, listening, and writing reports.

### Job Advancement

Traffic technicians usually start as assistants. With experience, they can move up to associate and possibly to senior positions, depending on the size of the department. Some traffic technicians might need to move to larger cities if they want to advance.

### Knowledge

Design, Building and Construction, Engineering and Technology, Law and Government, Customer and Personal Service, Public Safety and Security, Transportation, Telecommunications

### Work Experience

Some traffic technicians learn their skills on the job. You might begin as an assistant within a traffic operations center. You work with an experienced technician or engineer who teaches you the skills needed to do the job.

### Helpful High School Courses

Computer and Information Sciences, Drafting, English Language and Literature, Mathematics, Social Sciences and History

### Skills

Check that equipment is working properly, determine how a system is working and how it can be improved, adapt equipment as necessary, adjust actions in relation to others' actions, figure out the effect of system changes.

### Interests

Realistic interests. Enjoy work activities that include practical, hands-on problems and solutions; working outside with plants, animals, and physical materials such as wood, tools, and machinery. Often prefer to work outside.

Investigative interests. Enjoy searching for facts and figuring out solutions to problems mentally.

Conventional interests. Enjoy work activities that follow set procedures, routines, standards, data and detail; and working where there is a clear line of authority to follow.

# Using Other Career Information Sources

The information at the OOH and O*NET Web sites is also printed in books. The *Occupational Outlook Handbook (OOH)* is reprinted every two years in book form. The O*NET *Dictionary of Occupational Titles* describes almost 1,000 of the most common jobs in the U.S. Department of Labor's O*NET database. The descriptions include information about skills, earnings, abilities, education, projected growth, and more.

In addition to the printed versions of the *OOH* and *O*NET,* you will want to look through the *Guide for Occupational Exploration (GOE)*. It gives a definition and explanation of each of 14 different career interest areas. It also lists work groups and subgroups, and provides the information you need to understand the career area.

There are many career publications, magazines, audiovisuals, and other online sources of career information. Your career counselor, media specialist, and teacher will have some other great resources for you to explore. You can borrow or check out most of these sources for short periods of time to take home.

# Learning About Careers Through Hands-On Experiences

**Hands-on experiences**—actually spending time on work sites—provide a realistic way to explore and research careers. Employers like to hire people who already have some experience in the workplace. There are many ways for you to get hands-on experience in today's workplace.

*What interests and aptitudes should a person entering this career have?*

▶ **Career shadowing** is observing a worker and asking questions for a day or less in a field of work you find interesting. For instance, a student interested in becoming a lawyer could spend a day with a lawyer, following her around the office, observing what she does in the courtroom as part of the everyday work schedule, and asking appropriate questions. Many adults in your community are very willing to take part in career shadowing.

▶ **Part-time work** is working a few hours each week over months or years. It gives you an opportunity to gain knowledge and skills as well as earn money to prepare for the future. There is a variety of opportunities in your community. Some examples include retail work experience at the local mall or food service work at a food establishment in your community.

▶ **Temporary work** is agreeing to work full-time or part-time for only a few weeks or months. It gives you the chance to gain skills and earn money for a limited time. Some examples include summer jobs, such as detasseling corn or working at an amusement park. Winter jobs might include working at a Christmas tree farm or helping businesses conduct an inventory, counting and recording the number of items the company has on a specific date.

*Name two or three people or careers you want to career shadow.*

▸ **Internships** are opportunities to work in an industry through a school-related program to gain skills and experience, usually without pay. Internships are one of the most valuable experiences you can have as you explore career opportunities. Many employers hire their interns as employees. Examples of high school internship opportunities include working in schools, preschools, day care centers, health care facilities, or auto service/repair businesses.

▸ **Cooperative education** programs offer students opportunities to go to school and work for pay at the same time. Typically, they spend part of the day at school and part of the day on the job. **ICE** (Interdisciplinary Cooperative Education) is an example of a program offered in many high schools. Students receive credits, grades, and a salary for working in a career-related field as part of their daily class schedule. Some opportunities might include health care, child care, auto service, retail service, construction, or farm work.

▸ **Volunteering** is working without pay. In some communities, opportunities for paid work experience are limited. You might choose to volunteer because you strongly believe in a cause. Check out local hospitals, nursing homes, veterinary offices, schools, and food pantries for volunteering opportunities. In many schools and communities, students have the opportunity to participate in **service learning** programs. The students do community service projects such as cleaning up neighborhoods, planting flowers at the city park, visiting the elderly in nursing homes, or raising money for philanthropic (not-for-profit) organizations, such as March of Dimes or Bowl-a-Thons for Junior Achievement.

**ETHICS**

**Who Should Be Responsible for the Damage?**

John Mellar went into his office, leaned back into his chair, put his feet up on the desk, and accidentally kicked the company laptop. It fell onto the floor and shattered the display screen. John shrugged the whole thing off. He said, "Oh, well. The company can afford to fix it. Good thing it wasn't mine." What does John's attitude demonstrate?

▶ **Entrepreneurship** is creating your own job. You might have started out as an entrepreneur at a very young age. In fact, it might have been your first paid job. Did you set up your own lemonade stand in your front yard? If so, you are an entrepreneur. If you are a creative person with self-motivation, you can be quite successful in operating your own business. If you can recognize a need in your community, you could turn it into a profit. Examples might include house-sitting, pet care, lawn care, or setting up Web sites for individuals or companies.

Whatever your area of interest, you can find sources of career information to help you explore careers and make choices.

# Recording Information About Potential Careers

Many resources are available to help you learn about potential careers. Record your career information systematically. You will see the similarities and differences of various careers. This knowledge will also help you realize the importance of researching careers before making decisions.

The following questions provide you with a guide as you research and record information about different occupations.

▶ What career are you researching?

▶ What is the definition/description of the career?

▶ What skills or abilities are needed to perform this occupation?

▶ How much education and training is needed for this career?

▶ What are the possibilities for advancement?

▶ What is the **work environment** (the surroundings) like? For example: fast or slow pace, quiet or noisy, indoor or outdoor work.

▶ How many hours are spent working (hours per day, days per week, and overtime)?

▶ What is the location (large city, rural area, or coastal) of the work?

▶ What duties, responsibilities, or types of work performance are required for this career?

▶ What personality type is best-suited to this occupation?

▶ What values and lifestyle best match this career?

▶ What is the average yearly salary for this occupation?

▶ How many jobs are currently available within this occupation?

▶ What is the projected job outlook for this career?

▶ What careers are related to this career?

# Case Study: Who Benefits from Volunteering?

Acacia was an eighth-grader when she decided to become a teen volunteer at the local hospital. One day each week, she spent several hours in different parts of the hospital doing a variety of tasks—including making beds, filling water pitchers, delivering flowers, and talking to patients.

**How could this volunteer service help Acacia make decisions about her future career goals?**

## CAREER FACT

If you enjoy classes in English, government, health, and social studies, you may want to consider one of these careers:

▸ Correctional officer
▸ Emergency medical technician
▸ Firefighter
▸ Lawyer
▸ Paralegal
▸ Police officer

## Section 4-2: Review

### Understanding Key Concepts

1. List and briefly describe two sources of online career information.
2. What kinds of career information can you find in the *GOE*?
3. Give five specific examples of different types of hands-on experiences.
4. Describe the difference between part-time and temporary work. Give examples of each.

### Thinking Creatively

Which type of hands-on experiences do you believe will be most worthwhile for you? Why?

Who will you career shadow if you have the opportunity? Why is career shadowing worthwhile?

### Taking It a Step Further

Using the Internet, research volunteer opportunities in your local community, state, the United States, and even other countries. Then create a list of those that interest you the most.

**Honorable Grant Hawkins, Superior Court Judge**
**Criminal Division Chair, Marion County**

I am a trial judge, sitting on the Superior Court bench in Marion County. I manage the court as an administrator and preside over criminal cases. The court has a staff of eight in addition to me. There are a number of deputy prosecutors and public defenders who work exclusively in this court. There are two deputy sheriffs who routinely provide security and transfer prisoners. The court "family" can get quite large.

I have a B.A. from Wesleyan University in Middletown, CT. I also have a J.D. from Indiana School of Law, Indianapolis. When I was in high school, I thought I wanted to be a doctor. For 27 years after I was admitted to practice law, I had a private practice. I also held a contract as a public defender. You might say that I stayed in my entry-level position until I was elected to the bench.

In my free time, I enjoy the sports my body allows me to play. I also enjoy reading, and, because I am an elected official, I attend a number of community and political functions each month.

I am afraid I did not do too good a job of balancing my personal life and work during the early years of my career and my marriage. I spent too much time developing and maintaining my legal practice. As a result, I did not spend enough time with my children while they were growing up. I am sorry I missed that opportunity. Now that I am a judge, it is easier to find a balance. However, one of the reasons there is more time is that my children are grown up, and they aren't around enough for me to spend a lot of quality time with them.

# Chapter Review and Activities

The following sections can help you review the contents of this chapter and develop your workplace competencies.

## Key Concepts

Following are the key concepts presented in the chapter.

▸ Recognizing and defining the differences between jobs and careers will help you prepare for your future.

▸ As you begin to think about careers, it will be very important for your future to learn more about them through both informal and formal research.

▸ Careers are grouped in career clusters. You can find information about careers within these different clusters.

▸ Information about careers is available through a wide variety of resources—including the Internet, books, magazines, and videotapes.

▸ You can learn about careers through many different hands-on experiences—including career shadowing, part-time work, temporary work, internships, cooperative education, volunteering, and entrepreneurships.

▸ By researching and recording information systematically, you can learn more about potential careers.

## Key Term Review

Complete the following activity to review your understanding of the key terms.

| | | |
|---|---|---|
| advancement | formal research | part-time work |
| career | hands-on experiences | professional level |
| career cluster | I.C.E. | projected outlook |
| career shadowing | informal research | service learning |
| cooperative education | internships | temporary work |
| entrepreneurship | job | volunteering |
| entry level | networking | work environment |

You are the trainer for your local police department. Using at least 10 of the key terms in this list, write an article for the monthly newsletter, telling the employees about the types of training available to people seeking a career in law enforcement.

## Comprehension Review

Answer the following questions to review the main concepts in the chapter.

**1.** What are the differences between a job and a career?

**2.** What is the difference between entry- and higher-levels of employment?

**3.** How can you informally research careers?

**4.** How can you formally research careers?

**5.** Which hands-on experiences offer opportunities to learn about careers?

## School-to-Work

**Math:** Your boss is leaving for the day. On the way out, he tells you that the prices on all the 50¢ candy bars rose by 20 percent. Because you are the shift manager, he asks that you calculate the new prices and then make certain that the two other crew members and you change the prices on each candy bar. You know from the inventory report that the store has 15 boxes containing 12 bars. How will you calculate the new prices? How many candy bars must each crew member sticker if you have equal workloads? Write down the steps you would take to solve these mathematical problems and the correct answers.

**Social Studies:** Research the career clusters of law enforcement, firefighting, or public safety. In your opinion, what are the benefits and drawbacks involved with taking care of society?

**Writing:** Write a letter to someone currently employed in a career that interests you. In the letter, explain that you are seeking more information about that career, tell him why you are interested in it, and request to meet with (or at least talk to) him about the career.

**Science:** What does an NIEHS scientist do?

---

## Does This Job Interest You?

The following job is posted on the Internet. What education and experience are required? What requirement does this job have that most jobs do not have? What types of interests and skills should a person working in this position have? How could someone apply for the job?

| FIND JOBS | POST RESUMES |
| --- | --- |

### Emergency Services Director

**Salary:** $62,228–$82,451
Excellent fringe benefits

### Job Description

Our county government is seeking a Emergency Services Director to be responsible for the supervision of the 911 emergency dispatcher center for Fire, Police, Emergency Services (EMS); management of the county-wide emergency radio network; coordination of emergency planning for all man-made and natural disasters; management of the animal control division within the county; and coordination with Fire, EMS, and Law Enforcement of all disaster and Hazardous Materials responses.

### Job Requirements

Requires a Bachelor's degree in Emergency Management Planning or related field; training in situations affecting hazardous materials; eight years of experience in emergency communication, telecommunication, or hazardous materials, which includes four years in a management/supervisory capacity; and five years experience in emergency management and emergency contingency planning.

### Contact

**Department of Human Resources**
P. O. Box 654
St. Louis, MO 20050
111-475-4200  FAX: 111-475-4082

Apply Online

© JIST Works

# What career appeals to you?

Mechanics, Installers, and Repairers Careers

# Chapter 5

# Creating a Career Plan

## What You'll Learn

▸ Understand the steps to create a career plan

▸ Explore possible lifestyles

▸ Define your goal

▸ Consider educational options

▸ Evaluate your findings

▸ Make a decision

▸ Put your plan into action

▸ Determine your educational path

▸ Gain career experience

What if selecting a career were like playing a game show? What if you selected the "wrong" curtain? Fortunately, you can have control of your choices. This chapter will introduce you to the questions you should ask about careers, and it will suggest sources to use for career information.

*Before everything else, getting ready is the secret of success.*

*—Henry Ford*

# Section 5-1: Steps to Creating a Career Plan

As a young child, you might have pretended that you were a teacher, astronaut, doctor, or professional basketball player. You enjoyed living in your imaginary world. You could be anything you imagined in your imaginary world on any particular day.

As a teenager, you are now realizing that you need to be more realistic than you were in the world of your imagination. You also realize that you are in control of your life as you prepare for a successful career. As you continue to mature and explore careers, you need to create a career plan. You can do this by exploring your lifestyle, defining your goal, evaluating your possible career choices, considering your educational options, making a decision, and putting your plan into action.

*If you were a contestant on the Career Game Show, which curtain would you choose?*

## The Career Game Show

| | |
|---|---|
| Announcer: | "It's time for the Career Game Show! Please welcome our host." |
| Host: | "Are you ready? You have five seconds to select your career. Behind one curtain is a career as a doctor!" |

*(Loud cheering and wild applause)*

| | |
|---|---|
| Host: | "And behind another curtain is a career as a teacher!" |

*(More applause and cheering)*

| | |
|---|---|
| Host: | "But behind a third curtain is unemployment." |

*(Boos and hisses from the audience)*

| | |
|---|---|
| Host: | "But just one quick reminder before you select a curtain: This is what you will do for the next 40 years! Are you ready? Which curtain will you select?" |

# Explore Your Lifestyle

Your lifestyle is your way of living that reflects your values and attitudes; it is how you express yourself. How do you want to spend your day? What are the activities that you enjoy the most? To begin creating the lifestyle you want, identify your personality, aptitudes, interests, skills, and values. You can then narrow your choices to a few career groups or clusters that appear to be a good fit for you. Your next step is to evaluate those career-cluster choices through research. After researching your choices, you will be better prepared to determine which careers within the clusters are realistic for you, match your values, and fit the lifestyle you want for yourself.

It is important for you to realize that no one expects you to narrow your career choices to just one. At this time in your life, selecting just one career might mean ignoring other possibilities that could be better choices. Keep at least two or three in mind.

You will want to explore specific careers by comparing what you want or expect in a career and lifestyle to what the specific careers you have identified require or offer. Consider the following:

**Career outlook.** What will be the demand for your career choice 10 years from now? Why is this demand an important factor? Your research will give you predictions about the number of job openings in the future. Zack, for example, really enjoyed spending a day career-shadowing his uncle who is a plumber. He decided to research the career and discovered that there will be a demand for plumbers over the next several years.

**Focus of the work.** Do you prefer working with **data** (information, words, facts, numbers, or statistics), people, or **things** (objects such as machinery, computers, or tools)? Most careers involve working with all three categories, although usually more with one than the others. For example, auto service technicians work with all three categories, but most of their work is with things. Can you think of other examples?

**CAREER FACT**

Careers as mechanics, installers, and repairers can include appliance repair, auto mechanics, diesel mechanics, electrical repairers, heating and air conditioning technicians, millwrights, precision instrument repairers, and small engine mechanics.

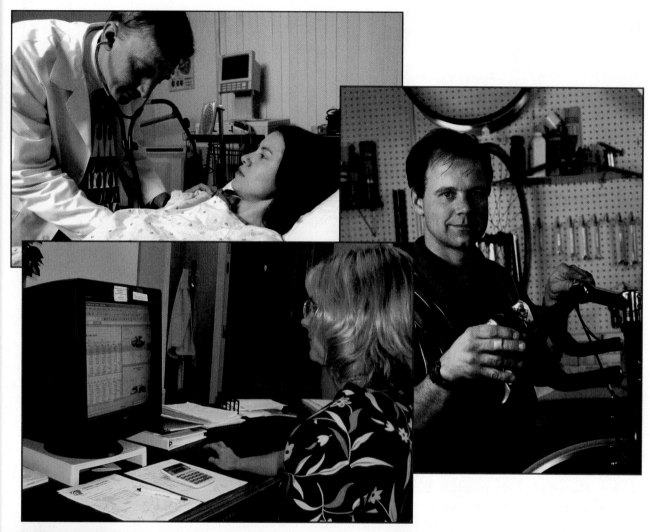

*Do you prefer to work with people, data, or things?*

**Education and training.** It is critically important to understand that in today's workplace you must be a **lifelong learner**; your education and training will never be finished. Even if you stay at the same job or career for 30 years, you will need to upgrade your skills, training, and knowledge. It is also important to realize that different jobs and careers have different education and training requirements. By 2016, about 65 percent of all workers will be in jobs that require more education or training than they can learn in a few weeks on the job, according to government predictions. Will you hang in there and go to school for two more years after high school to get a better job? Does obtaining a four-year bachelor's degree sound reasonable for you? Do you value education enough to get a doctorate degree? These are options you must consider while making your career plan.

**Responsibilities and tasks.** What will you actually be doing in the career you have chosen? What will the day-to-day tasks include? Do you do the same thing day after day, or does each day bring new experiences? Is the career fast-paced and stressful or easy with less pressure? Consider responsibilities and tasks carefully as you choose a career.

# Unemployment Rate by Level of Education

*How can you use the information in these tables in making decisions about your future?*

| Unemployment Rate | Level of Education |
|---|---|
| 1.4% | Doctoral degree |
| 1.1% | Professional degree |
| 1.7% | Master's degree |
| 2.3% | Bachelor's degree |
| 3.0% | Associate degree |
| 3.9% | Some college, no degree |
| 4.3% | High school graduate |
| 6.8% | Less than a high school diploma |

*Note: This data reflects annual averages for 2006 for full-time workers age 25 and older.*

*Source: Bureau of Labor Statistics, Current Population Survey.*

## Ten Fastest-Growing Occupations

| Occupation | Employment 2006 | Employment 2016 | Number of New Jobs | Percent Growth | Source of Postsecondary Education and Training |
|---|---|---|---|---|---|
| Network systems and data communications analysts | 262,000 | 402,000 | 140,000 | 53% | Bachelor's degree |
| Personal and home care aides | 767,000 | 1,156,000 | 389,000 | 51% | Short-term on-the-job training |
| Home health aides | 787,000 | 1,171,000 | 384,000 | 49% | Short-term on-the-job training |
| Computer software engineers, applications | 507,000 | 733,000 | 226,000 | 45% | Bachelor's degree |
| Veterinary technologists and technicians | 71,000 | 100,000 | 29,000 | 41% | Associate degree |
| Personal financial advisors | 176,000 | 248,000 | 72,000 | 41% | Bachelor's degree |
| Makeup artists, theatrical and performance | 2,000 | 3,000 | 1,000 | 40% | Postsecondary vocational award |
| Medical assistants | 417,000 | 565,000 | 148,000 | 35% | Moderate-term on-the-job training |
| Veterinarians | 62,000 | 84,000 | 22,000 | 35% | First professional degree |
| Substance abuse and behavioral disorder counselors | 83,000 | 112,000 | 29,000 | 34% | Bachelor's degree |

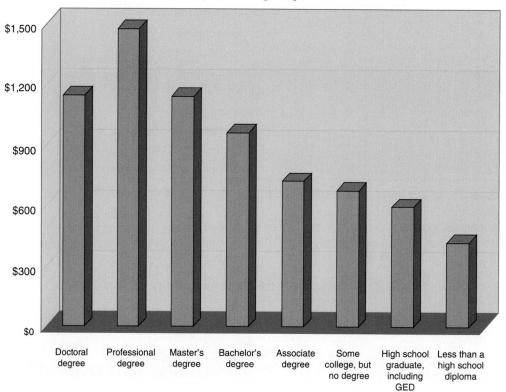

## Median Weekly Earnings by Education Level

$1,500

$1,200

$900

$600

$300

$0

Doctoral degree | Professional degree | Master's degree | Bachelor's degree | Associate degree | Some college, but no degree | High school graduate, including GED | Less than a high school diploma

Note: Median is the middle number in a set of ordered numbers, which means half of the workers at this level earn more and half earn less. Also, this data reflects annual averages for 2006 for full-time workers age 25 and older.

Source: Bureau of Labor Statistics, Current Population Survey

*How much schooling are you willing to complete to increase your earnings?*

---

### ETHICS

**Whose Job Is It To Be Respectful, Anyway?**

You were having a bad day even before you got to work. Your friends did not wait for you before school, you had to sit with strangers at lunch, and your teacher made fun of you in class because you flunked a quiz. The minute you stepped through the door, your supervisor growled, "Why are you late?" What will you say?

---

**Salary.** How much money do you expect to make each year? This is a very broad question that depends on many factors. They include how much education and training you have, how many years of experience you have, where the work is located (what part of the country), and how many people are available to fill the positions. You can find information about the **salary** (cash payment for work performed) to expect in each career you research.

**Skills and aptitudes.** Learning a skill is much easier if you already have the aptitude for it. If you can match your natural talents to careers that require the same abilities, you are on the road to success. Emily, for example, has always enjoyed helping and teaching others. During her high school career, she took a Cadet Teaching class and found out that she really enjoys working with five- and six-year-olds. She plans to attend college to become a kindergarten teacher.

**Values.** Your values should match the values required in a particular career. Michael wants to be an accountant. He knows that he will be expected to be very honest. Why is honesty important if you are considering being an accountant?

**Work environment.** What type of environment do you prefer to work in? Could you describe the "perfect" work setting? Do you like being indoors or outdoors? Could you spend 40 hours each week in an office with no windows? Would you be willing to work outdoors even if the temperature could range from 10 degrees in the winter to 90 degrees in the summer?

**Working hours.** If you could choose one of the following work schedules, which would it be: 8 a.m. to 5:00 p.m.? 3:00 p.m. to 11:00 p.m.? Midnight to 7:00 a.m.? Why? In some cases, you might be able to arrange **flextime** (employees set their schedules to fit their lives). For example, you might want to be home to meet a service technician or when your children get home from school at 4:00 p.m. By utilizing flextime, you could be at work by 7:30 a.m., take only half an hour for lunch, and leave work at 3:30 p.m.

The decisions you make about your career focus, amount of training, level of responsibility, desired salary, work environment, work hours, and the personal values that you want to emphasize in your job will determine your future lifestyle. What decisions will you make?

## Define Your Goal

What is your goal? Where do you want to go? Would you take a long trip without a road map to give you visual directions? Think of your high school career as a "road map" that will lead you to your destination and a successful career. If you want to be successful, you must plan your route, a specific path that leads to where you want to go. As you move from middle school to high school, your parents and you need to meet with your high school counselors to outline the different academic paths available and how they relate to different career choices. Your teachers can also help you identify goals and routes.

*What work environment do you prefer?*

It is important that you develop your own **personal road map**, a plan for reaching your career goals, early in your high school career. When you do, you can realistically work toward your career goals.

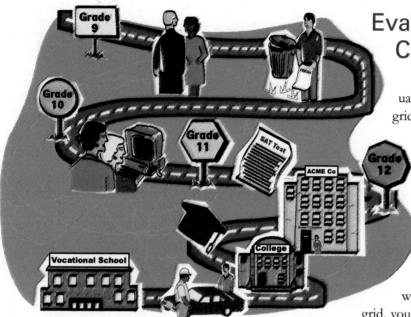

*What path will you take to career success?*

## Evaluate Your Possible Career Choices

You can use an expanded grid to evaluate possible career choices. To create your grid using paper, skip a couple of lines on a sheet of paper and then list all your possible career choices in columns across the top of the paper. Then, in the blank lines along the left edge of the paper, create a new row for each factor you think is important to consider, such as Career Outlook, Focus of the Work, Education and Training, or Responsibilities and Tasks. (If you want to use the computer to create the grid, you can use a spreadsheet or the Table feature in your word processing program.)

| | Career 1 | Career 2 | Career 3 |
|---|---|---|---|
| Career Outlook | 20% increase | 10% increase | 10% increase |
| Focus of the Work | Data | Data | People |
| Education and Training | Bachelor's | Associate | Master's |
| Responsibilities and Tasks | Research Writing reports Supervising | Research Writing reports | Interview Counseling Training |
| Salary | $50,000 | $35,000 | $75,000 |
| Skills and Aptitudes | Math Writing | Math Writing | Communications Human relations Management |
| Values | Attention to detail | Attention to detail | Helping others |
| Work Environment | Office | Office | Office Travel |
| Working Hours | 8 to 5 Some overtime | 8 to 5 | Variable |

*How would creating a chart like this help someone choose from among several career options?*

## Section 5-1: Review

### Understanding Key Concepts

1. What steps are involved in creating a career plan?
2. Why is it important for you to develop your own personal road map?
3. How does gathering information about yourself help you with creating a career plan?
4. What are the areas of information about yourself and careers that you can compare?
5. How can you organize your findings so that you can make a decision?

### Thinking Creatively

Why do children often have such strong beliefs about their future careers?

What causes them to abandon their dreams?

### Taking It a Step Further

Identify a career that you doubt you could (but would really like to) achieve: famous pop star, doctor, Supreme Court judge, or whatever. List every obstacle in your path and brainstorm ways to remove those obstacles. Then create a plan you could follow to achieve the career.

# Section 5-2: Considering Your Educational Options

After you consider career choices, you are ready to look more closely at the education and training needed for the choices. Global competition and today's economy have increased the need for postsecondary education and training. Some type of education and training will be required for any career you choose. Many options are available. You will need to decide which one(s) are best for you.

## Different Levels of Education

High School Diploma or GED

Proficiency Certificate

Associate of Science Degree (AS)

Bachelor of Science or Bachelor of Arts (BS/BA)

Master of Science or Master of Arts (MS/MA)

Educational Specialist (EdS)

Doctorate (MD or PhD)

*Do you understand what each of these levels of education requires?*

# High School Diploma or GED

GED (General Educational Development) tests measure whether a person has the knowledge and skill of a high school graduate. To earn a GED certificate, a person must score at a certain level on multiple-choice tests in reading, writing, social studies, science, and mathematics and write a satisfactory, timed essay. The GED enables people who are unable to complete a traditional high school education to continue their education and improve their job opportunities.

To receive a high school diploma, students must earn a certain number of credits. Students typically earn one credit for each class they pass. Some classes, such as English or mathematics, are required. Classes that students choose, such as foreign languages, music, or child development, are called *electives*. Students often question the value of required classes, but as the table of SCANS skills in Chapter 2 shows, today's employers expect all employees to have skills in reading, writing, and mathematics. However, some careers require more of one than others, as shown in the following list.

## Careers That May Interest You

| Requiring English | Requiring Math |
|---|---|
| Accountant | Accountant |
| Advertising Agent | Actuary |
| Arts Administrator | Aerospace Engineer |
| Banker | Air Traffic Control Analyst |
| Buyer | Applied Mathematician |
| Career Consultant | Architect |
| Civil Service Worker | Astronomer |
| Computer Programmer | Attorney |
| Customs and Immigration Agent | Civil Engineer |
| Editor | Communications Specialist |
| Health Service Worker | Computer/Engineer |
| Hotel and Catering Manager | Computer/Sales |
| Housing Manager | Computer Operator |
| Information Scientist | Cryptographer |
| Insurance Agent | Designer |
| IT Consultant | Ecologist |
| Journalist | Economist |
| Lawyer | Engineer |
| Librarian | Environmental Technologist |
| Market Researcher | Financial Analyst |
| Marketing Specialist | Information Scientist |
| Multimedia/Web Designer | Inventory Strategist |
| Nurse | Investment Banker |
| Occupational Therapist | Investment Manager |
| Officer in Armed Forces | Market Research Analyst |

| Requiring English | Requiring Math |
|---|---|
| Police Officer | Meteorologist |
| Politician | Network Programmer |
| Publicist | Operations Researcher/Analyst |
| Publisher | Physician |
| Radio/TV Personnel | Physicist |
| Real Estate Agent | Practical Nurse |
| Retail Manager | Research Scientist |
| Salesperson | Robotics Programmer |
| Social Worker | Software Developer |
| Systems Analyst | Statistical Analyst/Statistician |
| Teacher | Systems Analyst/Engineer |
| Writer | Teacher |

Grades are becoming more critical in today's schools as well. Grades have been used as a factor for entrance into college for a long time, but more and more employers also consider high school grades. What if your school board decided to drop the letter grade *D* from the grading scale? In other words, any grade below *C* would be considered failing. This would certainly be more compatible with today's workplace. What do you believe are some reasons why employers want employees who perform at a higher level than *D* work?

The successful student will know how to learn; unsuccessful students will have excuses why they can't learn. What are some of these excuses? How would you argue against these excuses? The successful student and most valuable employee will find ways to acquire education and training beyond high school.

Graduating from high school without a specific purpose or job preparation increases your chances of being unemployed. Dropping out of high school increases your chances even more. In times of **economic recession**, a period of economic decline when demand for work is low or even stops, the first workers to be laid off are typically high school dropouts. The choice will be yours. Will *you* choose to drop out or graduate?

# On-the-Job Training and Apprenticeship

Almost every job offers some on-the-job training (OJT) so that new employees can learn the specific skills necessary to working for a particular employer, such as using specialized equipment. The advantage of OJT is that trainees can earn money while they learn job skills.

In an **apprenticeship**, a person learns a trade while working for an employer. There are many occupations that require apprenticeships, as shown in the chart. Apprenticeships are centuries old. They date back to the 12th century in England. Men were **indentured** to an employer for about seven years. They had a legal contract for service with a specific trade. At the end of the seven years, the apprentice became a journeyman or craftsman and eventually a master craftsman who would indenture an apprentice of his own.

**DISCRIMINATION**

**Do You Have a Right to Regular Breaks?**

In your work as a data entry clerk, you get very tired after two hours of typing and staring at the computer screen. On a Web site on time management, you read that taking a 10-minute break can refresh your mind, protect your eyesight, and keep your wrists from getting Carpel Tunnel Syndrome. However, your employer refuses to allow any breaks other than your half-hour lunch. Can you sue him for discrimination or at least report him for poor working conditions?

**CAREER FACT**

The number of jobs for small engine mechanics is projected to increase because people are buying more motorcycles, boats, and lawn and garden equipment that will need repairs.

*What difference will it make in your life if you do not get your high school diploma?*

Today, apprenticeships range from one to seven years and include men and women. The apprentice receives on-the-job training and classroom instruction from craftspeople and journey workers (certified, experienced, skilled people).

## A Brief Listing of Apprenticeship Programs

| | |
|---|---|
| Carpenters | Plumbers |
| Millwrights | Pipefitters |
| Electricians | Sheet Metal Workers |
| Bricklayers | |
| Iron Workers | |

*Do you know anyone in an apprenticeship program? Are you considering one of these programs?*

## Career and Technical Education (CTE Schools)

**CTE schools** prepare students for the job market in very specific skills such as **cosmetology** (the art of styling hair, applying makeup, and grooming nails) or diesel mechanics. Sometimes these schools have other names, such as trade schools, technical colleges, business colleges, or conservatories. Most CTE schools look at trends in the labor market. Then they design programs for popular careers.

Programs can include many trades, but also include business and health-related careers—for example, certified nurse's aid (CNA) and licensed practical nurse (LPN), firefighting, emergency medical technician (EMT), computer aided design (CAD), and computer programming and repair. The schools have small classes and offer job-placement assistance after graduation. CTE school classes focus specifically on the career you have selected. The overall amount of time spent in class is often shorter than required in other **postsecondary** (after high school) programs.

**Projected Outlook for 2016**

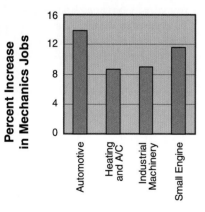

*What does this chart tell you about future opportunities in these careers?*

## A Brief Listing of CTE Programs

**Technology Training**

Computer Applications

eCommerce Design

Electrical Engineering Technology

Information Technology

Network Administration

Web Engineering

**Continuing Medical Education**

Dental Assistant

Health and Exercise Sciences

Health Care Administration

Massage Therapy

Medical Assistant

Medical Transcription

Nursing

Pharmacy Technician

Ultrasound Technician

X-Ray Technician

**Art Schools and Institutes**

Advertising

Culinary

Fashion Design

Fashion Merchandising and Marketing

Film

Graphic Design

Industrial Design

Interior Design

Photography

Web Design

**Career Education**

Automotive Technician

Aviation Maintenance

Electrician

Hospitality Management

Plumbing

Travel and Tourism

Welding

**Business Schools**

Accounting

Business Administration

Secretarial

Court Reporting

Criminal Justice

Homeland Security

Legal Assistant

Paralegal

*Is attending a vocational or tech prep school a good decision for you?*

**CAREER FACT**

The demand for appliance repairers is expected to grow slightly because appliances are becoming more complicated and expensive.

**COMMUNITY**

SkillsUSA is a career and technical student organization for high school and college students who are taking classes toward a career in technical, skilled, and service occupations. Members of SkillsUSA can participate in local, regional, and national competitions in a wide variety of skill areas, such as auto repair, electronics, food service, and health care. Visit your local chapter or the SkillsUSA Web site at www. skillsusa.org to find out more information.

# Military Training

Military training requires self-discipline and dedication. Can you name all the branches of the U.S. military?

To **enlist** or join a branch of the military, you must provide a Social Security number, driver's license, birth certificate, and proof of high school graduation or the equivalent. Next is the three-part screening process: physical, moral or ethical, and aptitude. If you pass the prequalification, you must go to a Military Entrance Processing Station (MEPS). You are then given further examinations, interviewed, and asked to take the Oath of Enlistment.

## The Cost of Education

How will you pay for the education you choose? Not only will you have to pay tuition (the cost of classes), but you may also have to pay for books, laboratory fees, food, and housing. Have you and your parents started saving for these future costs?

About half of the students in postsecondary education receive some sort of financial aid to help them pay for their education. Financial aid can include the following:

▶ **Scholarships and grants:** Federal and state governments, colleges, and community organizations give this money to students. Students may receive this money because of outstanding athletic, artistic, or academic achievement or because of financial need.

▶ **Work-study programs:** Students who qualify for this program earn part of their tuition money by working for their school or a nonprofit organization.

▶ **Student loans:** State and federal governments provide this money through schools and banks to qualified students to help with educational costs. When the students complete their education, they have to pay back this money with *interest* (a charge for borrowing money).

To apply for financial aid, students must complete the Free Application for Federal Student Aid (FAFSA). The government uses the financial information that students and their parents provide on this form, which can be completed online, to determine how much financial aid the students should receive.

*Is a military career for you?*

Each Armed Service has its own **basic training** (officially called Initial-Entry Training and informally called "Boot Camp"). This training develops the enlistees and helps them realize their potential. The training can vary between 6 and 13 weeks. However, the education doesn't end at basic training. Each Armed Service also offers advanced training that builds on the foundation established in basic training. The advanced training gives you the opportunity to strengthen your skills and gain new ones for specialized roles in the military. When you complete your time of service, the government pays for additional education.

Just a reminder to male students: Nearly all 18-year-old men living in the U.S. must register with the Selective Service. It's the law and your civic duty. In fact, most states require a young man to be registered with the Selective Service before renewing his driver's license. The easiest way to register is to go to www.sss.gov and register online. By registering, you also stay eligible for college loans and grants, job training, and federal jobs.

Females in the United States do not have to register. However, there are equal opportunities for males and females in today's military. You will have many opportunities to discuss career opportunities with the U.S. military while you are in high school.

## Colleges and Universities

If you attend a college or university after high school, you need to decide which college program will prepare you for your chosen career path. You have many choices, including the college to attend, the major (area of study) to pursue, and the classes to take.

## One- and Two-Year Community Colleges

One- and two-year community colleges offer full- and part-time degree programs and other programs. Full-time and part-time study can lead to a two-year **associate degree** and requires attending school several hours each day, several days per week. Just as with high school, attending school and studying will be your priority for several months or years as you work toward your career objective. Credits earned in an associate degree program will usually **transfer** to (be accepted by) another college or university.

Some people do not need two to four years of college to prepare for a career. They need a series of classes that teach specific skills for specific careers. These series of classes, called **certificate programs** or **diploma programs**, typically require completing several months to two years of classes. The certificate you receive verifies that you have the skills necessary to work in the particular career field.

Community colleges also often offer short courses that will help you upgrade your job skills. Short courses might last for only a few days or weeks. More and more short courses are being taught via the Internet.

## Four-Year Colleges and Universities

Approximately 2,000 accredited colleges and universities across the United States offer many of the same programs that the one- and two-year community schools offer, but also four-year programs of study. These four-year programs lead to a four-year **bachelor's degree**, either a Bachelor of Arts or Bachelor of Science. Many professional positions require a minimum of a bachelor's degree.

Universities are organized by a number of different schools or colleges for teaching and research. Each school or college within the university might offer both undergraduate- and graduate-level degrees. They also offer advanced study or specialized degrees in many areas, such as law and medicine. Which careers require a **graduate degree**? Which careers require an advanced degree—such as a **master's degree** or **doctoral degree**—that is earned after a bachelor's degree?

*What are the advantages of attending a college?*

## Purdue University - West Lafayette Campus Schools

Agriculture

Consumer and Family Sciences

Education

Engineering

Health Sciences

Liberal Arts

Management

Nursing

Pharmacy

Science

Technology ──────────→

Veterinary Medicine

**Educational Requirements in Technology**

Computer Repair —
Technical Certificate (CISCO)

Computer Programmer —
Associate Degree (2 years college)

Computer System Administrator —
Bachelor's Degree (4+ years college)

*What programs does the college nearest you offer?*

# Distance Learning

One of the newest sources of education is **distance learning** or Internet classes. These "virtual universities" exist only as Internet sites. This form of education can be helpful to people who live a great distance from a college campus or because of their jobs or personal lives can't take the time to go to a class several days each week.

## Section 5-2: Review

### Understanding Key Concepts

1. List three careers that require both math and English skills.
2. What is the difference between an apprentice program and a CTE school?
3. What are three advantages of selecting military training to receive your education?
4. What is the difference between a community college and a university?

### Thinking Creatively

What types of postsecondary schools are located near you?
What are the advantages of going to a postsecondary school that is far away from your home? What are the disadvantages?

### Taking It a Step Further

Research the topic of distance learning on the Internet. What courses are offered that interest you? What problems would you have if that were the only type of education available to you? Write a paper that discusses the Internet courses that interest you and the advantages and disadvantages of distance learning for you personally.

# Section 5-3: Developing a Career Plan

Two important actions you need to take early in your high school career are to make a decision about the career area that interests you and to begin planning. These action areas can affect whether you achieve your career goal.

## Make a Decision

"Jump in! Come on. Just jump in." Haven't you heard this at the swimming pool? It is a brave move in some cases, isn't it? How is selecting a career similar to just "jumping in"? Now is the time to make some choices. Which careers you choose to pursue will depend on many factors, but unless you begin now, it is unlikely that anything will happen at all. The good news is that if you set a goal, you are more likely to achieve it. Also, remember that **flexibility**, your willingness to change or adapt, is very important because you have many, many years to make changes in your life.

## Case Study: What Should Mariasha Do?

Mariasha loves to fix computers, televisions, and other electrical equipment. She enjoys finding the problem and fixing it. She also is very good at math, but found out after one semester of the class that she dislikes accounting.

**What career options should Mariasha consider?**

# Begin Planning

Planning is an important part of everyday life. It is also critical for reaching your goals. Individuals and groups have plans for reaching goals, whether it is a game, an event, or a career choice. What are some examples of planning?

To say that you're planning to win the game is good, but is it enough? You must be ready to put your plan into action. What equipment do you need? What skills does your opponent have? To decide that you are going to be a teacher is great, but what's your plan? What type of a teacher do you want to be? What degree will you need? The more specific your plan, the easier it will be to put your plan into action—and the more likely you will be to succeed.

In creating your plan, think of these specific issues for two different careers:

▶ Would I most like a career in which I work with data, people, or things?

▶ What work environment would I enjoy the most?

▶ What work environment would I enjoy the least?

▶ What physical requirements would I like for my job to have?

▶ What physical requirements would I not want my job to have?

▶ Would I like to own my own business?

Begin achieving your career goal by setting realistic short-term goals that will help you reach your long-term goal. These short-term goals are called **stepping-stone goals**. There are several advantages of setting stepping-stone goals. They help you achieve results and give you opportunities to make changes along the way.

## Determine Your Educational Path

You have thousands of schools to choose from. The following are some suggestions for selecting a school—whether you are considering a certificate program, a community college, or a university:

▶ Check to see whether the school is **accredited**—that it has met certain minimum standards by an accrediting agency in the U.S.

▶ Write or visit several schools before making a choice.

▶ Ask questions about course offerings, costs, job placement, and hours of instruction.

▶ Check to see whether local employers or government programs offer similar training at no cost.

▶ Talk with people who have attended the school.

First, narrow your choices. Then begin the admissions application process for each school. You can complete most of this process online, although paper applications are still available. Admission requirements for a four-year university are often very similar to those in the chart.

## Typical University Admission Requirements for Beginning Students

| High school diploma or GED | All applicants must either graduate from high school or have a GED. |
| --- | --- |
| Subject-matter requirements | Universities have subject-matter requirements in English, math, and laboratory science; some students might have foreign language requirements as well. |
| Quality requirements | Applicants who meet the minimum subject-matter requirements are evaluated on the basis of quality. Quality includes much more than just high school class rank; it also encompasses your probability of success, overall grade average, grade average in degree-related subjects, trends in achievement, SAT and/or ACT scores, and the strength of your college prep program. |

*What admissions requirements does the school that most interests you have?*

## Gain Career Experience

What do these activities have in common: babysitting, baling hay, delivering newspapers, and selling lemonade? These are all experiences that can contribute to your career plans. Every experience you have shapes your likes and dislikes, your skills and aptitudes, and your values and goals. How can a grade school experience such as selling lemonade affect your future career plans?

Plan hands-on experiences, actually working in the career environment, that allow you to explore careers. You can use career-shadowing, part-time work, temporary work, internships, volunteering, or entrepreneurships. You can also take part in cooperative education programs such as I.C.E. or service learning programs to learn more.

An important part of exploring careers and creating your own career plan is comparing the information about a career with your reactions to your experiences. For example, if you dislike mowing lawns because of the heat, you might not want to seek a career involving working outside in hot weather. On the other hand, if you enjoy working in the school bookstore, you might be interested in marketing and sales. Can you think of other examples?

Be aware, though, that most careers involve some activities that you might not enjoy. The goal is to choose a career that involves as many of your interests and as few of your dislikes as possible.

### Consider the Alternative

After reading this book, you should have a clearer idea about your primary career goal, which is the career you want most. As you work toward this goal, however, you also should consider alternative career goals.

Suppose your primary career goal has strict physical requirements, such as an athlete or a dancer. What happens if you are injured and can't meet those requirements? What if changes in technology or the economy eliminate jobs in the career you want? What if you aren't accepted into the professional school for your career?

To find alternative career goals, look at careers that are related to your primary career goal. Also, consider other interests and skills you have. Is self-employment a possibility? Remember that you are likely to change careers several times in your lifetime, so you shouldn't focus on only one career goal.

*What careers might interest someone who enjoys this type of work?*

**Scenario:** A school counselor interviews a student about his career plans.

**Roles:** A student and a counselor

**Discussion:** Answering the questions "who, what, when, where, why, and how," discuss the student's career plans.

## Case Study: What School Should Levi Attend?

Levi is a senior in high school and has been working for Overbeck Construction through the I.C.E. program. He likes working on construction equipment and wants to further his education in this career field.

**What are three options for Levi?**

**What are one advantage and one disadvantage of each option?**

---

### Section 5-3: Review

**Understanding Key Concepts**

1. What are two action areas of your career plan that you can definitely do right now?
2. What factors do you need to consider as you make educational choices?
3. What three types of admissions requirements do most postsecondary education programs have?
4. How can gaining career experiences help you determine your future career?

**Thinking Creatively**

How can earning excellent grades in school affect your adult life?

Can you think of any experience you had that didn't teach you something about yourself?

**Taking It a Step Further**

Using the Internet, find at least three schools that you might attend after high school. Look for one that is close to your home, another that is within your state, and the third one in another state or country. Prepare an expense grid that compares the costs of attending all three schools.

**Mike Hurst, President**
**Tune Tech, Inc.**

I own and operate an eight-bay auto repair facility in Indianapolis, Indiana. How did I get here? When I was in high school, I wanted to be a race car driver. I got my diploma and completed an A.A.S. degree in Mechanical Engineering Technology at Lakeland College in Mentor, Ohio.

I loved racing so much that I volunteered with a rally-racing team in Michigan, a team so respected that it gained factory support from the Oldsmobile division of General Motors. Through that volunteering, I made connections. Friends there found me a position on the crew of a NASCAR Cup team. The moral of the story: Always leave a good impression. You never know who you may be impressing.

Running a successful auto shop has enabled me to pursue my own motorsport goals. I've raced stock cars, sports cars, and rally cars, in which I won three national championships. I have competed in long-distance events, such as the *Car & Driver* magazine One Lap of America.

Lately I'm spending less time on racing and more time with my family. After 20 years of driving, I've stepped back and accepted the position of Club Rally Series Manager. I negotiate sanctions with event organizers and monitor the conduct of rally races nationwide for the 60,000 member Sports Car Club of America.

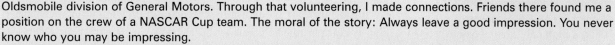

# Chapter Review and Activities

The following sections can help you review the contents of this chapter and develop your workplace competencies.

## Key Concepts

Following are the key concepts presented in the chapter.

▶ As you continue to mature and explore careers, you need to create a career plan by exploring your lifestyle, defining your goal, evaluating your possible career choices, considering your educational options, making a decision, and putting your plan into action.

▶ Your lifestyle reflects your values and attitudes.

▶ Compare what you want or expect in a career and lifestyle to what the specific careers you have identified require or offer, including career outlook, focus of the work, education and training, responsibilities and tasks, salary, skills and aptitudes, values, work environment, and working hours.

▶ Define your goals and determine a personal road map to success.

▶ Evaluate possible career choices.

▸ Carefully consider the education and training needed.

▸ There are many different levels of education available, and your choices will depend on the specific career.

▸ Making a decision about a career area and planning how to reach this goal are important.

▸ Set realistic goals, both short and long-term. Short-term goals are also called stepping-stone goals.

▸ Gain career experience.

▸ An important part of exploring careers and creating your own career plan is comparing the information about a career with your reactions to your experiences.

## Key Term Review

Complete the following activity to review your understanding of the key terms.

| | | |
|---|---|---|
| accredited | diploma programs | lifelong learner |
| apprenticeship | distance learning | master's degree |
| associate degree | doctoral degree | personal road map |
| bachelor's degree | economic recession | postsecondary |
| basic training | enlist | salary |
| CTE schools | flexibility | stepping-stone goal |
| certificate programs | flextime | things |
| cosmetology | graduate degree | transfer |
| data | indentured | |

The automotive company where you work is cutting 300 jobs. The supervisor has asked you to prepare and post a chart that lists and explains the different types of education available in your state. Use at least ten of the key terms in your chart.

## Comprehension Review

Answer the following questions to review the main points in the chapter.

**1.** What are the steps of making a career decision?

**2.** How can you evaluate what you discover about yourself and the careers that interest you?

**3.** What are educational options for people who do not want to go to a four-year college or university?

4. What are the degrees you can obtain at a four-year college or university?

5. How can you choose a school from among the many postsecondary options available to you?

6. How can experiences help you determine careers that might not interest you?

## School-to-Work

**Math:** Your salary is $43,500, and you have a sign-on bonus of $1,500. How much money will you be losing if you take an unpaid vacation of four days? Write down the steps you would take to solve this mathematical problem and the correct answer.

**Social Studies:** What are some attributes of a workplace? How can some of the attributes affect a family? Create a cause-effect chart that illustrates your ideas.

**Writing:** Write an e-mail message to an organization and request information about its purpose, openings for volunteers, and how to become a volunteer.

**Science:** Using the Internet or magazine articles, research high-definition television. Then write a report that explains how the technology works, discusses the advantages of the new technology, and lists the number of programs that your favorite TV network currently broadcasts in HDTV.

## Does This Job Interest You?

The following job ad was posted on the Internet. What education and experience are required? What requirement does this job have that most jobs do not have? What types of education, interests, and skills should a person working in this position have? How could someone apply for the job?

| **FIND JOBS** | **POST RESUMES** |
| --- | --- |

### Workover Rig and Truck Mechanic

| | | | |
| --- | --- | --- | --- |
| **Employer:** | Key Energy Services, Inc. | **Education:** | Trade school or apprenticeship |
| **Desired Expertise:** | Mechanic, Rig Mechanic | **Location:** | International, Egypt |
| **Experience:** | 5+ years | | |

### Job Description

Responsible for the maintenance and repair of a workover rig and truck project. Must be able to work on all aspects of light and heavy trucks. Good understanding of mechanical and electrical technology required. Must be able to train and develop national personnel and work with national clients. Must be able to plan maintenance and repair projects, including material requisitions. Contract has stringent performance standards that must be met safely.

Airfare provided by company to and from reasonable commercial airport.

### Job Requirements

Apply via e-mail.
To apply for this position, applicants MUST meet the following criterion:
Be located in North America.

### Contact

wrtm@aol.com

**Apply Online**

# What career appeals to you?

# Unit **2**
# Becoming Familiar with the Workplace

## Chapter 6: Developing Fundamental Workplace Skills

*Chapter 6 focuses on Construction, Mining, and Drilling careers.*

## Chapter 7: Searching for a Job

*Chapter 7 focuses on Transportation careers.*

# Chapter 8: Applying for a Job

Chapter 8 focuses on Industrial Production careers.

# Chapter 9: Excelling at the Interview Process

Chapter 9 focuses on Business Detail careers.

# Chapter 10: Understanding Workplace Issues

Chapter 10 focuses on Sales and Marketing careers.

# Chapter 6

# Developing Fundamental Workplace Skills

## What You'll Learn

▶ Improving your communication skills

▶ Developing teamwork skills

▶ Becoming a leader

▶ Using time-management strategies

The knowledge you gain while attending school or while working can help you become oriented to your new roles as an employee and co-worker. In those roles, you will have opportunities to develop many of the characteristics that employers seek. This chapter focuses on four of the basic skills everyone needs for starting a new job. They are **communication** (sending and receiving information), **teamwork** (working together for a common goal), **leadership** (guiding, influencing, and showing others the way), and **time management** (using time wisely).

*The journey is the reward.*

*—Taoist saying*

| Key Terms | | |
|---|---|---|
| active listening | efficiently | teamwork |
| brainstorming | leadership | teleconferencing |
| communication | negotiating | text messaging |
| competitive | nonverbal communication | time management |
| compromising | scanning | verbal communication |
| controlled leadership | shared leadership | voice inflection |
| delegating | skimming | win-win solution |

# Section 6-1: Improving Your Communication Skills

Have you ever played Gossip or the Telephone Game? One person shares a message with the next person, who shares it with the next, and so on until the last person in the line shares it with the group. It's pretty amazing what happens to that message as it is passed from person to person and each one hears and interprets it differently.

Communication involves understanding and being understood. Effective communication can

- ▸ Improve your image and lead to job success.

- ▸ Improve work relationships and career prospects.

- ▸ Reduce job stress and improve your quality of life.

- ▸ Help you achieve more powerful results and increase your earning potential.

*Why are some messages not interpreted in the way the speaker intended?*

# Verbal Communication

**Verbal communication** involves using words to give information to others. Words really do matter. Your words affect others. You can make an angry person angrier or less angry. How? Look at the person you are talking to and think about his needs and personality before you say anything. Then you can avoid misunderstandings and hard feelings. If you see that an angry friend looks as if she has a cold, for example, you can understand that her harsh words have less to do with you than how she's feeling. You can then answer her with kind words that might make her feel better.

Even a lack of words can affect others. If a neighbor greets you and you don't answer, for example, he might think either that you haven't heard him or that you are disrespectful. Your lack of response can create negative feelings.

## Speaking

Words also can affect your career. Every time you speak, people judge you by what you say. If you tell the truth, people will know that they can trust you. If you use proper grammar, correct pronunciation, excellent vocabulary, and courtesy, people respect and admire you and might even be willing to give you more responsibilities. What can you do if you know that your way of speaking isn't acceptable on the job?

▶ Read more. Read newspapers, magazines, and books that interest you. When your mind sees the correctly written language, it begins to think with that language.

▶ Read out loud. When your ear hears the words that you are reading, you will begin to feel more comfortable speaking that way.

| Qualities and Skills Employers Seek | |
|---|---|
| Communication skills (verbal and written) | Leadership skills |
| Honesty/integrity | Organizational skills |
| Interpersonal skills (relates well to others) | Self-confidence |
| Motivation/initiative | Friendly/outgoing personality |
| Strong work ethic | Tactfulness |
| Teamwork skills (works well with others) | Well-mannered/polite |
| Analytical skills | Creativity |
| Flexibility/adaptability | Grade point average (3.0 or better) |
| Computer skills | Entrepreneurial skills/risk-taker |
| Detail-oriented | Sense of humor |

*Reprinted from Job Outlook 2004, with permission of the National Association of Colleges and Employers, copyright holder.*

*How can something as simple as talking create problems among friends?*

▶ To improve your pronunciation, listen carefully to people speaking on the TV or radio news. The newscasters always try to use correct pronunciation.

▶ Work on improving your vocabulary. If you don't know the meaning of a word, look it up. Sign up to be on one of the free e-mail lists that automatically sends you a different word each day. An excellent vocabulary will lead you toward career success.

▶ Rules of courtesy gradually change over the years. In some workplaces, you are expected to address customers as Mr. or Mrs. Some bosses expect you to answer them with "Yes, sir," or "Yes, ma'am." Other workplaces are more casual. However, one rule remains: Speak respectfully to others. If you follow that rule even when you're angry, people think of you as a courteous person.

Words are not the only spoken message you give. Your **voice inflection** (the tone of your voice) sends a message. Even just one word can give entirely different messages, depending on the way it's spoken. Try these:

Say "No" with anger in your voice.

Say "No" calmly.

Say "No" as if you were confused.

Did you notice any changes inside yourself when you said "No" in three different ways? Often, our bodies and feelings follow our tone; that is, our words actually intensify our feelings, making them stronger.

## How Do You Talk on the Phone?

In today's technological world, people communicate in a variety of ways. In addition to face-to-face conversations, they often use the telephone for communication. Business telephone conversations follow certain rules of etiquette. When you are making a business phone call, follow these steps:

1. Speaking clearly and loudly enough to be heard, identify yourself and your company.

2. Say, "May I speak with ___?"

3. Thank the receiver of the call for connecting you with the person you're trying to reach.

4. Explain the purpose of your call in one or two sentences.

5. Ask the person you're calling whether this is a convenient time to talk.

6. If someone puts you on hold, it is okay to hang up after three minutes. Then call back and ask to leave a message.

If you are receiving a business phone call, follow these steps:

1. Give a short greeting, such as "Hello," and then identify your company and yourself.

2. Ask how you can help the caller.

If you have to put someone on hold, ask for permission first and wait for their answer. Why should you ask for permission? Sometimes a call can be a life-and-death emergency. At other times, people would rather return the call later. When someone does agree to being put on hold, update the person on hold on the status of the call every few minutes.

Today, you often see people using their cell phones as they are walking down the street or driving in vehicles (if it is legal in their state). You also see them receiving and sending calls in restaurants and many other public places. What are some rules of etiquette to remember when using cell phones in public?

- Be safe. Watch where you are walking! If you are driving, pull over to answer the phone or send a call.

- Be considerate. If you are in a public meeting, don't allow your cell phone to disrupt the meeting. Set your cell phone to vibrate or turn it off completely unless you are expecting an emergency call.

- Be respectful. If someone has chosen to spend time with you, don't waste your time together by talking on the cell phone.

- Be appropriate. The popularity of cell phone cameras raises questions of what is appropriate, what is company policy regarding pictures, and what is legal.

### DIVERSITY

**Why Won't He Take Any Money?**

Jacques, your next-door neighbor, is from a foreign country. Fortunately for you, he is a mechanic. Your old SUV still looks as pretty as a picture, but it won't run half the time. It never fails that when Old Blue doesn't start, your neighbor comes over, works with the wiring, and gets it started. You tried to pay him, but he won't accept gifts or money for helping you. What's up with that?

### CAREER FACT

Boilermakers make, install, and repair boilers and other large containers that hold liquids and gases. The boilers supply steam to huge engines in power plants; or provide heat and power in buildings, factories, and ships. Boilermakers also work with tanks that process and store chemicals, oil, and other products.

*Why does a cell phone frequently create more problems than it solves?*

**ETHICS**

**What Will You Do?**

If you see that one of your co-workers is assigned more work than you are and that he cannot possibly finish it in time, what will you do?

▶ Be cautious. **Text messaging** (using your phone to type and send a message) or *texting* is quick and convenient, but it is no substitute for clear verbal and written communication. What type of information are you sending and who might have access to it (credit card and telephone numbers, and so on)?

▶ Be courteous. **Teleconferencing** (meeting by electronic means) requires the same courtesies and communication skills as if you were meeting face-to-face.

## How Do You Handle Voice Mail Messages?

Voice mail has become a normal part of life. You probably have quite a bit of experience leaving messages for friends and family. However, in your role as an employee, you need to handle voice mail very professionally. If you have to leave a voice mail message, follow these steps:

**1.** Speak clearly and slowly.

**2.** Leave your name, phone number, and a brief message.

**3.** Say your name and number again at the end of the message.

If you are expecting phone calls about a job or if you have to record a voice mail message for a company, follow these steps:

1. Speak clearly and slowly.

2. Record your name, organization, and a brief message that states whether you are in the office that day, when to expect a call back, whom to contact if the call is urgent, and how to reach that person.

3. Always respond to messages promptly (within 24 hours is customary).

## Active Listening

Part of communication is speaking. Another part is active listening. **Active listening** involves more than just listening with your ears. It also involves understanding the spoken and unspoken message. You also can listen in the following ways:

▶ By giving your undivided attention

▶ With your eyes, looking at the person talking

▶ In silence, giving the person talking a chance to finish speaking

▶ By asking good questions that help the person talking explain concerns

▶ By hearing the emotion in the voice of the person talking

▶ By giving appropriate feedback (responding to what the person said)

*What unspoken messages do you give when you do not listen to someone who is speaking?*

As you can tell, becoming a good active listener requires effort and practice. However, if you are a good listener, you can avoid many misunderstandings between your parents and you or with brothers, sisters, and friends. Have you ever upset your parents because you didn't listen closely to the time you should be home? Have you been left waiting for friends to join you because of a misunderstanding about what time the group was meeting? Becoming a good active listener can help you avoid situations such as these and the problems and hurt feelings that result from the misunderstandings.

In today's workplace, everyone must actively listen to follow directions correctly. You must listen carefully to key words and make certain that you are interpreting the message in the way the sender intends.

In some instances, you might need to rephrase the message as a question to make certain that you understand. For example, if your employer tells you to arrange the folders, you could rephrase the request this way: "You need me to arrange the folders in alphabetical order by last name. Is that what you mean?"

## Writing

People once thought that we'd soon have a "paperless" society, but we still rely on paper correspondence. We also have e-mail and chatting, text messaging, and faxes (facsimile machines). All these forms of correspondence require written communication.

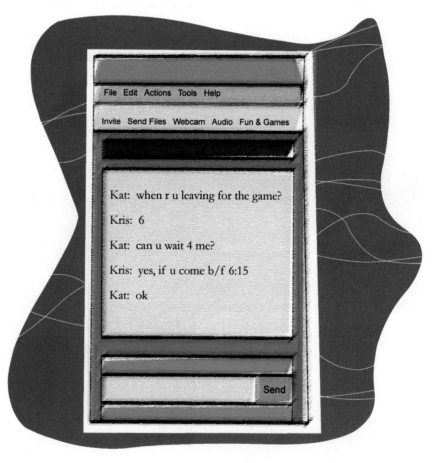

File  Edit  Actions  Tools  Help

Invite  Send Files  Webcam  Audio  Fun & Games

Kat: when r u leaving for the game?

Kris: 6

Kat: can u wait 4 me?

Kris: yes, if u come b/f 6:15

Kat: ok

Send

*How is instant messaging like writing a note or letter?*

**Message**

**Message for:** *Christina Leonardo*

**From:** *Juan Mendez*

**Date:** *4/20/12*

**Number:** *123-4567*

**Time:** *9:15*

**Message:** *Mtg has postponed until 10/12 Lme know if you are avail ckk that date*

**Taken by:** *bmt*

**Call Back ASAP** ✓

*Which communication is more effective? Why?*

**Message**

**Message for:** Christina Leonardo

**From:** Juan Mendez

**Date:** 9/20/12

**Number:** 123-4567

**Time:** 9:15

**Message:** The meeting has been postponed until 10/12. Let me know if you're available on that date.

**Taken by:** bmt

**Call Back ASAP** ✓

Writing is a very important workplace skill. The following tips can help you produce effective written communication:

▶ Correct spelling is absolutely essential and can affect your image and job success as much as verbal communication can.

▶ Proofread written correspondence for logic, good sentence structure, typographical errors, and misspellings before you send it.

▶ With handwritten communication, write as legibly as possible.

Whenever possible, use the writing process of prewriting, creating a draft, revising, editing, and proofreading your writing. Others will appreciate your efforts.

**CAREER FACT**

Demand for roofers is fairly constant even when new construction declines because roofs always need repairing and remodeling.

## Reading

Reading is the receiving end of written correspondence. The average employee spends several hours each workday reading. What reading might an employee need to do in a typical day? Two strategies you may want to use when you need to read are scanning and skimming.

*How can you quickly find a phone number in a telephone book?*

**Scanning** is looking through printed material to find specific information that you need to answer a question. To scan material, follow these steps:

1. Prepare to scan by looking to see how the material is organized—by numbers, letters, steps, or the words first, second, and so on.

2. Look for words that are **bold**; *italicized*; or in a different **font**, size, or **color**.

3. Move your eyes quickly down the page, looking for the specific information you need.

What are examples of printed material that you should scan?

**Skimming** is a way of reading to get a quick impression of printed materials to understand the topic and main points. Because you will receive a great deal of correspondence, it is worthwhile to learn this technique. Sometimes skimming is all that will be necessary to understand what you need to know. To skim material, follow these steps:

1. Prepare to skim by reading the title and name of the author and looking at the pictures.

2. Ask yourself *who, what, when,* and *where* is this material likely to be mainly about?

3. While your mind continues to ask questions, move your eyes down columns or in a zigzag pattern across long lines of print.

4. Look for exact names of people, places, things, ideas, and numbers.

5. Watch out for the words that can tell you *how* and *why*: *therefore, whenever, until, because,* and *instead.*

What are examples of printed material that you should skim?

There will be other times, however, when the material is much too important to scan or skim. You will need to read much more carefully for facts and details. What are examples of printed material that you must read carefully?

# Nonverbal Communication

**Nonverbal communication**, using facial expressions and body positions to show feelings, is also an important form of expressing yourself. What are some examples of nonverbal communication? How can you tell when someone is sad? What lets you know that a person is mad?

Many times you might not be aware of the nonverbal messages you are giving. Sometimes you might just be repeating facial expressions that another family member uses or a habit that you've formed. However, others might interpret your messages differently from what you intended. For example, you might frown when you're thinking deep thoughts, just as your mother does.

Friends might see you frowning and think that you're sad about something. The frowning is really just a habit you learned from your parent. Also, nonverbal communication can mean different things in different cultures. Did you know that, in some cultures, smiling is an expression of sadness? In others, looking directly into another person's eyes is a sign of disrespect. In yet others, shaking the head up and down means no.

Although you do not want to be self-conscious (or always thinking about what others are thinking of you), you do need to be aware that they are looking at your face and the way you hold your body for information about how you feel and what you are thinking. Just being aware of nonverbal communication and the messages that it can send others will make you a better communicator. Remembering that nonverbal communication can mean very different things in different cultures will help you to be more careful when you're with others.

Clear communication—whether it is spoken, written, or nonverbal—is especially important among group members. This is true whether you are planning a family outing, putting together a group science assignment for school, or completing a project at work. Without clear communication, the group cannot complete its tasks and reach its goals and objectives.

## Section 6-1: Review

### Understanding Key Concepts

1. What are three forms of communication?
2. How are the skills for active listening and reading similar? How are they different?
3. What are the differences between scanning and skimming reading material?

### Thinking Creatively

How can you tell when you're using acceptable spoken communication? Is it important to be able to write acceptably in every career?

How can you tell when your nonverbal communication is offending someone?

### Taking It a Step Further

You are the owner of a real estate company. Write a section for the policy manual for your employees on one of these topics:

▶ The standards for Web pages that advertise properties
▶ Etiquette and the proper use of the office phone
▶ Etiquette and appropriate use of e-mail
▶ The proper use of camera phones
▶ The proper use of cell phones

**TECHNOLOGY**

You probably have used instant messaging software (such as AIM or Yahoo! Messenger) to talk with your friends while you are on the computer. Many businesses and other organizations use a similar type of software to help employees in different locations communicate and share information easily. How is instant messaging with a friend different from instant messaging with a co-worker?

# Section 6-2: Developing Teamwork

Teamwork is the cooperative effort of a group of people acting together to achieve a goal. You have been a member of many groups in your life—including family, school, social groups, athletic groups, and musical groups, for example. You will continue to be a member of groups throughout your life. What are some examples of groups or teams you might belong to in the future? You might never have thought some of these groups as being teams, but they are.

One of the groups you will (or might already) be part of is your workplace team. Not only will it be necessary for you to be responsible for yourself on the job; you will also need to be prepared to work with others (and sometimes take responsibility for them). You also will need to help your employer's business succeed. Many of the teamwork skills needed in your workplace can also be helpful as you work and play with your family and friends. This section discusses teamwork skills needed in the workplace, but remember to think of ways to apply those skills to the activities you do at home and at your school.

Effective workplace teams must be able to

▸ Accept and work with different personalities.

▸ Solve problems.

▸ Identify and effectively assign roles based on the strengths and weaknesses of the individual team members.

The goal is for the team to be strong and successful.

Teamwork isn't a new concept, but it certainly is frequently emphasized in today's workplace. Why? Competition has caused today's companies to organize their workers into teams to address problems, create the best products, and provide the best services to their customers and suppliers. The companies must try to find win-win solutions to problems. A **win-win solution** deals with a problem in a way that is fair and beneficial for everyone. For example, you might find it very easy to talk to customers but really don't like running the cash register. Your co-worker is comfortable in working with the cash register but very shy. What would be a win-win solution to both of your problems?

Effective teams can make a difference. If a sports team works together well, the results can be quite positive—maybe even a winning season. However, there are many benefits of working as a team besides winning athletic competitions. As more and more companies realize the benefits of teamwork, they are reorganizing their workforce so that team members share responsibility and leadership. Can you think of some of the other benefits of having a workforce that works together as a team in today's workplace?

**CAREER FACT**

If you want a job that offers excellent opportunities but involves working outdoors frequently, risk of injury, and sporadic employment, consider being a glazier. What's a glazier? A glazier installs glass in buildings. Most glaziers work as helpers to learn the trade, but employers often prefer someone who has completed a 3- to 4-year apprenticeship program.

*How are a sports team, a staff, a club, and a class similar?*

Teams will work best when the team members function together effectively. It can take time for a team to learn to work effectively together. Team members need to get used to one another and learn how each person's strengths can help the team to be successful. In addition, each team member needs to have the character traits and skills that strengthen a team and avoid those behaviors that hurt the team.

## Character Traits that Build Teams

What do you think is necessary for teams to work together successfully? If you said communication, you are right! Teamwork requires very clear spoken, written, and nonverbal communication, as well as active listening. However, teamwork also requires some inner character qualities:

▶ Empathy (showing concern by helping each other)

▶ Fairness (each member doing his share of the work)

**CAREER FACT**

The construction-related occupation that loses the least amount of work time because of bad weather is the career of the elevator installer or repairer. A person in this career typically works 40 hours per week, but may have to work overtime or be on call 24 hours per day.

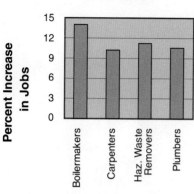

**Projected Outlook for 2016**

*What does this chart tell you about future opportunities in these careers?*

Respect (being open to the ideas and efforts of others)

Honesty (being truthful)

Integrity (choosing to do what is right)

Selflessness (sharing information and resources with other team members)

# Skills that Build Teams

There are also other critical skills that members of effective teams must have. You can develop these skills over time:

Flexibility is the willingness to change or adapt.

**Delegating** tasks is asking others to do a portion of the work.

**Brainstorming** is sharing ideas to come up with the best solution.

**Negotiating** is looking at all the options and then discussing the benefits and drawbacks of each to arrive at the settlement of a matter.

**Compromising** is making mutual concessions to, or giving in on, parts of team members' ideas to create a solution everyone accepts.

How can you develop these team-building skills?

---

<table>
<tr><td>

### Rules for Brainstorming

Brainstorming is an effective tool to cultivate, create, and develop ideas to solve worksite problems. But there are certain rules that will make a brainstorming session more successful:

- State ideas, but don't discuss them
- Record all ideas
- Expect wild ideas
- Be spontaneous
- Suspend judgments
- Quantity, not quality, of ideas counts
- Build on each other's ideas

</td></tr>
</table>

# Case Study: How Would You Spend $1,000?

Your school has received $1,000 from a local business. The only requirement is that every student must benefit from the way you spend the money.

**Using the "Rules for Brainstorming," what are some ideas for using the money?**

---

# Behaviors that Harm Teams

Some behaviors might prevent members from working effectively as a team:

▶ Not accepting responsibility for your actions or choices

▶ Distracting others from their work

▶ Being a troublemaker

▶ Trying to get attention

▶ Being too **competitive** (trying to outdo others)

These types of behaviors do not benefit anyone—individuals, the team, or the company. What could team members do to correct such negative behaviors?

As you begin a new job or career, recognize the strengths and knowledge that others will contribute to your success as well as to the success of the company you are working for. Make an investment in your work by being a contributing team member. You will discover a great deal of satisfaction in your career.

*How can disruptive behaviors harm a team?*

# Section 6-3: Becoming a Leader

Skill in leadership is required in many jobs and careers. You might have already experienced being a leader, or your classmates might have leadership experience. How effective are you as a leader? Do you enjoy leading others? Who do you know that you believe is a good leader? What makes that person a good leader?

It is unlikely that you will lead a group early in your career, but it is certainly a time to observe leadership styles and show your leadership qualities. Two types of leadership styles are the following:

▶ **Controlled leadership** is leadership that is forced on other people. Fear is often an outcome of controlled leadership. The members of the group fear that they might be punished or lose their jobs if they don't do what the leader says. Many times, this leads to feelings of hostility or feeling that they should just give up.

▶ **Shared leadership** gives everyone a chance to have a say in the way things are being done. Everyone is free to share ideas and opinions. The leader is a member of the group and has the responsibility of keeping the group on task. The leader is a facilitator (encourager) and helps the members feel confident, secure, and worthwhile.

Which type of leadership would you prefer? Why?

You can begin now to develop leadership skills. At home, completing your chores, maintaining good grades, and showing a respectful attitude usually earns you greater responsibility. Following through on the responsibilities usually earns you more freedom. If you are a member of a sports team, you will find that following the coach's instructions, having a good attitude, being respectful to teammates, and doing your best will result in others looking up to you. As a member of a club, you will find that volunteering to help with special projects, being faithful in your attendance, and being respectful to others might lead to a position as a club officer. By the time you complete your schooling, leadership skills will have become a natural part of who you are.

Because there is such a competitive global challenge in today's workforce, effective leadership is more important than ever. One person cannot accomplish everything; effective leaders must delegate tasks to others and then motivate them to complete the tasks. Not only is delegating and motivating others important, but leaders must also be willing to work hard themselves. Leaders must clearly understand the company's purpose and goals. They must educate and motivate the entire organization to understand and work toward achieving those goals, which requires effective communication from the top management positions throughout the entire company.

Leaders are responsible to the entire organization. Employees want to believe in their leaders and feel confident in their leadership. They want to trust them and look to them for wisdom. Leaders spend a great deal of time training and preparing future leaders for their organization. Being a leader is a privilege; however, with this privilege comes responsibility for a successful workforce. If a leader is not willing to take this responsibility, it is unlikely that the business will succeed.

## Qualities Companies Look For in a Leader

- ☑ Skilled in self-management
- ☑ Skilled in problem-solving
- ☑ Skilled in communicating
- ☑ Works well with others
- ☑ Even-tempered
- ☑ Flexible
- ☑ Sets a good example
- ☑ Has the respect of others
- ☑ Reliable
- ☑ Honest
- ☑ Has integrity
- ☑ Optimistic
- ☑ Creative
- ☑ Has a vision
- ☑ Willing to commit to the organization

## Section 6-3: Review

### Understanding Key Concepts

1. What is controlled leadership?
2. What is shared leadership?
3. Why is being able to delegate tasks so important to a leader?

### Thinking Creatively

Give an example of a situation in which controlled leadership is the best way to manage a group.

Give an example of a situation in which shared leadership is the best way to manage a group.

Is it important to develop leadership skills if you prefer being a follower?

### Taking It a Step Further

Robert K. Greenleaf is a former AT&T executive who coined the term "servant-leadership." Conduct an online search for the term and write an explanation of the characteristics of a servant-leader.

# Section 6-4: Using Time-Management Strategies

"Time is money!" What does this expression mean to you? What do you think it will mean to your employer? Wasting time or "killing time" can mean the difference between making a profit or losing money, which might eventually mean the difference between company growth or job layoffs. As an employee, you will be expected to work **efficiently** (not wasting anything). Time management means to use your time wisely. Again, observe and listen to your co-workers and supervisors. You will see both good and bad examples of time-management techniques. How can you use these examples to learn good time management skills?

An important part of time management is keeping track of all your deadlines and activities. Remember to use your calendar to record upcoming assignments and other tasks that you must accomplish.

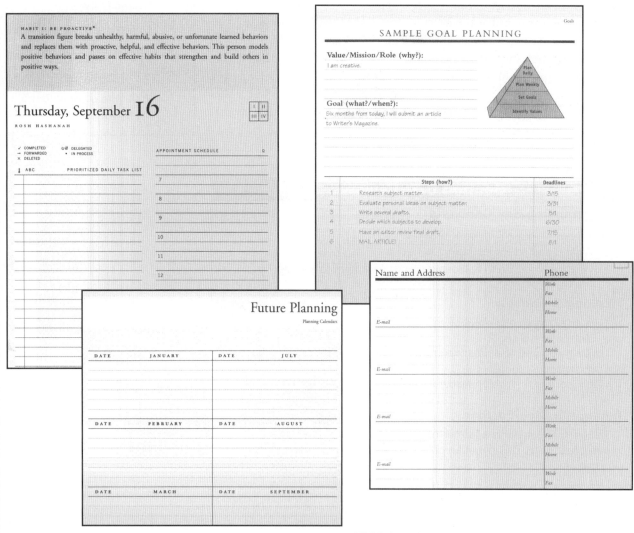

*Which time-management products would you find helpful?*

# Case Study: What Are They Doing That Is Wrong?

Jasmine and Kaitlyn are enrolled in a cadet teaching program at their local high school. For credit and a grade, they are working as teaching assistants at a local elementary school three hours every other day. Their responsibilities are varied and include copying papers on the copier located in the teacher workroom. Often there is food available, which they are welcome to eat. However, after finishing their tasks, they often linger for 15 minutes or longer before returning to the classroom.

**NETWORKING**

Find a leader in the community (a minister, politician, educator, or businessperson) to interview about the responsibilities and rewards of leading people. Share your findings as a one-minute speech.

**COMMUNITY**

Spend two hours shadowing the leader who you interviewed for the networking assignment. Write one paragraph of at least five complete sentences, describing your experiences with the leader and the impact that person is making on your community.

**What is being abused in this situation?**

**What would you tell Jasmine and Kaitlyn to do to improve their time-management skills?**

## Time-Management Tips

- Set deadlines for assignments or tasks and stick to the deadlines.
- Make a list of activities you need to accomplish and number them in order of importance or deadlines.
- Do difficult jobs first and get them finished early.
- Set aside a block of time to make telephone calls.
- Take a break when your energy needs recharging.
- Learn when and how to say "no" and avoid too much stress and fatigue.
- Keep your desk clear; throw away unimportant papers.
- Organize your files, using color-coding and labels.
- If someone asks to put you on hold during a telephone call, leave a message or call back later. (Remember your telephone manners.)
- Keep pen and paper by the telephone.
- If you have unexpected interruptions, avoid small talk and agree on another meeting time.
- If the unexpected visitor won't leave, you leave the workspace.

Use your thinking and problem-solving skills to create your own plan for using your time effectively. Time can never be replaced: After you use it, it's gone forever. Choose carefully how to spend it. You can use it to help others; you can use it to create unique expressions of yourself through music, art, writing, or body strengthening; or you can waste it, doing nothing. It's your choice.

## Section 6-4: Review

### Understanding Key Concepts

1. Why is it important for employees to work as efficiently as possible?
2. What are some time-management procedures students can follow to use time more effectively?
3. Why is the issue of time management so important?

### Thinking Creatively

What would you do if you owned a business and found one of your employees sleeping while he was supposed to be working?

Why is it important to take a break when you are working on a project that takes a long time?

How can you courteously handle someone who is interrupting your work?

### Taking It a Step Further

Prepare a time-management plan that the members of your family can use to effectively complete the weekly tasks required to maintain your home. Your plan should include strategies for managing the laundry, cleaning, and preparing meals. Print your plan as a spreadsheet or word-processing table.

## Spotlight on a Career

### Dennis R. Colter
### D. R. Colter Construction

I am the owner of a construction company, D. R. Colter Construction, and I build condos, houses, and small business buildings. I am responsible for talking with potential customers, taking care of all governmental permits, and drawing up house plans when customers do not already have them. I hire my framing and finishing crews, and I arrange for and schedule subcontractors to complete the plumbing, electrical work, roofing, and excavation. I also order all supplies for the projects and check each site every day to make certain that the work is being completed correctly. Really, I am responsible for every part of my business.

I always knew that I wanted to own my own business. While I was still a high school student, I worked for a plumbing company, and then I learned to operate a backhoe and other excavation equipment. I would dig the septic lines or prepare the soil for the houses my father's construction company was preparing to build. I even bought my first house while I was a senior in high school. I earned a high school diploma, and throughout the years I have taken a few college classes just for my own satisfaction. I also earned my real estate license.

Owning a construction business is stressful. The weather; local, state, and national economies; governmental regulations; competition from other companies; customers; supply companies; and crew members all impact the business. I have always enjoyed playing basketball, golfing, and water sports; they are my stress relievers. Attending professional basketball games and caring for my home are other activities I enjoy.

# Chapter Review and Activities

The following sections can help you review the contents of this chapter and develop your workplace competencies.

## Key Concepts

Following are the key concepts presented in the chapter.

▶ Communication involves both understanding and being understood.

▶ Verbal communication is the use of words to communicate a message. It involves speaking, active listening, writing, and reading.

▶ Nonverbal communication is the message sent through facial expressions and body language.

▶ Teamwork is emphasized in today's workplace.

▶ The character traits that build teams include empathy, fairness, respect, honesty, integrity, and selflessness.

▶ The skills that build teams include delegating tasks, brainstorming, negotiating, and compromising.

▶ Behaviors that harm teams include not accepting responsibility for actions or choices, distracting others from their work, being a troublemaker, trying to get attention, or being too competitive.

▶ Leadership is required in many jobs and careers. Now is the time to begin developing leadership skills.

▶ Know the qualities that companies look for in a leader.

▶ Controlled leadership is leadership that is forced on other people; shared leadership gives everyone a chance to have a say in the way things are being done.

▶ One person cannot accomplish everything; effective leaders must delegate and motivate other team members.

▶ Companies' profits depend on the efficiency and reliability of their employees.

▶ An important part of time management is keeping track of deadlines and activities.

▶ Time can never be replaced. Carefully choose how to spend it.

---

### ROLE-PLAYING

**Scenario:** An employee feels that he is not receiving the training he needs to be able to do his job well. He approaches the employer to express his frustration.

**Roles:** Employee and employer

**Discussion:** What tone of voice and body language did the employee and employer use? Were they effective in communicating with each other? What could they have done differently?

---

### TECHNOLOGY

Technical innovations in communications can help you in managing your time. Most computers include calendar programs, instant messaging, electronic reminders, and meeting planners. In addition, handheld devices such as the BlackBerry, iPhone, and other PDAs (personal digital assistants), including cell phones, can help you stay organized and give you reminders of family, social, and school events. For adults, this technology provides an instant link to employers, co-workers, and customers. This technology can minimize waiting time, simplify changing plans, and eliminate scheduling errors.

## Key Term Review

Complete the following activity to review your understanding of the key terms.

| | |
|---|---|
| active listening | scanning |
| brainstorming | shared leadership |
| communication | skimming |
| competitive | teamwork |
| compromising | teleconferencing |
| controlled leadership | text messaging |
| delegating | time management |
| efficiently | verbal communication |
| leadership | voice inflection |
| negotiating | win-win solution |
| nonverbal communication | |

You are the foreman of a construction crew whose members are not getting along. Most of the problems stem from the way the team members take extra-long lunch breaks and are careless with the company's equipment. Using at least ten of the key terms, write a brief message to the team about the problems, demonstrating shared leadership in your writing.

## Comprehension Review

Answer the following questions to review your understanding of the key concepts in the chapter.

1. What are two types of verbal communication and when do you use each one?

2. Why is being aware of nonverbal communication important?

3. Which qualities strengthen teamwork?

4. Why is shared leadership better than controlled leadership in most situations?

5. Which qualities should a leader have?

6. What are some tips for improving time-management skills?

# School-to-Work

**Math:** Write the steps you would take to solve this mathematical problem and furnish the correct answer.

> Mike makes $25.00 a week less than the sum of what Jason and Raul together make. Raul's weekly income would be triple Steven's if he made $50.00 more per week. Mike makes $285.00 per week, and Steven makes $75.00 per week. How much does Jason make?

**Social Studies:** On the Internet, research the topic of hierarchical leadership. Then write a paragraph that discusses the pros and cons of this leadership style.

**Writing:** Some of your crew members are goofing off at work and not completing their tasks on time. The supervisor will hold the entire team accountable for the task on Friday. Using the proper format, write a script of what you could say to your co-workers to describe the problem. Tell them how it is disrupting the workplace. Then suggest a possible solution to the problem. Close by asking your co-workers for feedback.

**Science:** Animals use body language to communicate. Conduct a keyword search on the topic of the body language of animals to find out how animals use their bodies to communicate emotions. Choose the animal that uses body language that most closely resembles people you know. Write a paragraph describing the animal's body language and showing the ways it is similar to the body language of people you know.

---

## Become a Better Speaker

Though you speak every day, you have to invest time and effort to become an effective speaker. Seek out speaking opportunities by taking speech courses, participating in class discussions, and joining speaking-oriented clubs, such as debating or drama.

When you have to make a speech, use these strategies:

▶ **Organize your ideas.** Use notecards or presentation software such as PowerPoint to create outlines of the main points you want to make. Find a logical sequence to the information so that a listener can follow along easily.

▶ **Know your audience.** Use a style of speaking that appeals to the people who are listening to you.

▶ **Practice.** Time your speech to make sure it is the right length. Also, test out any equipment you are using in your presentation to make sure that it is working correctly. Film yourself speaking or have a friend watch you to see how you could improve. This practice will help you be confident when you have to give your speech.

▶ **Look for feedback.** Make eye contact with your listeners to make sure that they understand what you are saying. Build in time at the end of your speech for questions or encourage your listeners to ask questions during your talk.

## Does This Job Interest You?

The following job is posted on the Internet. What education and experience are required? What requirement does this job have that most jobs do not have? What types of interests and skills should a person working in this position have? How could someone apply for the job? How could someone find out more about the job?

---

**FIND JOBS**    **POST RESUMES**

### GemXtracts Driller

> **Location:** West Africa

### Job Description

▸ Constructing resource models using GemXtracts software
▸ Grade control modeling
▸ Designing, cost estimating, and scheduling of drilling programs
▸ Supervision of diverse workforce

### Job Requirements

▸ Degree in Geology or Geological Engineering
▸ Overseas experience
▸ Gold experience

Our client requires drilling experts who are currently trained in GemXtracts software and available to move to West Africa. Candidates who have a minimum of three years' technical experience and some managerial experience should apply.

If you consider yourself a flexible and resourceful professional with a high degree of initiative, you could be the person required to contribute toward the success of our overseas client. This single or married status assignment offers an attractive U.S. expatriate compensation package.

### Contact

Qualified candidates are encouraged to apply without delay to:
GemXtracts Consultants Ltd.
61 Cameron, Suite 250
Hudson, New York 01234
Tel : 000-111-2222
Fax : 000-111-2223
Email : info@gemxtracts.com

**Apply Online**

# What career appeals to you?

# Chapter 7

# Searching for a Job

## What You'll Learn

▸ Determining what you offer an employer

▸ Deciding what job you want or don't want

▸ Organizing your job search

▸ Identifying potential employers

▸ Contacting potential employers

▸ Following through

With today's technologies, you can sit down at a computer and search for millions of jobs located all over the world. Some excellent job search sites are available. It is an interesting and worthwhile activity to research careers just to see what's "out there."

Finding a job may not be easy. Although some people will get really lucky and find a job right away, most people may have to look for several weeks or months. As a matter of fact, looking for that first job will be a job!

> *If a man wants his dreams to come true, he must wake up.*
>
> —*Anonymous*

| | | |
|---|---|---|
| classified ads | job leads | template |
| cold contact | letter of inquiry | United States Office of Personnel Management (OPM) |
| competitors | networking | wages |
| concise | private employment agency | warm contact |
| contact person | public employment agency | White Pages |
| fringe benefits | referrals | Yellow Pages |
| interview | screens | |
| JIST Card | self-directed job search | |

# Section 7-1: Preparing for a Job Search

Before you begin searching for a job, you need to answer two important questions. What do you offer an employer? What do you need or want in a job? These are questions that you must answer by thinking realistically about yourself.

## Determining What You Offer an Employer

How can an employer get in contact with you to set up an **interview** (a meeting) or take your application? Why would someone want to hire you? You need to have a quick way of letting an employer know who you are and why you are a good candidate for a job.

Michael Farr, author of *Young Person's Guide to Getting & Keeping a Good Job* (published by JIST Publishing), has developed a job search tool that he refers to as a **JIST Card**. He recommends that you place information that employers need to know about you on a small card, approximately the size of a three-by-five-inch index card. What types of information do you think you should include on the card?

Any employer will want to know these facts about you:

▶ **Your full name.**

▶ **Your phone number, including the area code.** (If you have a cell phone number or pager, you should include that number as well.)

▶ **Your e-mail address.** If you do not have an e-mail address, you can set up a free e-mail account from a variety of sources on the Internet. If you don't have access to the Internet, check your school and local libraries for Internet connections.

▶ **Type of position you are seeking.**

*What information will you put on your JIST Card?*

Mike Holten
123-456-7890
m_holten@aol.com

Desired position: Transportation

Skills: Comfortable with all age groups, attentive to customer needs, completed two semesters of small engine courses, volunteered for pit crew for two years, completed sophomore year of high school

Personal Qualities: Attentive to details, punctual, reliable

> ▶ **Your skills.** Describe your skills by listing your education, extracurricular activities, and life experiences. Be sure to include transferable skills (for example, being a careful listener) and job-related skills (such as being good with customers).

> ▶ **Special conditions.** You may want to include a note about the number of hours that you are available.

> ▶ **Your self-management skills.** List at least three self-management skills on the last line of your JIST Card.

When you write down this information about yourself, you will have a clear picture of exactly how valuable you can be to the right employer. You will also have a self-marketing tool. You can give it to people who are helping you find a job or to prospective employers so that they remember you and can easily contact you.

To create a good first impression of you as an employee, make sure that your JIST Card has no mistakes and looks attractive. If you use a computer to create your JIST Card, you can print it whenever you need one. Be sure to keep several with you throughout your job search).

## ETHICS

### What Is Fair?

You are in a contest at work to see how many bottles of lotion you can sell. One of your co-workers talked with a woman who wanted to buy some, but she left her credit card in the car. She went to get the card, and your co-worker went to the back of the store to accept a delivery. The customer has returned with her credit card. What will you do?

# Deciding What You Want or Don't Want

The second step of searching for a job is deciding what you want or need from a job—as well as what you don't want. Do you want just any job? Are you willing to do anything? What will you do if you receive two job offers? How much time do you want to spend looking for a job?

**WAITRESSES & WAITERS, DISHWASHERS, & PREP COOKS NEEDED IMMEDIATELY.**

Please apply in person at "The Large Round Bale," 111 N. Main Street, Anytown, USA

*Would you consider applying for this job?*

## On-the-Job Competency

### How Important Is It That You Go to Work?

Most employers provide vacation days and holidays off, but you must arrange to use these days in advance. Otherwise, you are expected to show up for work when you are scheduled. Good attendance is important to the company, other employees, and customers. For example, how would you feel if you were taking a trip and the pilot of your plane just decided not to show up and the flight had to be cancelled? What if you were part of a NASCAR racing crew and the chief mechanic decided not to attend the race?

## CAREER FACT

Careers in transportation might include air traffic controllers, bus drivers, pilots, railroad workers, taxi drivers and chauffeurs, truck drivers, and water transportation occupations.

Carefully think about the following:

▶ **Working hours.** Will this job provide you with enough hours to earn the money you want or need? Will you have to work more hours than you feel you can handle?

▶ **Job location.** How will you get to and from work? How long will it take you to get there? How much will a vehicle and fuel cost? How much will other forms of transportation cost (such as subway or bus)? Realistically, you should subtract these costs from your salary.

▶ **Workplace responsibilities.** How much responsibility do you want? Can you handle it? Remember that you will be given time to learn.

▶ **Co-workers.** Many people decide whether to take a job, keep a job, or leave a job based on the people they work with. You need to feel like you "fit in" and will become comfortable with the people you will be working with. If you have the opportunity to interview for a job, ask yourself, "How do I feel about the people I met during the interview?"

▶ **Company policies.** Are you willing to work for a company with many policies or rules? Or would you be happier working in a place with few rules? Before you accept the job, find out about the company policies.

▶ **Wages. Wages** are the money paid to employees. Is the company offering you enough money to cover the expenses you will have in traveling to and from work? Is the hourly rate offered to you comparable to the rate offered by the company's **competitors** (companies trying to get business from the same customer)? When will you get a raise?

▶ **Fringe benefits. Fringe benefits** are the extras that a company provides in addition to wages. Will you be offered any type of insurance plan? Will the company pay for part of your insurance? What other benefits does the company offer? Will you earn vacation days or sick leave days? Will you have to join a union and pay dues? Do you have to pay for your own uniform?

Answering these questions will help you decide whether you should apply for the job, whether to accept the job if it is offered to you, or whether you should continue to look for something that fits you better.

It usually isn't hard to find an entry-level job because they are plentiful in most areas. These jobs are typically low-paying, part-time, and (in many cases) boring. For some of you, just having a job will be good enough. Others will want to find "the" job. It might require more time and effort on your part to actually get what you really want unless you are very lucky.

# Case Study: How Important Are Co-Workers?

Chelsea interviewed for a summer job with a clothing store not far from her home. One of her friends worked there last summer and told her it was a great place to work. During the interview, the manager said that Chelsea would be responsible for arranging the displays, stocking the clothes, and cleaning the dressing room and store. The interview went well. As Chelsea was leaving the company, however, she saw a classmate working there with whom she doesn't get along with very well. The manager called the next day and offered Chelsea the job, giving her two days to decide whether to take the job.

**What are some things Chelsea needs to consider?**

## Section 7-1: Review

**Understanding Key Concepts**

1. What are two questions that you should answer before you even begin looking for a job?
2. What information should you include on a JIST Card?
3. How can you use a JIST Card?
4. What are factors you may want to consider as you make a decision about a job?

**Thinking Creatively**

How can you decide which of your skills to include on a JIST Card?
How can you decide which job factors are critical for your satisfaction at work?

**Taking It a Step Further**

Create a chart that lists the factors involved in making a decision about a job. Then interview at least five people to find out which factors are important to them and why. Write two paragraphs discussing what you discovered in your research.

# Section 7-2: Beginning Your Job Search

Searching for a job can be a little frightening and perhaps overwhelming. The following sections share information that you can use when beginning your search: how to organize the information that you will be collecting and where to begin in your search for potential employers.

## Getting Organized Before You Begin

Depending on local employment openings and your job interests, you will soon find some **job leads** (information about a business or company that is hiring workers) that you think you might be interested in checking out. It is very important to establish a system for organizing your job search. A system accomplishes two things. It reduces the time to find a job and can help you get a better job than you might otherwise find.

Michael Farr, in *Young Person's Guide to Getting & Keeping a Good Job* (published by JIST Publishing), recommends that you record job lead information on an index card. If you don't have index cards, you can use a small notebook. If you enjoy using computers, you may want to develop a system on your home computer or personal digital assistant (PDA), which is a handheld computer such as a BlackBerry. Whichever system you choose, the type of information you record for each company will be the same. It may include name of the company, telephone number and/or e-mail address, address (including directions or map) or Web page, **contact person** (the person you need to speak to), job title or type of work available, and information about the specific business or industry (what it does or makes).

**Company:** *Five Seasons Athletic Club*

**Contact Person:** *David Freitz*

**Phone number/e-mail address:** *(123) 456-7890 df@fiveseasons.com*

**Source of lead:** *Uncle Evan*

**Notes:** *4/10 called. Mr. F. on vacation, returning 4/15. Mr. F. said he'd have a shuttle bus driver opening in one week. Asked me to complete app asap. 4/16. Completed app onsite. 4/17 Mr. F. called to schedule interview at 10 a.m. on 4/19.*

*How can keeping all the information about a job lead in one place help you?*

After deciding on the system you want to use to organize your job search, create a **template** (a form to use as a guide) for recording information about each job lead. Then you are ready to start making contacts—in person, by telephone, or via e-mail—and recording information about job leads.

## Case Study: What Should Deshawn Do Next?

Deshawn will be a sophomore in high school next year. He is looking for his first summer job. He wants to make enough money to go to movies with friends and buy some new video games. His parents have suggested that he needs to also start saving for college. He stops by the following businesses and inquires about jobs: a food service restaurant, hardware store, nursing home, the local veterinarian's office, and a supermarket. The good news is that everyone is accepting applications for the summer!

**What should Deshawn do next?**

# Identifying Potential Employers

Before you can apply for a job, you must identify potential employers. Three job search methods are networking, self-directed searching, and using employment agencies.

## Networking

**Networking** just means talking to people and gathering information about a need you have. Quick! Name three people who could help you find a job. One of the fastest and easiest ways to find out about available jobs is talking to your parents, other relatives, friends, and neighbors. Maybe you think this is an unfair way to get a job, but the reality is that this is how many people get started in a company or find jobs. Networking is an excellent way to learn about jobs before they are announced publicly because employers prefer to hire from **referrals** or recommendations made by current employees.

In fact, about 40 percent of all jobs are filled by people who learn from someone in the organization or business that a job is likely to become available. This is known as a **warm contact** (getting help from people you know). Look at the chart to see how networking can benefit you when you are looking for a job.

Make certain that you give each person in your network one of your JIST Cards. They will then have the information they need to talk about you with potential employers or they can even give the employer your JIST Card.

## Networking Can Result in Thousands of Contacts

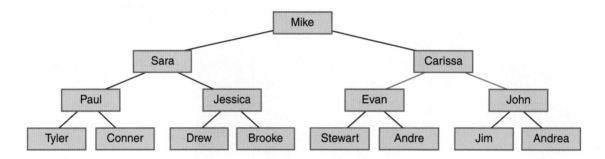

If you ask each referral for two names and follow through, your network will soon look like this:

| Alex | Bonnie | Charley | Danielle | Jeanne | Karl | Lisa | Matthew | Nicole | Richard |
|---|---|---|---|---|---|---|---|---|---|
| Tomas | Bret | Cindy | Emily | Franklin | Jose | Katrina | Lee | Maria | Nate |
| Rita | Alberto | Chris | Debby | Ernesto | Helene | Isaac | Joyce | Kirk | Leslie |
| Patty | Rafael | Sandy | Tony | Valerie | William | Andrea | Barry | Chantal | Dean |
| Gabrielle | Humberto | Ingrid | Jerry | Karen | Lorenzo | Melissa | Noel | Olga | Pablo |
| Rebekah | Sebastien | Tanya | Arthur | Cristobal | Edouard | Gustav | Hanna | Kyle | Laura |
| Nana | Paloma | Rene | Sally | Teddy | Vicky | Ana | Bill | Claudette | Danny |
| Grace | Henri | Ida | Joaquin | Kate | Larry | Mindy | Nicholas | Peter | Sam |

*How can you build a network of contacts?*

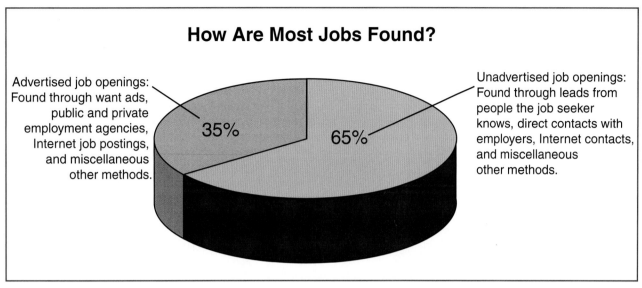

## How Are Most Jobs Found?

Advertised job openings: Found through want ads, public and private employment agencies, Internet job postings, and miscellaneous other methods.

**35%**

**65%**

Unadvertised job openings: Found through leads from people the job seeker knows, direct contacts with employers, Internet contacts, and miscellaneous other methods.

*What would you conclude after reading this chart?*

## Self-Directed Job Searching

You can look for jobs on your own, called a **self-directed job search**. To conduct a self-directed job search, use the Internet, the telephone directory, and classified ads; or look around your community to find businesses that might be interested in hiring you.

### Using the Telephone Book

You can use telephone books (print or online) to find potential employers. If you know the names of companies where you'd like to work, you can find their telephone numbers and addresses in the **White Pages** telephone book. Often, this version is arranged in two sections. The residential section lists home telephone numbers. The business section arranges the information alphabetically by the first word in each business's name.

If you don't know the actual names of businesses, use the **Yellow Pages** telephone book. The business categories of the Yellow Pages make it easy to find companies in your areas of interest. This book also has two sections. They are the Index and the actual Yellow Pages of business ads and contact information. The Index is an alphabetical listing of each category and its page numbers. For example, if you are interested in working in food service, look under the business category "Restaurant," in which you will find the page numbers of restaurant ads. When you turn to those pages, you will find an alphabetized list of food service establishments, including the telephone numbers and addresses. Make a job lead card for each employer you want to contact.

When you use the telephone book to look for a job, you have no guarantee that the company is actually hiring. Where can you go to find information about companies that are actually hiring?

> **CAREER FACT**
>
> Air traffic controllers earn high pay and have good benefits, but must work quickly and efficiently. They must give total concentration to their work to make certain that pilots receive the correct instructions. Being responsibile for the safety of so many lives can be exhausting and can cause mental stress.

## Internet Video and the Job Search Process

Improvements in technology have made it easier than ever before to create, view, and distribute video on the Internet. A quick search of the popular site YouTube reveals numerous videos, some serious and some silly, about finding a job.

Some jobseekers hope to stand out from the crowd by creating video resumes or introductions in addition to a traditional resume. A video resume is a one- or two-minute video in which jobseekers introduce themselves, describe their qualifications, and explain why they would be good employees. Some video resumes include music or special titles, but most of them are a simple shot of a person from the waist up in one location. Career sites such as Vault and CareerBuilder.com have added features to let jobseekers post video resumes in addition to traditional ones.

If done well, video resumes give jobseekers a chance to show their personalities and possibly their creative and technical skills. If done poorly, video resumes give thousands of YouTube members something new to ridicule. Employers in conservative industries, such as finance, may frown on a video resume. Because video resumes may reveal race, religion, disabilities, and other characteristics not found on a traditional resume, many employers may not want to view video resumes for fear of legal action concerning discrimination if the jobseekers on video do not get job interviews.

Video interviews are another way that video technology is being used in the job search process. In this type of interview, the job applicant typically goes to an office with a webcam and a monitor that shows the job interviewer in another location. The applicant listens to the questions and then gives his or her answers while looking at the webcam. In addition to helping employers save on travel expenses, video interviews make it easy for employers to compare interviews without relying on their notes and to share interviews with other managers.

Whether you are creating a video resume or participating in a video interview, following these guidelines will help you make the best video impression:

▶ Practice being in front of a camera so that you will be more comfortable and confident.

▶ Dress professionally.

▶ Minimize distractions by clearing away any clutter that will appear onscreen and controlling background noise.

▶ Speak clearly and slowly and look straight into the camera.

▶ Be enthusiastic and show your personality, but stay focused on presenting your job skills.

## Using Classified Ads

Many companies use their local newspapers to advertise job openings. The newspaper section of advertisements that includes job openings is called **classified ads**. Each newspaper organizes this section differently, but each has an index that lists its subsections of ads such as Homes, Cars, and Job Openings. Usually, the ads for jobs are also placed in alphabetized categories such as Administrative, General, Health Care, Professional, Restaurant, Sales, Trade, and so on. The General section usually lists entry-level jobs.

What can you do if you don't subscribe to a newspaper at home? Your school library or public library probably has a subscription to your local newspaper. Can you think of other ways to gain access to the classified ads?

Many times classified ads use abbreviations or special words. Each newspaper's classified ad fees are usually based on the number of lines the ad uses. The abbreviations save space and money for the buyers of the ads.

---

### HIRING

Food service restaurant now hiring FT Asst Mgrs., Exe fringe, Qualified individuals with restaurant mang. exper. call Jackie at 111-2222 M–F. EOE

*What do you notice about this ad? Do you understand what it says?*

---

## Using the Internet

In this technological age, many newspapers list their classified ads section online. Some even offer a section specifically for hourly jobs. To access your newspaper's Web site, enter the newspaper's name as a keyword in a search engine such as Google. You probably will see a Jobs link. Clicking that link will take you to a window in which you can select the area of employment that you are seeking.

Another way to use the Internet in your job search is to go to a specific company's Web site, such as BestBuy.com. The Web site probably has a link to employment opportunities or careers where you can find a listing of job openings. If you don't see the link, look for the link to company information. You can often find job openings listed in that section of the site.

You can find job-search engines on the Internet, such as Monster. Using these search engines can be overwhelming and frustrating for someone seeking a part-time job in a local community. However, they are excellent resources for finding more information about higher-level jobs or jobs at other locations.

## Looking Around Your Community

Don't underestimate the importance of keeping your eyes open throughout your self-directed job search. You can use this method as you go about your daily routine. As you walk or drive through your community, look for "Help Wanted" or "Now Hiring" signs. Check bulletin boards and announcement boards at your local supermarkets, businesses, schools, or churches. What are some other ways to conduct a self-directed job search?

# Using Employment Agencies

Organizations that help people find jobs are employment agencies. Some employers choose to hire employees through these agencies. The agency **screens** applicants, looking carefully at their qualifications and finding the person who best meets the needs of the company.

The two types of employment agencies are public and private. The major difference between the two is that the services of a **public employment agency** are free, and a **private employment agency** charges a fee. Companies can list job openings with either or both types of employment agencies. Do you have any employment agencies in your community?

Public employment agencies will provide counseling services. Sometimes they help you prepare for the job interview and help arrange the interview. Sometimes you have to do these yourself. Public employment agencies include state employment service offices and the USAJOBS Web site, sponsored by the **United States Office of Personnel Management (OPM)**, the human resources office for the federal government. To find out more information about these agencies, enter your state's name and the keywords "workforce development" in an Internet search engine or look in the state government telephone listings under "employment services."

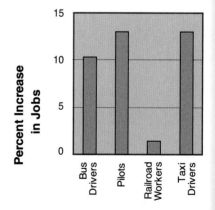

**Projected Outlook for 2016**

*What does this chart tell you about future opportunities in these careers?*

*Why would someone go to a public employment agency to find a job?*

If you use a private employment agency, make certain that you understand how much of a fee will be charged, who will pay it, how long you have to pay it, and whether it will be given back to you later. Make sure that you understand the contract completely before you sign it. If you don't understand the terms of the contract, ask questions. It is a legal document, and if you sign the contract and don't follow it, you could end up in court.

## Section 7-2: Review

### Understanding Key Concepts

1. What is networking and how can you use it in a job search?
2. What is a warm contact?
3. What methods can you use to conduct a self-directed search for a job?
4. Why do some companies hire employment agencies to find applicants for positions?
5. What is the difference between a public and private employment agency?

### Thinking Creatively

Why do some people find looking for a job so difficult, whereas others seem to enjoy the search?

When should someone hire an agency to find a job?

### Taking It a Step Further

Using the Internet, research a federal or state Workforce Development site for information about available jobs. Then go to an Internet job search site, such as Monster, and research jobs for the same area. Write a paragraph comparing the differences and/or similarities of jobs listed on the sites.

# Section 7-3: Contacting Potential Employers

As you record contact information on each job lead, make sure that you take a few minutes to find more information about the specific company and industry. Doing so will make you more comfortable when you are talking with the employer. You can also show how interested, organized, and professional you are.

When you have the information you need about a specific business or have seen a classified ad that gives a phone number, contact the business. Make a phone call, stop in, or write the employer to see whether the company is hiring. Contacting a person you do not know is called making a **cold contact**.

## Use the Telephone

According to career author Michael Farr, using the telephone is one of the most efficient ways of looking for work. Not only do you avoid spending time traveling and save money on transportation, but you also can talk to many organizations in a very short period of time. The following tips will help you use the telephone in your job search.

1. Overcome your shyness up front. After all, what's the worst thing that can happen to you when you are talking on the phone? Focus on the fact that you are offering to meet the employer's need, not asking for a favor.

2. Write a script and practice what you are going to say. Remember to keep it short and to the point. A script is especially helpful if you suddenly feel shy.

*What would you say if you had to talk on the phone to a potential employer?*

3. Before you make the call, make sure that you know how to use good telephone skills by speaking clearly and professionally.

4. Try to get the name of the supervisor or manager of the department in which you want to work before you call. When you call, ask for that person by name.

5. If you are told that the company is not hiring, say that you are still very interested in working for the company or a similar company. Ask for referrals to other companies.

You may think that calling an employer sounds frightening and that you would not feel comfortable trying this. That's okay because there are still many other methods used to look for a job. However, many organizations recognize and appreciate people who are assertive and show initiative. This approach may or may not work, but it is better than not trying at all. By making that first contact, you have made an impression and you may even be considered for a future job.

## Visit the Company in Person

If you do not like to use the telephone, or if a company provides its address in a classified ad, visit a company in person. When you do so, you have a greater opportunity to contact the correct person.

One thing to keep in mind if you make a personal visit is that your appearance and behavior are important. Dress appropriately, in a way that will make an employer feel that you will represent the company well. Also, go prepared. You will have to speak to someone. You can use the telephone script as the basis for your conversation with the person who greets you. You may be asked to give information about yourself. Be sure to take your JIST Card with you.

*What would you say to a receptionist if you want to know whether the company has any job openings?*

When you visit the company, ask to speak with the person who would actually hire you for the position in which you are interested. Again, it is very important for you to research information about the company before you arrive. Because this person is likely to be very busy, you should keep your visit short and focused on your intent. You will want to ask the following questions: "Are you hiring right now?" "Will you be hiring in the future?" Explain why you are interested in working for the company, give the person your JIST Card, and thank him or her.

# Write to the Company

If you are not in a hurry to get a job, are uncomfortable with calling or visiting the company, or if a company's classified ad requests that you send an e-mail message, fax, or **letter of inquiry** (a letter asking for an application or more information), you may want to write to the company. Be sure to use the five phases of writing in communicating with the company.

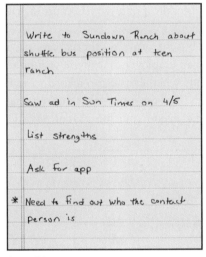

*Prewriting*

Write to Sundown Ranch about shuttle bus position at teen ranch

Saw ad in Sun Times on 4/5

List strengths

Ask for app

\* Need to find out who the contact person is

*Drafting*

Dear ?

Hello, I saw your ad in the Sun Times about a shuttle bus driver position. I have a good driving record.

Please send me an application. Mail it to me at the address below.

Thanks.

*Revising*

Dear ?,

Hello, I saw your companys ad in the Sun Times about a shuttle bus driver position.

I have a good driving record.

Please mail me an application at my home addresss. If you don't mind, I will call you in two weeks.

Sinceerly,

*Editing and Proofreading*

Mr. Adams
Dear ?,

Hello. I saw your companys ad for a shuttle bus driver position in the *Sun Times* on 4-5. April 5th on I am a dependable, I get along well with people, and I have a good an excellent driving record.

enclosed
Please mail an application to me in the self-addressed, stamped envelope. If you don't mind, I will call you in two weeks to discuss the position and my application.

Thank you in advance for your time.
Sincerely
Sinceerly,

*Final*

Dear Mr. Adams,

Hello. I saw your company's ad for a shuttle bus driver position in the *Sun Times* on April 5th. I am dependable, I get along well with people, and I have an excellent driving record.

Please mail an application to me in the enclosed self-addressed, stamped envelope. If you don't mind, I will call you in two weeks to discuss the position and my application.

Thank you in advance for your time.

Sincerely,

Your message should be **concise** (short and to the point). It should include information about who you are, your interest in the company, and your qualifications for the position. You should provide contact information, a time that you will follow up on your letter of inquiry, and a JIST Card. Remember that when you are writing letters, neatness and courtesy count!

# Follow Through

Following through is possibly the most important part of the job search. If you call or visit an employer, always send a thank-you note or e-mail message. The note will not only remind the employer that you are interested in working for the organization, but will also show that you have good manners. Send this note to the person with whom you spoke, thanking her for the time and information provided. You should restate your interest in working for the company and ask that the company contact you if an opening becomes available in the future.

It is also acceptable to ask if you may call back to check on the status of your inquiry. Just remember to write in a friendly, polite way because it will most certainly help you get the job.

In some cases, you will be offered a job right away; in other situations, it may be several weeks before you hear from an employer. If you are waiting to hear about a specific job, you need to decide whether you can afford to wait or continue following up on other job leads. Today's job market dictates that you pursue several job leads at the same time, even if one job is your favorite.

Dear Mr. Adams,

Thank you very much for inviting me

to interview for the shuttle bus driver

position. I am very impressed with

your company, especially the training

you provide for your drivers.

Thanks again for sharing your time with

me. I will call you next week when I return

from my trip to Texas.

Sincerely,

*How might sending a thank-you note help you get a job?*

Now you know what it is going to take to look for that first job. Assuming that you are in school full-time and may also be involved in one or more extracurricular activities, your time will be very limited. That's why it is very important to take a systematic approach and organize your time to get the results you want. The more contacts you can make, the more interviews will result. The more interviews you have, the sooner you will find a job. Remember there is someone out there who wants to hire you. But that won't happen until you take the initiative.

## Section 7-3: Review

### Understanding Key Concepts

1. What is a cold contact?
2. What are three ways to contact a company about a job and what are the advantages and disadvantages of each?
3. Why is following through after making initial contact so important?

### Thinking Creatively

Which type of contact—warm or cold—is easier for you? Why?

What thoughts might run through the minds of potential employers when they post job-opening ads?

### Taking It a Step Further

Prepare a template for either a letter of inquiry or a follow-up thank-you note, leaving blanks for information that will change.

## Spotlight on a Career

### David Randolph, Locomotive Engineer
### CSX Transportation

I am a Federal Railroad Administration (FRA) Certified Locomotive Engineer employed by CSX Transportation. I have been working in engine service for 35 years. I am responsible for the safe and efficient operation of diesel-electric locomotives in yard and road operations. I must know and comply with all federal and state laws, CSX operating rules, and other railroads' rules. I'm tested every three years on the federal rules and annually on my company's rules. I am expected to make the correct decision, and everything depends on several factors: power, car count, weather, and operating conditions.

I graduated from high school and was hired by the Monon Railroad. Experience has been my main source of education. After a series of tests, I received a promotion to engineer. Education for an engineer is an ongoing process. The rules and equipment are constantly changing; keeping up-to-date is part of the job. However, the training is different today. New employees are required to attend a school prior to being hired. They must work as trainmen for at least a year. Further training is based on seniority: The company announces dates for an Engineer class, and trainmen are chosen based on the dates they were hired. After five weeks of classroom work and testing, the students are sent to the field for 11 weeks of on-the-train training. With the passing of written tests and qualifying rides, they become engineers.

The balancing act of home, family, and working on the railroad can be difficult. Most railroad jobs are 24/7 because employees are on call. Then they can spend time in a motel at the other end of a trip, waiting for a train to take back home. I've been told that railroading gets into your blood, and I am proof that this is true. When I am not working, I photograph, collect, and build model trains. When I go on vacation, I like to hike, camp, and take pictures of trains.

# Chapter Review and Activities

The following sections can help you review the contents of this chapter.

## Key Concepts

Following are the key concepts presented in the chapter.

▸ Before you begin searching for a job, you need to answer two important questions: What do you offer an employer? What do you need or want in a job?

▸ To determine what you can offer, place information that employers need to know about you on a small card (referred to as a JIST Card).

▸ The second step in searching for a job is deciding what you want or need from a job—as well as what you don't want.

▸ It is very important to establish a system and organize your job search.

▸ Before you can apply for a job, you must identify potential employers.

▸ Networking is an excellent way to learn about jobs before they are announced publicly.

▸ You can look for jobs on your own (called self-directed job search) by searching the Internet, using the telephone directory, checking classified ads, or looking around your community.

▸ Organizations that help people find jobs are employment agencies. The agencies screen applicants who best meet the needs of the company. There are two types of employment agencies: public and private.

▸ When you have gathered the necessary information you need, contact the business by making a phone call, stopping in, or writing the employer to see whether the company is hiring.

▸ One thing to keep in mind if you make a personal visit is that your appearance and behavior are important.

▸ If you choose to write to the company, your message should be concise and should include information about who you are, your interest in the company, and your qualifications for the position.

▸ Following through is possibly the most important part of the job search. If you call or visit an employer, it is always a good idea to send a thank-you note or an e-mail message.

## Key Term Review

Complete the following activity to review your understanding of the key terms.

classified ads
cold contact
competitors
concise
contact person
fringe benefits
interview
JIST Card
job leads
letter of inquiry
networking
private employment agency

public employment agency
referrals
screens
self-directed job search
template
United States Office of Personnel
  Management (OPM)
wages
warm contact
White Pages
Yellow Pages

You are the manager for an airline company that is laying off 35 percent of its staff. You have been asked to give a presentation on where to search for jobs. Using at least 10 key terms, create a short multimedia or written presentation for the employees who will begin searching for different jobs.

## Comprehension Review

Answer the following questions to review the contents of the chapter.

1. What two steps should you take before you begin a job search?

2. What is networking and why is it important?

3. Of the three methods of making cold contacts mentioned in this chapter, which is the most efficient?

4. Why is visiting a company an effective way to locate a job?

5. What information should a letter of inquiry include?

6. What are three ways to follow up on a job lead?

## School-to-Work

**Math:** Write the steps you would take to solve this mathematical problem and then provide the correct answer:

A job placement agency is charging you a flat fee of $150 and 5 percent of your annual income and sign-on bonus. Company A has offered you a salary of $46,000 and a 3 percent sign-on bonus after 90 days. They also agreed to pay half of your placement fees if you stay with the company for one year. Company B offered a salary of $51,000 with no bonus and no sharing of placement fees. Which offer should you accept?

**Social Studies:** Create a family occupation tree that includes grandparents, great-grandparents, uncles, aunts, and any other relatives or in-laws. Underneath each person's name, list job titles and responsibilities

**Writing:** Write a **letter of inquiry** to an employer who just told you that his company is hiring. In the letter, identify the position that interests you. Also, tell him why you find that particular job interesting and why you would be a good candidate for it. Close by thanking the employer for his time.

**Science:** Why has the United States never sent humans to Mars? What might we gain from doing so? What are some of the skills and characteristics that will be required by the astronauts who go? Conduct research online, and then prepare either a report with illustrations or a presentation to answer these questions.

. . . . . . . . . . . . . . . . . . . . . . . . . . . . . . . . . . . . . . . . . . . . . . . . . . . .

## Does This Job Interest You?

The following job is posted on the Internet. What education and experience are required? What requirement does this job have that most jobs do not have? What types of interests and skills should a person working in this position have? How could someone apply for the job? How could someone find out more about the job?

| FIND JOBS | POST RESUMES |
|-----------|--------------|

### Corporate Pilot

**Company:** Savvy Logistics, Inc.
**Contact Name:** HR Department
**Address:** 10 East Main Street

**City State Zip:** Imperial Valley, MT 00112
**Fax:** 000-111-2222
**E-mail:** jweber@savvy.com

### Job Description

Western U.S.-based agricultural company seeks a qualified pilot. Aircraft include a Mitsubishi MU2 and Cessna Caravan.

### Job Requirements

Applicants must demonstrate a proven record of safety along with strong customer service skills. Ideal candidate must be qualified in one or both aircraft. Salary commensurate with experience. Bilingual preferred. Must live or be willing to relocate to Imperial Valley.

### Contact

To apply, please submit resume and flight experience, along with a cover letter indicating qualifications for piloting MU2 and/or Caravan and your philosophy of a properly run corporate flight department. Only applicants who submit a cover letter, as indicated, will be considered for the position. Submit cover letter and resume by e-mail (in confidence). EOE.

**Apply Online**

# What career appeals to you?

# Chapter 8 Applying for a Job

## What You'll Learn

▶ Creating a superior resume

▶ Writing a cover letter

▶ Preparing a portfolio

▶ Applying for a job

▶ Taking additional steps to employment

Applying for a job is hard work. The better prepared you are, the greater your chances of success. To be successful when you apply for a job, you need some important job search tools and tips for completing applications.

*Success is that old ABC—ability, breaks, and courage.*

*–Charles Luckman*

background checks
birth certificate
convicted
cover letter
employment application
employment tests
Fair Labor Standards Act

felony
job applicant
misdemeanors
NA
negotiable
onsite
philosophy

portfolio
references
resume
Social Security
transcript
work permit

# Section 8-1: Getting an Employer's Attention

When you are looking for a job, you probably will be in competition with several other applicants. How can you get the right kind of attention from an employer? How can you stand out as a quality employee?

Three tools that work together well to make a positive impression on a potential employer are a resume, a cover letter, and a **portfolio** (a collection of samples of your work). Before you even get to the stage of completing an application for a job, you probably will want to prepare all three. Well-written resumes and cover letters and interesting portfolios can get the attention of even the busiest employers.

## Create a Superior Resume

What is a resume? A **resume** is a summary of information about a person: the contact information, education, skills, activities, and recognitions you've received. A resume gives you a chance to point out your strengths and abilities, showing that you are prepared to work. A superior resume is one that is so attractive and well-written that it increases your chance of getting the job. Why is a resume such an important job-searching tool?

Today, many classified ads request a resume, even for entry-level jobs. Employers receive dozens or even hundreds of resumes for a particular job. Most employers skim through the resumes and read just a few carefully. All this is done without ever meeting the job applicant face to face! The resume might be the first and only impression that the interviewer or employer has of you; its content and appearance are critical.

How do you create a resume? You can find literally thousands of books, Web sites, and computer programs that can provide you with samples of resumes as well as tips and pointers on resume writing. There is no one right resume for every job situation. The key is to write a resume that focuses on your strengths that directly apply to the job you are seeking.

A JIST Card is a mini-resume that contains your full name; your phone number, including the area code; your e-mail address; the type of position you are seeking; your skills; special conditions, such as specific hours you are available; and your self-management skills. Resumes should expand on that information, including these components:

▶ **Contact information.** This information includes your name, address, telephone number, and e-mail address.

▶ **Career profile.** The career profile lists the position you want and summarizes your career goal.

▶ **Main sections.** These sections are organized according to your work, volunteer, or extracurricular experiences; education; skills; and personal interests that relate to your career objective.

▶ **Highlights.** Highlights can include awards, accomplishments, and recognitions you have received.

You will also need a separate list of references. **References** are the names of and contact information for people who will recommend you for employment. Always remember to ask people whether you can list them as references. Also, remember to choose references who are appropriate for the job that you are applying for.

Remember these important points as you create your resume:

▶ **Highlight the skills that are appropriate for the job.** For instance, if you are applying for a job as a cashier, emphasize strong math skills. If you are seeking a job as an amusement park ride supervisor, emphasize your child care experience.

▶ **Stress what you offer rather than just what you are looking for.**

### CAREER FACT

Careers in industrial production might include book binding, dental lab technology, machine work inspection, factory management, printing, silversmithing, tool setting, welding, and woodworking.

---

**Dean Grant**
123 Darlton Court
Columbus, OH 41103
123 345-6789
d_grant@aol.com

Objective: A position in manufacturing

Areas of Accomplishment

Manufacturing
- Completed two semesters of industrial design courses
- Completed two semesters of welding courses
- Completed two semesters of time management

Additional Skills
- Detailed record keeper
- Neat appearance
- Punctual, reliable, outgoing, friendly, and honest

Education:
Center High School, Diploma
Columbus, OH

---

*What could you put in your resume that focuses on your strengths?*

▸ **Always write a resume that is applicable to the particular job.** If the employer is looking for someone with a solid work history, highlight your dates of employment that show your work record. Or if the employer is more interested in what you can do, emphasize your skills that directly apply to the job.

You will probably want to use a word processing program to create your resume. What do you gain by having an electronic version of it rather than a handwritten or typed one?

How can you get your resume to the right person? Find out the name of the person who supervises the specific job you seek within the company. After you have identified this person, send your cover letter and resume directly to that person.

When should you take a resume to a company personally? When should you e-mail it or mail it? If it is convenient, and if the company does not specifically ask that you mail a resume, deliver it in person. Having an employer associate a face with a resume usually increases your chances of getting an interview. If you are applying for a job that is not in your local area, it is acceptable to e-mail or mail your resume with a cover letter. For example, if you live in New York and you are applying for a job in Texas, it makes sense to send it by e-mail or mail because of the distance involved. Some companies might require the use of e-mail or mail for resumes and cover letters.

**CAREER FACT**

Although most industrial production management positions require a college degree, there is no specific educational program for that career. Most applicants have a bachelor's or master's degree in industrial engineering, management, or business administration.

# Prepare an Interesting Cover Letter

If you are visiting a prospective employer, you can just take your JIST Card or resume with you. However, if you are replying to a request for a resume in a classified ad, you need to mail the resume. What would an employer think if he or she opened a letter and it contained only a sheet of paper with information about a stranger? What could you include in the envelope that would introduce you and the resume?

A **cover letter** is your way of introducing your resume and asking for an interview. A cover letter should contain at least three paragraphs:

▸ The opening paragraph should introduce you to the employer, telling who you are and why you would be a good employee for the company. Open with an unusual approach to get the employer's attention.

▸ The second paragraph is the main part of the letter. It gives your qualifications, accomplishments, and successes to convince the employer that you offer value to the company.

▸ The final paragraph closes the letter by thanking the person for the opportunity to introduce yourself, asking for an interview, and saying that you will contact the employer with a phone call to follow up on your application—unless you know that the company does not welcome phone calls.

Whenever you mail a resume, be sure to include a cover letter. If you e-mail a resume, use your cover letter as the e-mail message.

## Strategies for Writing Winning Cover Letters

Wendy S. Enelow and Louise Kursmark, authors of *Cover Letter Magic* (published by JIST Publishing), offer these five strategies for writing cover letters:

▸ Make it easy for someone to understand "who" you are. Clearly communicate that information at the beginning of your cover letter. For example, you can write "I am a sophomore in high school and want to pursue a career in ____"

▸ Include the information that you know about the company or the position for which you are applying. Tell specifically how your experience can meet the company's needs.

▸ Explain why you want to work for this company in particular. Tell the company what it is doing right that caught your attention. For example, a sentence like "I buy most of my clothes at your store" lets an employer know that you know and like the products you would be selling.

▸ Be sure that your cover letter is neat, clean, and well-written. It should be attractive and not over-designed.

▸ Double-check, triple-check, and then have someone else check your letter to be sure that it is error-free! Even the smallest of errors is unacceptable.

## DIVERSITY

### Why? Why? Why?

Every time you give your co-worker an instruction, she begins asking questions. Why do I have to do that? Who is going to help me? How do we do that? For how long? Where? You would think that she was writing a book. Why does she ask so many questions?

## ETHICS

### How Trustworthy Are You?

Your employer asked you to work the early shift tomorrow because she has to go with her son to court. She said that she knew she could trust you not to tell anyone else. The next day, one of your co-workers asks why you came in early. What will you say?

123 Darlton Court
Columbus, OH 41103

April 4, 20xx

Mr. David Freitz
24 Main Boulevard
Columbus, OH 41103

Dear Mr. Freitz,

I enjoyed talking with you on the phone today about the manufacturing position that will soon be available at your company. As you requested, I am enclosing my resume and will come to the facility to complete an application tomorrow.

On my resume, you will see that I have demonstrated an interest in manufacturing by completing courses in industrial design and welding. I have also studied principles in time management. With the knowledge these courses have provided, I am confident that I can make an outstanding contribution to your company.

I look forward to learning more about your facility and the position you have available tomorrow.

Sincerely,


Dean Grant

*How can a cover letter help you get a job?*

## On-the-Job Competency

### What Should You Wear to Work?

Your job requires you to work with a conveyor belt (a continuously moving belt that carries products from one point to another). How is that factor going to impact how you dress for work? What should you wear? What should you not wear? Why? Regardless of where you work, what should you wear to work?

## DISCRIMINATION

### Is Your Employer Guilty of Discrimination?

Your father and mother are Muslims from an Arab country, and you were not born in the United States, although you've lived here since you were six months old. When you applied for a job as an airport safety security guard, you indicated on the application that you were a Caucasian and a citizen of the United States. Now your supervisor has discovered your nation of origin and says that you're fired. Are you being discriminated against?

# Develop a Portfolio

More and more employers are asking for portfolios as part of the job application process. The portfolio can be a useful tool to show your best work and to describe the ways in which your work has improved over time.

You will want to base your choices of what you place in your portfolio on the job you are seeking. For example, if you are applying for a job in fashion design, you can include samples of your best designs. If you are applying for a job as a cashier, you might want to include copies of your math grades. Can you think of other examples?

You might include this information in your portfolio:

▸ A statement indicating that the items reflect your original work and should not be copied.

▸ An introductory letter that describes your **philosophy** (beliefs about yourself and others as well as career goals)

▸ Your resume

▸ Letters of recommendation

▸ School **transcript** (the record of your grades)

▸ Copies (not originals) of writing samples such as reports, research papers, journals, or Web pages

▸ Math samples and/or problem-solving samples

▸ Computer projects

- Designs (art work, brochures, photographs, PowerPoint presentations)
- Volunteer service projects, newspaper articles, photos, or other documentation to show activities in which you have been involved
- Awards and certificates
- References and thank-you letters that recommend you or show how much you are appreciated

What would you place in your portfolio?

Use a three-ring binder of good quality that looks professional and attractive. Get some clear sheet protectors to hold your papers and documents.

You can organize your portfolio in many different ways, depending on your career objectives and career goals. Your resume should be located toward the beginning of your portfolio. Look at your resume carefully. Can you give proof of the information in your resume? For example, if you listed training in first-aid as one of your skills, do you have a certificate that you can copy for your portfolio? To show that you have strong math skills, highlight your math grades on your transcript, and include it in your portfolio. You could also include letters of recommendation from the references listed on your resume.

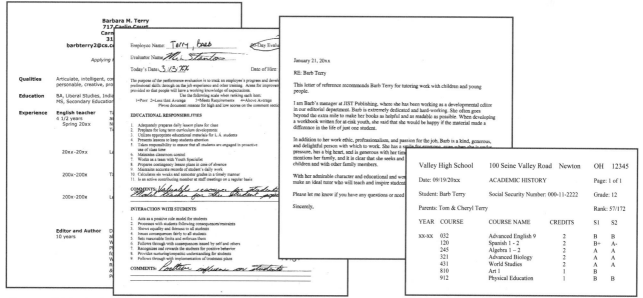

Can you think of other items you would place in your portfolio?

With today's technology, an electronic portfolio is an excellent option because you can store the information on a hard drive or removable media. Electronic portfolios do not require physical space as traditional portfolios do. Also, you can easily send them by e-mail to a prospective employer. If you have the computer skills and creativity, or want to improve your skills, create an electronic portfolio. Be sure to use multimedia such as videos, graphics, sound, and pictures.

## Section 8-1: Review

### Understanding Key Concepts

1. What are the goals of a resume, cover letter, and portfolio?
2. What information should you include in a resume?
3. What is the purpose of a cover letter?
4. How is a portfolio different from a resume?
5. What is an advantage of an electronic portfolio?

### Thinking Creatively

What would be the advantages and disadvantages of preparing resume and cover letter templates?

When should you start working on your portfolio?

### Taking It a Step Further

Make a list of all the electronic equipment someone would need to create a digital portfolio. Then write a paragraph explaining the steps one would have to follow to create the portfolio.

# Section 8-2: Filling Out an Employment Application

**E**mployment application forms request information about you, your education, and your work experience. Most companies require you to fill out an application form for any job.

Application forms can vary from company to company, but they also have many similarities. Some of the forms might be one page long; others might be two or more pages. Look over the sample application form. What information can you answer easily? What information are you not able to answer unless you have it written down and with you?

Use the following tips when filling out an application form. These tips are for paper application forms, but also can apply to electronic applications (job applications completed using a computer).

## Tip 1: Ask for a Second Application

When you ask for an application, request two copies. You can use one as a rough draft and the other as the final version.

# Tip 2: Ask for Permission to Take the Application Form

Ask if you can take the application form home with you. Doing so gives you time to think about your answers. Having more time allows you to think about paragraphs before you write them or attach a resume stressing your qualifications for the job.

Do not be surprised if the employer asks you to complete the application onsite. Many employers do not allow applications to leave the premises. They want to make certain that the applicant is the person who completed the application.

# Tip 3: Read the Entire Application Before You Start

Always read the entire application form before you start filling in the blanks. Think about your answers. Notice where they go. Plan how to use the space you have for each answer.

**APPLICATION FOR EMPLOYMENT**
(Pre-Employment Questionnaire)    (An Equal Opportunity Employer)

**A. PERSONAL INFORMATION**

DATE _____

SOCIAL SECURITY NUMBER _____

NAME _____
LAST    FIRST    MIDDLE

PRESENT ADDRESS _____
STREET    CITY    STATE    ZIP

PERMANENT ADDRESS _____
STREET    CITY    STATE    ZIP

PHONE NO. _____ ARE YOU 18 YEARS OR OLDER? ☐ YES ☐ NO

ARE YOU EITHER A U.S. CITIZEN OR AN ALIEN AUTHORIZED TO WORK IN THE UNITED STATES? ☐ YES ☐ NO

**B. EMPLOYMENT DESIRED**

POSITION _____ DATE YOU CAN START _____ SALARY DESIRED _____

ARE YOU EMPLOYED NOW? _____ IF SO, MAY WE INQUIRE OF YOUR PRESENT EMPLOYER? _____

EVER APPLIED TO THIS COMPANY BEFORE? _____ WHERE? _____ WHEN? _____

REFERRED BY _____

**C. EDUCATION**

| | NAME AND LOCATION OF SCHOOL | NO. OF YEARS ATTENDED | DID YOU GRADUATE? | SUBJECTS STUDIED |
|---|---|---|---|---|
| GRAMMAR SCHOOL | | | | |
| HIGH SCHOOL | | | | |
| COLLEGE | | | | |
| TRADE, BUSINESS, OR CORRESPONDENCE SCHOOL | | | | |

**D. GENERAL**

SUBJECTS OF SPECIAL STUDY OR RESEARCH WORK _____

SPECIAL SKILLS _____

ACTIVITIES (CIVIC, ATHLETIC, ETC.) _____
EXCLUDE ORGANIZATIONS, THE NAME OF WHICH INDICATES THE RACE, CREED, SEX, AGE, MARITAL STATUS, COLOR, OR NATION OF ORIGIN OF ITS MEMBERS.

U.S. MILITARY OR NAVAL SERVICE _____ RANK _____    PRESENT MEMBERSHIP IN NATIONAL GUARD OR RESERVES _____

**E. FORMER EMPLOYERS.** LIST BELOW LAST FOUR EMPLOYERS, STARTING WITH LAST ONE FIRST.

| DATE MONTH AND YEAR | NAME AND ADDRESS OF EMPLOYER | SALARY | POSITION | REASON FOR LEAVING |
|---|---|---|---|---|
| FROM | | | | |
| TO | | | | |
| FROM | | | | |
| TO | | | | |
| FROM | | | | |
| TO | | | | |
| FROM | | | | |
| TO | | | | |

**F. REFERENCES.** GIVE THE NAMES OF THREE PERSONS NOT RELATED TO YOU, WHOM YOU HAVE KNOWN AT LEAST ONE YEAR.

| | NAME | PHONE NUMBER | BUSINESS | YEARS ACQUAINTED |
|---|---|---|---|---|
| 1. | | | | |
| 2. | | | | |
| 3. | | | | |

**G. PHYSICAL RECORD**

DO YOU HAVE ANY PHYSICAL LIMITATIONS THAT PRECLUDE YOU FROM PERFORMING ANY WORK FOR WHICH YOU ARE BEING CONSIDERED? ☐ YES ☐ NO IF YES, WHAT CAN BE DONE TO ACCOMMODATE YOUR LIMITATION?

_____

IN CASE OF EMERGENCY, NOTIFY _____
NAME    ADDRESS    PHONE NO.

"I CERTIFY THAT THE FACTS CONTAINED IN THIS APPLICATION ARE TRUE AND COMPLETE TO THE BEST OF MY KNOWLEDGE AND UNDERSTAND THAT, IF EMPLOYED, FALSIFIED STATEMENTS ON THIS APPLICATION SHALL BE GROUNDS FOR DISMISSAL.

I AUTHORIZE INVESTIGATION OF ALL STATEMENTS CONTAINED HEREIN AND THE REFERENCES LISTED ABOVE TO GIVE YOU ANY AND ALL INFORMATION CONCERNING MY PREVIOUS EMPLOYMENT AND ANY PERTINENT INFORMATION THEY MAY HAVE, PERSONAL OR OTHERWISE, AND RELEASE ALL PARTIES FROM ALL LIABILITY FOR ANY DAMAGE THAT MAY RESULT FROM FURNISHING SAME TO YOU.

I UNDERSTAND AND AGREE THAT, IF HIRED, MY EMPLOYMENT IS FOR NO DEFINITE PERIOD AND MAY, REGARDLESS OF THE DATE OF PAYMENT OF MY WAGES AND SALARY, BE TERMINATED AT ANY TIME WITHOUT ANY PRIOR NOTICE."

DATE _____ SIGNATURE _____

DO NOT WRITE BELOW THIS LINE

INTERVIEWED BY _____ DATE _____

_____

HIRED ☐ YES ☐ NO POSITION _____ DEPT. _____

SALARY/WAGE _____ DATE REPORTING TO WORK _____

APPROVED: 1. _____ 2. _____ 3. _____
EMPLOYMENT MANAGER    DEPT. HEAD    GENERAL MANAGER

*What are some typical mistakes job applicants make when filling out a form if they don't look carefully at it? What happens to applications that are not filled out properly?*

# Tip 4: Follow the Instructions

Read the instructions on the application carefully. If the instructions ask that you print or type information, it is important to follow them. Printing rather than cursive writing and using ink are usually preferred because they are easier to read. What do you think employers do with applications they cannot read? What do they think about applicants who do not follow the instructions?

# Tip 5: Write Neatly

Neatness counts! If you are completing a paper application, write slowly and carefully, forming each number and letter carefully. Think about each answer and avoid making erasures or crossing through answers. You might even want to carry an erasable black ink pen with you just for completing applications. Recopy your application if it is messy; it is better to ask for another application form than to submit one that is messy. What message does a messy application give an employer about you?

# Tip 6: Answer All Questions Completely

Answer all the requests for information on the application form. Avoid using abbreviations on the job application unless they are requested or the writing space is very limited. In some cases, your abbreviations might have a different meaning or the person reviewing your application might not understand them.

There is one exception. In some cases, the information might not apply to you. If it doesn't, put the letters **NA**, (which means "not applicable" or "does not apply") in the blank or draw a line through the blank. The employer looks for thoroughness in your answers, so don't leave anything blank. What are some examples of information that might not apply to you?

# Tip 7: Provide Accurate Information

Be honest about any information you provide. Lying is not only dishonest, but it also is illegal. After you have signed and dated an application form, it becomes a legal document. The employer has the right to keep it on file. In many cases, employers will conduct **background checks** (investigating past and present information about you from former employers, schools, and the police). They also will check with your references (recommendations from another person about your character, ability, attitude, and so on).

If you give false information, your application will be rejected. If the lie is discovered after you are employed, you can and probably will be fired. In certain cases, you might even be sued. Can you think of a situation in which an employer might want to fire or sue an employee for lying on an application?

# Tip 8: Know Your Rights

It is illegal for an employer to ask whether you have ever been arrested. It is legal to ask "Have you ever been **convicted** (found guilty by law) of a felony?" (A **felony** is a serious criminal offense such as murder or burglary.) An employer might also legally ask questions about **misdemeanors** (a less serious offense such as theft) if it could affect your ability to do a job. When filling in the job application, you can write "no" if you were arrested but not convicted of a felony or misdemeanor.

# Tip 9: State the Specific Position You Want

In the Position blank on the application, be specific about the kind of work you want. Do you really mean "anything" or do you mean "any job?" If at all possible, give a specific job title such as "cashier," "cook," "detailer," or "sales clerk." The person reading the application then knows exactly what position interests you rather than wondering how much you know about the company and whether you are really serious about working.

# Tip 10: Be Careful About What You Write for the Expected Pay Amount

The application might have a blank entitled "Expected Pay" or "Wage Requirement." If so, try to keep your answer general. Write "standard pay for the job" or "**negotiable**" (it can be arranged through discussion and bargaining). Requesting too much money on your application form might eliminate you from getting the job. Underesti-mating your pay makes you look uninformed about the job. The way you answer these questions tells the employers how much you know about the work and whether your expectations of the salary are realistic.

If you know someone who has a position similar to the one you are seeking and you feel comfortable doing so, ask her what the starting salary at her company is. Then you can write the word *approximately* and that amount on your application.

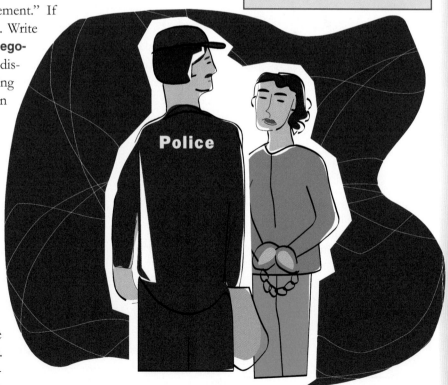

*Why would employers have concerns about hiring accounting clerks or warehouse workers who have been arrested for theft?*

# Tip 11: Add the Finishing Touches to Your Application

Before you turn in the completed application, proofread it. Check for errors in spelling, grammar, and blank spaces. Then make sure that you sign the application form where it asks for your signature. Also, put the correct date on the form. Without your signature and date, the application is not complete. What will most likely happen to your application form if you turn it in without your signature?

# Tip 12: Follow Up

Ask the employer about the procedure for learning the status of your application. *Be persistent, but don't be a pest!* Always follow up by calling, e-mailing, or writing a thank-you letter to the employer.

The preceding tips are useful whether you are submitting the job application in paper form, online, or using a computerized application form.

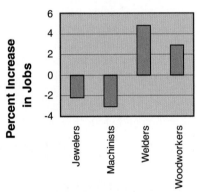

**Projected Outlook for 2016**

*What does this chart tell you about future opportunities in these careers?*

---

## Case Study: How Could the Anger Have Been Prevented?

Isabel was looking for a new job and went to a local industry's employment office. She asked for an application form. The industry's policy was that applications had to be filled out **onsite** (at the place of the business). As the receptionist handed the application form to Isabel, Isabel asked if she could borrow a pen or pencil because she didn't have one with her. Several minutes later, Isabel asked if she had to fill in all the information because she didn't know the addresses or telephone numbers of her references. The receptionist told Isabel that she needed that information and that her application could not be completed without it. At that point, Isabel was totally frustrated; she tore up the application and walked out of the office.

**What did Isabel do wrong?**

**Why do you think the industry requires that applications be filled out onsite?**

---

We can certainly understand Isabel's frustration, but, as a **job applicant** (a person looking for a job), she made several mistakes. How could her frustration have been avoided? You can rewrite the story!

# Section 8-3: Taking Additional Steps to Employment

Submitting a resume or filling out an application is just a first step to getting a job. Every company has a unique process. Many ask applicants to take employment tests and submit additional documentation.

## Complete Employment Tests

Some companies require all their applicants to take **employment tests**, either as paper-and-pencil or computerized tests. Employment tests might be skills tests, such as typing accuracy and words-per-minute. Sometimes, employers give tests to measure your knowledge. Other times, the tests check your honesty or personality characteristics. You certainly have the right to refuse to take these tests, but if you want the job, you will probably have to take them.

## Comply with Drug Testing and Other Possible Conditions of Employment

Drug testing is a requirement for employment at many companies. In most cases the testing is legal. Your signature on the job application gives a

### TECHNOLOGY

If an employer were to search for information about you on the Internet, what would he or she find? Is there video of you doing something crazy on YouTube? Are there pictures of you partying on Facebook? Do you complain about your current boss on your blog? These things can create a negative impression about you and can prevent you from getting the job you want. Do an Internet search on yourself and try to remove (or request that others remove) anything that employers might consider objectionable before you apply for a job.

company the right to request a drug test. If you accept the job offer, you might have to pass pre-employment checks and/or tests. Employers consider these tests to be "conditions of employment." These conditions can be in effect even after you have started with the company. Company policies usually determine the time and methods of testing. The costs of drug testing are usually covered by the company.

Drug testing as a condition of employment is a long-term situation. There is no simple answer as to how long drugs will remain in a person's system. If there's a drug out there, there is a drug test for it! The best solution is to avoid using drugs and alcohol. Drugs have *no place* in work society today and *never will*.

Another example of a condition of employment occurred when a recently hired employee lied about some information on the employment application. This employee was fired. As long as you have been honest in your answers on the application, you will not have this problem.

## Submit Additional Documentation

In addition to the job application form, companies must have other documents before they can hire you. Make sure that you have these documents in your possession or portfolio or know how to access them quickly:

▶ Social Security card

▶ Birth certificate

▶ Work permit (if you are under age 18)

*Do you have all these forms of identification?*

## Social Security Card

The United States has a program called **Social Security** that is based on a simple concept. While you work, you pay taxes into the Social Security system. When you retire or become disabled, you, your spouse, and your dependent children receive monthly benefits based on your reported earnings. Also, your survivors can collect benefits if you die.

To maintain an accurate record of your wages or self-employment earnings that are covered under the Social Security Act and to monitor your record when you start getting Social Security benefits, the United States government requires that you have a nine-digit Social Security number (abbreviated as SSN). The SSN is used for other purposes as well. The annual tax forms your parents complete each year ask for their and your SSNs. Also, many organizations, such as schools, colleges, military, and businesses use the number as a form of identification. To get an SSN, contact your local Social Security office or call 1-800-772-1213. If you are not an American citizen, contact the nearest immigration service to receive appropriate documents for you to work legally in the United States.

When you are in middle or high school, you should ask your parents if you can have access to your SSN. You can memorize the number so you can record it on forms when required. Carry a copy of your Social Security card with you. An employer will need to make a copy of your Social Security card and submit it with other documentation to the federal government.

### What Do the Digits in Your Social Security Number Represent?

The numbers assigned in the SSN have significance. The first three digits are assigned by the geographical region in which you were residing when your number was obtained. The remaining six digits in the number are more or less randomly assigned. To date, more than 400 million different numbers have been issued. It will not be necessary to reissue numbers for a long time because one billion combinations are possible.

## Birth Certificate

To prove your age and place of birth, you need a **birth certificate**, which is an official document issued by the Department of Health in the county and state where and when a baby is born. Some hospitals give a certificate that includes hand and feet prints to the parents of each child born there. The certificate is cute and is a nice souvenir, but it is *not* an official document (although some places might accept it). It will be worth your time and effort to obtain an official copy of your birth certificate before you begin your job search if you don't already have a copy. You can order an official copy of your birth certificate from the county or state in which you were born.

### Career Fact

The careers of jewelers, precious stone and metal workers, and silversmiths require learning the trade through vocational or technical schools, distance-learning centers, or on the job. About 51 percent of these workers are self-employed, operating their own stores or repair shops. Some specialize in designing and creating custom jewelry.

## Work Permit

If you are under age 18, you might need a **work permit** for most non-farm jobs, depending on your state laws. To get a work permit, see the designated person in your school. You have to actually be hired before you can get a work permit, but you cannot work until the work permit is completed. Making certain that your employer, the school, and you fill out all the information will require some work on your part.

Getting a work permit sounds like a hassle, but the process is actually designed to protect *you*. Laws defining work permits come from important

## Child Labor Laws Included in the FLSA

You must be at least 16 years old to work in most non-farm jobs.

You must be at least 18 years old to work in non-farm jobs declared hazardous by the Secretary of Labor.

If you are 14 or 15 years old, you may work these hours:

> 3 hours per school day, but no more than 18 hours per school week

> 8 hours per non-school day, but no more than 40 hours per school week and between 7 a.m. and 7 p.m. (except between June 1 and Labor Day when nighttime work hours are extended to 9 p.m.)

Different rules apply in agricultural employment.

*Which regulations apply to you?*

legislation called the **Fair Labor Standards Act** (FLSA). FLSA sets minimum standards for both wages and overtime. It also establishes the procedures for paying wages and regulations related to child labor.

## Case Study: Is the Employer Breaking the Law?

Jenifer, age 16, is working at the local convenience mart several evenings during the week and on the weekends. She works an average of 32 hours each week. She really likes the extra money and doesn't mind working that many hours. However, her employer has asked her to stay and close the store at midnight at least twice.

**Is it legal for Jenifer to work that late?**
**What should Jenifer do?**

## Section 8-3: Review

### Understanding Key Concepts

1. Which types of tests do employers sometimes give and what are their purposes?
2. In addition to a job application, which documents are needed for employment?
3. What is the purpose of work permits?

### Thinking Creatively

Do you think employers should be able to require a prospective employee to take a drug test?

Why does the government need to know when children are born?

### Taking It a Step Further

Research your state laws regarding the employment of teens. Then create an electronic or printed brochure or PowerPoint presentation that fully explains the laws to a specific audience: either for teens, their parents, or employers.

## Spotlight on a Career

**Crisanta Fasano, Ph.D., Senior Research Scientist**
**Eli Lilly and Company**

As a Senior Research Scientist at Eli Lilly and Company, I meet with the development, manufacturing, regulatory, quality, laboratory, and engineering groups to develop ways to test the processes for making medicine. When I worked with other companies, I was responsible for developing new medicines, testing the medicines, problem solving, and checking for quality.

In my junior year of high school, I got very interested in chemistry. I thought that becoming a chemist would give me opportunities to understand what, how, and why things happen. I pursued my bachelor's degree in chemistry in Manila, Philippines. I was hired as a chemistry laboratory instructor in one of the universities and then as a quality engineer in a big corporation in the Philippines. I then moved to the United States and completed a doctorate in physical organic chemistry from Southern Illinois University.

I am an active member and officer of the Toastmasters Club. I attend dancing classes to learn ballroom dancing. I hike, watch movies, watch ball games, enjoy the theatre, exercise, travel, and visit family and friends.

I balance work with life by recognizing my priorities—that life is not all about making money. It is about doing the things that I enjoy the most and finding fulfillment in knowing that what I am doing makes a positive impact on society. My priority is taking time to build relationships and appreciate the beautiful things that life has to offer.

# Chapter Review
# and Activities

The following sections can help you review the contents of this chapter.

## Key Concepts

Following are the key concepts presented in the chapter.

▶ The better prepared you are when applying for a job, the greater your chances of success.

▶ When you are looking for a job, three tools work together well to help you make a positive impression on a potential employer: a resume, cover letter, and portfolio.

▶ A resume is a summary of information about a person.

▶ A cover letter is a letter that introduces you and requests an interview.

▶ A portfolio is a collection that shows your work and development over time.

▶ Most companies require you to fill out an application form that requests information about you, your education, and your work experience.

▶ Although application forms can vary from company to company, they also have many similarities.

▶ In addition to the job application form, companies must have other documents before they can hire you. Make sure that you have your Social Security card and number, birth certificate, and perhaps a work permit (or know how to access them quickly).

▶ Employment testing might be part of the qualifications for employment.

▶ Drug testing is mandatory for employment in many jobs.

## Key Term Review

Complete the following activity to review your understanding of the key terms.

| | | |
|---|---|---|
| background checks | felony | portfolio |
| birth certificate | job applicant | references |
| convicted | misdemeanors | resume |
| cover letter | NA | Social Security |
| employment application | negotiable | transcript |
| employment tests | onsite | work permit |
| Fair Labor Standards Act | philosophy | |

You are the office manager for a computer-manufacturing plant. Using at least 10 of the vocabulary words, write a statement that gives application instructions to job applicants.

## Comprehension Review

Answer the following questions to review the contents of the chapter.

1. What are three tools you can use to get a prospective employer's attention? How do the tools differ?

2. How can you make certain that your application for employment is neat?

3. Why are following the instructions, writing legibly, and being truthful so important when you are completing an application for a job?

4. How do employers use the way the applicants complete the blanks for the specific position and salary requirements?

5. What additional steps often must be taken after submitting a resume or application?

## School-to-Work

**Math:** Write the steps you would take to solve this mathematical problem and the correct answer:

You are preparing an electronic portfolio to use in your job search. You have four color diagrams of machines you created that you need to scan, as well as three black-and-white reviews from your current employer. One copying service charges $1.45 per color scan and $1.05 per black-and-white scan. Another service charges the same rate for both types of scans: $1.30. Which service should you use?

**Social Studies:** Find someone in your community who is a veteran of the U.S. military services. Interview that person to find out how the person applied for the position, how the salary compared to other jobs, what the requirements were for the position, whether the training was adequate for the tasks and responsibilities on the job, and so on.

**Writing:** Write a cover letter and resume that you can use in your job search.

**Science:** What are pyrotechnic devices? How do they work? What skills are needed to use the devices? How much training is required to obtain the needed skills? What is the average entry-level salary for a job that uses the devices? Conduct research online, and then prepare either a one-page paper with illustrations or a presentation, answering these questions.

## Does This Job Interest You?

The following job is posted on the Internet. What education and experience are required? What requirement does this job have that most jobs do not have? Which types of interests and skills should a person working in this position have? How could someone apply for the job? How could someone find out more about the job?

| FIND JOBS | POST RESUMES |
| --- | --- |

### Manager

**Company:** ThinkingEnergy.com
**Location:** Atlanta, GA 30305
**Salary/Wage:** $60,000.00–65,000.00 USD/year

**Status:** Full-Time, Employee
**Job Category:** Industrial Production
**Career Level:** Manager (Manager/Supervisor of Staff)

Use the employer's preferred method to send your resume—click Apply Online!

### Job Description

International manufacturing firm in NE Atlanta is seeking a hands-on Project Manager to work within the manufacturing engineering department. Candidate will be responsible for new equipment, manufacturing projects from receipt of order through shipment, installation, and warranty period. Responsibilities include conferring with customers regarding design configuration; documentation and contractual requirements of individual projects; engineering job-specific components; issuing engineering package to production; efficiently dealing with production, installation, and warranty issues as they arise.

### Job Requirements

Candidate must have 5+ years exp within an industrial manufacturing environment, have 5+ years exp with AutoCAD (must be fully proficient or expert in LT 2002), have the ability to read blueprints, and have previous project management/project expediting exp. Previous supervisory skills and/or exp within a power plant or pulp and paper industries preferred, but not required. Prefer manufacturing exp as a project manager, not in construction. Excellent opportunity with a very profitable 40-million-dollar North America operation, a division of a world-wide operation, with 180 employees.

Questions you will be asked:

▶ Are you available and interested in a direct hire position in NE Atlanta? Why would you consider this location?

▶ Please detail your overall exp in project management in an industrial capital equipment manufacturing environment. Do you have 5+ years exp?

▶ Detail your AutoCAD experience. What releases have you worked with? How long?

▶ Do you have any power generation or pulp and paper industry exp?

### Contact

manager@thinkingenergy.com

( Apply Online )

# What career appeals to you?

# Chapter 9

# Excelling at the Interview Process

## What You'll Learn

▸ Preparing for an interview

▸ Getting through the interview

▸ Taking action after the interview

A **job interview** is a meeting between an employer and a person seeking the job. The interview gives each an opportunity to get to know the other. The job seeker and the employer or interviewer have some things in common. What do you think they are?

This chapter will help you sharpen your interview skills and help you prepare to be more successful during the interview process.

*Any activity becomes creative when the doer cares about doing it right, or doing it better.*

*—John Updike*

# Section 9-1: Preparing for an Interview

Many people start worrying about the interview and talk themselves into negative states of mind. Don't do this to yourself! Think positively about your strengths. The following sections have some suggestions for helping you prepare for the interview.

## Investigate the Company

Remember to do some research so that you know some facts about the business that is interviewing you. This will help you make a good impression.

*What do you think the job seeker and employer have in common during the interview process?*

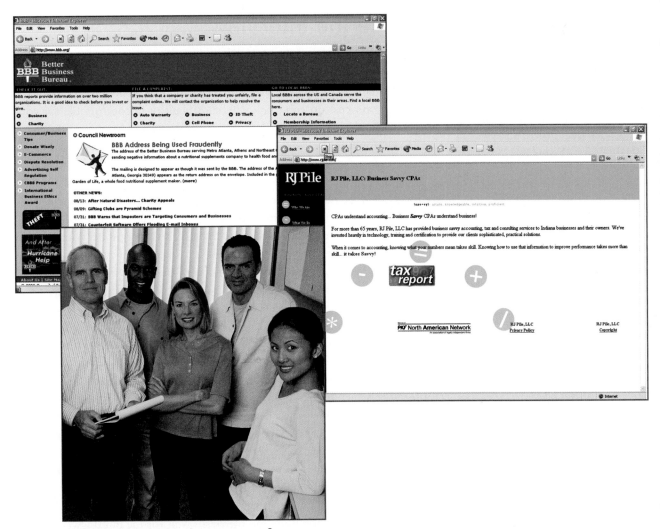

*Where can you go for information about a company?*

How can you get more facts about the company? One of the fastest and easiest ways to learn about a company is to check out its Web site if it has one. You can also check with your librarian to find information in resource books. For inside information, talk to people who work for the company. Also, you can contact the local Better Business Bureau or Chamber of Commerce for information.

Research answers to the following questions:

▶ What is the size of the company; that is, how much business does it do?

▶ How many employees work for the company?

▶ What does the company produce or what services does the company provide?

▶ Who are the company's competitors?

▶ What are the company's reputation, values, and mission statement?

Family and friends help form your attitude. Positive encouragement helps motivate you toward achieving your future goals and career success. Unfortunately, criticism from family and friends can have a very negative effect on your attitude toward future achievement. However, you are responsible for your life. You can choose to use a positive mental attitude (PMA) to overcome the negative and be successful in your own life. Who has encouraged you the most? Have you overcome criticism or a negative attitude? Have you encouraged someone else?

DIVERSITY

### Why Is He Always Late?

Your co-worker is always late. You can call him to remind him to be to work on time, but he still comes in late. You even gave him a watch so that he would know the time. Is he lazy? Is it that he cannot tell time?

# Practice the Interview

Before you go to your first interview, take some time to practice. You can practice in front of a mirror or with a friend. Or even better, practice with an adult who might actually have some interviewing experience. What about the interviewing process do you think will be difficult or uncomfortable for you?

What should you practice? You should rehearse every part of the interview, from entering the front door to leaving through it. Know what you are going to say to the **receptionist**, the person who greets visitors as they walk in. Receptionists are often asked to give their impression of the person applying for the job; be pleasant and friendly when you enter the reception area.

If you are unaccustomed to meeting strangers, prepare what you will first say to the interviewer. What do you think would be appropriate? Most people say "Hello," and then tell the person their name and why they are there. Practice answering the most common interview questions. Some of the most common questions are shown in the following list. Be sure that you have practiced answering these questions before you go for the interview.

Think of questions that you could ask the interviewer. You might want to take a list of questions with you to the interview. Practice asking your questions. You can also practice leaving the interviewer's office and the building. This might seem like a great deal of practicing, but doing so will make you feel more comfortable, which in turn will improve your performance in the interview.

Allow the actions of the interviewer to guide your actions. For example, wait for the interviewer to extend her right hand to shake hands; then offer your right hand in return. Also, wait until the interviewer sits or indicates that you should sit. Do not move the chair to a different position. Remember, this is the interviewer's office and the furniture has been arranged as she wants it to remain. Do not lean on the interviewer's desk or lay your personal belongings, such as purse or notebook, on the desk. Wait for the interviewer to indicate that the interview is completed. When the interviewer stands at the end of the interview, you stand. Remember to thank the interviewer for the time she spent with you.

## Ten Questions Interviewers Often Ask

1. Why don't you tell me about yourself?
2. Why should I hire you?
3. What are your major strengths?
4. What are your major weaknesses?
5. What sort of pay do you expect to receive?
6. How does your previous experience relate to the jobs we have here?
7. What are your plans for the future?
8. What will your former employers (or references) say about you?
9. Why are you looking for this sort of position—and why here?
10. What kind of transportation will you use to get to your job?

The interviewer might ask you other questions, too. If you can answer these questions comfortably, the other questions will seem much easier also.

# Plan to Dress Appropriately

Why is it important to be **well-groomed**, or clean, for an interview? How can you tell if a person is well-groomed? Why should you be **appropriately dressed**—wearing clothing that is acceptable or even a little nicer than what you might wear to the job?

Studies have shown over and over that the **first impression** (the initial reaction to seeing something or someone new) is critically important. Within just a few seconds, people judge those they are meeting for the first time. Many times they base their judgment solely on appearance.

Good grooming includes being clean. Having a clean body, clean teeth, clean hair, clean fingernails, clean clothes, and clean shoes are all very important. If any of these good grooming habits are lacking, an opportunity for getting the job will suffer.

Also, consider your hairstyle and dress style. Extremes attract attention, but such attention can be negative. What extremes in dress should you avoid during an interview? Most interviewers indicate that visible body art, such as tattoos, decorated nails, multiple earrings, and other body piercings, is not appropriate for the workplace. They suggest that you cover tattoos and remove excessive jewelry for interviews and for work.

Being **conservative** (or wearing business-like clothing) is recommended. For instance, applying for an office position might require a shirt and tie for guys, and dress pants or a skirt and blouse for girls. On the other hand, an interview for a job in an auto repair shop would call for clean pants and a collared shirt for males or females.

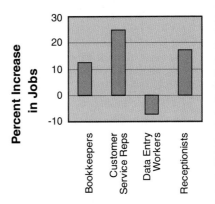

**Projected Outlook for 2016**

*What does this chart tell you about future opportunities in these careers?*

## CAREER FACT

Careers in business detail might include administrative office detail, bookkeeping, customer service, office management, and records processing.

*What is appropriate attire for an interview?*

# Know Where You Are Going

Make sure that you know the location of the interview before you leave. If at all possible, practice traveling the route you will take to the interview. If you are driving, know where you are supposed to park. If you are taking public transportation, know which bus stop or subway stop will get you where you are going. Locate the appropriate entrance and the correct floor.

# Allow Extra Time to Get There

**Punctuality** (being on time) is an important part of making a good impression. Arrive 10 or 15 minutes before the interview to have enough time to catch your breath, relax, and regain your poise. Arriving early also shows that you value the employer's time and that you are dependable and organized. It is also very important to arrive early because employers expect employees to be prepared to begin working on time.

Arriving early also gives you the opportunity to greet the receptionist. Remember to be polite and friendly. More than likely, the receptionist is the person you talked to first when you inquired about a job opening. Thank her for any help offered. Keep in mind that the receptionist is often the **front line** for the interviewer. The front line is the first person you meet who is evaluating your behavior. The interviewer might listen to your conversation with the receptionist or ask the receptionist to evaluate your behavior while you were waiting.

*Why is it important to know where you are to go for the interview?*

# Case Study: What Could Keon Have Done Differently?

Keon had scheduled an interview at 9:00 a.m. with Ward Real Estate. He thought he left home in plenty of time, but he had to drive around the block twice before he was lucky enough to find a parking spot a short distance from the real estate office. When he got out of his car, it was already 8:55 a.m. He opened the door to the building, hurried into the lobby, and discovered that the office was located on the third floor. It was 9:03 a.m., past the time for his interview!

**How could Keon have avoided this situation and arrived for his interview on time?**

---

## Section 9-1: Review

### Understanding Key Concepts

1. How can you investigate a company?
2. Why is a first impression so important in a job interview?
3. What are three tips you would share with a friend to help him sharpen his interview skills?

### Thinking Creatively

Why is interviewing so difficult for most people?

If you were an employer, what questions would you want a prospective employee to answer?

What are some questions a person should always ask the interviewer?

### Taking It a Step Further

The government says that employers cannot ask certain questions. Conduct an online search to find out which questions are considered illegal.

---

# Section 9-2: Creating an A+ Interview

The interview is the employer's time to look at you carefully, ask questions, listen to what you say, and answer the questions you ask. This gives the interviewer an opportunity to decide whether you are the best candidate for the job.

The interview is also a good time for you to look carefully at the interviewer and the environment, and to consider whether this is the right job for you. You do not have to accept the job. You might have more than one job offer, or you might have time to wait before accepting a job. You might want do so if you are confident that something better will become available.

The first interview might take just a few minutes. It is usually less than an hour, especially with entry-level jobs. The interview for more advanced jobs could take several hours and more than one interview. Be aware that interviewers have different styles. Be prepared for each of these:

▶ **The Talker.** This interviewer does all the talking, so all you have to do is sit and listen. You might think that this is an "easy interview," but remember that "the talker" might be checking out your listening skills.

▶ **The Questioner.** This interviewer asks you many questions very quickly and might be trying to create a stressful situation. Your responses determine whether you will be considered for the job.

▶ **The Passive.** It is very difficult to "read" this type of interviewer (someone who does not express his thoughts or feelings). It might be difficult to know how you are doing. Even if the interviewer might appear passive, he is forming impressions about you.

▶ **The Note Taker.** This interviewer writes down everything you say, which can be very distracting. Remember that this is a normal interview process for "the note taker." It also might be the structure that the company needs to follow. Or it might be just the interviewer's way of keeping track of what you say.

## DISCRIMINATION

### What Constitutes Religious Discrimination?

When the local florist hired you, you made certain that she knew that you were not available for working on Saturdays. You specifically told her that Saturday was your Sabbath, the one day of the week when you attended church and did absolutely no work. Valentine's Day falls on Sunday this year, and everyone in the shop is expected to work until all the flowers are ready to be delivered. You reminded your employer that you cannot work on Saturdays. She said that you would be fired if you didn't do your part. You offered to come in at midnight on Saturday, but she said that would be too late. If she fires you, has she discriminated against you?

*What would you say each of these people is thinking?*

# Watch Your Nonverbal Behavior

Have you ever been told, "It's not what you say; it's what you do"? What does this mean? **Nonverbal behavior** is what a person does rather than what she says. What are some examples of nonverbal behavior?

## Your Attitude

Your **attitude** (the way you look at life and act toward others) can affect your chances of being successful in life as well as getting a job. Employers are looking for people with good attitudes. In fact, some research indicates that attitude is the number one criteria in hiring new workers. It is so important that employers usually take the time to question people you listed as references about your attitude. Employers would rather hire a person with fewer job skills and a good attitude than one who has the skills but a poor attitude. Why do you think this is true?

Employers look for good communication skills, acceptance of differences as strengths, and a willingness to be involved in the job. It is important to show these qualities to create a positive first impression. Other characteristics of a positive attitude in today's workplace include

- ▶ Cheerfulness
- ▶ Dedication
- ▶ Punctuality
- ▶ Reliability
- ▶ Working well with others

## Your Body Language

As employers ask questions, they observe your **body language** (the messages you send through the way you move your body) to find out what kind of attitude you have. They know that your attitude will affect your performance in the workplace. Body language is important during an interview. Some positive uses of body language during an interview include shaking hands, looking the interviewer in the eyes, and sitting up straight. Do not cross and uncross your legs, pop your knuckles, or play with your hair.

*Why are these behaviors inappropriate?*

# Watch How You Talk

The following suggestions can help you have a successful job interview. Not all of these suggestions apply to every job; use the ones that best fit your situation.

▶ Speak **enthusiastically** (eagerly and with interest). Showing an active interest in the job and the person interviewing you will impress your interviewer.

▶ Speak clearly. Do not eat anything or chew gum. Doing so could cause the interviewer to have difficulty understanding you. It also detracts from your appearance.

▶ Speak correctly. When you are talking with friends and family, you can relax and use their **dialect** (the accepted vocabulary, grammar, and pronunciation of an area or group in society). When you are in an interview, you are in a different setting and should use the dialect that is appropriate for that setting. How can you switch from one dialect to another?

▶ Always be honest. Do not try to cover up something from a past job with a lie. It is better to admit your mistake and show the interviewer that you are willing to learn from past mistakes than it is to lie.

▶ Do not "bad-mouth" former employers. It is always better to be fair and kind-hearted than to sound like a complainer or a troublemaker.

▶ Do not overemphasize salary. It should never be the first question you ask about the job. If the interviewer asks you to name a salary or wage, ask him what the pay range is for the job.

During an interview, think carefully about everything you say before you say it. The interviewer will be listening for indications that you are the right person for the position that needs to be filled.

# End the Interview Strongly

You want to end the interview as strongly as you began. Here are some tips for accomplishing just that:

▶ When the interviewer lets you know that the interview is over, take just a few seconds to summarize your strengths. For example, you might say, "I believe that you will find that my skills in dealing with customers and my attention to detail will make me an asset to your staff."

▶ If you want the job, tell the interviewer that you want it.

▶ Arrange a time to contact the employer. For example, you could say, "I probably will have other questions. When is the best time for me to call you with them?" Remember to follow up when you said you would. Your follow-up will show your organizational skills.

- Thank the interviewer for her time.
- Say something cheerful as you leave, such as "Have a good day" or "I enjoyed meeting you."

## Case Study: Which Teen Would You Hire?

Mrs. Bernfield interviewed two different teenagers for a job in the Dietary department at the local nursing home. The first teenager indicated that school was okay and the teachers were okay, but she didn't like homework and would rather do anything than listen to other people talk. The second teenager said that he enjoyed school, had a B average in his Nutrition and Foods class, and enjoyed helping people.

**What type of attitude does each of these teenagers have?**
**Whom would you hire?**
**Why?**

### Section 9-2: Review

**Understanding Key Concepts**

1. What are the four types of interviewers and how do they differ?
2. What are some attitudes that employers expect from an employee?
3. How should you talk during an interview?
4. What can you do to end the interview positively?

**Thinking Creatively**

How can a person change nonverbal behavior that might be sending negative messages to others?
What kind of talking should you avoid during an interview and why?

**Taking It a Step Further**

Watch an interview between a TV journalist and a celebrity. Did the journalist do or say anything to make the celebrity feel comfortable? Did the celebrity seem confident or nervous? What did he do that gave you that impression?

# Section 9-3: Taking Action After the Interview

The interview is over. You did your best, but you do not know whether the employer is going to offer you a job. What should you do? What if you find out that you did not get the job? What will be your reaction?

## Send a Thank-You Note

Send a thank-you note to the interviewer. In the note, remember to also include the names of other people who spent time talking to you or gave you a tour of the business. Why do you think sending a thank-you note is important?

Write a thank-you note to Mrs. Martinez, Still Advertising, about my interview for the part-time summer position: Marketing Assistant.

Need to look up the address and Mrs. Martinez' title for the envelope.

*Prewriting*

Dear Mrs. Martinez,

Thanks for interviewing me. I enjoyed the interview very much. I hope you know how much I want the job.

*Drafting*

Mrs. Martinez,
Still Advertising
123 Main Street
New York, NY 00111

Dear Mrs. Martinez,

Thank you for the interview today.

Getting to know you and learning About Still was very intresting. I appreciate having the opertunity to meet you. Thank you for your time. I hope you know how much I want the job.

*Revising*

Mrs. Martinez,
Still Advertising
123 Main Street
New York, NY 00111

Dear Mrs. Martinez,

Thank you for meeting with me today.

I appreciate having the ~~opertunity~~ *opportunity* to meet you. I enjoyed interviewing for the part-time Marketing assistant position so much. Learning about your company and the position was very ~~intresting~~ *interesting*.

Thank you for your time. I will call you next week.

*Editing and Proofreading*

Mrs. Martinez, Vice President of Marketing
Still Advertising
123 Main Street
New York, NY 00111

Dear Mrs. Martinez,

Thank you for meeting with me today. I appreciate having the opportunity to meet you. I enjoyed interviewing for the part-time Marketing assistant position so much. Learning about your company and the position was very interesting.

Thank you for your time. I will call you next week.

*Final*

A thank-you note is a message that says that you appreciate something. In the case of an interview, sending a thank-you note shows your awareness that someone has given you an opportunity to become part of a company and has taken time from his schedule just for you. Employers are often surprised and impressed by the applicant who takes the time to send a thank-you note. The note makes him think of you one more time.

To show that you are definitely interested in the job, send the note within 24 hours after your interview. You can mail it or send it by e-mail. An advantage of a mailed note is that it cannot be deleted as easily as an e-mail message can.

## Evaluate Your Performance

Evaluating your performance is an important part of developing skills. The information you gain from evaluating yourself can help you improve your performance. It is especially good to evaluate yourself after the interview. Make notes about your interview while it is fresh in your mind. What kinds of questions could you ask yourself?

What should you do if you call an employer and find out that you did not get the job? Do not express anger or sadness. Instead, say "Thank you for the opportunity to interview for the position." If you have the opportunity, ask the employer if she knows anyone else who might be hiring. If you are polite, the employer might remember how well you acted in a difficult situation, and contact you if the chosen candidate turns down the job or if another position becomes available.

If an employer does not choose you, you might feel angry or discouraged. It is perfectly normal to be disappointed if you don't get the job. Did you know that lots of people are turned down many times before they get a job? Do not spend a long time blaming yourself or feeling sad. Do not take your anger out on others. Remember that even if you don't get the job, this has been a good experience.

How was my body language?

    Did I make eye contact with the interviewer?

    Was I friendly?

    Did I smile?

    Did I show enthusiasm?

    Did I give the interviewer a firm handshake?

    Did I show signs of nervousness?

How was my language?

    Did I speak clearly and correctly?

    Was I honest?

    Did I show that I was familiar with the company?

Notes: _____

_____

_____

*How can evaluating your performance after an interview help you?*

If you find yourself going to job interviews but always being rejected, ask yourself if it is because of your attitude, body language, or appearance. Read more about job interviewing skills, practice job interviewing, and just keep trying. Eventually, you will find the right match for you.

## Reasons Employers Give for Not Hiring Someone

When employers were asked why applicants were not hired even though they were qualified for the job, they gave one or more of the following reasons:

- Ate food or drank beverage during the interview
- Brought other people or pets to the interview
- Cell phone rang during the interview
- Chewed gum during the interview
- Criticized former employers
- Failed to make eye contact with the interviewer
- Immature attitude
- Job application was incomplete or sloppy
- "Know-it-all" attitude; asked no questions
- Lack of enthusiasm
- Lack of manners
- Lack of **tact** (style or grace)
- Late to the interview
- Lazy; not willing to take initiative
- Limp handshake
- Low ethical (morals and values) standards

- Made excuses for weaknesses
- No career goals
- Wanted job for only a short period of time
- Overly nervous
- Non-participant in extracurricular or community activities
- Not serious about getting a job–just shopping around
- Not willing to start at the bottom and work way up
- Poor grammar and speech
- Poor personal appearance
- Prejudiced
- Too much emphasis on how much they will be paid
- Uninformed about the company

## NETWORKING

Find a teen who has interviewed for a job recently and ask him to describe the experience.

## COMMUNITY

Make a list of the companies in your area that hire students. Contact three of the companies to find out the qualities expected of teen employees. Prepare a poster or presentation of your findings.

# Decide Whether to Take the Job (or Not)

If an employer offers you a job, you must decide whether you will accept the job. What will you do if you receive two job offers? What if you think you need to spend a little more time looking for a job? Carefully think about the following:

- **Working hours.** Will this job provide you with enough hours to earn the money you want or need? Will you have to work more hours than you feel you can handle?

- **Job location.** How will you get to and from work? How long will it take you to get there? How much will a vehicle and fuel cost? How much will other forms of transportation cost (such as subway or bus)? Realistically, you should subtract these costs from your salary.

- **Work responsibilities.** How much responsibility do you want? Can you handle it? Remember, you will be given time to learn.

- **Co-workers.** Many people decide whether to take a job, keep a job, or leave a job based on the people they work with. You need to feel like you "fit in" and will be comfortable with the people you will be working with. How did you feel about the people you met during the interview?

- **Rules, rules, rules!** Are you willing to work for a company with a lot of rules? Or would you be happier working in a place with few rules? Before you take the job, find out about the company rules.

▶ **Salary and benefits.** When will you get a raise? What other **benefits** does the company offer? Will you earn vacation days or sick leave days? Will you have to join a **union** (a group of workers who form an organization to protect its interests and require members to pay dues)? Do you have to pay for your own uniform? Will you be offered any type of insurance plan? Will the company pay for part of your insurance?

Answering these questions will help you decide whether you should accept the job, which job to accept, or whether you should continue to look for something that fits you better. Remember that no job is perfect. You can be comfortable in accepting a job that meets your most important needs..

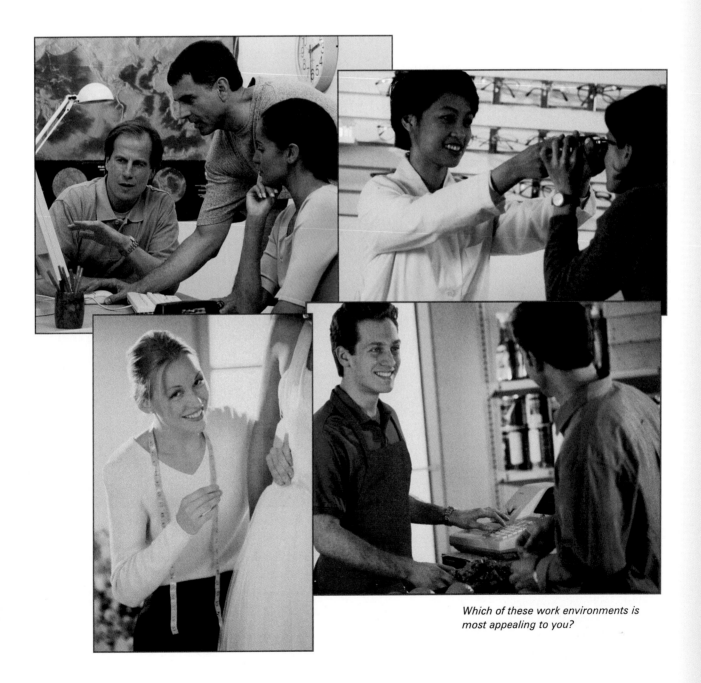

*Which of these work environments is most appealing to you?*

## ROLE-PLAYING

**Scenario:** Role-play a situation in which an employer interviews a potential employee.

**Roles:** Employer, potential employee, and possibly observers

**Discussion:** Was the applicant prepared for the interview? Did she appear to have knowledge of the job for which she was applying? Did the applicant exhibit appropriate body language and attitude? Did she speak appropriately? At the end of the interview, did the applicant summarize her strengths, arrange a time to follow up on the interview, thank the interviewer for the time given her, and leave with a positive statement, such as "Have a good day"?

# Case Study: Would You Hire Cody?

Cody had an interview with Mr. Valdez for a part-time position at Valdez Auto Service. Cody ignored the Do Not Enter sign posted by the door, walked up to Mr. Valdez, and started talking. Mr. Valdez had to drop what he was doing to keep Cody away from an area where sparks from welding were likely to catch his sweatshirt on fire.

**Mr. Valdez:** "Cody, please come in to my office. Have a seat and let's talk. Tell me about yourself."

**Cody:** "Uh, there's really not much to tell. I'm 16 years old, and I need some kind of work."

**Mr. Valdez:** "I see. Why do you think you want to work here in our auto service department?"

**Cody:** "Uh, one of my friends said it's a neat place to work. Oh, and he said I can work on my own truck here when there isn't anything else to do. I really like working on trucks."

**Mr. Valdez:** "Thank you for coming in, Cody. I'll be in touch."

**Cody:** "Uh, okay."

**Based on the information in this situation, would you hire Cody? Why or why not?**

**What suggestions would you make to Cody before he goes to another job interview?**

## CAREER FACT

If you enjoy classes in accounting, computer software, English, and math, you may want to consider a career in business detail.

## Section 9-3: Review

### Understanding Key Concepts

1. How can sending a thank-you note to an interviewer help you get a job?

2. What should you do if you are not chosen for a job?

3. What are some factors to consider when deciding whether to accept a job offer?

### Thinking Creatively

What would you say to a friend who is angry because an employer chose another applicant?

What can people do to change if they find that employers are afraid or unwilling to hire them?

### Taking It a Step Further

Conduct an online search for information about handling rejection. Then prepare a presentation on your findings.

## Spotlight on a Career

### Lynette Swanson, Tax Preparer
### Huth Thompson

I have been an accountant for the past 17 years. I did not plan it this way, but just fell into it. In high school, I had no great aspirations for any particular career. Getting married, having children, and being a homemaker seemed to be the ticket. I took business classes in high school and worked as a secretary after graduation. I was married at age 18 and continued to be a secretary at the university that my husband was attending. A month after his graduation, we became parents. I then started my stay-at-home mom role at the age of 21. Two more children arrived by the time I was 25.

I guess I started to get antsy to do something to earn extra money, so I worked at a retail store part-time and took classes as a part-time student in the Purdue School of Pharmacy. Then I worked at an accounting firm and found that I thrived on all the number lingo and tax jargon so much that I took accounting and tax-preparation classes.

I now work for the president/owner (both a CPA and a lawyer) of a small firm. I prepare all the individual tax returns, corporate tax returns, personal property tax returns and payroll tax returns; consult with clients on tax issues and governmental tax notices; and handle the bookkeeping, payroll services, tax projections, and tax research. I use the computer and have to know many software programs. I also read, conduct research, and attend seminars to keep up with tax laws and changes.

I work a 40-hour week except during a tax season. From January 2 through April 15, I work between 60 and 70 hours per week. My family always helps with cooking, shopping, and household chores when I am extremely busy, and we hire a cleaning service once a week.

I relax by reading, taking part in outdoor activities, and getting together with friends and family. I adore our four grandchildren and spend as much time with them as I can.

# Chapter Review and Activities

The following sections can help you review the contents of this chapter.

## Key Concepts

Following are the key concepts presented in the chapter.

▶ Prepare for an interview by investigating the company, practicing answering interview questions, planning how you will look, knowing where you are going, and allowing extra time to get there.

▶ Be aware of different interviewer styles.

▶ When you are in the interview, watch your nonverbal behavior (the messages you send through your attitude and body language) and speak enthusiastically, clearly, correctly, honestly, and positively without emphasizing money.

▶ As the interview draws to a close, summarize your strengths, arrange a time to follow up on the interview, thank the interviewer for the time given you, and leave with a positive statement such as "Have a good day."

▶ Within 24 hours of the interview, send a thank-you note to the interviewer.

▶ Evaluate your performance so that you can improve with each interview.

▶ If you are offered a job, think about factors in a job that are important to you as you decide whether to accept it.

## Key Term Review

Complete the following activity to review your understanding of the key terms.

| | | |
|---|---|---|
| appropriately dressed | first impression | receptionist |
| attitude | front line | tact |
| benefits | job interview | Talker |
| body language | nonverbal behavior | union |
| conservative | Note Taker | well-groomed |
| dialect | Passive | |
| enthusiastically | Questioner | |

You are an accountant in need of a part-time employee to do filing. The manager of the human resources department just requested that you give her a description of the type of employee you are seeking. Using eight of the key terms, write a description of the ideal employee for this position.

## Comprehension Review

Answer the following questions to review the main concepts in the chapter.

**1.** What can you do to prepare for an interview?

**2.** What is nonverbal behavior and how can it make a difference in an interview?

**3.** How can you make certain that you do not lose an opportunity for a job simply by talking the wrong way?

**4.** What should you do before you leave an interview?

**5.** After the interview is over, what can you do to make a good impression and remind the interviewer of you?

**6.** How can you decide whether to accept a job offer?

## School-to-Work

**Math:** Your interview is scheduled for 2:30 p.m., and you have to take city transportation to get to the interview. You will have to transfer buses three times, and then you'll have to walk for about 5 minutes from the bus stop to the location of the interview. It takes you 30 minutes to shower and get dressed and 5 minutes to walk to the stop for Bus 240. Which buses should you take if you want to get to the interview no less than 15 minutes early, using this bus schedule table? What is the latest you should begin getting ready?

| | | | | |
|---|---|---|---|---|
| Bus 240 comes to your street | 11:30 | 12:10 | 1:40 | 2:20 |
| Bus 431 meets Bus 240 | 11:45 | 12:25 | 1:55 | 2:35 |
| Bus 502 meets Bus 431 | 12:05 | 1:30 | 2:10 | 2:55 |

**Social Studies:** Do you think that age, gender, or race make a difference in the interview process? Check out sources on the Internet that discuss discrimination in the interview process.

**Writing:** Write a thank-you note in response to an interview. In the note, identify the position for which you interviewed. Tell why you are interested in working for the company and in holding that position, and why you would be a good candidate for it. Close by thanking the employer for her time.

**Science:** Why is the changing of the climate getting so much attention from scientists? What causes the climate to change, and what impact will that have on the future of the earth and its people? Research the topic of global warming and then prepare either a paper or a presentation, answering these questions.

## Does This Job Interest You?

The following job is posted on the Internet. What education and experience are required? What requirement does this job have that most jobs do not have? What types of interests and skills should a person working in this position have? How could someone apply for the job? How could someone find out more about the job?

**FIND JOBS** | **POST RESUMES**

### Senior Financial Analyst

| | | | |
|---|---|---|---|
| **Location:** | Universal City, CA | **Travel:** | No travel |
| **Job Type:** | Full-time | **Education:** | 4-year degree |
| **Experience:** | 5 years | | |
| **Minimum Salary:** | $85,000 | | |

### Job Description

In this high-visibility position, you will prepare quarterly corporate reports. The mandatory work week is Sunday through Thursday, and you must be willing to work overtime at quarter ends to meet corporate deadlines.

### Job Responsibilities

Prepare Monday morning business report
Prepare weekly cash flow report and quarterly cash flow reconciliation
Reconcile monthly investments in unconsolidated subsidiaries to respective entity in general ledger
Help prepare annual tax analyses and governmental filings
Perform analyses of consolidated reports
Maintain prior year's P&L restatements
Special projects as required

### Job Requirements

BA or BS in Accounting required; CPA preferred. Excellent analytical, organizational, and communication skills. Proficiency in Microsoft Word and Excel. Multitask oriented and flexible with ability to work with minimal supervision. Accurate with attention to detail. Team player orientation.
EOE

For prompt consideration, click the orange Apply Online button below, which links to the Universal Jobs page. Click "Vivendi/Universal Entertainment" in the upper left of the page, and then click "Search Openings." In the "requisition" field, type **694BR**, and follow the instructions to submit your resume.

( Apply Online )

**What career appeals to you?**

# Chapter 10 Understanding Workplace Issues

## What You'll Learn

▶ Understanding health, safety, and legal issues

▶ Taking advantage of entry-level jobs

▶ Looking at ethics in the workplace

▶ Taking on more responsibility

▶ Dealing with diversity and gender equity

▶ Solving work performance problems

▶ Developing conflict resolution strategies

A full-time job will give you an opportunity to learn much more about the workplace and society and your role in both. The knowledge gained before you begin a full-time job can help you avoid unnecessary mistakes and problems and put you on a path to career success. In this chapter, you learn about health, safety, and legal issues in the workplace. You also look at solving the problems that usually arise when people of different backgrounds work together.

*Experience is one thing you can't get for nothing.*

—Oscar Wilde

## Key Terms

| | | |
|---|---|---|
| advancements | glass ceilings | promotions |
| compensation | initiative | sex-role stereotypes |
| conflicts of interest | I-statements | sexual harassment |
| conflict resolution | mentor | standards of conduct |
| cost-of-living pay increase | merit pay increase | stereotyping |
| co-workers | monopolizing | wage discrimination |
| discrimination | organizational values | whistle blowing |
| diversity | performance appraisal | work ethic |
| entry-level job | price fixing | |
| ethics | probationary period | |

# Section 10-1: Understanding Health, Safety, and Legal Workplace Issues

Every workplace should have a health and safety policy. Additionally, the United States government has established many rules and regulations to deal with the problems of workers, including **discrimination** (treating a person or a group differently or unfairly because they are a different race, gender, age, culture, or so on). The government also monitors wages, hours, and health and safety issues. These issues are controlled through the U.S. Department of Labor, established in 1913.

An issue controlled by the U.S. Department of Labor is Workers' Compensation laws. These laws provide **compensation** (money or services received to make up for a loss) to workers who are injured on the job. Individual states also set up some of the Workers' Compensation laws. All employers are required by law to provide workers' compensation benefits, including

▶ Medical payments for a work-related injury or disability

▶ Rehabilitation services such as physical therapy

▶ Death benefits, including burial expenses (costs), paid to the worker's family

Other regulations include

▶ **The Americans with Disabilities Act (ADA).** This legislation protects people with disabilities who qualify for employment from being discriminated against simply because of their disability. Examples might include people with cancer, cerebral palsy, epilepsy, or HIV/AIDS.

▶ **The U.S. Environmental Protection Agency (EPA).** Environmental protection laws protect workers from long-term exposure to dangerous substances or polluted air. Some of the laws include the Clean Air Act and the Clean Water Act.

▶ **The Social Security Act.** This federal law provides Social Security insurance to all employees who pay the FICA tax for a certain length of time. Your parents probably applied for your Social Security number when you were born. However, if you do not have a number, you need to apply for one as soon as possible. Otherwise, you will not be eligible for this benefit.

▶ **Occupational Safety and Health Administration (OSHA) Act.** This act, which was passed in 1970, established a government agency that sets standards and policies governing facilities and procedures in the workplace. This agency works with business and industry to ensure safe working conditions. It also does inspections at work sites to make sure that any unsafe conditions are corrected.

Unfortunately, even with all these acts and government agencies looking out for you, accidents still happen. Sometimes they occur because of unsafe working conditions that weren't caught and corrected in time. Employees who are not being responsible for their own safety create a hazardous work environment as well. Can you think of workers' actions that might create health and safety hazards?

*How has the government taken care of its working citizens?*

Here are some suggestions for taking responsibility for your own health and safety:

▶ **Don't abuse substances such as alcohol, drugs, and tobacco.** Using or abusing any of these substances can create dangerous situations in the workplace, not just for the user, but for anyone else who has to work with or comes in contact with the user. In many cases, it is illegal to use these substances because they cause mental and physical impairments. For example, a person who has used too much alcohol could cause a serious injury to himself or someone else, even resulting in death. Studies show that second-hand smoke exposes nonsmokers to the same health risks as the smoker. Also, drugs cause serious side effects and can lead to accidents and even death.

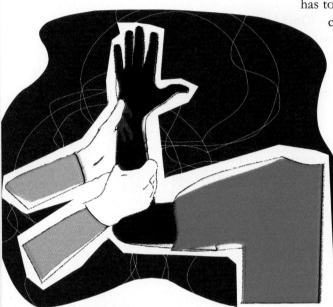

*Would you know what to do if you had to take care of someone who was bleeding profusely?*

Today, many businesses and industries require drug tests (that reveal the presence of drugs in a person's body) as part of their pre-employment policy. They also have regular drug testing programs for all their employees. If employees have drug problems, employers might refer them to a drug treatment program. The employers would rather pay the price to help employees recover from their addictions than allow them to injure themselves or several other employees. The injuries could cost the company thousands and sometimes millions of dollars. Why do many employers choose to help rather than fire employees with drug problems?

▶ **Wear protective clothing.** Goggles, hard hats, ear protectors, gloves, and safety shoes are all examples of protective clothing that employees must wear to reduce their chances of injury. Wearing protective clothing is a good habit to form and can even be applied to your life right now. Can you think of some ways?

## Universal Precautions for Prevention of Transmission of HIV and Other Bloodborne Infections

Universal precautions, as defined by the Centers for Disease Control (CDC), are designed to prevent the spreading of human immunodeficiency virus (HIV), hepatitis B virus (HBV), and other bloodborne pathogens when providing first aid or health care. Under universal precautions, blood and certain body fluids of all patients are considered potentially infectious for HIV, HBV, and other bloodborne pathogens.

Universal precautions recommend using protective barriers such as gloves, gowns, aprons, masks, or protective eyewear to reduce the risk of exposure of the health care worker's skin or mucous membranes to potentially infective materials. In addition, universal precautions recommend that all health care workers take precautions to prevent injuries caused by needles, scalpels, and other sharp instruments or devices.

Pregnant health care workers are not known to be at greater risk of contracting HIV infection than are health care workers who are not pregnant; however, if a health care worker develops an HIV infection during pregnancy, the infant is at risk of infection resulting from perinatal transmission. Because of this risk, pregnant health care workers should be especially familiar with, and strictly adhere to, precautions that minimize the risk of HIV transmission.

▶ **Follow safety regulations at work.** Why do bus drivers have to stop at all railroad crossings? Why do truck drivers have to stop after driving so many hours? There are reasons for these rules, and they all have to do with safety! These rules require employee cooperation.

Other issues are a direct result of the way you take care of your body, mind, and relationships. They include worker fatigue or tiredness, stress, and violent crimes. These are all serious issues in today's workplaces. Many businesses and industries will provide training and education to help employees deal with these issues.

Another issue about which some employers are required to train employees is that of bloodborne pathogens. Employers might be required to inform employees about universal precautions.

## Case Study: Whose Fault Is It Anyway?

Katie had just started her new job at a local restaurant as a dishwasher, and she hoped to become an apprentice chef by the end of the school year. She was running a load of dishes through the automatic dishwasher when suddenly she felt as if she had something in her eye. As the evening went on, her eye became very irritated and red. When she got home from work, her mom decided that she should go to the emergency room. The doctors discovered a small fleck of metal in her eye! A piece of metal had flown off of the automatic dishwasher and into her eye. Without treatment, it could have caused serious eye damage. When she called her employer, he asked whether she had worn goggles while washing dishes. The work policy was that goggles must be worn when using the dishwasher. She had not.

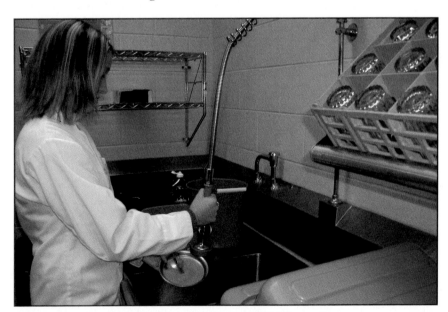

**Who was responsible for the damage to Katie's eye?**
**Who was responsible for paying her doctor bill?**
**Should she be paid for days missed at work until her eye heals?**

## Top 10 Most Dangerous Jobs

Fishers

Pilots and Flight Engineers

Logging Workers

Structural Metal Workers

Refuse and Recyclable Material Collectors

Farmers and Ranchers

Electical Power-Line Workers

Roofers

Drivers/Sales Workers and Truck Drivers

Agricultural Workers

(Taken from www.bls.gov)

*What dangers are you willing to accept when you are working?*

**CAREER FACT**

Careers in sales and marketing might include advertising sales, marketing management, real estate sales, retail sales, sales representation, sales worker supervision, and telemarketing.

## Understanding Key Concepts

1. What U. S. government department oversees the treatment of employees?
2. Name four acts that protect employees and tell what each does.
3. What can employees do to prevent accidents in the workplace?

## Thinking Creatively

Why should a government play a role in protecting its citizens in the workplace?

How can you decide when an employer is responsible for safety and when an employee is responsible?

## Taking It a Step Further

Research one of the federal employment laws, and prepare a PowerPoint or multimedia presentation that lists the specific protections the law provides employees.

# Section 10-2: Taking On the Role of Employee

You will probably hold several jobs and even change careers several times in your lifetime. Remember that every job is a learning experience. Eventually, you will find the job or career that matches your values and goals. You will want to stay at that job for many years.

Right now, however, you should look at your **entry-level job** as a "stepping stone" or a beginning job on a path to your ultimate career. There is so much you can learn and do as you challenge yourself to be the best employee in each of your entry-level jobs. There will be many short-term and long-term rewards for having a flexible and open attitude.

How many students in your class have jobs right now? Of those who have jobs, how many plan to find different jobs in the future? What are some reasons for finding a different job? Do you think anyone in your class plans to remain at a current job throughout life? Why or why not?

To take full advantage of entry-level jobs, you need to

▶ Be the best employee you can be. Do the work assigned to you to the best of your ability.

*Why would a company choose to promote someone in an entry-level position to a management role?*

▶ Take the **initiative**, which means to do things that need to be done without being told. Your employer and **co-workers** (the people who work with you) will definitely notice and remember.

▶ Try new experiences. You might discover that they are enjoyable or easier than you expected.

▶ Learn, learn, learn. Take advantage of every opportunity to get more training or education in your job. Many companies provide work-release time or even pay for further education and training.

As you follow these suggestions, you will discover many opportunities to learn on the job and make progress toward your career goals. However, you might have to face some practical issues as you adjust to your role as a new employee. How can you decide whether an action is right or wrong? Do you know how to work with people from other cultures or of the opposite gender? Is the work you perform on the job acceptable? When will you be ready to take on more responsibility?

## Practicing Ethics in the Workplace

**Ethics** (the code of values of a person, organization, or society) provide the **standards of conduct** (established guidelines) for what we believe is right and moral. The adults in your life have taught you ethics and modeled ethical behavior since you were born. Organizations do the same thing. All of society is based on trust, believing that others will do good. Can you think of some examples of people or organizations society trusts?

**Organizational values** (values that each organization expects of itself) often include reliability, fairness, commitment, honesty, and respect for its employees and customers. Each organization also expects that its members avoid **conflicts of interest** (when a company or government official gets personal gain from official business). Have you seen news stories of unethical or questionable business practices? What would it be like if businesses and industries could cheat and lie to you without taking the responsibility for their actions?

For example, is it ethical for a company to build and sell houses made of defective materials? Is it ethical for a company to take advantage of its employees by not paying them for time worked? For some of you, these questions will be easy to answer. For others, you might have difficulty. Ethics, unlike enforceable laws, come from within your family, community, the company you work for, and you.

Some government regulations include antitrust laws that prevent a company from **monopolizing** (businesses with no competition) or **price fixing** (an agreement between competitors to set the price of products). What would happen if only two companies sold computers, and they agreed that they would sell their computers for $5,000 to $5,500 each? Or what if only one company sold candy bars, and they sold them for $5.00 each? Would these practices be ethical? Would they be legal?

*Who is responsible when a company makes defective products?*

Individuals, organizations, and government can work together to encourage ethical behavior. When individuals report unethical behavior to authorities, they are **whistle blowing**. Can you think of some situations in which an employee might be a whistle blower? An organization that promotes ethical behavior is the Better Business Bureau. Do you have a Better Business Bureau in your community? Finally, government regulations help enforce ethics in the workplace.

**CAREER FACT**

If you enjoy classes in art, business, economics, or marketing, you may want to consider a career in sales and marketing.

Just as an organization must have good ethics, employees should demonstrate good **work ethics**. That is, an employee should be willing to work hard and to do a job well. Practicing good ethics strengthens a business. How can having good work ethics as an employee help you be more successful?

## What Are Good Work Ethics?

Courteous, businesslike behavior

Being truthful

Taking responsibility for actions

Treating others respectfully

Working in a safe manner

Not gossiping or telling secrets

Protecting the environment

Working for the good of the business

Being concerned about the community around the business

*What happens when businesses or employees do not practice these good work ethics?*

# Dealing with Diversity

Today's workforce has changed drastically in recent years. This change is a direct reflection of changes in the U.S. population. According to a recent issue of *American Demographics*, the United States census showed

> At 12.3 percent of the population, people who identify themselves as 'Black' are a large group—but no longer the largest minority. In the 2000 Census, Hispanics jumped to 12.5 percent of the population, from just 9 percent in 1990, and narrowly edge out African Americans as the nation's largest minority group. Whites still make up a 75 percent majority of the U.S. population—but that share is shrinking fast. Although only 3.6 percent of the U.S. population identify themselves as Asian, 22 percent of Asians have income (money they earn) of $100,000 or more, a share that is nearly double the U.S. average. Less than 1 percent of the population is Native American, but that number is expected to rise faster than average over the next five years. The newest category, counted for the first time in the 2000 census, is Multiracial, accounting for 2.4 percent of the U.S. population (many of which are under age 18).

**Diversity** can be defined as the presence of a variety of people (including employees) of different races, religions, nationalities, abilities, and ages, and both genders. Minorities and women will have more opportunities in the future than in the past. They will have better jobs and better choices of jobs. They will be better paid than in the past. This change in the work force also means that employers will have a larger group of potential employees to choose from.

---

**DISCRIMINATION**

**Have You Been Sexually Harassed?**

Working for Mrs. R. is something else. A couple of weeks ago, you wore a sleeveless T-shirt to work because you knew that you'd be landscaping the area in front of the office. As Mrs. R. explained which flowers she wanted you to plant beside the sidewalk, she kept putting her hand on your arm. When you picked up the tray of flowers, she reached out and grabbed your left bicep and said something like "My, how strong you are." You felt uncomfortable but didn't say anything. Was Mrs. R. guilty of sexual harassment?

**DIVERSITY**

**Why Does Her Family Follow Her Everywhere?**

One of your co-workers seems to be joined at the hip with her family. They bring her to work and stay for what seems like forever. Then they are back at least a half hour before quitting time. What makes people act like that?

---

*Why is it important to be accepting of other people?*

The changes in the workforce will affect everyone. Employers should hire the best people with the best training and education regardless of their race, gender, or age. **Stereotyping** (judging other people because of their appearance, age, gender, or race) probably will no longer be accepted. Workers will have to learn how to overcome problems resulting from diversity.

What does this mean to you? How do you think this will affect you? What are your beliefs about the roles of men and women in the work force? Because the gender and ethnic makeup of the work force is changing, it is very important for employers and employees to be open to different ideas, cultures, and personal styles.

For example, increased workplace diversity has changed what is considered acceptable language. The word *man* has been used for centuries to refer to both men and women. In recent years, however, this has become less acceptable, and many terms have been changed to be "sex-fair." For example, how have these words been changed? Mankind? Chairman? Fireman? Policeman?

Today, women make up more than half of the workforce! However, **sex-role stereotypes** (roles assigned to people based on their sex, not personal interests or skills) affect the careers available to women. Women make up only 25 percent of the nontraditional occupations. Why do you think this is true? How would you respond to the following survey?

Would you say the following traits describe men only, women only, or both men and women?

▶ Aggressive     ▶ Careful     ▶ Responsible

▶ Athletic     ▶ Easily excited     ▶ Self-confident

▶ Better at math     ▶ Educated     ▶ Smart

▶ Capable     ▶ Make better decisions

If you said men only or women only for any of these responses, you are stereotyping! The correct answer is that these traits can describe both men *and* women, depending on their personal interests and skills. If you have a tendency to stereotype men or women, *you* have a problem. It could lead to problems for you in today's workplace.

Political freedom and equality are values on which the United States of America is founded. Discrimination is unlawful. There are laws preventing **wage discrimination** (unequal pay for equal work). However, inequality in the workplace still occurs. **Glass ceilings**, or barriers to **promotions** or **advancements** (positions that offer higher pay and more responsibilities), still exist: Minority groups still receive unequal pay and fewer advancement opportunities. Pregnant women and families with children still might not be treated equally in the workplace.

Another form of discrimination is sexual harassment. The Equal Employment Opportunity Commission (EEOC) defines **sexual harassment** as "unwelcome sexual advances, requests for sexual favors, and other verbal or physical conduct of a sexual nature." Victims of sexual harassment can be women or men. The harasser doesn't even have to be of the opposite sex.

Follow these guidelines if you are discriminated against or sexually harassed:

1. Tell the person who discriminated against you or the harasser that the behavior is not acceptable and that it must stop immediately.

2. Write a letter to the person, giving details of the behavior and what you will do if it doesn't stop. Make sure that you date the letter, sign it, and keep a copy. Give the letter to the person with a witness present.

3. Keep a written record of any incidents and your responses.

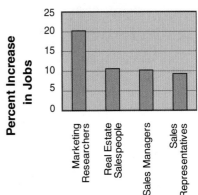

**Projected Outlook for 2016**

*What does this chart tell you about future opportunities in these careers?*

*Do you think a woman should do this job? Why or why not?*

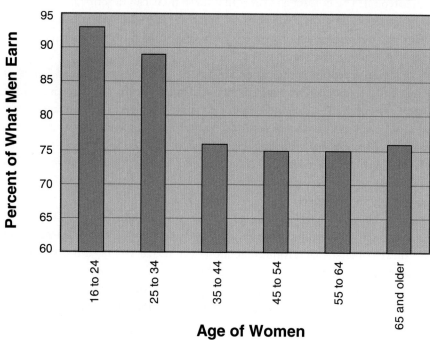

## Women's Salaries vs. Men's Salaries

*Percent of What Men Earn* (vertical axis: 60, 65, 70, 75, 80, 85, 90, 95)

*Age of Women* (horizontal axis: 16 to 24, 25 to 34, 35 to 44, 45 to 54, 55 to 64, 65 and older)

**4.** Follow the grievance policy in your employee handbook. Tell your supervisor or human relations department.

**5.** File a complaint with the Equal Employment Opportunity Commission.

**6.** If you are still not getting satisfactory results, consider filing a lawsuit.

It is very unlikely that you will ever get to Step 6. Usually a stern warning to the harasser is enough for the behavior to stop. But remember that the law is on your side. You don't have to put up with harassment and discrimination.

The workforce is changing and will continue to change. There are many laws to prevent and/or stop discrimination. Most importantly, this has to begin with you. As you enter this changing world of work, try your best to accept, adapt to, and value diversity. How can you do that?

## Case Study: Can Stereotyping Cause an Innocent Person to Be Fired?

Mandy is a newly licensed real estate agent, and Zach is a broker with the same real estate company. Zach trains the new real estate agents, deciding when they have met the company standards and have completed the training. Mandy knows that she's good at her work and that she ought to feel confident about her ability, but Zach said women should not work and kept questioning her competence, refusing to sign off on her training. One day, about a week after one of those times when Zach refused to approve Mandy's work, she is called to the office of the owner of the company. He asks her why her training is not yet completed. Then he calls Zach into his office.

---

**CAREER FACT**

Real estate agents often work evenings and weekends. They also are on-call; that is, they must be available when their clients need them. To be a real estate agent, you must complete a course, take an exam, be sponsored by an agency, and get a license. A real estate agent's income is a portion of each sale of a property.

---

What are possible reasons for the way Zach is treating Mandy?
What should the owner say to Mandy and Zach?
How might the situation affect Mandy's and Zach's jobs?

# Evaluating Your Work Performance

You might have heard employers or your parents make this comment: "It's so hard to find good help these days." What do you think they mean? Do you think this is true? The United States government passes laws to protect employees from unfair employers and hazardous workplace conditions. Who protects an employer from employees who don't care or actually hurt the business?

The employer has the responsibility to oversee the performance of each employee. Sometimes they assign a **mentor** (an advisor and role model) when an employee first begins working with an organization. This mentor can give you feedback, answer questions, and give advice that will prepare you for your own personal career advancement.

Many workplaces have some type of **performance appraisal** (a written evaluation of job performance). Most employees start out with a 90-day **probationary period** (a trial period of work) in which their work will be watched very carefully. For some employees, this probationary period could last six months or longer. Compare this type of evaluation to ways you are evaluated at school. Both include evaluations of your quality and quantity of work, dependability, attendance, punctuality, and appearance. Can you think of other examples?

Most businesses review your work once or twice each year. In most cases, a positive review will include a pay raise. There are two types of raises. A **cost-of-living pay increase** is given to workers to keep up with rising costs, typically amounting to two to five percent of your current salary or wages.

*When is mentoring effective?*

### Who Is Responsible for You?

Taking good care of the environment is important, but have you ever thought about another endangered species—you? There are many dangerous choices teens can make. If you don't take good care of yourself, who will? Take good care of yourself by doing the following:

▶ Avoid the caffeine in chocolate, cokes, coffee, and tea.
▶ Exercise weekly.
▶ Drink eight glasses of water every day.
▶ Eat five or six servings of fruits and vegetables a day.
▶ Sleep eight hours a night.

### On-the-Job Competency

### How Can You Keep Customers?

Whenever a customer buys something from you, you have a chance to strengthen your relationship with him so he will keep coming back. What are some ways you can do that?

Normally, this has nothing to do with how well you are doing in your job. A **merit pay increase** means that the employee has performed at an exceptional level, but might remain at that level and continue to improve or move up in the organization.

What could be some consequences for employees who are performing below expected performance standards? What could happen to those performing above the standards, including exceptional work?

It is just as important to do a self-evaluation and ask yourself questions such as, "Have I worked to the best of my ability? Have I been doing a good job?" If you answer "yes" to these questions, you have nothing to fear from an evaluation by your employer.

## Case Study: What Do the Driver and Passengers Expect?

Your date and you are going to the prom, and you will have a chauffeur-driven limousine pick up you and two other couples at your house, take you to dinner, and then take you all to the prom. When you make the arrangements with the limo service, you tell the person the date, place, and time of the prom. You are asked for a down payment: half the total cost of the limousine service.

What are your expectations of the driver and his or her performance?
What are the results if your expectations are met?
What are the consequences if your expectations are not met?
Now put yourself in the place of the driver. What expectations does the driver have?
What consequences could occur if the driver's expectations are not met?

# Taking On More Responsibilities

People have the ability to handle a great deal of work at once. As you become more familiar with your workplace and your specific job, you will be able to take on more responsibilities.

You will want to make a good impression on your employer. One of the best ways to accomplish this goal is to look for work that needs to be done. Employers look for and appreciate employees who take initiative. Another way to make a good impression is to network with your co-workers and supervisors to get their support and backing. As you are recognized for your excellent work ethic and teamwork, you will have the opportunity to take on even more responsibilities.

Taking on more responsibility in the workplace might result in career advancement or promotion within an organization. You might notice an opening posted on the bulletin board and choose to apply. Or your supervisor might recommend you for a promotion because of your initiative and positive performance appraisals. In today's workplace, you probably will not be promoted just because you are next in line but because you are the person best suited for the position.

*What responsibilities does a supervisor have?*

It is said that the best predictor of future performance is past performance. What does this mean to you?

Usually you will want to take advantage of being offered more responsibilities, and you will look forward to promotions. But there might also be some disadvantages to being promoted. Can you think of any disadvantages? What could happen after you are chosen to be a supervisor of your former co-workers? Are you willing to give a lot more time and energy to being a successful supervisor? Are you willing to take on more stress? How will you feel when you are criticized by your employees? Do you think you would be willing to take on these disadvantages?

## Section 10-2: Review

### Understanding Key Concepts

1. List four ways to take advantage of an entry-level job.
2. Why are ethics so important for companies and employees?
3. Why is knowing how to handle diversity so important in the workplace?
4. What are the differences and similarities between a performance appraisal and an evaluation at school?
5. What are two types of pay increases and how are they different?
6. How can you find out about and be considered for career advancements?

### Thinking Creatively

How can a stepping-stone job help someone in a future career?

Even if you haven't had a paid job yet, do you think people ever get jobs while in school and then keep them for the rest of their lives?

### Taking It a Step Further

Can any entry-level job help you develop skills you can use in any profession? Using the following list, find one skill that is specific to the "Summer Job" identified and then describe how you can use that skill in each occupation listed.

| Summer Job | Occupation |
|---|---|
| Nanny | Computer Programmer |
| Paper Carrier | Psychologist |
| Fast Food Worker | Housing Contractor |
| Lawn Caretaker | Journalist |

# Section 10-3: Facing Problems in the Workplace

Learning that a company has chosen you as an employee usually will make you feel happy and excited. In the beginning, the employer seems kind, the co-workers seem helpful, and you might even plan how you are going to spend your paycheck. You might think that life will be much better. In reality, becoming an employee might add more stress to your life and might give you another opportunity to use your problem-solving skills. What problems can occur in any job?

## Solving Work-Performance Problems

When you accept a job, you have every intention of displaying a good work ethic, of doing well for your employer. However, you might find that you do not perform as well as the employer expects or needs you to. Why do these performance problems occur?

First, your poor performance might be due to personal problems that interfere with your work. If that is the case, you need to decide what your priorities are. If your family or schoolwork needs your attention, but your job takes too much of your time, which is more important? Whatever your answer is, deal with that first. What do you think would be some options for you?

Second, your poor performance might be the result of not understanding your employer's expectations or knowing what your job is. If your employer does not have a written employee handbook (a book that includes company policies, procedures, and guidelines), you cannot know exactly what is expected of you. Employees need standards and examples. They need to be able to read the handbook and be comfortable with asking questions.

Third, you might not have the skills, resources, or training to do the job. You might have been told to watch and ask if you have questions. However, you might feel uncomfortable asking questions, thinking that you will look silly or that you will be told your work is "bad." You might also have watched others but still not understand how to do the work.

In situations like these, the employer is partially responsible for your poor performance. You did not get the information or resources that you need. However, you are also responsible for observing other employees, asking questions, and getting help when needed.

Unfortunately, sometimes poor performance is just a matter of choice. You might find yourself choosing not to do a good job. It is the employer's responsibility to give you some type of feedback on your performance. It can be either a formal reaction from an official source or an informal reaction from co-workers. If you feel that you just cannot do a good job for this particular company or that this job does not match your values and goals, consider looking for a job that is better for you. Realize that if you decide to stay but continue to do poor work, you might be fired.

# Accepting Criticism

Accepting criticism is very difficult. Criticism makes people feel embarrassed, angry, and stressed. How do you react to criticism? Since you were a small child, you have taken criticism for inappropriate behavior. Maybe it was for hitting your younger brother or sister or for talking in class without permission. Did you retaliate or fight back? Were you angry? Did you take it out on someone else?

As hard as it is to believe, criticism can be good for you. A coach's criticism improves a player's skills. Teachers' criticism improves the students' skills. Supervisors' criticism improves the employees' skills. You get the picture. Your attitude toward criticism will influence how you will get along with your supervisor as well as other employees and your future with the company.

You do have choices if you believe the criticism is unfair:

▶ Accept the criticism and change your behavior or attitude.

▶ Tolerate the criticism, but make no adjustments.

▶ Leave the company.

> **COMMUNITY**
>
> Research the history of your community and prepare a report or presentation that describes the diversity (or lack of diversity) in your community.

## Case Study: What Should Tricia Have Done?

Tricia was instructed to copy papers for an upcoming meeting. About halfway through the job, the copy machine jammed. Tricia had worked in the office for only a few weeks and had never encountered this problem before. She pushed a few buttons, opened a few doors on the copier, but really didn't know what to do. She decided the best thing would be to just walk away from the machine and try again later. When the next person tried to use the copier, he was very upset that he had to take the time to reset it before he could use it.

**NETWORKING**

Find someone from another culture or religion. Interview the person to discover how that culture is different from yours.

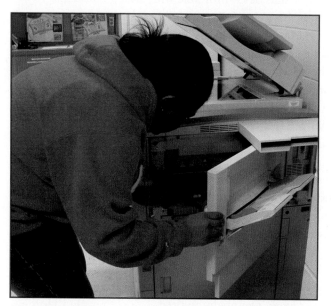

**What does Tricia's reaction reveal about her?**

**CAREER FACT**

Opportunities for door-to-door salespeople, news and street vendors, and telemarketers are expected to decline. Opportun-ities for securities, commodities, and financial services sales agents are expected to increase at the same rate as other occupations. However, the former group of salespeople needs only on-the-job training; the latter group must pass a licensing exam.

# Resolving Workplace Conflicts

At some point, you will most likely encounter an employer or supervisor you don't like. You might also discover that you have co-workers you don't like, either. One of the main reasons employees leave jobs is because of conflicts with employers and/or co-workers.

The first step of resolving any conflict is to ask yourself "Who has the problem?" If you find that you have conflicts with your employers, supervisors, co-workers, or other people in your life, could the problem be you? Can you use the problem-solving process to resolve the problem within yourself?

Positive interpersonal relationships require thought and work on your part. Do you

▶ Know what your supervisor and co-workers expect from you?

▶ Understand how your work impacts the business?

▶ Do your fair share of the work?

- ▸ Have a cooperative, positive attitude?

- ▸ Treat people with respect by greeting them and asking for (not demanding) help when you need it?

- ▸ Ignore gossip, inappropriate language and jokes, and trouble makers?

You don't need to memorize that list. Just remember the Golden Rule: *Do unto others as you would have others do unto you.* That one principle can guide you in all your relationships.

Using the problem-solving process of defining the problem, selecting a goal, analyzing your solutions, making a plan, taking action, and evaluating the results can be effective when you're the only person involved in the process. However, what do you do when you have looked closely at yourself and realized that others are creating a problem for you or see *you* as the problem? How can you resolve this type of conflict? You need to use **conflict resolution** (solving problems between opposing forces).

For example, you might not understand the instructions your employer or supervisor gives, or you might feel that she is showing favoritism to one of your co-workers and treating that person better than everyone else. Your co-workers might be giving you all the hard work or treating you disrespectfully. You might be worried about the safety of the place where you work. Use the problem-solving steps to decide what is wrong and what you can do about it. In the case of a conflict with another person, you probably will need to communicate with others about the problem. Follow these conflict-resolution guidelines:

- ▸ **Always respect the chain of command.** Don't go over your supervisor's head by talking to her supervisor unless you have no other choice. If you do, you probably will have to deal with negative consequences, such as having to deal with your supervisor's anger.

- ▸ **Wait until you have calmed down.** If you confront your supervisor or demand a meeting when you are really angry, you will not be able to think rationally and might say things you would not say when you have had time to think about the situation.

- ▸ **Ask the supervisor (or the secretary, if there is one) to schedule a meeting at a convenient time.** Asking is using proper business etiquette and will take you much further than demanding.

- ▸ **Arrive on time for the meeting.** Follow proper business etiquette when entering your employer's office and stand until you are offered a seat.

- ▸ **Be prepared to state the problem.** Keep a cool head and maintain a positive attitude by thinking of the problem as an opportunity to learn and grow as a person.

*Do unto others as you would have them do unto you.*

*—The Golden Rule*

**ROLE-PLAYING**

**Scenario:** A male teen applies for a position at a day care center.

**Roles:** A male teen and the hiring manager at the day care

**Discussion:** How comfortable did the teen seem with regards to being considered for the job? How comfortable was the manager with the idea of hiring a male? Can males take good care of children?

*We have a responsibility to ourselves to meet our own needs.*

*—Mary Treffert*

▶ **Keep in mind that your goal is to understand others.** Try to understand the feelings of all the people involved in the problem, not just your own.

▶ **Look for a win-win solution to the problem.**

▶ **Use I-statements.** With **I-statements**, you tell others what you think or feel without blaming anyone.

Which one of these statements do you believe is less threatening to another person, and why?

"You've got to get this mess straightened out, or you're going to have a disaster!"

**or**

"I believe there is a serious problem, and it needs our attention fast!"

## Section 10-3: Review

### Understanding Key Concepts

1. What three choices do you have if your supervisor criticizes your work performance?
2. What is conflict resolution? How is it different from and similar to problem solving?
3. How can you resolve problems on the job?

### Thinking Creatively

What are the responsibilities of a supervisor?

### Taking It a Step Further

Use the Internet to research on the topic of mentoring. Then think of a skill, ability, or character quality you have that you could share with someone else. Create a program for doing so. Make sure that your program includes the following:

▶ A list of the objectives (exactly what you think needs to be taught)
▶ A description of and a method for recruiting the typical person needing the mentoring
▶ At least five mentoring activities
▶ A performance evaluation that measures whether the skill, ability, or character quality improved
▶ A feedback form the mentored person completes

**Tanya Stellpflug, Room Leader**
**Abercrombie and Fitch**

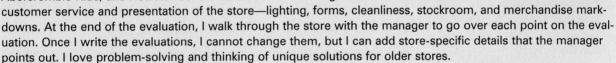

I am a Room Leader for Abercrombie and Fitch, which means that I am part of a traveling team that crosses the country to open up new stores. Our responsibilities include training the managers and the brand representatives. During the week before a store opens, we set up the tables; build walls; and train new employees on using cash registers, presentation, and customer service. It's a great feeling to see a new store open and then be able to head home knowing that the job is complete.

While I'm waiting for a new store to open, I also travel to Abercrombie and Fitch, Abercrombie Kids, and Hollister Co. stores in the surrounding area and evaluate them on customer service and presentation of the store—lighting, forms, cleanliness, stockroom, and merchandise markdowns. At the end of the evaluation, I walk through the store with the manager to go over each point on the evaluation. Once I write the evaluations, I cannot change them, but I can add store-specific details that the manager points out. I love problem-solving and thinking of unique solutions for older stores.

When I was in high school, I wanted to be a French teacher, so I earned bachelor's degrees in French and Women's Studies from the University of Wisconsin–Madison. However, my work experiences in college moved me into an entirely different area. While in college, I was a Sales Associate at Urban Outfitters. I worked as a Manager-in-Training at Urban Outfitters and as an Assistant Manager at a Hollister Co. store before accepting my position on the New Store Opening Team.

To keep balance in my life, I read, swim, call my friends, eat out, and shop. My days off are precious to me, so I try to squeeze in as much family and friend time as I can.

# Chapter Review and Activities

The following sections can help you review the contents of this chapter.

## Key Concepts

Following are the key concepts presented in the chapter.

▶ Health, safety, and legal issues in the workplace are so important that the United States has created the Department of Labor to make certain that employers treat employees properly.

▶ The government has passed four acts to monitor employment: The ADA protects people with disabilities, the EPA monitors the environment, the Social Security Act collects retirement funds, and OSHA monitors safety and health in the workplace.

▶ Employees must accept responsibility for their safety by not abusing substances such as alcohol and drugs, wearing protective clothing, and following safety regulations in the workplace.

▶ Entry-level jobs prepare you for careers if you strive to be the best employee you can be, take the initiative, try new experiences, and learn on the job.

Writing an e-mail to a supervisor, co-worker, or customer is different than writing to a friend. There are certain procedures, or etiquette, that you should follow when sending an e-mail at work:

▸ Write an informative subject line that clearly explains what the message is about.

▸ Start your message with "Dear Mr. or Ms....," unless you are on a first-name basis with the person.

▸ Avoid using abbreviations in your message. They can be confusing and are too informal for work. You should avoid using emoticons, such as :-), for the same reason.

▸ Keep your message short, one screen if possible, and to the point. Separate your ideas by starting each one on a new line or numbering them. This formatting makes the message easier to read quickly.

▸ Read your message before you send it. Make sure there are no spelling (use the spell check feature) or grammar errors.

▸ Societies are founded on ethics—doing what is right. Businesses and employees must make ethical decisions if our society is to be successful.

▸ The workplace is becoming more diverse as people of different races, nationalities, religions, genders, ages, and abilities work together.

▸ As you become more comfortable in a job, you might want to take on more responsibility. Your employer will probably give you a performance appraisal that will evaluate your work and help you determine whether you need to make improvements or whether you are ready for an advancement.

▸ If your employer criticizes your performance, you will need to either change your behavior or find different work.

▸ To resolve conflict in the workplace, use the problem-solving steps and communicate with those with whom you have the conflict.

## Key Term Review

Complete the following activity to review your understanding of the key terms.

| | |
|---|---|
| advancements | merit pay increase |
| compensation | monopolizing |
| conflicts of interest | organizational values |
| conflict resolution | performance appraisal |
| cost-of-living pay increase | price fixing |
| co-workers | promotion |
| discrimination | sex-role stereotypes |
| diversity | sexual harassment |
| ethics | standards of conduct |
| entry-level job | stereotyping |
| glass ceiling | wage discrimination |
| initiative | whistle blowing |
| I-statements | work ethic |
| mentor | |

Your employer has asked you to write a short set of procedures for handling problems in the workplace. Use at least 10 key terms in your explanation.

## Comprehension Review

Answer the following questions to review your understanding of the key concepts in the chapter.

**1.** What types of protection does the United States government offer workers?

**2.** What can be the role of entry-level jobs?

3. What ethics standards are required of businesses, and what standards do most employers require of their employees?

4. What types of diversity are seen in the workplace today?

5. What are three choices you can make if you are given negative feedback on your work performance, and what are the benefits of each?

6. Why is conflict resolution so important?

. . . . . . . . . . . . . . . . . . . . . . . . . . . . . . . . . . . . . . . . . . . . . . . . . .

## School-to-Work

**Math:** Write down the steps you would take to solve this mathematical problem:

> You earn $10.50 per hour. Your employer tells you that he is giving you a cost-of-living pay raise of 3.5 percent, and that, because you do such excellent work, you will receive a merit pay raise of $.50 per hour. How much will you be making per hour?

**Social Studies:** The ADA established many provisions other than employment for the disabled. One of those provisions is equal access to buildings. What does that mean for buildings of historical importance? Must each one be renovated, thereby destroying its authenticity? Research the law to find out just how it impacts that type of building. Then locate one historic building, discover whether those accommodations have been made, and prepare either a report or a PowerPoint presentation that discusses the provisions that have been made for the disabled at the building.

**Writing:** One of the best ways to avoid sexual harassment is to clearly give others the message that you do not welcome inappropriate conduct without displaying a hostile attitude toward people who might be just trying to be nice. Write a brief script between a male and a female co-worker in which one is beginning to sound a bit flirtatious and the other clearly, firmly, but kindly sets the boundaries for the relationship.

**Science:** The EPA plays an important role in protecting our environment. Using Google, Yahoo!, or your favorite search engine, type the key words *Environmental Protection Agency*, browse through some of the sites, and choose a topic to research. Using the information you collect, prepare a brochure or PowerPoint presentation about the issue you choose.

. . . . . . . . . . . . . . . . . . . . . . . . . . . . . . . . . . . . . . . . . . . . . . . . . .

## Does This Job Interest You?

The following job is posted on the Internet. What education and experience are required? What requirements does this job have that most jobs do not have? What types of interests and skills should a person working in this position have? How could someone apply for the job? How could someone find out more about the job?

---

**FIND JOBS**  **POST RESUMES**

### Marketing & Sales—Professional Sports Teams

| | | | |
|---|---|---|---|
| **Company:** | SportsWorks | **Job Type:** | Entry Level—New Grad Marketing Sales |
| **Location:** | US-IN-Indianapolis | **Required Education:** | 4-Year Degree |
| **Base Pay:** | $35,000 | **Required Experience:** | College |
| **Employee Type:** | Full-Time Employee | **Required Travel:** | Negligible |
| **Industry:** | Sales-Marketing | **Relocation Covered:** | No |

### Job Requirements

To be considered for positions in this highly competitive sports industry, candidates should possess the following characteristics:

Be passionate about sports and the business of sports. Ability to work in a fast-paced team environment. Sales and/or marketing experience. Flexible schedule. Willing to travel. Ability to relocate. Good network in the sports industry.

PLEASE NOTE: All applications will be replied to via e-mail. Due to the high response and confidentiality of this search, we are not accepting phone calls or faxes in response to this position.

### Contact

hr@sportsworks.com

**Apply Online**

---

## Staying Safe on the Job

Every year thousands of teenagers end up in the emergency room because of work-related injuries. The Fair Labor Standards Act prohibits workers under the age of 18 from operating potentially dangerous equipment such as cars and trucks, meat slicers, and circular saws, but there are other hazards in the workplace. A hazard is anything that can hurt you mentally or physically. These hazards include everything from knives and hot grease to stress, noise, and repetitive motion. Follow these guidelines to stay safe at work:

▸ Always take the time to follow safe work procedures.

▸ Make sure you have been trained on equipment before you try to use it. Don't be afraid to ask questions about safety procedures.

▸ Be on the lookout for potential hazards, such as slippery floors. Tell your supervisor about any unsafe conditions that you see.

▸ Read the labels of any chemicals that you use on the job, such as cleaning products or pesticides, so that you are aware of any risks involved.

▸ Find out what you should do in case there is an emergency. Know where safety equipment, such as a fire extinguisher, is kept. Your employer should have emergency plans in place.

Remember, you have the right to work in a safe environment. If you feel threatened or uncomfortable at work, talk to your supervisor. If your supervisor does not help you, discuss the issue with your parents.

**What career appeals to you?**

# Unit 3 Accepting Responsibility for Your Life

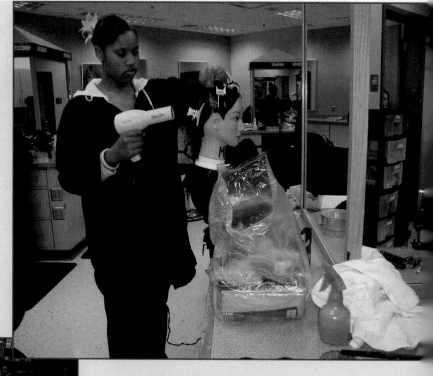

## Chapter 11: Taking Your Place in the Global Community

*Chapter 11 focuses on Recreation, Travel, and Other Personal Services careers.*

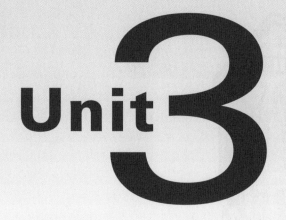

## Chapter 12: Managing Your Money

*Chapter 12 focuses on Education and Social Service careers.*

236

# Chapter 13: Becoming a Responsible Consumer

*Chapter 13 focuses on General Management and Support careers.*

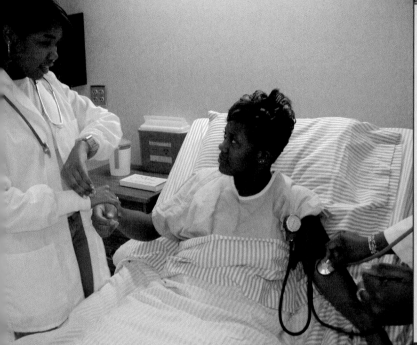

# Chapter 14: Successfully Handling Adult Roles and Responsibilities

*Chapter 14 focuses on Medical and Health Services careers.*

# Chapter 15: Designing Your Tomorrow Today

*Chapter 15 focuses on Military Services careers.*

# Chapter 11

# Taking Your Place in the Global Community

## What You'll Learn

▶ Understanding the American economic system

▶ Competing in a global economy

▶ Becoming a contributing member of society

U nless you live alone on an island, you are part of a community. You may feel as if you are not very noticeable or important in it, but you still are part of it. As you accept jobs, begin your career and move toward an independent life, your role in your community will automatically increase. You must understand how your community works economically and globally so that you can add to its success.

*No one is so important that everyone knows him; no one is so small that no one knows him.*

*(Unknown)*

calculated risk
capitalism
civic responsibility
competition
consumers
deflation
demand
democracy
economic system

efficiently
entrepreneur
free enterprise system
globalization
goods
income taxes
ingenuity
inflation
prejudiced

profit
recessions
services
small business
special-interest groups
supply
textiles
trends

# Section 11-1: Understanding the American Economic System

Have you ever traveled to different parts of the United States? If you have, you may have noticed that the cities are different from the country. Small towns are different from the suburbs. One thing remains constant: The people and their communities depend on one another. This dependence exists because of the American **economic system**: the way a society produces, sells, and uses goods and services.

The people who formed our government decided that it should be based on shared leadership—a **democracy** (the form of government in which the citizens give power to leaders whom they choose). The Founding Fathers also

*How do events in Washington, D.C., impact our economy?*

decided to base the economy on an economic system called the **free enterprise system**. This system (also called **capitalism**) is one in which individuals and private businesses are free to organize and operate without government control.

The U.S. government does sometimes step in and tell a business what it can and cannot do. The government's role in that situation is to protect people or other businesses. If a business is polluting the environment, the pollution might cause thousands of people to develop the risk of cancer, for example. The government may require the business to stop polluting and clean up (or pay for cleaning up) the affected area. However, governmental officials can lose their jobs if they take advantage of their power and try to control businesses.

The freedom from government control that the free enterprise system gives is not found in many other countries around the world. In some countries, the government completely controls what and how many products are made available to the people. How would you feel if that were true of the United States? How do you think this would affect you? How do you think this would affect your family?

Why and how does the free enterprise system work? Some of the most important principles of the system are the law of **supply** (the goods or services available) and **demand** (what people want), and competition between companies to win customers by having lower prices or better goods and services.

## Consumers, Goods, and Services

**Consumers** are the people who spend money to buy goods and services. The term **goods** refers to products that can be produced, and **services** refers to doing work for people. Based on these definitions, which of the following represent goods and which represent services?

▶ Babysitting

▶ Airplane flight

▶ Haircut

▶ Fast food

▶ Computer software

Sometimes the difference between goods and services is not as obvious as you may think. In some cases, the product can be both.

In a free enterprise system, the goal of business and industry is to make a **profit** (the money that's left after the company pays its expenses). A company can return its profits to the owners and investors, or it can purchase new equipment or even other companies. Some of the profit might be given back to support community activities (such as scholarships, Little League, or health care). To increase profits, most companies work hard to operate **efficiently** (without waste). Working efficiently also means savings to the consumer.

*Which of these items are goods and which are services? Are any of them both goods and services?*

*What are the advantages and disadvantages of making a soda dispenser accessible to customers?*

One example is the sale of fast-food soft drinks. Having customers get their own drinks saves employee time, so the price of the drinks might drop. At the same time, the customers receive free refills, which save the customers money. Can you think of other ways a company can improve efficiency and increase profits? Some fast-food service industries are experimenting with totally automated restaurants. How would this improve efficiency and increase profits? How do you feel about this concept?

## Supply and Demand

The law of supply and demand is important because it impacts every part of our economic system. Supply and demand, simply stated, determines which companies survive and which don't. When a company tries to sell goods or services that few consumers want, the company usually goes out of business.

Typically, the law of supply and demand says that as a good or service becomes more popular, the more expensive and harder to find it becomes. On the other hand, when goods or services are easy to get or are no longer popular, their prices go down. Here's an example: How easily could you sell a copy of your local newspaper if it were two weeks old? What if the date on the newspaper were 1864?

# Competition

Another important principle that affects businesses in a free enterprise system is **competition**. When businesses compete against each other, the cost or quality of the goods or services usually changes.

Look at soft drinks again. What if only one business sold soft drinks? It could charge just about any price for the drinks. What if the government could set the price of the soft drinks at a fixed rate? The consumer would have to pay that price. However, if many businesses sell soft drinks, they compete against each other for the consumer's business. What are some examples of companies that compete with one another in your community?

One of the things historians and economists can track is how well the American free enterprise system does. From its beginning, the United States has faced bad and good times economically. During the bad times, also called **recessions**, people quit spending money. Prices drop (called **deflation**), workers are laid off, and companies go out of business.

---

## Business Owners and Investors

Many small businesses are owned by just one person. This type of business is called a *sole proprietorship,* and it is the simplest and least expensive way to organize a business. The owner makes all of the decisions about how the business is run and takes on all of the financial responsibility for the business. Because sole proprietorships are small, their owners often have difficulty getting business loans and have to either use their own savings or borrow money from family and friends. If the business fails, the owner could lose all of his or her money as well as his or her job. If the business succeeds, the owner can keep all the profit.

In a *partnership,* two or more people share the responsibilities and the rewards of running a business. The main advantage of a partnership is that each partner can contribute his or her talents to improving the business. For example, one partner may excel in marketing, and another may be great at developing new products. In some cases, one partner provides the money to start the business, and the other partner runs the business. All partnerships need a legal document that explains each partner's responsibilities, states each partner's share of the profits, and establishes a process for handling disagreements or even ending the partnership.

A *corporation* is a business that has its own legal identity that is separate from its owners. Corporations can be owned by just a few people or thousands of people. To gain money and spread out financial risk for the business, corporations divide ownership of the business into shares of *stock* and then sell them to people known as *stockholders* or shareholders. The stockholders elect a board of directors to make major decisions about how the business is run.

If a corporation performs well and earns profits, the stock becomes more valuable and can be sold for a higher price than the stockholder paid for it. If the corporation loses money, the stock is worth less, and the stockholders lose money. If you look at the stock market listings in the financial or business section of your local newspaper or on the Internet, you will notice that stock prices go up and down all the time. Investors make money in the stock market by buying stock in companies that they think will earn more profits in the future. Although investing in the stock market can be risky, it also can be a great way to increase your wealth if you are able to wait out the ups and downs of the stock market and carefully research the corporations in which you want to invest.

---

## Why Was She So Upset?

Adara came to work very upset. All morning long, she wouldn't talk. In the afternoon, she finally shared what was bothering her. The night before, she had watched a criminal investigation program on TV in which the villain was supposedly an Arab sheik, dressed in a turban and wearing a mustache. Then that morning she happened to watch part of a cartoon with her younger brother. Again, the villain was an Arab. Adara said that she just couldn't handle it anymore. What was her problem?

## The Changing Value of $100

$2,000 — $1,923
$1,500
$1,420
$1,114
$1,082
$1,000
$727
$618
$500
$362
$181
$128
$0

1916  1926  1936  1946  1956  1966  1976  1986  1996

**Year**

(y-axis label: Equivalent in 2006)

*How has the value of $100 changed over the years?*
*(Data based on Consumer Price Index statistics)*

*Is it important for the average person in the U.S. to understand our economy?*

The opposite occurs during good times. This creates a situation in which production of goods and services cannot keep up with consumer demand. Spending and prices rise (called **inflation**). Many things happen to the economy when it is experiencing deflation or inflation. What are some things that happen to families during deflation and inflation?

Why is it necessary for you to understand how a free enterprise system works? Even if you are a very small part of the free enterprise system, knowing more about how it works will prepare you for making wise career decisions and setting career goals. If recent **trends** (the general direction the economy is going) continue and if predictions come true, more jobs will be available in the service careers. As you explore careers, consider what and how many job openings will be available in these various career fields. Who knows? You may even want to start an entirely new career field. To learn more about recent trends or the outlook for a career field, check out the Department of Labor Web site.

## Case Study: Why Did the Prices Change?

The *Cumberland Avenue* band was extremely popular among teenagers and young adults. Everyone wanted to go to the concerts, and people bought the band's CDs as quickly as they came on the market. In addition, concertgoers bought the band's T-shirts and posters at each performance. Because of the band's popularity, it charged very high prices for its products, and consumers were willing to pay those prices.

Then a new band, the *J Thomas Band*, began to enjoy quick success, becoming popular almost overnight. Its concerts began selling out in advance, and CDs sold out in nearly every store. *Cumberland Avenue* fans quickly became fans of the new band, and demand for *Cumberland Avenue*'s concerts and products dropped off drastically.

As a result, demands for the *J Thomas Band* music and products and services went up—and so did their prices. The *Cumberland Avenue* band had to lower its concert tickets and prices for its products.

**What happened to prices when the *Cumberland Avenue* band was popular?**
**What happened to prices when the popularity of the *Cumberland Avenue* band was low?**
**What do you think will eventually happen to the *Cumberland Avenue* band? Why?**
**What do you think will eventually happen to the *J Thomas Band*? Why?**

# Entrepreneurs

How many businesses have you owned and operated? Chances are that you have tried at least one of these: selling lemonade from a stand in your front yard, raking leaves, shoveling snow, house-sitting, or baby-sitting. If so, you already have experience as an **entrepreneur** (someone who owns and operates his or her own business). What did it take to start your own business? Are you still in business today? If not, why not?

Most entrepreneurs start out as **small business** (an independently owned and operated business) owners. In the United States, the small business owner is the foundation of our free enterprise system because the majority of businesses by far are small businesses. What are the names of some small businesses in your community?

Even many of our largest companies started out as small businesses, perhaps even in the basements of people's homes, garages, or living rooms. When Charlotte Fowkes was fired from her job, for example, she turned her hobby of creating "diaper cakes" for baby shower gifts into an online business. Three years after she created Baby-Cakes.com, demand for her product was so great that she opened a traditional store. Charlotte showed how **ingenuity** (cleverness) and creativity can lead to success in entrepreneurship.

You may know other examples. The company Mrs. Fields Cookies started in someone's kitchen. The Wright brothers built the first successful airplane in their bicycle shop. Check out other examples by entering the key words "successful entrepreneurs" in a search engine online.

*Entrepreneurs (those who start businesses) average 3.8 business failures before final success. What sets the successful ones apart is their amazing persistence. There are a lot of people out there with good and marketable ideas, but pure entrepreneurial types almost never accept defeat.*

*—Lisa Amos*

*Which has more impact on the U.S. economy: big businesses or small ones?*

## Business Plans

If you want to be an entrepreneur, you need to write a business plan, which is a document that describes your business idea, establishes goals for your business, and explains in detail how you will reach those goals. Entrepreneurs use business plans to help them get business loans, find business partners, and attract employees. A business plan must answer the following questions:

1. Who are you and what is your business idea? Why are you the right person to start this business?
2. Who are your customers? What kind of advertising or marketing plan will you use to reach them?
3. What will it cost to start your business? How much money will it cost to operate the business on a daily basis? Where will you get this money? If it is a loan, how will you pay it back?
4. Who is your competition? What will you do differently?
5. How will you run the business? What goods or services will you offer? How will you deliver those goods and services to the customer? Where will the business be located? Where will you get your supplies? Who will be your employees?
6. What prices will you charge for your goods and services? How will you collect and keep track of the money you earn and pay your expenses?
7. When do you think you will start to make a profit? How will you make your business grow?

Go back and reread the quotation at the beginning of this section. How many businesses fail before the entrepreneur finally succeeds? Starting your own business is a risk (a gamble, a chance that can lead to success or failure). If you can make a calculated risk, your chances of success are much greater. A **calculated risk** is one in which you analyze possible outcomes (step 3 in the problem-solving process) before you make a decision. It takes a special kind of person to take a calculated risk and turn it into a success story. Are you willing to take the risk? Do you have the resources (including patience, ingenuity, and self-confidence) to transform an idea into a successful business?

## Section 11-1: Review

### Understanding Key Concepts

1. What is a free enterprise system?
2. Compare and contrast the terms *goods* and *services*.
3. What are the important principles in a free enterprise system?

### Thinking Creatively

Why do you think the Founding Fathers of the United States chose a shared leadership form of government?

Why is entrepreneurship so important to a free enterprise system?

Do you have an idea for a new business you could start?

### Taking It a Step Further

Research these three economic systems: subsistence, socialist, and Buddhist. Choose one and prepare a PowerPoint presentation on a government that uses or used it, its benefits, and its drawbacks.

# Section 11-2: Competing in a Global Economy

No doubt you have heard of globalization, but what on earth is it all about? The term **globalization** means that the entire world is connected economically, politically, or culturally. Historically, globalization has been around for centuries, beginning with international trading and people moving to other countries, especially to the United States. With increased use of technology, including the Internet, globalization has become a reality and touches your life in interesting ways (many that you don't even know about).

What if work can be done anywhere at much lower costs, which in turn produces higher profits? What if brainpower can be used anywhere, regardless of the language spoken? If you owned a company, what would you do? For example, before 1965, the U.S. imported (or bought from other countries) less than 10 percent of **textiles** (cloth or fabric used to make clothes). By 1990, imports accounted for 35 percent of the textiles used. Today, more than 75 percent is imported! This is just one example of how sales of foreign-made products are affecting producers in the U.S.

To remain competitive or become more competitive, U.S. companies must lower costs and respond better to consumer demand. They must develop skills to produce high-quality goods at competitive prices. Those are great challenges to today's businesses and industries. Are these changes good or bad for the consumer?

There is much debate about whether globalization is a good or bad thing. Supporters say that it has led to greater understanding of other cultures. Those cultures learn about the American economic and political systems.

**COMMUNITY**

Subway and Domino's Pizza are examples of franchises. A *franchise* is a business where a local business owner pays a fee to and signs a contract with a national company for the right to use a certain business idea or brand name. Find out more about how franchises work by talking to a local franchise owner or visiting the Small Business Administration's Web site at www.sba.gov.

**CAREER FACT**

Job opportunities for personal and home care aides are expected to increase rapidly because of the increase in the number of elderly people. Other reasons for the increase in opportunities are that the pay is low, and the training requirements are low. However, the emotional demands involved in the work are great.

*Do you know that McDonald's has 30,000 outlets in about 119 countries?*

*What are ways in which a global economy has impacted your life?*

Critics say that America's gain has been at the expense of other countries and has even made the poorest people poorer. Others maintain that globalization actually hurts the American economy by moving jobs to other countries that have lower wage costs.

Countries are learning more about each others' political, economic, and social structures. More and more goods, services, technology, and information are being shared. Some U.S. companies are involved in partnerships with companies from other nations. Other U.S. businesses are moving their manufacturing operations to other countries such as Mexico, China, and India. No longer is the question "Will the United States be involved?" Now it is "What does the United States need to do to remain successful in a global economy?"

## Section 11-2: Review

### Understanding Key Concepts

1. What is globalization?
2. Why has globalization been increasing?
3. How is globalization changing the world?

### Thinking Creatively

What are some of the "hidden" ways that globalization affects people?
Is it fair for a free enterprise system to have to compete against businesses supported by their governments?
What can American businesses do to remain successful in a global economy?

### Taking It a Step Further

Search through Web sites to find out what other countries think about American companies. From your findings, form strategies that American companies can use to win the trust of their customers in other countries.

# Section 11-3: Becoming a Contributing Member of Society

By this point in your life, you have probably learned that with freedom comes responsibility. If you have the freedom to go to an activity without an adult, for example, you are free from adult supervision. You are responsible for your behavior. That certainly is true when you live in a country with a democratic government like that of the United States. As a citizen of the United States, you are free to work, live, worship, and speak, but you are also responsible for your government. What responsibilities do you think a citizen of the United States has?

On the other hand, the U. S. government accepts the responsibility for many areas of its citizens' lives. What responsibilities does the government accept in your life? Fulfilling those responsibilities costs money. But how does the government get its money?

## Accepting Civic Responsibility

The attitudes you have toward your community and nation will shape the quality of life for everyone. **Civic responsibility** means responding to the rights, privileges, laws, and policies of your community in an informed, committed, and positive way. This is an adult role that you learn. You will need to use your studying and active listening skills to learn how your community operates and how the decision-making process impacts public policy. You also must recognize the value of serving your country or community.

Civic responsibility includes voting and obeying the laws. Voting is one of the most important civic responsibilities that you will have. You have the right and the responsibility to select the candidates that you believe best represent you and your values. In what year can you vote in the presidential election for the first time?

Obeying laws is another responsibility you have as a citizen. The United States Constitution, a federal law, is the highest law in our country. The levels of government established by the Constitution—cities, counties, and states—are also responsible for setting and enforcing laws. You must obey those laws.

*And so, my fellow Americans: ask not what your country can do for you—ask what you can do for your country.*

*—President John Fitzgerald Kennedy, Inaugural Address, 1960*

### COMMUNITY

Plan a community project that reinforces the message of this chapter: Every citizen needs to help the community. Your project can be anything from creating an anticrime campaign to cleaning up an eyesore or picking up trash to volunteering at a senior citizen's center, day care, or political organization.

### Examples of Different Levels of Government Responsibilities

| Federal | State Government | Cities and Counties |
| --- | --- | --- |
| Military protection | State police protection | Fire and police protection |
| Interstate highways | State highways | Streets and roads |
| Equal opportunity in education laws | Postsecondary education | Elementary and high school education |
| Equal opportunity in employment laws | Divorce and marriage laws | Public health laws |

*Does one person's vote make a difference?*

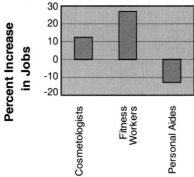

**NETWORKING**

Contact leaders of a small group in your community to see whether the group needs teen volunteers to help on a project.

**Projected Outlook for 2016**

*What does this chart tell you about future opportunities in these careers?*

**ETHICS**

**Is It Too Much Work?**

Eight inches of snow fell last night. Unfortunately, it was preceded by a freezing rain, and underneath all the snow was a thick sheet of ice. It's your turn to shovel the sidewalk in front of the office. You're tempted to shovel just a narrow little path. What will you do?

There is much more to civic responsibility, however, than just voting and obeying the law. Today's society is faced with many social problems. What do you believe are some serious problems facing your neighborhood, nation, and the world? Have you ever tackled some of the problems as an individual or through an organization such as Boy Scouts or Girls Scouts of America, 4-H, or a church youth group?

The following issues are ones that many American citizens believe should be resolved. These issues will be passed on to your generation to solve. They will impact you, your family, friends, community, the United States of America, and the people around the entire globe.

## Crime

From burglaries in our own homes to global terrorism, crime impacts every part of our world. Crime has been on the rise for many years. One issue that has been very evident is the increase of violence in our schools, especially that involving guns. As a result, school administrators have begun programs to provide for the safety of all students: security cameras, metal detectors, in-school suspension programs, bans on backpacks and book bags, and more strict dress codes, to mention a few. Most of you have very strong feelings about these programs, but the reality is their purpose is to keep you safe.

On a larger scale, law enforcement and gun control are issues that are dealt with at every government level—local, state, national, and even international—every day. What can you do to help with these issues?

## Education

The "No Child Left Behind" law states that every child has the right to an education. However, many American students are still dropping out of school every year. These students often become unskilled laborers in our workforce or spend a good part of their adult lives unemployed. Also, studies indicate that those students who do graduate still fall behind other nations, especially in math and science. The reality is that the United States must compete with the other nations in today's international economy.

What would you do to improve education? How would you raise funds for public and private education? What would you do to encourage students to stay in school? Is the United States affected by the educational systems in other countries?

## Environmental Problems

Most Americans enjoy today's technologies. In fact, no society has experienced the standard of living and quality of life experienced today. But at what price? You have certainly heard about global warming and pollution. Many scientists believe that the threat to our environment is so great today that it is a threat to human existence!

Created in 1970, the Environmental Protection Agency (EPA) enforces laws and regulations to improve our environment. Unfortunately, solutions to environmental problems often conflict with individual goals and **special-interest groups** (people with particular concerns).

### On-the-Job Competency

**Why Should Kristin Adjust Her Approach?**

Kristin is a young instructor at the local fitness club. Her job is to motivate and lead the club's clients to reach their fit-ness goals. Kristin is an out-standing athlete with seemingly boundless energy, and she expects the same from her clients. However, some of the clients seem to pull away and resist Kristin's leadership. What does Kristin need to under-stand? How could she lead more effectively?

*Can a small group of people with a common concern make an improvement in the environment?*

It would be very easy to argue for and against different issues that affect farmers, manufacturers, and the transportation industry, for instance. Can you think of any specific examples you have read about or seen in the news recently? How do the environmental decisions made in the United States impact the planet Earth?

## Diversity

Every human being has the right to "life, liberty, and the pursuit of happiness," according to the *Declaration of Independence*. However, some people's attitudes become **prejudiced**. Their thoughts and behaviors become fixed. They resist new information without any proof or evidence. Their attitudes become destructive. This problem is complicated because of social influences from family, friends, and the media. Unfortunately, prejudice brings out the worst in some people.

The reality is that today's communities have many different racial, ethnic, and religious groups. How can you work to reduce prejudice in your community or the world?

Crime, education, environmental problems, and diversity are just a few of the social issues that confront our world. Being a responsible citizen is not easy. It requires knowledge, commitment, and a willingness to be involved. You need to understand the issues that face your community and then communicate your opinion to the leaders. How can you let your leaders know what you're thinking?

*What causes people to be prejudiced against others? How can someone with prejudice against others overcome it?*

Some of you may choose to become more involved than others by taking an active leadership role. You may choose to run for a public office at your local or state level. Some of you may choose to represent your country as a senator or representative or even a higher office. But each of you can make a difference. It is your civic responsibility to do so.

# Paying Taxes

What does the word *taxes* mean to you? What does it mean to your parents? How much do you actually know about taxes? **Income taxes** are paid to support government services at local, state, and federal levels. Sales taxes are taxes collected when someone makes a purchase. The tax is usually a percentage of the cost of the item purchased. Property taxes are taxes charged for owning land or other goods.

Taxes pay for many services in your local community, including your public library, police, and fire protection. State taxes pay for teachers' salaries and maintaining the roads you drive on, as well as for many other services. Federal taxes pay for military protection; regulating the safety of foods, prescriptions, and over-the-counter drugs; transportation systems; environmental needs; and so on. Laws created by elected lawmakers establish the taxes on workers' incomes, purchases, and some types of properties.

*Where will this agency get the money to meet its financial responsibilities?*

## Triton Fire Department Budget

The Triton Fire Department budget for Fiscal Year 2011/2012 is $10,520,562 and is broken down into the following categories:

| | |
|---|---|
| Fire Protection: | $ 6,831,286 |
| Paramedic Services: | $ 2,835,497 |
| Disaster Preparedness: | $ 69,451 |
| Weed Abatement: | $ 3,328 |
| Equipment Replacement: | $ 781,000 |
| Total Budget | $ 10,520,562 |

## Section 11-3: Review

### Understanding Key Concepts

1. What does civic responsibility involve?
2. What social issues face responsible citizens?
3. What are three types of taxes?

### Thinking Creatively

Do you really live in a free country if you have to pay taxes and obey laws?

Why is voting so important?

### Taking It a Step Further

Prepare a brochure, poster, or PowerPoint presentation that informs teenagers of their civic responsibilities.

## Spotlight on a Career

### Deborah Koh, Owner
### Enos Salon and Spa

I own a salon and spa at Fort Benjamin Harrison. I am a cosmetologist, massage therapist, permanent makeup artist, accountant, advertising director, and maintenance supervisor. Those are quite a few hats for one person to wear. However, I find that my clients are friends, not customers, which makes my efforts seem worthwhile.

When I was in high school in Korea, I set a goal of being a research scientist. After getting my diploma, I studied cosmetology so that I would have a way to support myself while I attended college.

In college, I majored in chemistry and had a minor in biology. After I graduated from college, I achieved my goal. I accepted a position as a research scientist. In it, I developed devices for measuring LDL (low-density lipoprotein) cholesterol. The company where I worked was quite small—less than 100 employees. Getting to know my co-workers gave me an opportunity to meet people with different educational and cultural backgrounds. I enjoyed adjusting to the diversity. However, I knew that I wanted to own my own business and develop strong relationships with people. I quit my job and started my salon.

My greatest struggle in owning a business is trying to balance my work with my personal life. A beginning business takes a great deal of time and energy. In my limited free time, I enjoy shopping with my three children, cooking, and singing.

# Chapter Review and Activities

The following sections can help you review the contents of this chapter.

## Key Concepts

Following are the key concepts presented in the chapter.

▸ The American economy is a free enterprise system, based on the key principles of supply and demand of goods and services, competition, and entrepreneurship.

▸ Advancements in technology have led to a global economy, in which countries around the world compete for business.

▸ As people mature, they should take on more responsibility for the society in which they live.

▸ Civic responsibilities include voting, being aware of issues within society, and supporting the government financially through taxes.

## Key Term Review

Complete the following activity to review your understanding of the key terms.

| | | |
|---|---|---|
| calculated risk | efficiently | profit |
| capitalism | entrepreneur | recessions |
| civic responsibility | free enterprise system | services |
| competition | globalization | small business |
| consumers | goods | special-interest groups |
| deflation | income taxes | supply |
| demand | ingenuity | textiles |
| democracy | inflation | trends |
| economic system | prejudiced | |

Write a paragraph to someone from another country about the way the American economy operates, using at least 10 vocabulary words.

## Comprehension Review

Answer the following questions to review your understanding of the key concepts in the chapter.

1. Explain how the free enterprise economic system works.

2. What challenges does globalization create for the United States economic system?

3. What are your civic responsibilities?

4. What problems face our society?

5. What is the purpose of taxes?

## School-to-Work

**Math:** Write down the steps you would take to solve this mathematical problem:

> Your gross pay is $1,538.47. The federal tax withheld is $211.13, the state tax is $48.75, the local tax is $10.04, and the F.I.C.A. tax is $109.68. What percentage of your pay goes to those taxes?

**Social Studies:** Find someone in your community who has fought for the United States. Interview that person to find out more about the cause for the conflict and the person's experiences in combat.

**Writing:** Research one of these topics: an issue facing our society, the way taxes are spent, or the cost of health care. Then write a letter to your Senator or member of Congress about the topic, suggesting an alternative. Close the letter by thanking the politician for his attention to the issue and willingness to serve the people of your state.

**Science:** Research the elements of simple machines, find three images of the elements you find most interesting, and create a presentation showing the elements with captions explaining how they work.

## Does This Job Interest You?

The following job ad was posted on the Internet. What education and experience are required? What requirement does this job have that most jobs do not have? What types of education, interests, and skills should a person working in this position have? How could someone apply for the job?

| FIND JOBS | POST RESUMES |
|-----------|--------------|

### Immediate Opening for USCG Licensed Captain

Reeve Enterprises
P.O. Box 210
New York, NY 00001

### Description

IMMEDIATE OPENING FOR USCG LICENSED CAPTAIN to run 63-foot Gold Coast Sailing Catamaran 3-1/2 hour day sailing and snorkeling trips for cruise ship passengers in St. Thomas, U.S. Virgin Islands. Come work in "America's Paradise"—U.S. Virgin Islands!

### Requirements

Must be good with crew and passengers and be experienced in boat maintenance. Vessel is equipped and well-maintained with two Honda 50 HP four-stroke engines. Ability to drive our company's other 100-foot motor vessels to alternate as relief captain would be an advantage. Ideal position for a Captain and spouse (mate or hostess) to operate virtually their own business.

### Contact

Send resume to John Reeve at jreeve@attglobal.net or fax to 300-775-3191.

( Apply Online )

**What career appeals to you?**

*Education and Social Service Careers*

# Chapter 12

# Managing Your Money

## What You'll Learn

▶ Being responsible with the money you earn

▶ Understanding financial services

▶ Using other people's money

▶ Creating a plan for using your money

Do you manage your money, or does it manage you? Do you decide when to spend your money (and on what), or do you just go along with the flow? Do you just hope that you'll have enough money to do all the things your friends do and all the things you want to do? Getting oriented to the workplace involves learning a new role as manager of the money you earn so that it enables you to live the kind of life you want. In this chapter, you will learn about earning money, the businesses that will help you manage your money, how to use other people's money, and how to create a plan to manage your money.

> *He that is of the opinion money will do everything may well be suspected of doing everything for money.*
>
> —Benjamin Franklin (1706–1790)

## Key Terms

| | | |
|---|---|---|
| annual percentage rate (APR) | co-signing | interest |
| automated teller machine (ATM) | credit | mortgage |
| automatic deposit | debit card | online services |
| bankruptcy | debt consolidation | principal |
| certificate of deposit (CD) | down payment | savings account |
| check register | finance charge | spending plan |
| checking account | fixed expense | transit (ABA) number |
| checking account balance | flexible expense | |
| consumer counseling services | impulse buying | |

# Section 12-1: Being Responsible with the Money You Earn

One of the most exciting parts about beginning to work is the knowledge that you will be earning money—your own money. You may need that money to pay for car insurance, to save for college, or to contribute to your family's income, but the money is yours. How would you spend a paycheck?

## Understanding a Paycheck

When you receive your first paycheck, you can calculate your wages by multiplying your hourly rate times the number of hours you work. You may be surprised at the amount on the paycheck. Why did you receive only part of the total amount you earned? Your paycheck stub (the part that often accompanies the check itself) tells the whole story. It shows the following information:

▶ Dates of pay period

▶ Gross pay or the total amount of earnings

▶ Deductions or the money taken out of the total amount of earnings.

▶ Net pay (also called take-home pay) or the gross pay minus deductions

▶ Total hours worked

▶ Other pay for working overtime (more than 40 hours per week) or bonuses (extra money for excellent work)

Don't throw your paycheck stubs away; they are important. The law requires you to keep them for at least three years for tax purposes.

You might choose to have some money taken from your pay, such as health plans, life insurance, savings and retirement plans, professional and/or union dues, charitable contributions (giving money to good causes) and stock purchases. Other required deductions are federal and state income tax (money paid from worker's income to support the government) and FICA (Social Security). These required deductions are the largest ones taken from your paycheck. How does your employer know how much to deduct from your paycheck?

Every time you begin a new job, you must fill out a W-4 tax form. Your employer uses the number of withholding allowances that you write on the W-4 form to find how much money to deduct from each of your paychecks. You can claim one allowance for yourself, one for your spouse (if you are married), and one for each of your dependents (the people you support financially). The total money deducted from all your paychecks in one year usually comes close to equaling your annual tax bill. How do you know what that bill is?

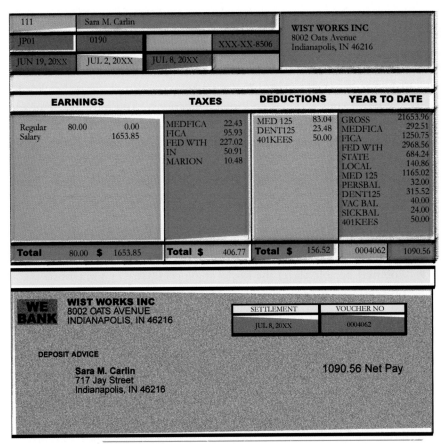

*Can you explain the parts of a paycheck and stub?*

**a** Control number   22222   Void ☐   For Official Use Only ►
OMB No. 1545-0008

| **b** Employer identification number | **1** Wages, tips, other compensation | **2** Federal income tax withheld |
| --- | --- | --- |
| **c** Employer's name, address, and ZIP code | **3** Social security wages | **4** Social security tax withheld |
| | **5** Medicare wages and tips | **6** Medicare tax withheld |
| | **7** Social security tips | **8** Allocated tips |
| **d** Employee's social security number | **9** Advance EIC payment | **10** Dependent care benefits |
| **e** Employee's first name and initial  Last name | **11** Nonqualified plans | **12a** See instructions for box 12 |
| | **13** Statutory employee  Retirement plan  Third-party sick pay | **12b** |
| | **14** Other | **12c** |
| **f** Employee's address and ZIP code | | |
| **15** State  Employer's state ID number   **16** State wages, tips, etc.   **17** State income tax | | |

Form **W-2** Wage and Tax Statement

Copy A For Social Security Administration — Send this entire page with Form W-3 to the Social Security Administration; photocopies are **not** acceptable.  Cat. No. 10134D

**Do Not Cut, Fold, or Staple Forms on This Page — Do Not C**

*What are the purposes of these forms?*

---

‑ ‑ ‑ ‑ ‑ Cut here and give Form W-4 to your employer. Keep the top part for your records. ‑ ‑ ‑ ‑ ‑

Form **W-4**   **Employee's Withholding Allowance Certificate**   OMB No. 1545-0010

Department of the Treasury
Internal Revenue Service  ► Your employer must send a copy of this form to the IRS if: (a) you claim more than 10 allowances or (b) you claim "Exempt" and your wages are normally more than $200 per week.

**1** Type or print your first name and middle initial  Last name   **2** Your social security number

Home address (number and street or rural route)   **3** ☐ Single ☐ Married ☐ Married, but withhold at higher Single rate.
Note: If married, but legally separated, or spouse is a nonresident alien, check the "Single" box.

City or town, state, and ZIP code   **4** If your last name differs from that shown on your social security card, check here. You must call 1-800-772-1213 for a new card. ► ☐

**5** Total number of allowances you are claiming (from line **H** above **or** from the applicable worksheet on page 2)  **5**
**6** Additional amount, if any, you want withheld from each paycheck  **6** $
**7** I claim exemption from withholding for 20XX, and I certify that I meet **both** of the following conditions for exemption:
  • Last year I had a right to a refund of **all** Federal income tax withheld because I had **no** tax liability **and**
  • This year I expect a refund of **all** Federal income tax withheld because I expect to have **no** tax liability.
  If you meet both conditions, write "Exempt" here  ►  **7**

Under penalties of perjury, I certify that I am entitled to the number of withholding allowances claimed on this certificate, or I am entitled to claim exempt status.

**Employee's signature**
(Form is not valid unless you sign it.) ►    Date ►

**8** Employer's name and address (Employer: Complete lines 8 and 10 only if sending to the IRS.)   **9** Office code (optional)   **10** Employer identification number (EIN)

For Privacy Act and Paperwork Reduction Act Notice, see page 2.   Cat. No. 10220Q   Form **W-4**

---

*Why are ATM machines both helpful and harmful?*

Every year you will receive a W-2 form from your employer by January 31. The W-2 states your earnings and total deductions. You must file state and federal tax return forms by April 15 for the previous year's earnings. In the required tax forms, you calculate the amount of money you still need to pay or any refund owed to you from the government. You can get the forms you need to complete in four ways:

▸ State and federal governments send you the forms if they have your correct address.

▸ You can download the forms from government Web sites.

▸ You may be able to get the forms at a local library or some post offices.

▸ Tax-preparation software provides the forms.

## Using Financial Institutions

What do you do with the money that you earn? Will you keep it in your purse or pocket until you've spent it all? Should you store it in a safe place in your room?

One of the first steps you will want to take after you begin receiving a regular paycheck is to open checking and savings accounts. A **checking account** is an account that usually has a small fee for each use. You may pay for each time you write a check or use an **automated teller machine (ATM)** (a banking machine that gives you 24-hour access to banking services), an ATM card (a plastic card you can use only with the ATM machine), or a **debit card** (a card that lets you withdraw the money for a purchase from your bank account without writing a check). A **savings account** is an account that pays you a small amount of money (called **interest**) for maintaining a balance and from which you rarely withdraw money.

You will need to carefully select the business that you trust with your money. You can choose a bank, which welcomes everyone, or a credit union. Membership in a credit union often is not open everyone. Instead, it is limited to people who are in the same occupation (such as teachers) or belong to a certain community or association (such as a club). You may want to talk with your parents, neighbors, and friends to get their feedback on which one they like the best.

Remember that many financial institutions are available. You will want to shop around for the one that best meets your needs. When making your decision, use the problem-solving step of comparing alternatives. Check and compare the features that each institution offers, such as

▶ Charges for checking accounts

▶ Interest rates for savings

▶ Convenient hours

▶ Deposit insurance (FDIC)

▶ Interest rate charged for loans

▶ Location of bank

▶ 24-hour online and ATM services

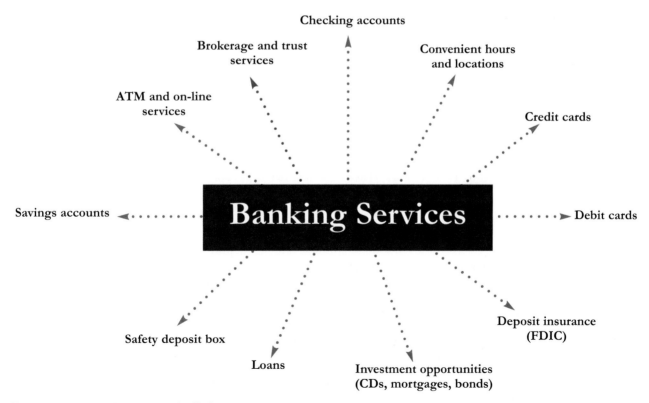

*How many services does your bank offer?*

*What information is required on a personal check?*

**DISCRIMINATION**

**Is This a Case of Gender Discrimination?**

You just learned something interesting. When you were walking past the employee lockers, you saw a piece of paper on the ground. You picked it up, turned it over, and saw the check stub for the only female who works in your position. Her hourly rate is $1.00 lower than the hourly rate of three other guys and you who were all hired on the same day. Is she being discriminated against because of her gender?

Before you open a checking account, ask whether the business has a required minimun balance (a certain amount of money that you must always have in your account). Ask about free checking. Other questions you need to ask are these: How many checks can you write each month for free? What is the charge for additional checks? When can you have a debit card? How much does the institution charge when you don't have enough money in the bank, called nonsufficient funds (NSF), usually a flat fee for each bounced check (a check written for more money than you have in your account)? Many financial institutions will also provide **online services** so that you can manage your money from your computer.

Opening a savings account is very similar to opening a checking account. You might choose to open an account at the same bank where you have your checking account, or you might select a different financial institution. Again, shop around for the best interest rate.

Some accounts, called negotiable order of withdrawal (NOW) accounts, are available. They combine the benefits of checking and savings. These accounts typically require a larger minimum balance, but you earn interest on your account balance and have no service charge for transactions.

## Using Checking Accounts

When you open your checking account, you will receive a box of blank checks from the bank. At the upper-right corner of the check is the check number. At the bottom of each check are three numbers: the **transit (ABA) number** (the numeric code for your bank), your checking account number, and the check number again.

When writing a check, make sure that your writing clearly communicates the important information. You need to write the date in the line provided. You can write out the month, day, and year: May 15, 2006. If you prefer, you can just use two-digit numbers and hyphens: 05-15-06. In the line that has the words *Pay to the Order of*, write out the name of the person or company you are paying.

In the short line beginning with the $, use numbers to write the amount of the check: $1504.25. In the line that ends with the word *Dollars*, write out the number words of the amount of the check: One thousand five hundred four and $^{25}/_{100}$. If the line has blank space after the written number, draw a line to the word *Dollars*. Doing so prevents anyone from changing the amount of the check.

In the *For* line, you can write your account number if you're paying a bill or a reminder to yourself about the purpose of the check. Then write your signature on the line above the check number. You're not finished with the check, though, until you record it in the check register.

The **check register** is a little booklet of pages of blank columns and rows for recording the date, check number or type of withdrawal, the name you wrote in the *Pay to the Order of* line or source of the deposits, the amount of each withdrawal, and any deposits. You also use the check register to keep track of your account balance. What type of math would you have to do to keep accurate records of your balance?

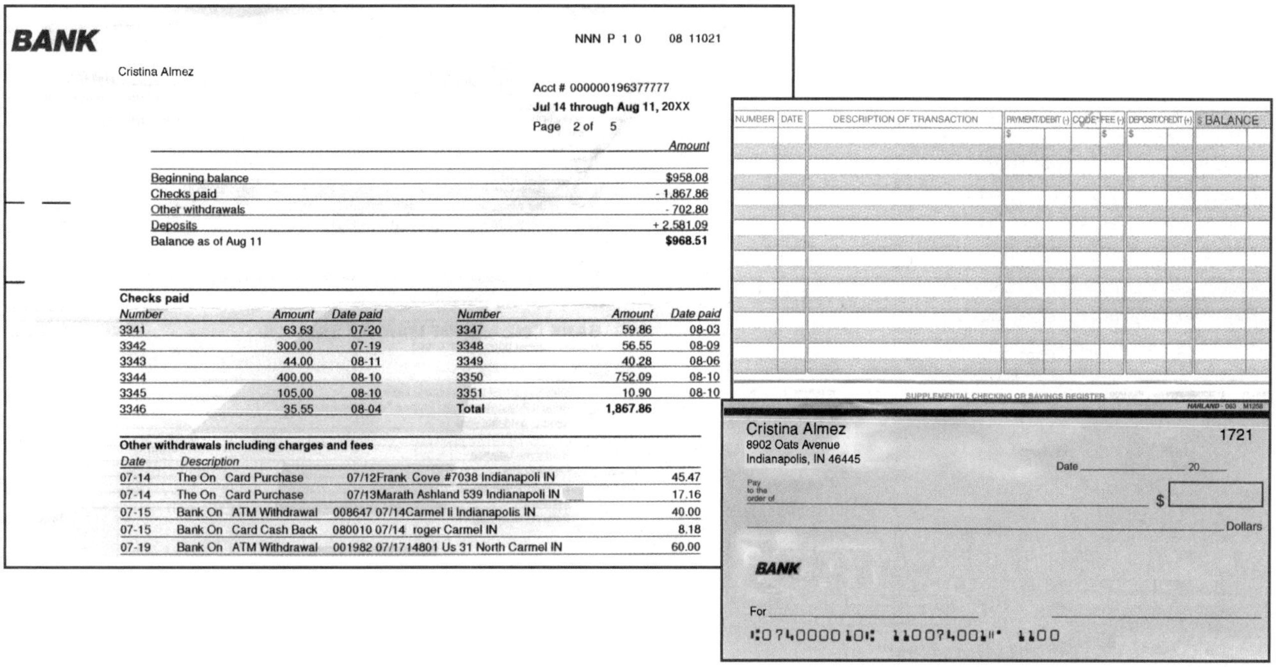

**BANK** NNN P 1 0 08 11021

Cristina Almez

Acct # 000000196377777
Jul 14 through Aug 11, 20XX
Page 2 of 5

| | Amount |
|---|---|
| Beginning balance | $958.08 |
| Checks paid | - 1,867.86 |
| Other withdrawals | - 702.80 |
| Deposits | + 2,581.09 |
| Balance as of Aug 11 | $968.51 |

Checks paid

| Number | Amount | Date paid | Number | Amount | Date paid |
|---|---|---|---|---|---|
| 3341 | 63.63 | 07-20 | 3347 | 59.86 | 08-03 |
| 3342 | 300.00 | 07-19 | 3348 | 56.55 | 08-09 |
| 3343 | 44.00 | 08-11 | 3349 | 40.28 | 08-06 |
| 3344 | 400.00 | 08-10 | 3350 | 752.09 | 08-10 |
| 3345 | 105.00 | 08-10 | 3351 | 10.90 | 08-10 |
| 3346 | 35.55 | 08-04 | Total | 1,867.86 | |

Other withdrawals including charges and fees

| Date | Description | | |
|---|---|---|---|
| 07-14 | The On Card Purchase | 07/12Frank Cove #7038 Indianapoli IN | 45.47 |
| 07-14 | The On Card Purchase | 07/13Marath Ashland 539 Indianapoli IN | 17.16 |
| 07-15 | Bank On ATM Withdrawal | 008647 07/14Carmel li Indianapolis IN | 40.00 |
| 07-15 | Bank On Card Cash Back | 080010 07/14 roger Carmel IN | 8.18 |
| 07-19 | Bank On ATM Withdrawal | 001982 07/1714801 Us 31 North Carmel IN | 60.00 |

| NUMBER | DATE | DESCRIPTION OF TRANSACTION | PAYMENT/DEBIT (-) | CODE | FEE (-) | DEPOSIT/CREDIT (+) | $ BALANCE |
|---|---|---|---|---|---|---|---|

SUPPLEMENTAL CHECKING OR SAVINGS REGISTER

Cristina Almez
8902 Oats Avenue
Indianapolis, IN 46445

1721

Date ____ 20__

Pay to the order of ____ $

____ Dollars

BANK

For ____

⑆074000010⑆ 110074001⑈ 1100

*Do you know how to write a personal check, record it in the check register, and balance a checkbook?*

You may also receive an ATM bank card and a password (a secret word or number that only you know) to access the ATM. You can use the ATM card to make deposits and withdraw cash from your checking account. You should record every ATM transaction into your check register.

To deposit a check that is written out to you, you must *endorse* it (sign the back of the check) and fill out a deposit slip. When you give these items to the teller, he or she will give you a receipt showing the amount you deposited and the date. Be aware that you may not be able to withdraw this money right away because it takes about a day or so for a check to *clear* (for the bank to verify that the check is valid).

By keeping track of your **checking account balance** (money you have in your account) and not spending more money than you have in checking, you can avoid bouncing checks. However, if you make a mistake and deduct more from your account than it has, the results can be costly and embarrassing. The bank will charge you a flat fee (usually $20 or more) for each overdraft. Those charges can equal an annual rate of 1,000 percent or more. In addition to the charge the bank makes, the company receiving the bounced payment will usually charge you from $25 to $40. A bounced check of $5.00, for example, could result in a $45 charge.

Each month, your bank will send you a statement—either through the mail or on your computer. This statement lists checks, ATM transactions, deposits, and service charges. Always check the bank statement against your check register, a process called checkbook balancing. If you find a mistake and can't balance your check register against your bank statement, contact your bank for help. It is very unlikely that your bank made a mistake, but it can help you get your account back on track.

**ETHICS**

**What Do You Do When No One Is Looking?**

You are the last one to close up the store. It is your job to count the total money in the cash drawer at the end of the day; leave four $5s, three $10s, two $20s, and $10 in change in the drawer; prepare a deposit slip; and take the extra cash to the night deposit box at the bank. No one would have any way of knowing whether you wrote down the correct amount. What will you do?

## Using Saving Accounts

The paperwork involved in tracking a savings account is usually much simpler than that of a checking account. If you're using the savings account the right way, you are depositing money into it on a regular basis. You rarely withdraw money from it. You just record a deposit onto the register and add it to the previous balance.

If you have your checking and savings accounts with the same institution, your monthly statement will list the transactions and current balance of both. If you have the savings account with another institution, you will receive regular statements. They may arrive quarterly (once every three months), not monthly.

When you get your first job, make up your mind to set aside a certain percentage, perhaps as much as 10 percent, of every dollar you earn. Although 10 percent might not seem to be very much if you're earning $1,000 per month, it will add up. In one year's time, you will have saved $1,200 plus the interest earned on the savings. In 20 years, you will have saved $24,000 plus the interest. If you deposit a certain amount of money into a savings account and never add additional funds, your balance will still increase, but at a slower rate.

| Year | Beginning Balance | Interest Rate | Yearly Interest | Ending Balance |
|------|-------------------|---------------|-----------------|----------------|
| 2009 | $500.00 | 0.0235 | 11.75 | $511.75 |
| 2010 | 511.75 | 0.0235 | 12.03 | 523.78 |
| 2011 | 523.78 | 0.0235 | 12.31 | 536.08 |
| 2012 | 536.08 | 0.0235 | 12.60 | 548.68 |
| 2013 | 548.68 | 0.0235 | 12.89 | 561.58 |
| 2014 | 561.58 | 0.0235 | 13.20 | 574.77 |

*How does your savings grow?*

## Automatically Depositing Your Paycheck

Many people choose to use **automatic deposit** (the employer deposits each paycheck directly into an employee's account or accounts). Automatic deposit is convenient because you don't have to make a trip to the bank to deposit paychecks before you can begin spending your money. If your employer offers automatic deposit, you must complete the paperwork to set it up. On the form, you can choose whether to deposit the entire amount into checking, savings, or a combination of both. You will be asked to submit a blank check or deposit slip with the word *Void* written across it for each account that is to receive money. The form gives your employer the correct transit or ABA numbers and your account numbers. When you choose to use automatic deposit, you still receive a paycheck stub from your employer, but the check portion is marked *Void*.

**Are You a Worrier?**

Do you wonder "What if I don't have enough money or time? What if I can't make it on my own? What if I don't get accepted into the program that I want?"

Retrain your brain to think this way:

▶ It's okay to feel uneasy about a new situation.

▶ Worrying doesn't solve problems; problem solving solves problems.

▶ I have or can find the tools I need to face whatever comes my way.

▶ I will set goals, think of possible solutions, and act on the best one.

### DIVERSITY

**Does Being Loud Mean That You're Losing Control?**

One of your co-workers gets very loud whenever anything goes wrong. He never apologizes because he says that's what he's feeling, and he has a right to express it. You feel as if he will lose control and go berserk because no one in your family ever yells. You always discuss problems calmly. Whose method is right?

Automatic deposit is an excellent way to save money. You can deduct a certain amount from your paycheck to be deposited to your savings account. The benefits of automatic deposits to your savings account are two. You usually will not even notice the change in your paycheck. You probably will not be tempted to withdraw the money from the savings account.

## Looking at Other Banking Services

Financial institutions provide many more services besides checking and savings accounts. These services will become more important to you as you earn more money, have money to invest, or need larger sums of money. For example, a **certificate of deposit (CD)** pays a higher rate of interest to customers than a savings account pays, but you must deposit a larger amount of money and leave it in the bank for a longer period of time or else the bank will charge you a substantial early withdrawal penalty (a fee for taking the money out early).

Banks also provide safe deposit boxes (a small box inside a secure vault to hold valuables such as important documents, jewelry, coins, and so on), travelers' checks, and **consumer counseling services** (a service that gives advice to people who do not manage money well). Banks also provide credit services, consumer loans, and mortgages (discussed in the next section).

## Ways to Save

| Type | Description | Advantage | Disadvantage |
| --- | --- | --- | --- |
| Passbook Savings | Any amount of money can be deposited. | Can open account with even very small amounts of money. Easy to take money out if needed. Insured by FDIC. | Very low interest. Interest rates can change. |
| Certificate of Deposit (CD) | Money needs to be invested for a specific amount of time (usually six months to several years). Interest is paid on the balance. | Guaranteed fixed rate of interest. Rate better than passbook savings. Insured by FDIC. | Must deposit larger amount. Money not easily available. Penalty for withdrawing money early. |
| Money Market or Mutual Funds | Many investors combine their money. | Pays higher interest than passbook savings. Money can be withdrawn anytime. | Minimum deposit required. Interest rates vary. |
| U.S. Savings Bond | Insured by government. Government borrows your money and pays it back. | Guaranteed by U.S. Treasury. No taxes on income until you turn bond in for money.* | Have to store the bonds, which may cause problems. |

*For example, $25 buys a $50 bond in seven years, and the bond continues to earn interest beyond $50 until you cash it in (turn it in for money).

*What type of savings plan would you choose? Why?*

# Section 12-2: Using Other People's Money

There will be times in your life when you will not have enough money to make an important purchase. You will need to use other people's money to buy the item on credit. The word *credit* comes from a Latin word meaning "trust." Financial institutions and businesses (called creditors) trust you to pay them back when you use **credit**, or borrow money. When you borrow money, you take on a new role with certain responsibilities: You become a debtor. You are responsible for paying back the money you borrow. Credit bureaus keep a credit rating report, a record of every time you purchase something on credit and whether you make your payments on time and for the correct amounts. A good credit rating is one of the best financial tools you will ever have.

Extending credit to people is the main way that banks, other financial institutions, and finance companies make money. For every dollar loaned to a person, the company makes money. **Finance charges** are the total dollar amount paid by the borrower for using the money. Those charges are based on the amount of money you borrow and the interest rate at which you agree to borrow it. The **annual percentage rate (APR)** is the percentage cost of credit that you pay on a yearly basis.

When you are saving money, you want the interest rate to be high. When you are borrowing money, you want the interest rate to be low. If you borrow $1,000 for one year from a bank and it charges you 15 percent APR, for example, you will pay the bank $150 for using its money. The bank then uses the $150 to pay interest on the savings people have in the bank. The remainder is the bank's profit.

Banks aren't the only financial institutions that loan money to people. A credit union is another type of lending institution. Its interest rates are usually low. Remember that you must be a member to borrow money from a credit union. A consumer finance company is a financial institution that specializes in making loans. It usually charges a higher interest rate because it is willing to loan money to people with poor credit or no credit rating.

## Borrowing Money

If you want to borrow money (also called applying for credit), you have to fill out a credit application. It is very important to read the application carefully. Answer each question truthfully.

Buying anything on credit is quite costly! Your responsibility as a good consumer is to shop around for the best credit options. When you are comparing loan or credit card offers, read all paperwork and ask the following questions before you sign:

▶ What is the minimum monthly payment?

▶ What is the APR (annual percentage rate)?

▶ If the interest rate is adjustable, how much can it increase at one time?

▶ What is the maximum interest rate?

▶ Does the loan have annual and transaction fees?

The APR is the most important comparison you will make.

Not everyone can buy on credit. They may not have a good credit rating. If you are under age 18, you cannot get credit. Typically, if you don't have a job, you cannot get credit. And, if you have chosen not to pay or couldn't pay back credit in the past, you cannot get more credit (or you will have to pay very high interest rates).

Many young people are dependent on adults to help them establish a credit rating and buy on credit. An adult can choose to help you by **co-signing** (signing a legal contract that states that the adult will be financially responsible for your loan or credit card debt if you don't pay on time). This positive step can help you establish your own credit as long as you make your payments. Another step is to open a savings account. Having one helps you establish a credit record.

*How is filling out a credit application similar to filling out a job application?*

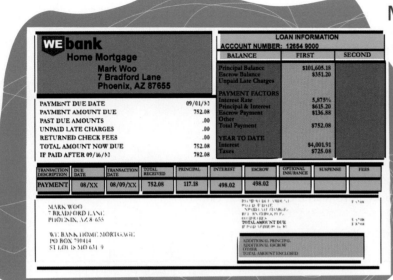

| | | | LOAN INFORMATION | | |
|---|---|---|---|---|---|
| | | ACCOUNT NUMBER: 12654 9000 | | | |
| | | BALANCE | FIRST | SECOND | |

**WE bank**
Home Mortgage
Mark Woo
7 Bradford Lane
Phoenix, AZ 87655

| | | | | |
|---|---|---|---|---|
| Principal Balance | | | $101,605.18 | |
| Escrow Balance | | | $351.20 | |
| Unpaid Late Charges | | | | |
| | | | | |
| PAYMENT FACTORS | | | | |
| Interest Rate | | | 5.875% | |
| Principal & Interest | | | $615.20 | |
| Escrow Payment | | | $136.88 | |
| Other | | | | |
| Total Payment | | | $752.08 | |
| | | | | |
| YEAR TO DATE | | | | |
| Interest | | | $4,001.91 | |
| Taxes | | | $725.08 | |

| PAYMENT DUE DATE | 09/01/XX |
|---|---|
| PAYMENT AMOUNT DUE | 752.08 |
| PAST DUE AMOUNTS | .00 |
| UNPAID LATE CHARGES | .00 |
| RETURNED CHECK FEES | .00 |
| TOTAL AMOUNT NOW DUE | 752.08 |
| IF PAID AFTER 09/16/XX | 782.08 |

| TRANSACTION DESCRIPTION | DUE DATE | TRANSACTION DATE | TOTAL RECEIVED | PRINCIPAL | INTEREST | ESCROW | OPTIONAL INSURANCE | SUSPENSE | FEES |
|---|---|---|---|---|---|---|---|---|---|
| PAYMENT | 08/XX | 08/09/XX | 752.08 | 117.18 | 498.02 | 498.02 | | | |

MARK WOO
7 BRADFORD LANE
PHOENIX, AZ 8 655

WE BANK HOME MORTGAGE
PO BOX 790414
ST LOUIS MO 631 9

*How much is being paid in interest?*
*How much is being paid in principal?*

# Mortgages

Most people use credit to buy a home. According to the National Association of Realtors, the median price of a home today is about $224,000. Most people don't have that much money in their checking or savings account. They choose to borrow the money using a form of credit called a **mortgage**. To qualify for a mortgage, you usually must have a good credit rating and make a **down payment** (a beginning payment that is a certain percentage of the total cost of the item). Each month, you make a payment to the institution. A portion of the payment pays the **principal** (the amount borrowed). The other portion pays the interest on the mortgage.

# Installment Credit

Another type of credit is called installment credit. As with mortgages, the total amount of the installment credit is divided into smaller parts and paid at specific times, usually once each month. Typically, the lender requires a down payment. The more expensive the item, the higher the down payment. Installment credit is usually used for big items such as a car, swimming pool, or appliance.

# Credit Cards

All too often, Americans also choose to purchase many other items on credit including clothes, entertainment, food, gasoline, and personal items. You might say that "buy now and pay later" has become the American way. Why is this so common?

More than likely, your parents receive advertisements in the mail and on the Internet for credit card and loan opportunities several times each week. Credit cards make purchasing very easy. But it is also every easy to overspend. Do you know anyone who has gotten into serious credit card debt?

Major credit cards such as American Express, MasterCard, and Visa are called multipurpose credit cards. Typically, banks sponsor these cards. When businesses let their customers use major credit cards, the businesses must pay the bank that issued the card a small fee for each charge made. The customer who is the cardholder also makes a monthly payment for the interest and for the charges that month or for the unpaid balance. The banks are making money both from the businesses and from the customers of the businesses.

Credit cards can also be single-purpose cards. Gasoline credit cards and department store credit cards are examples. Each card is valid at only one particular business. Again, the cardholder pays the business for interest on charges made or the unpaid balance on a monthly basis.

## Handling Debt Problems

It is estimated that more than 35 million people in the United States have a debt problem. Many people face serious debt problems today for several reasons, including college expenses, layoffs and salary cuts, and family emergencies.

Using your communication skills and the problem-solving process is important if you ever find yourself facing serious debt problems. The first step is to notify your creditors of the problems as soon as you realize that you will not be able to make payments. Then you need to find out what your alternatives are before you make a decision. There are many ways to handle financial problems, including debt consolidation, debt consolidation loans, or—as a last resort—**bankruptcy**, a condition in which a person or business cannot pay debts.

In a **debt consolidation**, you ask a nonprofit organization to arrange lower payments and interest rates with your creditors. You then stop using credit for your current purchases. Instead you make one payment to the debt consolidation service, which sends portions of that payment to each of your creditors.

*Why do people sometimes overspend when using credit cards?*

Studies predict that job opportunities for special education teachers will increase because the number of special education students is rising, and there is a shortage of qualified teachers. Special education is a general term that covers many areas: speech or language, mental retardation, emotional, hearing, sight, physical disabilities, and other health problems. Special education teachers design and then teach specific lessons for their students.

## Know Your Rights

As a debtor, not only do you have definite responsibilities, but you also have specific legal rights. The United States government has established several credit acts to protect you:

▶ The Equal Credit Opportunity Act requires a creditor (the organization loaning the money) to notify you within 30 days whether you have been approved for a loan. If you were denied, it must tell you specifically why or tell you how you can request that information.

▶ The Fair Credit Reporting Act requires that credit agencies share your file with you. If you are denied credit, they must tell you the specific reason.

▶ The Truth in Lending Act limits your liability for lost or stolen credit cards and ensures that you receive monthly statements from the issuer of your credit cards.

▶ The Fair and Accurate Credit Transactions Act of 2003 ensures that all citizens are treated fairly when they apply for a mortgage or other form of credit.

When you are aware of your rights, you can protect yourself from companies that might try to take advantage of you.

*What can too much debt do to a person or a family?*

A debt consolidation loan is similar to the debt consolidation service, but you get a loan to pay off all your other creditors. You then make payments on that one loan. However, a debt consolidation loan might encourage people to continue to live beyond their means, which can lead to bankruptcy.

A bankruptcy has two purposes. It gives the creditors a fair share of the debtor's money or property, as determined by the National Bankruptcy Act. It can be voluntary or involuntary. Second, bankruptcy gives the debtor a fresh start. Many times people believe that bankruptcy is the only option. However, bankruptcy is not the best choice because it can

▶ Ruin your chances of getting a loan

▶ Leave a bad mark on your credit report for 10 years

▶ Keep you from getting the job you want

▶ Severely hurt your financial future

It is important to seek financial counseling help when you cannot solve credit problems. Check your local telephone directory or use key search words online such as "credit counseling."

# Case Study: Should Jessica Buy a Truck?

Jessica is a junior in college and is working with a financial counselor to help her figure out how she can manage her debts and afford to buy a truck. She is $40,000 in debt at age 21. How did this happen?

▸ Her college expenses are $16,000 per year, which include tuition, books, and room and board. Her parents pay her tuition ($5,000 each year), she saves $1,000 from her summer job, and she receives $10,000 each year in student loans (which she does not have to repay until she graduates).

▸ After receiving "free" credit cards, she maxed out two cards at $5,000 each. She is able to pay only the minimum amount due on the credit cards, which is just the interest.

▸ Her part-time job gives her about $100 a week from which she must pay personal expenses, bus fare, and the credit card bills.

**Can Jessica afford a truck?**
**What would you advise her to do?**

## Section 12-2: Review

### Understanding Key Concepts

1. In the context of this chapter, what is credit?
2. How can a teenager establish a good credit rating?
3. What should you do if you cannot pay your bills?

### Thinking Creatively

Explain how borrowing money from a bank, a credit union, and a consumer finance company differ.

Why is it important for the United States government to oversee organizations that extend credit to consumers?

What are the advantages and disadvantages of filing for bankruptcy?

### Taking It a Step Further

Research three credit card companies. Create a spreadsheet that compares their services and interest rates. Then write a paragraph of at least five complete sentences, comparing and contrasting the companies. Your concluding sentence should state which credit card you think is the best.

# Section 12-3: Creating Your Own Spending Plan

How can you avoid getting into credit trouble? Begin now to think about your role as the manager of your money. Many people don't like the word *budget* because it sounds so negative. Unfortunately, they don't budget properly because they've never been taught how. Financial advisors suggest that instead of creating a budget, you create a **spending plan** (a plan for saving and spending your income). But where do you begin?

## Keep Track of Your Spending

The best way to begin creating a spending plan is to keep track of every expense, even snacks and soft drinks, for one month. This tracking takes a great deal of time, but it's not difficult. Using a list like the one showing Jessica's income and expenses, write down all your income and expenses.

You'll be recording two kinds of expenses: fixed and flexible. **Fixed expenses** are those you pay every week or month; **flexible expenses** can vary and are not the same every week or month. Keeping track of all those expenses will probably be a major eye-opening experience for you! It is amazing how they quickly add up.

The cost of ownership is one area of expense that your record keeping will reveal. It's really easy to forget that the cost of owning something is frequently more than its purchase price. One of the best examples is a car or truck. What expenses will you have to pay when you own a vehicle? Those operating expenses add up very quickly.

*Everyone wants to experience "the great American dream," but what is needed most is a solid money management plan.*

*—Personal Money Management*

**Impulse buying** is buying things without thinking about the consequences. It can add up to big amounts. Writing down every thing you spend and taking a good look at your list will help you identify your "spending leaks." Then avoid these leaks by not using shopping as a form of entertainment. Do not go to the mall to socialize with friends or just spend time. Usually those trips to the mall result in some spending, even if it's just for food or small items.

## Case Study: What Did Jessica Discover?

Monthly Income: $400

Monthly Expenses:

    Groceries and personal items - $140

    DVD - $15

    Rock concert ticket - $40 (charged on her credit card)

    Souvenir T-shirt from rock concert - $20

    Dinner date - $30 (charged on her credit card)

    Rent - $350 (included in college loan)

    Cell phone bill - $40

    Credit card bill - $75 (remember that she owes $10,000)

    Savings - $0

**How much did Jessica spend in cash?**

**How much did she charge?**

**Which of these expenses are fixed and which are flexible?**

**Does she have any cash left over? Could she save any money?**

**In addition to Jessica's $10,000 of debt on two credit card bills, how much did she charge this past month?**

**Is there hope for Jessica?**

# Follow the Three Rules for Responsible Money Management

How can you control your spending? How can you keep from getting into too much debt? Consider these three rules for responsible money management:

- ▶ Live within your means.
- ▶ Take care of your future.
- ▶ Maximize your pleasure.

*What happens when people do not control their spending?*

## Live Within Your Means

The first rule, living within your means, requires that you not allow your expenses to exceed your income. Expenses today are very different from those in the past. In the past, food, shelter, clothing, and financial security were the requirements. Today, many young people have their own computer and their own cell phone. Do you have to have these items? If you are to live within your means, what can you do without?

To live within your means, you must develop patience. The "can't-wait" attitude can be a real money management trap. Many young people want to start out where their parents are now. What they forget is that they must be patient. It took their parents 20 or 25 years of working, saving, and doing without to get to a comfortable financial position.

To live within your means, you need to ignore commercials, ads, and sales flyers. You will find that many times you want more than you actually need, partially because the media constantly sends the message to "buy, buy, buy!"

To live within your means, you must be a wise shopper. Never purchase products and services without comparing prices and values. To be wise in your shopping, read labels. Check warranties (companies' promises to fix or replace defective equipment), and read contracts. Avoid salespeople who pressure you to buy immediately.

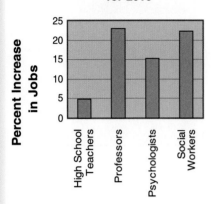

**Projected Outlook for 2016**

*What does this chart tell you about future opportunities in these careers?*

*What must you have in order to survive?*

## Take Care of Your Future

Avoid overusing credit. Credit itself is neither good nor bad. It can be a real help when you need it, but it can also get you in deep debt if you don't use it carefully. If you do have to use credit, remember three key points:

▶ Shop around for the best credit terms.

▶ Keep track of your credit expenses.

▶ Remember that everything you purchase on credit today impacts your financial future.

To feel comfortable about your financial future, you must have cash on reserve. Financial advisors recommend that you maintain enough cash savings to cover three months' expenses. Knowing that you have that money to fall back on in an emergency can give you a sense of security.

Plan for large expenses. Everyone has financial obligations that are due at different times during the year: Set aside some money each week to meet those expenses. Insurance payments are one example. If you currently own a car and must pay insurance of $130 per quarter (four times each year), how can you plan ahead to pay this insurance bill? The money you save for large expenses should be in addition to your cash savings.

Determine your financial goals, based on your values, and then decide what your priorities are. What is one of your future financial goals? Is it going to college? Is it buying a new car or truck? Maybe it's traveling. Of your goals, which one is the most important to you? Which one is the least important to you? Begin definite savings for each of your financial goals. Even small savings of two dollars each week will eventually add up.

The issue of retirement plans is one that in your mind seems so far away that it is not worth your time to discuss. But now is the time to consider retirement plans. Begin the habit of saving money now. The sooner you start saving, the more time your money has to grow.

*When should you create a financial plan for your retirement?*

Many retirement plans are available, including employer's pensions or profit sharing plans; tax-sheltered savings plans, such as a 401(k); individual retirement accounts (IRAs); and your own personal savings. You will need to ask questions. Talk to someone you trust: your employer, your bank, your credit union, or a financial advisor. You need to know these facts about retirement:

▶ Retirement is expensive. Experts estimate that you need about 70 percent of your preretirement income to maintain your standard of living when you stop working.

▶ Social Security pays the average retiree only about 40 percent of preretirement earnings.

▶ Financial security does not just happen. It takes planning, commitment, and (yes!) money.

▶ Less than half of all Americans have put aside money specifically for retirement.

▶ You can't retire with security unless you really prepare for it. That means facing up to reality and beginning to take action for tomorrow as well as today.

▶ Putting away money for retirement gives you freedom when you want it—and deserve it.

▶ The average American spends 18 years in retirement.

Many Americans guess when determining their retirement needs. Don't be one of them. Find out more. Save now and beat the retirement clock.

## An Overview of Retirement Plans

| Plan | Definition | Advantages | Disadvantages |
|---|---|---|---|
| Employer's pension and retirement | Employee has money deducted from paycheck. Some employers match employee contributions. | Money is deducted automatically. Employer's matching funds are free gifts. | Employer may not offer good investment options. |
| Profit-sharing | An employer gives a portion of the company's earnings to a retirement account for each employee. | The account is free. | Contributions are impacted by the company's profits. Can be difficult for a business to process. |
| Individual retirement account (IRA) | A person establishes an account and contributes no more than a maximum amount established by the government. | Provides a way to save additional money for retirement and defer or avoid paying taxes. | Penalties for early withdrawal. Unclear and changing regulations. |
| Personal savings | A person deposits money into an account. | The owner has total control over the money. | Easy access to money can increase difficulties in saving. |

*Which of these retirements plans would you use? Why?*

## Maximize Your Pleasure

How can you get the maximum pleasure from your hard-earned money? The only way to get more from your money is to know what you value the most and then make sure that you spend your money on what you value.

Decide in advance what you want to do with windfalls (unexpected income). What will you do with your tax refund? How will you use that $50 birthday gift? Will you spend it on impulse buying? Instead of spending your windfall on something you don't really have to have or won't even want six months from now, consider putting it toward credit card expenses or putting some of it into your savings for a financial goal. Above all, make sure that you spend it on what you truly value.

By successfully managing your money, you can "maximize your pleasure." You can buy that new car or truck, take a vacation, or even start thinking about sending your own children to college!

**NETWORKING**

Find and interview someone to get information about educational loans.

**COMMUNITY**

Create a presentation, brochure, poster, and/or article about wise spending for the school newspaper, local paper, local TV/radio station, or school Web site.

*What do you value enough to invest your money in?*

## Section 12-3: Review

### Understanding Key Concepts

1. What is the first step toward creating a spending plan?
2. What are the two types of expenses and how can you identify them?
3. What are the three rules of responsible money management?

### Thinking Creatively

How much money is enough?
How can you personally distinguish between a need and a want?
How can you tell that you've taken good care of your financial future?

### Taking It a Step Further

For one week, keep track of everything you spend by recording it on in a chart. At the end of the week, analyze your spending and write a paragraph that discusses your current spending habits and what they reveal about your values.

## Spotlight on a Career

**Peggy Wild, Ph.D., CFCS**
**State Specialist for Family and Consumer Sciences Education**
**Indiana Department of Education**

I work with about 1,150 Indiana teachers of Family and Consumer Sciences and related courses. One of my main responsibilities is coordinating the development of curriculum for Family and Consumer Sciences departments in middle schools, high schools, and career preparation schools. Another responsibility is providing professional development opportunities for teachers. I am also responsible for helping others understand and value Family and Consumer Sciences programs.

I earned a B.S. degree in Family and Consumer Sciences Education in 1968; a B.A. in Elementary Education; an M.S. in Family and Consumer Sciences Education; and the PhD. in Secondary Education, with a major in Family and Consumer Sciences and concentrations in curriculum and assessment. All four degrees are from the University of Arizona.

I knew I wanted to pursue a career in Family and Consumer Sciences, but I was not sure which area I would pursue. The excellent faculty in Family and Consumer Sciences Education at the University of Arizona helped me sort out all my options and select the education major as my career.

During high school and college, I had part-time and volunteer jobs in the food industry, in early childhood education, and in a human services agency. Because my position includes developing curricula for students who are in those career paths, my work experiences in those areas have given me firsthand knowledge of what the curriculum needs to include.

Reading is my main interest: I read science fiction, mysteries, historical novels, biographies, and self-improvement books. I also enjoy hiking, antiquing, traveling to new places, and visiting friends and relatives.

I have struggled my whole career to figure out how to maintain a balance between work and life. However, my appreciation of the value of my profession and the contributions it makes to society makes my working hours pleasurable, and the learning it requires seems more like leisure than work. I am renewed by looking creatively at how I use my time.

# Chapter Review and Activities

The following sections can help you review the contents of this chapter.

## Key Concepts

Following are the key concepts presented in the chapter.

▶ Money is one of the fundamental tools for living successfully in our society.

▶ One of the most exciting parts about beginning to work is the knowledge that you will be earning your own money and receiving a paycheck.

▶ Look at your paycheck stub carefully to understand why you receive only part of the total amount you earned.

▶ Every year you must file state and federal tax return forms by April 15 for the previous year's earnings.

▶ One of the first steps you should take after you begin receiving a regular paycheck is to open checking and savings accounts.

▶ You need to carefully select the financial institution that you trust with your money.

▶ When writing a check, make sure that your writing clearly communicates the important information.

▶ If you're using a savings account the right way, you are depositing money into it on a regular basis and rarely withdrawing money from it.

▶ When you get your first job, set aside a certain percentage of every dollar you earn.

▶ Automatic deposit is convenient because you don't have to make a trip to the bank to deposit paychecks before you can spend your money.

▶ Financial institutions provide many more services besides checking and savings accounts.

▶ When you borrow money, you take on a new role with certain responsibilities, including paying back the money you borrow.

▶ Credit bureaus keep a credit rating report. A good credit rating is one of the best financial tools you will ever have.

▶ When filling out a credit application, read the application carefully and answer each question truthfully.

▶ Shop around for the best credit options.

> ## TECHNOLOGY
>
> The Internet makes it easy to bank, pay bills, check investments, and shop from a home computer. It also makes it easy for people to commit crimes such as identity theft. Identity theft is when someone uses your name, Social Security number, or other personal information without your permission to steal from you or to commit other crimes.
>
> To protect your valuable personal information while you are online, do not respond to or click links in any e-mail that requests that you update or confirm your account or other personal information, even if the e-mail looks like it's from your bank or credit card company. This scam is called phishing because thieves use it to fish for information that they can steal.
>
> Don't download any files unless you know and trust the source, and don't click links in pop-up windows. Doing so may install spyware on your system. Spyware is software that monitors and controls how you use your computer. You can protect your computer from this type of software by installing a firewall, antivirus software, and the most recent versions of the operating system (such as Windows) and Web browser.
>
> Finally, always look closely at your bank and credit card statements for any unusual withdrawals or purchases or incorrect information. Talk to the bank or credit card company right away if you notice something suspicious.

- The United States government has established several credit acts to protect you. Know your legal rights.

- There are many ways to handle financial problems, including debt consolidation, debt consolidation loans, or bankruptcy. If you realize that you won't be able to make payments, notify your creditors.

- Keeping track of your expenses is the best way to begin creating a spending plan.

- Avoid impulse buying.

- Follow the three rules for responsible money management: Live within your means, take care of your future, and maximize your pleasure.

## Key Term Review

Complete the following activity to review your understanding of the key terms.

| | |
|---|---|
| annual percentage rate (APR) | down payment |
| automated teller machine (ATM) | finance charge |
| automatic deposit | fixed expense |
| bankruptcy | flexible expense |
| certificate of deposit (CD) | impulse buying |
| check register | interest |
| checking account | mortgage |
| checking account balance | online services |
| consumer counseling services | principal |
| co-signing | savings account |
| credit | spending plan |
| debit card | transit (ABA) number |
| debt consolidation | |

You are a social worker who must explain banking and financial services in a workshop for people who have just immigrated to the U.S. Using at least 10 key terms, write a brochure or create a poster or PowerPoint presentation for the group.

## Comprehension Review

Answer the following questions to review your understanding of the key concepts in the chapter.

1. What is the difference between gross and net pay?

2. How are banks and credit unions similar, and how are they different?

3. How are checking and savings accounts similar, and how are they different?

4. What is credit, and how can a teenager establish a good credit rating?

5. What are the two types of expenses, and how can you identify them?

6. What are the three rules of responsible money management?

## School-to-Work

**Math:** You invest $1,000 in a CD that yields 6% annual interest, but you must leave the money in the bank for two years. How much interest will you receive at the end of those two years? Write down the steps you would take to solve this mathematical problem.

**Social Studies:** Governing bodies create budgets to determine the amount of tax dollars to set aside for each service provided to the residents. Research the previous year's budget for your city, town, or county. Prepare a chart of those expenditures. Do you agree with the way the governing officials spent the taxes? Write a paragraph that discusses your findings and opinion.

**Writing:** Research the key words *electronic banking*. Then write a paragraph, explaining the advantages and disadvantages of electronic banking.

**Science:** How do scientists determine the age of rocks and fossils? Conduct research online, and then prepare either a paper with illustrations or a presentation to answer this question.

## Does This Job Interest You?

The following job ad was posted on the Internet. What education and experience are required? What requirement does this job have that most jobs do not have? What types of education, interests, and skills should a person working in this position have? How can someone apply for the job?

---

**FIND JOBS**    **POST RESUMES**

### Theatre Arts Assistant Professor (Design/Technical Theatre)

**College:** Los Rios Community College District
**Job Location:** New York, NY
**Duration:** Full-time, tenure-track position

### Instructional Assignment

The primary instructional assignment will involve teaching Rehearsal and Production, Children's Theatre, Stagecraft, and Lighting. The assignment also can include theatre courses such as Costume Construction, Stage Make-Up, Arts Management, Introduction to the Theatre, and other theatre courses as needed.

### Requirements

1. Have a Master's degree from an accredited institution in drama, theatre arts, or performance completed by August 12, 20XX; OR, have a bachelor's in drama, theatre arts, or performance AND a master's in comparative literature, English, speech, literature, or humanities.
2. Have sensitivity to and understanding of the diverse academic, socioeconomic, cultural, disability, and ethnic backgrounds of community college students.

### Salary

Entering annual salary varies from $38,331 to $63,550 depending upon units and degrees completed at accredited colleges/universities and on verified experience.

### Benefits

The District offers medical/dental plans to employees and eligible dependents—either at no cost, or on a pro-rated basis, depending on the number of hours worked and the plan(s) selected.

### Contact

Please apply online at http://www.nyccd.edu/hr/Facultyapplication.htm

( **Apply Online** )

**What career appeals to you?**

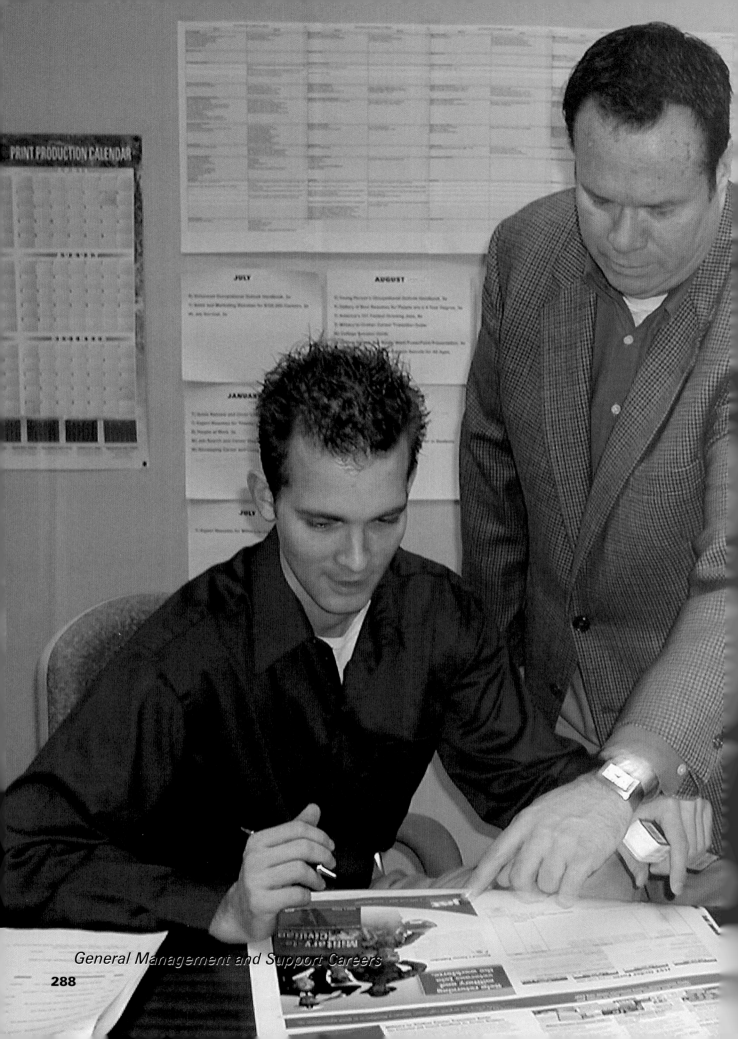

# 13 Becoming a Responsible Consumer

## What You'll Learn

▸ Developing independent living skills

▸ Planning for your future

Moving from childhood to adulthood is not easy. However, most people will choose to become financially responsible and independent. Independent living (supporting yourself) requires a great deal of skill, one you develop by having patience and overcoming mistakes. As you move toward adulthood you will gain control of your life. You will be able to make wise financial choices and decisions in your role as a consumer. You will find a place to live, make arrangements for your own transportation, make sure that you have adequate insurance, and buy food and clothing. You will even plan for your retirement.

*Today's youth are part of our economy and will grow to become the consumers of tomorrow. It is essential that children understand the purpose of advertising, and how they can use it to make better informed consumer choices.*

*—Mike Johnston,*
*CIM's International Chairman*

## Key Terms

| | | |
|---|---|---|
| beneficiary | house brands | policyholder |
| benefits | hygiene | premiums |
| claim | impulse purchases | renter's insurance |
| co-payment | insurance | security deposits |
| deductible | landlord | tenant |
| foreclosure | lease agreement | unit prices |
| generic brands | life insurance | |
| homeowner's insurance | loss leaders | |

# Section 13-1: Developing Consumer Awareness

Before you go shopping for anything, be aware of the advertising tools that companies use to convince you to buy their products. Keep your eye out for advertising techniques. You will see them in printed ads, commercials, and even the language of salespeople:

## Ten Advertising Techniques That Can Trap You

| Technique | Description |
|---|---|
| Avant-Garde | Be the first one to get the product. |
| Bandwagon | To be part of the crowd, use the product. |
| Glittering Generalities | The product is good because of the words used in the ad. |
| Hidden Fears | The product will save you from danger. |
| Humor | The ad makes you laugh so you are attracted to the product it presents. |
| Magic | Nearly magical ingredients make the product more effective than others. |
| Patriotism | You prove your love for your country when you use the product. |
| Plain Folks | The product is a good value because ordinary people prefer it. |
| Snob Appeal | Using the product makes you better than other people. |
| Testimonial | The product is good because a famous person says so. |

Have you ever noticed the advertising on the Internet? You will find some unique strategies businesses have developed just for the Internet.

*Can you identify the advertising techniques used in these three ads?*

## Three Internet Advertising Techniques

| Technique | Description |
| --- | --- |
| Awards and Competitions | A Web site gives its visitors a list of other Web sites to rate. The "award" is a little graphic with the contest sponsor's logo on it. The winner then posts the award and creates a link to the contest sponsor's Web site. |
| Free Stuff | A company puts its logo, name, and Web site address on a mouse pad, screensaver, or small item and sends it to Web site visitors who request it. The Free Stuff link can be added to sites that list free stuff, doubling the advertising power. |
| Special Offers | A company advertises special offers only on its Web site so that visitors check it regularly, knowing that they will find deals there that they cannot get at any other place. |

As a consumer, you have the responsibility to choose products based on these factors, among others:

▶ Is it good for you physically?

▶ Is it good for your spending plan?

▶ Is the company producing it taking good care of its employees, customers, and the environment?

Can you think of additional factors to consider when you make purchases? Being a responsible consumer means that you make choices based on needs, not wants. On the other hand, buying products and services to impress others is called **conspicuous consumption**. It is not a responsible behavior. Try to make careful decisions about your spending—even if you really value or want the products or services you are considering. When you buy what you cannot afford, you create serious financial problems for your future.

---

### Section 13-1: Review

**Understanding Key Concepts**

1. What is conspicuous consumption?
2. What are the 10 advertising techniques used to convince people to buy products?
3. What are three criteria for deciding whether you're making a responsible purchase?

**Thinking Creatively**

Does the United States have a problem with conspicuous consumption? Support your answer with examples.

Give an example of a purchase you have made that does not meet the three factors that show someone is being a responsible consumer.

**Taking It a Step Further**

Choose three advertising techniques from the chart and find examples of commercials or ads that use that technique.

---

# Section 13-2: Choosing a Home

Have you thought about where you want to live after high school or college? There are different housing options for every lifestyle. Something you will quickly realize is that the costs of housing will make up the largest part of your budget. What is included in housing costs? A general rule to follow is that your housing costs should not exceed more than one-fourth of your take-home pay. You will spend the other three-fourths of your pay on essentials plus non-essentials (purchases that are nice but not necessary).

Become familiar with many types of properties. There are several ways to get this information, including checking out ads on the Internet; talking to a real estate agent; networking with family, friends, and co-workers; reading the classifieds; or just looking for "For Rent" signs. As you are shopping for a place to live, definitely ask residents who live in an area what they like and dislike about it before you make your decision. Ask the owner of the property for its true cost, which could include the amount of the damage or security deposit and the approximate cost of the utilities. Make sure that you look inside the properties you are considering. Take time to find

▶ A convenient place so that you can get to work quickly and be close to family, friends, and the areas where you will spend most of your leisure (free) time.

▶ The nicest property that you can afford. After all, you're going to be spending many hours in the place.

▶ A place that makes you feel safe and comfortable.

## Renting Versus Buying a Home

One issue to consider when you are ready to move into your own place is renting versus buying. There are advantages and disadvantages of each of these choices. Typically, young people begin by renting an apartment or house. It is a way of keeping expenses down. Also, renting is a better option if you are not planning to stay in the same area very long. Some of the advantages of renting include the following:

▶ Rent payments are usually less than mortgages.

▶ A **security deposit** (also called damage deposit) is money you pay to cover any damage to a rented home. Security deposits required for renting are much less than down payments for buying houses.

▶ The maximum possible debt from renting typically does not exceed a one year-lease agreement. A house has a 15- to 30-year mortgage.

▶ You are not responsible for repairs to a property you rent.

▶ Relocating is easier if you have a career opportunity in another location.

*Can you ever see yourself renting an apartment?*

Mr. H., your employer, is the worst boss ever. He wants all the utensils returned to the same position in the drawers. All the price tags have to be placed at exactly the same spot on every container. He goes ballistic if the cash register drawer is even a penny off. It seems as if nothing you ever do pleases him. Just once you'd like for him to ask you how you're feeling and praise your work. How can the two of you ever get along?

After you choose a place to live, your roommates and you will need to fill out a housing application form. This form asks for the following information:

▸ Your current address, phone number, and how long you've lived at your address.

▸ The make, model, and license number of your vehicle.

▸ The name, address, and phone number of your employer.

▸ The name of your bank and your checking and savings account numbers.

▸ The names and account numbers of any credit cards, consumer finance companies, or other loans you have.

▸ The names, addresses, and phone numbers of personal references. You can use the same ones you used on employment applications.

▸ Permission to contact the credit bureau to verify your financial record.

## CAREER FACT

If you enjoy classes in accounting, economics, business, or government, you might want to consider a career in general management and support.

APARTMENT RENTAL APPLICATION

DATE: _____

(Please Print)

APPLICANT: Last _____ First _____ M/I ___ S.S. No.: _____ D.O.B. _____

SPOUSE: Last _____ First _____ M/I ___ S.S. No.: _____ D.O.B. _____

TO BE WED _____ SINGLE _____ MARRIED _____ WIDOWED _____ SEPARATED _____ DIVORCED _____

PERSONS TO OCCUPY APARTMENT OTHER THAN LESSEE:
NO OTHER PERSONS WILL BE PERMITTED
TO LIVE ON PREMISES (1) _____ D.O.B. _____
(2) _____ D.O.B. _____

### RESIDENCY

PRESENT ADDRESS: _____ CITY: _____ STATE: ___ ZIP: _____

PHONE: _____ LENGTH OF TIME: _____ OWNS: _____ RENTS: _____

LANDLORD OR MORTGAGEHOLDER: _____ ADDRESS: _____ PHONE: _____

MONTHLY PAYMENT: $ _____ REASON FOR MOVING: _____

FORMER ADDRESS: _____ CITY: _____ STATE: ___ ZIP: _____

LANDLORD: _____ ADDRESS: _____ PHONE: _____

LENGTH OF TIME: _____ MONTHLY PAYMENT: _____ REASON FOR MOVING: _____

### EMPLOYMENT

EMPLOYED BY: _____ PHONE: _____

ADDRESS: _____ CITY: _____ STATE: ___ ZIP: _____

POSITION: _____ INCOME: $ _____ LENGTH OF TIME: _____ SUPERVISOR: _____

FORMER EMPLOYER: _____ PHONE: _____

ADDRESS: _____ CITY: _____ STATE: ___ ZIP: _____

POSITION: _____ INCOME: $ _____ LENGTH OF TIME: _____ SUPERVISOR: _____

SPOUSE EMPLOYER: _____ PHONE: _____

ADDRESS: _____ CITY: _____ STATE: ___ ZIP: _____

POSITION: _____ INCOME: $ _____ LENGTH OF TIME: _____ SUPERVISOR: _____

ADDITIONAL INCOME: $ _____ PER _____ SOURCE: _____

### CREDIT

BANK NAME: _____ ADDRESS: _____

LIST CREDIT CARDS: 1. _____
2. _____
3. _____

DRIVER'S LICENSE NO.: _____ TAG NO.: _____ MAKE: _____ YEAR: _____ LOAN: ❑ YES ❑ NO

DRIVER'S LICENSE NO.: _____ TAG NO.: _____ MAKE: _____ YEAR: _____ LOAN: ❑ YES ❑ NO

CAR LOAN: NAME AND ADDRESS: _____ CITY: _____ STATE: ___ ZIP: _____

### PERSONAL INFORMATION

WHOM SHOULD WE CONTACT IN CASE OF PERSONAL EMERGENCY:

NAME: _____ RELATIONSHIP: _____ PHONE: _____

ADDRESS: _____ CITY: _____ STATE: ___ ZIP: _____

HOW DID YOU HEAR ABOUT US: ❑ DRIVE BY ❑ YELLOW PAGES ❑ PERSONAL REFERRAL
❑ APARTMENT GUIDE ❑ FOR RENT MAGAZINE ❑ APARTMENT SHOPPER GUIDE ❑ HOMESTORE.COM
❑ OTHER ❑ RESIDENT REFERRAL, WHO? _____

DO YOU OWN A PET? _____ IF SO, WHAT TYPE? _____ WHAT WEIGHT? _____

DO YOU OWN A MUSICAL INSTRUMENT? _____ IF SO, WHAT KIND? _____

HAVE YOU OR ANY OCCUPANTS EVER BEEN CONVICTED OF OR PLED GUILTY OR "NO CONTEST" TO A FELONY OR MISDEMEANOR? _____

*How is a leasing application similar to an application for a job? How is it different?*

To avoid delays in the landlord's processing of the application, make sure that the information you provide on the application is accurate. The **landlord** (owner of the apartment) uses the information on the application to decide whether you are capable of taking care of the property and paying the rent. To make that decision, responsible landlords verify your credit rating. They also contact the people you listed as references. Some landlords require you to pay an application fee. That fee covers the cost of requesting a credit report and long-distance phone calls. It is not refundable.

When the landlord is satisfied that you are reliable, you are nearly ready to finalize the agreement. Before you sign a lease, carefully inspect the property you are renting (not one just like it). Look closely for the following problems:

▶ Signs of water damage on the ceiling. If you see brown or gray circles, you can be certain that water has been a problem.

▶ Dirt or damage throughout the property (on the walls, floor, doors, light fixtures, appliances and cabinets in the kitchen, and bathroom fixtures and cabinets). Most landlords will refuse to return the total of your security deposit if you are responsible for dirt or damage to any part of the property.

▶ Broken or loose windows or exterior doors. You can be held responsible for broken windows or doors. Even more important, though, is the fact that your utility cost will be greater if the property is not properly protected from the weather, not to mention possible risks to your personal safety.

*What is the purpose of a lease agreement?*

If your inspection reveals any problems in the property, refuse to sign anything until the problems are corrected. Prepare a written list of all the problems. Ask that they be corrected within a certain time period, request a reduction in your rent, or just refuse to rent the property. One of the worst choices you can make is to accept the landlord's word that the problems will be corrected and move in without a written listing of the problems that both the landlord and you sign. Landlords know that after you move in, you are likely to accept the poor conditions of the property rather than move.

When you are satisfied with the property, read the **lease agreement** (a contract between the landlord and you) carefully. If you don't understand something, ask questions. As the **tenant** (the person paying rent), you have certain responsibilities to the landlord. You must pay your security deposit. You must pay the correct amount of rent on time. You must be careful with the property and follow other terms in the lease. The landlord also has responsibilities to you: to maintain the property and to notify you in advance of any changes in the ownership of the property. The lease is a legal document that is enforceable by law. After signing the lease, you probably will have to make a security deposit and pay at least one month's rent before you can move in.

Some young people buy homes instead of renting them. Buying a home is the "American dream." There are definite advantages, which include the following:

▸ It usually increases in value over time.

▸ It gives you a sense of community, stability, and security.

▸ You are free to decorate it and landscape the yard.

▸ You do not have to rely on someone else to maintain the property.

The disadvantages of buying a home are these:

▸ You must have enough cash to pay the closing costs and make a down payment.

▸ You are responsible for the property.

▸ If you can't make the mortgage payments, you could face **foreclosure** (the mortgage company takes the property away from you without paying you anything for the money you invested in it).

▸ If you need to move to a different area, you have to sell the house or find someone to rent it from you.

## Income and Recommended Total Monthly Housing Expense

| Annual Income | Monthly Housing Expense |
| --- | --- |
| $15,000 | $350 |
| $20,000 | $467 |
| $25,000 | $583 |
| $30,000 | $700 |
| $35,000 | $817 |
| $40,000 | $933 |
| $45,000 | $1,050 |
| $50,000 | $1,167 |
| $55,000 | $1,283 |
| $60,000 | $1,400 |
| $65,000 | $1,517 |
| $70,000 | $1,633 |

*How much will you have to earn to have enough money to pay for your housing and live comfortably?*

Be a responsible consumer. Until you can afford a down payment, closing costs, and mortgage payments, you are better off to view the dream of owning a home as a long-term goal.

## Living with Roommates

You might want to begin your independent life by sharing your living space with roommates. You will find a lot of similarities between living at home with your parents and siblings and living with one or more people who are not related to you.

There are distinct advantages and disadvantages of having roommates. The number one advantage is that you can share expenses and responsibilities. Another advantage is that you will not be alone. The biggest disadvantage in having roommates is the conflict that can occur when you are sharing living space with other people, even if you choose to live with your best friend. What is the role of a roommate? How can you avoid conflicts, and how can you resolve them when they occur?

It is an excellent idea to lay some ground rules and discuss some issues *before* you agree to live with a roommate. For example, you should talk about

▶ **Expenses:** How will you share expenses such as rent, utilities, and groceries?

▶ **Personal space:** Are you going to share a bedroom? If there is more than one bedroom, and one is bigger, who gets the biggest bedroom?

▶ **Housekeeping:** What are your rules for housekeeping? What if one of you likes a "little clutter" and the other is a "clean freak?" Who does the dishes?

### On-the-Job Competency

**Do You Know What Others Are Thinking?**

Many people assume that they know what others are thinking just by watching their facial expressions and body language or interpreting what they say. However, those assumptions can keep you from truly understanding others and, even worse, can create barriers. If your friends left for lunch without you, how would you react?

*How would you feel about sharing your living space with another person?*

▶ **Food:** Who does the cooking? What if your roommate eats your food or offers your food to his or her guests?

▶ **Privacy:** How will you feel about your roommate's "friend" moving in for a few weeks or even months?

▶ **Atmosphere:** When do you need "peace and quiet?" What is your preference for music and television? What if your needs conflict with your roommate's needs?

▶ **Parking:** Does the property have adequate parking? If not, what agreement will you make on who parks in the most convenient location?

▶ **Ending the living arrangement:** What happens when you or your roommate decides to move?

By communicating clearly before you begin sharing a living space, you can avoid many misunderstandings. When you do have problems, practice shared leadership. Work together to solve the problems by using your problem-solving skills: Define the problem. Determine your goal. List and analyze possible solutions. Make a plan. Take action, and evaluate the results.

## Furnishing Your Home

Many young people furnish their first living spaces in "early attic"—leftovers from your parents. You might already own items that you can use, but you need to purchase many other items, whether your apartment is furnished or unfurnished. You will need small appliances such as a toaster and mixer, bedding, dishes, cookware, kitchenware, lamps, and towels, for example. You will want to purchase some of these items new. You can also purchase many used items at garage sales and thrift stores. You can also save money by

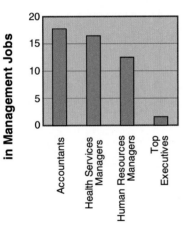

**Projected Outlook for 2016**

*What does this chart tell you about future opportunities in these careers?*

*Where would you go to get furniture for your first home?*

refinishing furniture, building your own, or buying pieces that you can use for more than one purpose, such as a futon, which can be a sofa or a bed.

Whatever you choose for your place to live, you will find out that you have some very important decisions to make. Some of your decisions will be good ones, and some will not be so good. The good news is that you already know the process for solving problems. You will learn from all your decisions. Listen to adults who "have been there." Many young people move out on their own for a while and for many reasons, including personal and financial, find themselves moving back home with their parents. It is good to have that "safety net" to fall back on until you are ready to try again.

---

### Section 13-2: Review

**Understanding Key Concepts**

1. What are the advantages of buying a house?
2. What are the advantages of renting?
3. What is the difference between a housing application and a lease agreement?

**Thinking Creatively**

When do you think you'll be ready to buy a home?
How can sharing an apartment be both a negative and positive experience?
What should you check for when trying to find a place to live?

**Taking It a Step Further**

Gather information about apartments and starter homes in your community and use Microsoft Excel or another spreadsheet program to make a grid that compares the benefits and costs of renting versus buying.

---

# Section 13-3: Making Arrangements for Your Transportation

Depending on where you live, you will want to consider your transportation options carefully. If you live in a large city that has public transportation, buying a vehicle might not be necessary. A car could even be a financial burden you don't need at this time. However, in some areas you need to provide your own transportation. If you choose to have your own, you will want to think carefully before purchasing your first vehicle.

If you could buy any vehicle in the world, what would it be? That dream vehicle is your want, but what do you really need? What would be a reasonable choice? There is much to learn about owning and operating a vehicle, but many people find this a very exciting and nonthreatening experience.

### TECHNOLOGY

Architects, engineers, and designers of all kinds use computer-aided design (CAD) programs to create plans for everything from large buildings to small components for manufacturing. To try out CAD for yourself, do an Internet Search for "room design programs" to find a free program to use to rearrange your bedroom. To create a room design, you will need to know the measurements of the room. What else should you consider?

*Which transportation options are available for you, and which ones are you willing to use?*

## Buying a Vehicle

Use your problem-solving skills when making a decision about transportation. Ask these questions before you purchase a vehicle:

▶ How much am I willing to pay to purchase the vehicle?

▶ How much will monthly payments be?

▶ What do I really *need?*

▶ Why do I need a vehicle?

▶ Can I afford the cost of maintaining this vehicle: gas, license plates and taxes, replacement and repairs, and insurance?

▶ Will this vehicle make my life better, or what will I have to give up?

When you have decided to purchase a vehicle, you will certainly want to shop around. What are some options available? As you do your research, check out different makes, models, and options you want and can afford. Magazines such as *Consumer Reports* and online services such as Edmunds will provide you with evaluations and histories of different vehicles, as well as target prices. The seller must honestly share information about the history of the vehicle with you. Remember also that car dealers are usually willing to bargain and negotiate the final selling price.

Because most young people do not have enough money to pay cash for a vehicle, they must get a loan. Shop around for the best interest rates. Read the purchase contract carefully before you sign it. Make sure that you fill in all the blanks on the contract or draw a line through them. More than likely, you will not be able to obtain a loan on your own and will need a co-signer (an adult willing to take financial responsibility for the amount of money borrowed). Make certain that your name is on the loan along with the adult's name; having your name on it will help you begin establishing your own credit rating.

## Case Study: What Options Does Sierra Have?

For Sierra's sixteenth birthday, her dad took her to look at used cars. She found a blue one that she really liked. After looking the car over carefully inside and out and asking several questions about the cost, mileage, miles per gallon, and previous owner, she asked if she and her dad could take it for a test drive. Much to her dismay, the car would not start. Her dad encouraged her to leave and check out cars at another dealership. Sierra did not want to leave.

**What would you have recommended Sierra do? Why?**

## Taking Care of Your Vehicle

After you have purchased your vehicle, find a responsible, honest auto service technician. This might be someone your parents or friends already know and trust. If not, ask around and check with the Better Business Bureau in your community. When you own a vehicle, you must make sure that it is safe at all times. How can you do that?

*Can you think of additional responsibilities you have when you own a vehicle?*

In addition to a safe vehicle, you must drive safely. Unfortunately, many teens have traffic accidents. You too have a high chance of having an accident during the first six months after you begin driving. To reduce those chances, remember the following:

▶ Always buckle your seat belt before driving. Make sure that your passengers are buckled up as well.

▶ Pay attention to your driving at all times. Don't let music, cell phones, or passengers distract you.

▶ Drive defensively. Don't assume that other drivers are watching out for you.

▶ Never drive when you are using alcohol or drugs. Never get in a vehicle with a driver who does.

▶ Obey the laws. Drive the speed limit and use your side and rearview mirrors when changing lanes.

▶ Use common sense and slow down when driving in fog, snow and ice, or heavy downpours.

# Section 13-4: Making Sure That You Have Adequate Insurance

One thing we know about life is to "expect the unexpected." Because none of us have a crystal ball, we really don't know what tomorrow will bring. One way to plan for life's unexpected events is to buy **insurance**. It pays a company to protect you financially from problems, such as ill health, fire, or accidents. Can you name different kinds of insurance? You can buy insurance for just about anything. Professional athletes can have their legs insured. Pianists can have their hands insured.

Insurance has its own language. You need to understand these terms.

▶ An insurance policy is a legal contract between the **policyholder** (the person buying insurance) and the insurance company. The policy tells you who and what is covered, how much the insurance company will pay, and how much the insurance will cost. As with any legal contract, read it carefully and ask questions about anything you don't understand before you sign it. It is just as important to know what the policy doesn't cover as what it does cover. Why do you think this is true?

▶ The insurance company will pay you for your losses depending on the terms of your insurance policy. **Benefits** are the money paid for the loss.

▶ The **beneficiary** is the person receiving the benefits, usually the policyholder. In the case of the death of the policyholder, the money will go to another beneficiary, usually a parent, spouse, or child.

*Who will pay for damage, injury, or death?*

▶ A **claim** is a notice to the insurance company to pay for a loss. You will need to notify the insurance company via a telephone call, or in writing if you have a claim. You might be required to go to the office of your insurance company representative to file your claim.

▶ The **deductible** is the portion of the loss that you pay. To reduce the cost of your premiums, you can choose to pay a certain portion of a loss before the insurance company pays the remaining costs.

▶ **Premiums** are the payments the policyholder makes to the insurance company. This amount is usually paid monthly, quarterly, or yearly.

Once again, it's important to shop around to keep insurance costs down. Know the type of insurance you need. Buy only as much coverage as you need. Ask about premium costs and deductible options. You probably will need only the basics: home, automobile, health, and life insurance.

## Home Insurance

If you decide to buy a home, you will want to purchase **homeowner's insurance** that protects your house, the contents of your home, and the land your house sits on. Usually you pay your homeowner's insurance to your mortgage company. That company pays your insurance company. Having the insurance paid through the mortgage company reassures your mortgage company that your property is protected by insurance.

Even if you rent, you still need insurance. You and the other tenants could lose everything if the rental property burns down or is destroyed by a natural disaster. The landlord carries insurance that covers the building and land. As a renter, you are responsible for finding an insurance company and purchasing your own insurance. **Renter's insurance** protects your personal belongings. Always keep a list of the items in your home.

# Automobile Insurance

Most states have laws requiring drivers to have insurance. When you apply for a driver's license or purchase a vehicle license plate, you can find out what the requirements are from your state's Bureau of Motor Vehicles.

A standard automobile insurance policy can include these types of coverage:

▸ Collision insurance covers the cost of repairs to your car. It also covers damages to your car if you are hit by an uninsured motorist (a driver who is not insured).

## Personal Property Inventory

### Living Room

**Furniture**

| Qty | Item | Manufacturer | Date Purchased | Price |
|---|---|---|---|---|
| | Sofa/Couch | | | |
| | Love Seat | | | |
| | Chairs | | | |
| | Wall Units/Bookshelves | | | |
| | Tables | | | |
| | | | | |
| | | | | |

**Electronics**

| Qty | Item | Manufacturer | Make/Model | Serial Number | Date Purchased | Price |
|---|---|---|---|---|---|---|
| | Television | | | | | |
| | DVD Player | | | | | |
| | Stereo | | | | | |
| | | | | | | |
| | | | | | | |

**Accessories**

| Qty | Item | Manufacturer | Date Purchased | Price |
|---|---|---|---|---|
| | Carpeting | | | |
| | Lamps | | | |
| | Window Coverings | | | |
| | | | | |

*What are the benefits of keeping an inventory of the things you own?*

▸ Comprehensive insurance covers your car for other reasons, including fire, hail damage, theft, and vandalism.

▸ Liability insurance covers damage or injury that you cause to others (other passengers in your vehicle or the other driver or passengers in that vehicle). It also covers property damage to the other vehicle. It does not cover your injuries or damage to your car.

▸ Medical payments insurance covers your medical expenses. It also covers the medical expenses of your passengers.

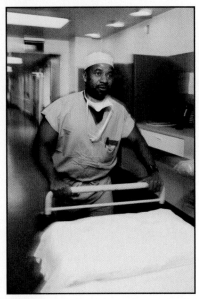

*How will you pay for medical expenses if you don't have health insurance?*

▶ Uninsured motorist insurance covers you against drivers who do not have liability insurance. This insurance might not be necessary, depending on your other coverage.

Some states have a type of insurance called no-fault insurance. Each policyholder's own insurance company pays a part of the claims, no matter who is at fault. This works particularly well if there is a disagreement about who is at fault. Disagreements delay the settling of the insurance claims.

Be a responsible consumer when it comes to automobile insurance. Investigate these ways of reducing your auto insurance premiums:

▶ Ask about insurance discounts such as those for good students, airbags, anti-theft devices, two or more cars on a policy, or a history of safe driving.

▶ Buy only the coverage you need.

▶ Drive carefully.

▶ Increase your deductible. You will pay more if you have a claim, but your premiums will be much lower.

▶ Shop around and get quotes from several insurers.

▶ Take driver education classes.

## Health Insurance

Because the cost of health care is so expensive and is continuing to rise, health insurance is very important. One serious disease, illness, or injury could cost you thousands of dollars in medical bills. Many businesses provide health insurance and life insurance plans for their employees. It is a wise financial decision to participate in these group plans because they will save you money. However, if this is not an option for you, you can enroll in an individual plan. Individual coverage can be expensive.

There are basically three different types of health insurance protection:

▶ Major medical covers doctor visits, prescription drugs, medical testing, hospital, and surgical expenses. You will be responsible for deductibles. However, you can choose your doctors and hospitals.

▶ Health Maintenance Organizations (HMOs) cover all health costs. You are responsible for a small **co-payment** (the set portion of the total cost that you pay). Your choice of doctors and hospitals might be very limited with an HMO, however.

▶ Preferred Provider Organizations (PPOs) might charge you higher premiums and higher co-payments than an HMO, but you will have a greater choice of doctors.

Ask your parents about the health insurance they have. What are the advantages and disadvantages of their insurance program? Some people might not be able to afford insurance or choose not to have insurance.

What happens when these people become sick or injured and need medical assistance?

## Life Insurance

There are many life insurance choices. **Life insurance** provides money to your beneficiaries when you die. There is also life insurance that will provide you money after you reach a certain age. Depending on your age and health, you need to consider the following when you are shopping for life insurance:

▶ Do I have anyone who depends on me for my paycheck?

▶ How much life insurance do I need?

▶ What will the premium costs be?

▶ Does my employer offer life insurance benefits?

*Why is life insurance important if you are responsible for a family?*

---

### Section 13-4: Review

**Understanding Key Concepts**

1. Which types of insurance does a young person living independently need?
2. What are the basic types of automobile insurance coverage?
3. What are the three basic forms of health insurance?

**Thinking Creatively**

Is purchasing insurance just a waste of money?
How can you lower the cost of your automobile insurance?
How should your role in your family affect your decision about life insurance?

**Taking It a Step Further**

Contact an insurance company in your community or go on the Internet and find out how much the auto insurance would cost if you were 18 and had to pay for the policy on your favorite vehicle.

---

# Section 13-5: Taking Care of Yourself

Most people put a great deal of time, thought, and energy into finding a place to live, the transportation they use, and insurance. They do research and comparison-shop when making these decisions. However, the less-expensive items you purchase can waste your time and money more than you may anticipate. Carelessness in the way that you spend both can ruin your life.

## Meeting Your Physical Needs

Did you skip any meals yesterday? How important is it to eat regularly? Do you get at least 30 minutes of exercise every day? How are you handling stress?

Have you ever heard anyone say: "Good health is everything?" What do you think they mean? Good health is an important part of a quality life. A healthy diet (what you eat), adequate exercise, and enough rest will help you control your own health.

▸ **Eat smart!** The MyPyramid food guidance system shows the guidelines for getting the nutrients (substances in food that the body needs to stay healthy) that you need each day. These guidelines were developed by the U.S. Departments of Agriculture and Health and Human Services.

▸ **Exercise!** People who exercise don't get sick nearly as often as those who do not exercise at all. Teenagers (and children) need at least one hour of physical activity every day. In addition to building strength, exercise reduces stress and makes you feel mentally alert. What do you like to do for exercise?

▸ **Get enough sleep!** Almost everyone needs at least eight hours of sleep each night. Some experts have suggested that teenagers need up to 10 hours of sleep because their bodies and brains are still growing. Sleep restores and recharges your body and brain. If you are not

*Why is eating the right kinds and right amounts of foods important in creating a healthy life?*

getting enough sleep, your concentration isn't as good and your body is tired, so you are much more likely to have accidents.

▶ **Stay on top of your health!** Regular doctor, dentist, and eye doctor (ophthalmologist) appointments are very important for maintaining and controlling good health. Following good **hygiene** (keeping your body clean) habits will also not only make you feel healthier but look healthy as well. What are some good hygiene practices?

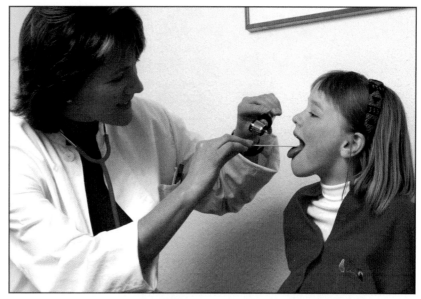

*How often should you see a doctor, dentist, and ophthalmologist?*

▶ **Stay away from substances that can harm your mind and body!** There are many substances that can cause serious damage to your mind and body and even kill you, including drugs, alcohol, tobacco, and inhalants. Most of them are illegal for teenagers to buy or use, but more importantly can become addictive (creating a physical or psychological need) and might destroy not only the person using them but also family members and other loved ones.

▶ **Manage your stress!** Everyone experiences stress. When was the last time you experienced stress? How did you handle it? Stress is normal; it is neither good or bad. But when you react to stress in a negative way, and your body doesn't return to normal, you will experience many side effects such as headaches, chest pain, anger, or depression. The best way to deal with stress according to health experts is to identify the cause and then do something about it.

Independent living is a goal of many teenagers, but it brings responsibility for yourself. This responsibility includes leading a healthy lifestyle. Eat right. Exercise. Get enough sleep. Follow the rules of good hygiene. Get regular medical checkups. Live drug-free. Personal lifestyle choices and career demands often create stress. Coping with stress involves recognizing the problem and finding strategies to control and reduce it.

# Buying Food

Food is a necessity and one of the largest expenses in your spending plan! How much do you think your family spends on food each week? The amount you spend on food depends on several factors, including how often you eat at home, how often you eat out, what you eat, and how many people you are feeding. How can you make responsible decisions as a consumer of food?

The average grocery store stocks thousands of items that you can purchase and then eat at home or take to work. However, many people choose to eat out several times each week rather than prepare food at home. How often do you and your family eat out each week?

When you are on your own, you will want to carefully consider how you spend your grocery money. Now is a good time to practice this skill. Here are some ways skillful shoppers get the most from their food dollars:

- **Plan meals ahead and make a shopping list.** These will allow you to do several things: buy less-expensive foods, plan for leftovers, organize your shopping trip to save you time and energy, and save money by not making **impulse purchases** (buying items without planning ahead).

- **Use coupons.** You can find manufacturers' coupons in newspaper supplements, in magazines, through the mail, and on the Internet. Many stores provide their own coupons as well. Occasionally, stores also offer double and triple coupon days; take advantage of these opportunities. You can save up to 10 percent on your total grocery bill by using coupons. That is a significant savings over several months.

- **Read supermarket advertisements for weekly and seasonal specials.** During certain times of the year, foods sell for lower prices. For example, strawberries are in season in the spring; corn-on-the-cob and green beans are priced right in the summer. The best time to buy turkeys is near Thanksgiving, when the supply is plentiful. Every week, stores offer special prices on certain items called **loss leaders** (priced at or below cost) to get customers into the store because typically they will buy more than just that one particular item.

- **Compare the prices of various sizes of a product.** You should check the **unit prices** (the cost of one standard measure of a product, such as its cost per ounce) of each size. Read the unit price information displayed on the shelves below the food items, or take your own calculator and figure the unit price yourself. Don't always assume that the bigger size is the better bargain because that is not always true.

- **Try generic brands (brands that have no trademark).** These are definitely less expensive than brand-name products and often cost less than **house brands** (private-label goods that are frequently packed for stores by the same companies that package nationally advertised brands). Generic brands have nearly the same nutritional value as the brand names, but might not taste or look as good. You will have to try each product for yourself and make your own judgments.

- **Read the labels.** They give you very useful information. In addition to telling you the nutritional information, labels tell you the number of servings per container. They tell you how the product is packed. They give a breakdown of the actual ingredients in the product (listed on the

*How important is it to learn how to shop for groceries?*

label from most to least). You can also find the manufacturer's address on the label if you wanted to contact the manufacturer.

▶ **Watch where you shop.** The type of store determines the prices you pay. Supermarkets typically have the lowest prices and have a large selection of products. Convenience stores charge higher prices, but are just that—more convenient.

Several of these tips also apply when you eat meals away from home. Many restaurants offer coupons and often run specials. By planning ahead where to eat and what to order, you can save quite a bit of money. In some cases, one or two people can eat out as inexpensively or even less expensively than if they had bought the food at the grocery store and prepared it at home.

Also remember that friends and family might be good for one or two free meals each week if you are close enough to come over for a "home-cooked" meal. Thank them sincerely for the great food, and they will invite you back over and over again.

*When should you buy the less expensive brand, and when should you buy the more expensive one?*

## Buying Clothing

The clothes you wear reflect who you are: your lifestyle and your personality. In today's society, clothing is a basic necessity. However, the amount of money spent on clothing can really vary from person to person. Whether you enjoy the latest fashion trends and buy clothes to update your wardrobe or prefer to spend your money on other things, you will want to create a clothes spending plan. Regardless of the value you place on clothes, how can you make good decisions about your clothing purchases?

Being a responsible consumer of clothing means that you don't make purchases based solely on what is in style, what you like, or the price. Before you buy, consider these factors:

▶ **Where will you be wearing the clothes?** Choose clothes that are appropriate for the setting. Wearing inappropriate clothing can cause problems: You might feel self-conscious, create a safety hazard at work, or even reduce your chances of promotion because you present an unprofessional image.

▶ **Does the item fit properly?** Improperly fitting clothes are not only very uncomfortable, but might actually create a safety hazard in the workplace.

▶ **Will the item wear well?** If it falls apart after you wear it a couple of times, you know that you have not made a good investment.

*How do you decide which items to purchase?*

**NETWORKING**

Find three people who have families and ask them to describe their first home after becoming independent from their parents. Write a comparison of the experiences of those you interviewed.

Here are some tips for making your clothing allowance stretch a little further:

▶ **Learn about clothing.** By reading labels, recognizing quality, and following care instructions, your clothes can last a lot longer. For example, if a label identifies the fabric content as 100 percent cotton, there is a good chance the clothing item will shrink quite a bit. If it is dry clean only, you will have an extra expense in caring for that clothing item.

▶ **Watch for promotional sales.** Almost every store will have promotional sales, which temporarily reduce prices. If you can wait just a few weeks, more than likely the clothing item you "want" will go on sale. You can save up to 30 percent off the regular price. For example, if a shirt was originally sold for $48 and is currently on sale at 20 percent off, how much are you saving? What is the promotional sales price of the shirt?

▶ **Clearance sales are even better bargains.** Stores do not want clothing that is not selling. They always need to make room for new clothes arriving in their stores. To make room for the new items, stores reduce prices from 50 percent to 75 percent to get rid of clothes that have not sold. If you aren't quite as concerned about wearing the latest fashion, you can shop clearance sales to add to your basic wardrobe and get a lot more for your clothing-spending dollar.

▶ **Check out resale shops and second-hand stores.** If you are really looking for bargains, either of these sources for used clothing can meet your needs. Many times, resale shops have brand-name clothes in excellent condition at very reduced prices. Second-hand stores such as Goodwill or Salvation Army have a good variety of clothes donated by people. The profits from the sales of clothes go back into the community to support philanthropic (charitable) projects and help needy families.

**COMMUNITY**

Locate a neighborhood playground in your community and organize a group to clean it up.

*If you had limited funds, where would you shop for clothing?*

## Case Study: How Does Shopping for Clothes Change When You Have to Pay for Them?

Parker has always bought his clothes at Hollister (or rather Parker's parents have bought his clothes at Hollister). Now that he is on his own, he is responsible for buying his clothes. Last week, he bought two shirts and a pair of pants because some of his things from last year are out-of-date. He used up his entire clothing allowance for the next three months! He still needs a new pair of shoes and might need a winter coat. He is considering opening a charge account at the clothing store.

**What do you think Parker should do? Why?**

### Section 13-5: Review

**Understanding Key Concepts**

1. How can you take good care of yourself?
2. What are three tips for stretching your food dollar?
3. What are three factors to consider before buying new clothes?

**Thinking Creatively**

How can being healthy help your career?

Why should you look through your closet before you go shopping for clothes?

How could peer pressure cause problems when you go shopping?

**Taking It a Step Further**

Take an inventory of all your clothing. Are there any clothes in your wardrobe that you can no longer wear? Are there clothes you don't want to wear any longer? Come up with a plan to take care of these unused clothing items.

**John Roscka, Funeral Director**
**Miller-Roscka Funeral Home**

I have owned and operated my funeral home business for the past seven and a half years. My responsibilities as a funeral director include removing bodies; preparing bodies for burial or cremation; meeting with families to make decisions about funeral services; and directing visitations, funerals, and burials. I have enormous amounts of paperwork to complete, and as the owner, I am responsible for overseeing the maintenance of the funeral home, receiving payments for our services, paying bills, advertising, and public relations.

My educational background includes graduating from high school, attending general education classes at Ancilla College, and completing a program at Worsham College of Mortuary Science in Chicago. After I graduated mortuary school, I had to pass the National Board exam and complete a one-year apprenticeship with a licensed funeral director. Then I had to pass the state licensing test. Finally, I was a fully certified funeral director.

I began working at a funeral home when I was a junior in college. I washed the cars, worked at visitations and funerals, and did general work around the mortuary. These experiences showed me what the job of a funeral director consisted of. I knew that I would enjoy a career as a funeral director.

Free time is hard to come by in the funeral business. I am on call 24 hours a day, seven days a week. The only way I truly get away from the job is to leave on vacation. Even then, sometimes things come up that make it necessary for me to cut my vacation short. I sometimes work odd hours. I miss some family activities. However, I try to spend as much time as possible with my family when I am not busy at the funeral home. Why? Sometimes I go for a week or two with nothing much happening. Then I may have four or five funerals in one week and have to work 16 to 18 hours a day.

# Chapter Review and Activities

The following section can help you review the contents of this chapter.

## Key Concepts

Following are the key concepts presented in the chapter.

▶ Independent living skills include finding a place to live, making arrangements for your own transportation, making sure that you have adequate insurance, buying food and clothing, and taking care of yourself.

▶ The better your self-management skills, the better your independent living skills will be. Now is a good time to start practicing many of these skills as you prepare for independent living.

▶ Be aware of the 10 advertising techniques that can trap you.

▶ Being a responsible consumer means that you make choices based on needs, not wants.

▶ Buying products and services to impress others is called conspicuous consumption and is not a responsible behavior.

- A general rule to follow is that your housing costs should not exceed more than one-fourth of your take-home pay.

- One issue to consider when you are ready to move into your own place is renting versus buying. There are advantages and disadvantages of each of these choices.

- There are distinct advantages and disadvantages of having roommates. The number one advantage is that you can share expenses and responsibilities.

- Depending on where you live, you will want to consider your transportation options. Use your problem-solving skills when making a decision about transportation.

- One way to plan for life's unexpected events is to buy insurance. Types of insurance include homeowner's, health, life, and automobile.

- Good health is critical to a quality life. This includes leading a healthy lifestyle: eating right, exercising, getting enough sleep, following the rules of good hygiene, getting regular medical checkups, living drug-free, and dealing with stress.

- Being a responsible consumer of clothing means that you consider where will you be wearing the clothes, whether the items fit properly, and whether they wear well.

## Key Term Review

Complete the following activity to review your understanding of the key terms.

| | |
|---|---|
| beneficiary | insurance |
| benefits | landlord |
| claim | lease agreement |
| co-payment | life insurance |
| deductible | loss leaders |
| foreclosure | policyholder |
| generic brands | premiums |
| homeowner's insurance | renter's insurance |
| house brands | security deposits |
| hygiene | tenant |
| impulse purchases | unit prices |

You are the manager of a consumer debt-reduction company. Using at least 10 key terms, write an advice column for your company's newsletter that tells readers how to manage their money.

# Comprehension Review

Answer the following questions to review your understanding of the key concepts in the chapter.

1. What is conspicuous consumption and what three factors can you consider as you make purchases to avoid conspicuous consumption?

2. What are some advertising techniques that companies use to entice consumers to buy their products?

3. What factors should you consider as you decide whether to buy or rent?

4. What factors should you consider before buying a vehicle?

5. Describe the different types of insurance that a young person needs.

6. How can you take good care of yourself?

# School-to-Work

**Math:** Write down the steps you would take to solve this mathematical problem:

> You are shopping for cleaning supplies and are trying to watch how much you spend. Your favorite laundry detergent costs $4.35 for 64 ounces or $7.38 for 96 ounces. Which one is the better value?

**Social Studies:** Make a list of everything you believe are necessary to have a "good life." Illustrate the "good life" by making a collage with pictures and words from magazines.

**Writing:** Create a realistic budget for a single person who lives alone in an apartment. In the budget, include the cost of rent, utilities, maintaining a vehicle, insurance, food, clothing, and entertainment.

**Science:** What is the science of biomechanics? Which countries have developed strong educational programs in that area?

## Does This Job Interest You?

The following job is posted on the Internet. What education and experience are required? What requirement does this job have that most jobs do not have? What types of interests and skills should a person working in this position have? How could someone apply for the job?

| FIND JOBS | POST RESUMES |
|---|---|

### Plant Manager

| | |
|---:|---|
| **Location:** | NE New Mexico |
| **Compensation:** | $80,000 to $100,000 plus bonus |
| **Job Type:** | Operations/General Management |

### Description

As the Plant Manager for a 300+ non-union, high-volume facility, you will be responsible for continuing to drive lean initiatives and all facets of production. Focus on leadership, coaching for supervisors, staff and building teams.

### Requirements

**Qualifications:** Six Sigma, Black Belt preferred
**Experience:** 5–7 Years
**Education:** Bachelor's Degree

Apply Online

## Shopping Online

The Internet can be a great tool to use to compare prices or locate hard-to-find items. However, shopping online involves risks that you won't find at the local mall. Follow these guidelines when you buy online:

▶ Only buy from companies or sellers you know and trust. Check for a physical address and phone number on the Web site and make sure the company has been in business for a while.

▶ Read the Web site's policies on shipping, returns, and privacy. Make sure that you understand all the charges involved in getting your order. Also, find out how the site will use the private information you provide when you place an order. If this information is hard to find or understand, don't buy from that site.

▶ Provide financial information only on a secure order form. Check for a lock icon in the status bar or a Web address that begins with https (the s stands for secure) to indicate that the order form is secure. Never send your financial information through e-mail.

▶ Keep records of everything you order. Save copies of or print online receipts, e-mail confirmations, or anything else relating to your order. That way you will have the information you need if there is a problem.

▶ Pay with a credit or charge card so that you are protected by the Fair Credit Billing Act. Under this law, you don't have to pay more than $50 if someone charges your card without your permission. Also, you can stop payment if you have a conflict with the company about your order. Another alternative is to set up an account with an online payment service, such as PayPal. This way, you can pay for things without having to give the seller a credit card number. The service is useful when you buy things from auction sites.

# What career appeals to you?

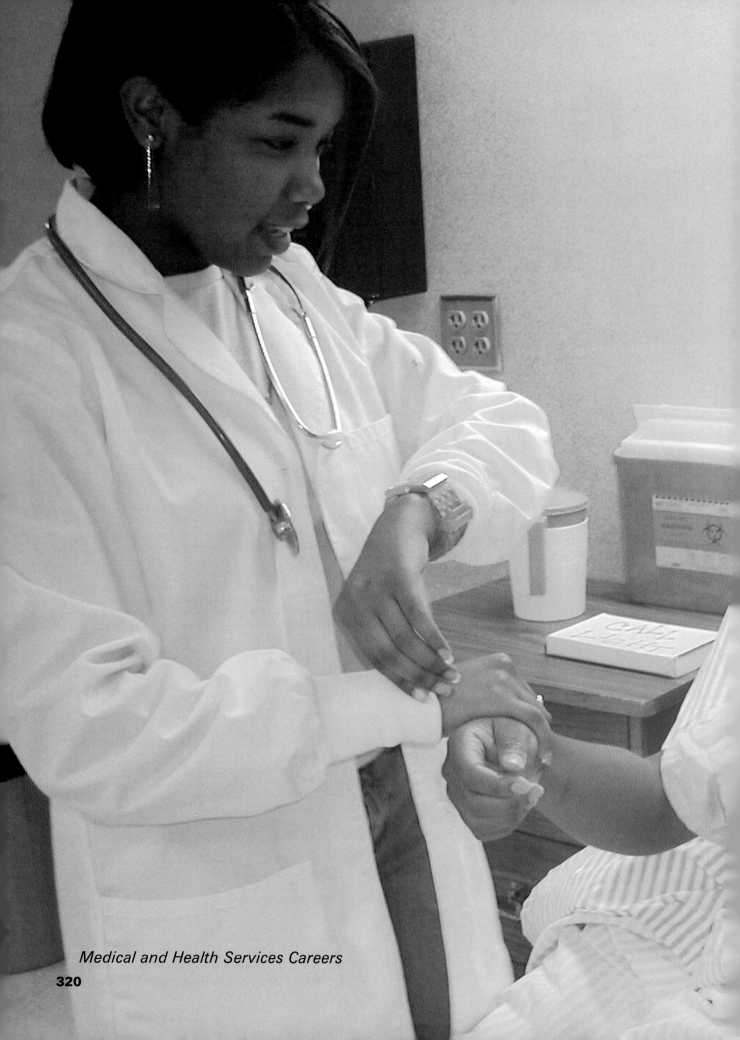

# Chapter 14

# Successfully Handling Adult Roles and Responsibilities

## What You'll Learn

▶ Expanding your personal life

▶ Including dating in your lifestyle

▶ Recognizing love

▶ Beginning your own family

▶ Creating a successful marriage

▶ Preparing for parenting

▶ Balancing your personal, family, and work life

Within the next 15 years, you will experience many changes. You might have finished your education, accepted a job related to your career choice, moved into your own home, and begun a family. How will you handle these changes in your roles and responsibilities? How will you begin preparing for changes today?

*Love at first sight is easy to understand; it's when two people have been looking at each other for a lifetime that it becomes a miracle.*

—*Sam Levenson*

# Section 14-1: Expanding Your Personal Life

One of the best gifts you can give yourself is the gift of freedom and living on your own for a while. Do you think you would enjoy living alone? What are some advantages and disadvantages of living alone?

During alone time, you can learn more about yourself as an individual. You can get a clear understanding of your strengths and your likes and dislikes. With that self-awareness, you can begin to create the lifestyle that you truly want, not one that your family, friends, or even co-workers expect of you.

## Including Dating in Your Lifestyle

After you clearly know yourself, you might find that you want to develop meaningful relationships with other people. You might choose to begin dating. **Dating** is when two unmarried people spend time together. How old should a person be when he or she begins dating?

In the United States, dating usually begins during the mid- to late teen years. You have the choice of whom to ask and what to do on a date. You can arrange the dates at school or parties, by telephone and the Internet, or through friends.

When you think of dating, you typically think of teenagers. But remember that dating can take place any time during a person's life. Some people choose not to commit to a permanent relationship and date during their entire lifetime. For others, divorce or death of a spouse can mean starting to date again when they are middle aged or elderly. Do you know any middle-aged or elderly people who are dating?

## Why Do People Date?

What is the purpose of dating in American society today? You might say that dating is for fun and enjoyment. Dating, as we know it today, became acceptable only after World War I. Historically, young people met at church functions or through their parents or parents' friends.

Dating customs in other countries are very different from ours. Many countries allow only chaperoned dates. Some countries still arrange marriages, so dating is not an accepted custom.

*Can you tell whether these couples are just friends, are dating, or are married?*

Dating has two main purposes. First, it helps you learn how to get along with others. Second, it prepares you for more serious, permanent relationships that will lead to marriage. By dating different people, you will learn the qualities you want in a marriage partner. You also discover the qualities you find unacceptable.

The dating process can go through several stages:

▶ **Stage 1 is group dating (going out with several people to an activity).** Group dating is more comfortable for teens because they will be with friends and can act more naturally than if they were alone with a girl or guy. Group dating activities might include a sports activity, a dance, a movie, bowling, or skating.

▶ **Stage 2 is single dating (might include several different dating partners).** After you have had some experience, you will feel more confident about going on a single date and pairing off as a couple. Single dating activities could include the same things as group dating.

▶ **Stage 3 is paired dating with one exclusive dating partner.** You have reached a point in a relationship where you have as much concern for your dating partner's feelings as your own. You will look more closely at qualities in a partner to decide what is important to you.

In *Men Are from Mars, Women Are from Venus* (published by HarperCollins), author John Gray says that dating is like aiming at a target. Each person you date shows you what you like and don't like in a relationship. Each moves you closer to the center of the target, the person with whom you can share the rest of your life. When you see dating as a learning experience, you can handle

*Do people in your culture practice these stages of dating?*

breakups more easily. You know that you are gaining a clear picture of what you need from a relationship. You are getting ready for a long-lasting one.

## Whom Should You Date?

What factors will you consider when choosing someone to ask out for a date? People are often attracted to certain physical characteristics. What is most important to you? Is age an important factor? If age is important to you right now, remember this: Girls mature more quickly than guys in American culture. However, this gap narrows as teens near adulthood. In addition to the physical characteristics and age issues, consider the following:

▶ **Background.** Having similar cultural, racial, and family beliefs or principles; level of income; and education can help create a healthy relationship.

▶ **Goals and values.** At the beginning of your dating experience, goals and values might not be very important to you. As you progress toward a more serious, loving relationship, you might begin thinking about issues that matter to you the most. Having the same goals and values will keep your relationship strong.

- **Interests.** There are several advantages for couples who have common interests, including enjoying the same activities, being able to talk about common interests, and spending more time together.

- **Personality.** It's true that "opposites attract" because we often look for people who have qualities we lack. For a relationship to last longer, however, the couple's personalities need to be similar enough that they are comfortable with one another.

The following list gives traits and behaviors that are good signs in a dating partner. Although no one might fit all of them, you can use them as a general guide. If you are dating someone you really like who has some of these qualities but not all of them, how you can improve your relationship? If you find that your current dating partner has very few of the qualities, you might want to consider whether you want to continue the relationship.

- Shows an interest in you and your feelings and activities as well as in his own

- Respects your physical and emotional boundaries

- Is comfortable and secure enough within herself to be satisfied with attention from you and does not need to constantly seek out attention and admiration from others

- Is finished with previous significant relationships

- Can manage his own responsibilities

- Can balance the need for control with the ability to be flexible when appropriate

- Is reliable; follows through on prearranged plans; shows up on time

- Is comfortable discussing her own feelings

- Has had one or more personal friendships for at least several years

- Enjoys affection and physical intimacy

- Has a positive, optimistic outlook on life

- Has a good sense of humor

- Takes responsibility for his own life, his own feelings, and the consequences of his own decisions without blaming others

- Takes care of herself physically and emotionally

- Can receive constructive feedback from others without getting defensive

- Knows how to resolve conflict in a constructive manner, or is willing to learn how to do so

**DISCRIMINATION**

**Can You Be Fired for Getting Pregnant?**
You have just found out that you are pregnant. Your employer got really mad when she found out and said that you are fired. Is that legal?

**CAREER FACT**

Careers in medical and health services can include dental hygienists, dentists, doctors, clinical technologists, nurses, orthodontists, pharmacists, physical therapists, psychiatrists, and surgeons.

- Expresses anger in an appropriate manner
- Does not feel that people are controlling when they express their legitimate needs, but at the same time does not have to do everything other people want.

**ETHICS**

**Where Does Patience Begin?**

You have five customers waiting in line, and the customer you are assisting now is using change to pay her bill. In the meantime, her three little children are fussing and fighting. What will you do?

## Case Study: Should This Couple Stay Together?

Travis and Lauren are seniors in high school. They have been dating since they were sophomores. Until just recently, Lauren thought Travis was the man she wanted to marry and spend the rest of her life with. But lately they have been discussing their future plans. Lauren is beginning to realize that what she values and what Travis values as far as future educational plans are very different. Lauren has been accepted to a pre-pharmacy program at a major university several hours away from her hometown. This program will require at least six years of college. Travis, on the other hand, wants to stay in his hometown and go directly into the workplace. He believes that he does not need to go to college because he wants to be an auto repair technician. He can get the training where he is currently working.

**CAREER FACT**

Opportunities for dentists are growing more slowly than for other health-care careers because dental hygienists and assistants handle more of the tasks.

**What would you recommend to Travis and Lauren?**

# What Are the Rules for Dating?

As you prepare to date, your childhood experiences will affect the way you believe you should behave. More than likely, you will treat your date the same way your parents have treated each other. Think about this very carefully! Is this the way you want to treat a date? When parents have a loving relationship and treat one another with kind words and thoughtful gestures, they provide a good model to follow. However, when parents argue frequently or show little affection for one another, they model behaviors you want to avoid in your own dating relationships.

What is **dating etiquette**? There are certain skills you need and rules (manners) to follow when you are taking on the role of a date. These rules require practice. For example, honesty, planning ahead, and knowing how to arrange a date are just a few issues to consider as you begin to date.

Honesty is important during any stage of dating. If you need a dating partner only for the dance and don't want to go any further than that, for example, let the person know ahead of time. There will be times when you will have to break a date. Let your date know as soon as possible and suggest another time. Most people will understand when something comes up and you give them an honest explanation. Never lie! Occasionally, a dishonest person will break a date because he or she has a "better opportunity." Remember the consequences are that if you do this, you will soon get a reputation for being dishonest.

*How do you treat your date or expect to be treated?*

Planning ahead is important when you are dating. The more formal the dating activity, the more planning that might be necessary. For instance, attending a prom requires a great deal of planning. Buying or renting the clothes and accessories, purchasing flowers, arranging transportation, and sometimes making dinner reservations all take planning.

Know how to ask for a date. Being prepared and knowing what you are going to say will save you embarrassment and show that you have good manners. Be specific about your plans when you call. This will help the other person decide whether to accept. Do not expect an immediate answer because many young people need to check with parents or employers and cannot accept right away.

> **CAREER FACT**
>
> If you enjoy classes in anatomy, health, physical education, or psychology, you might want to consider a career in medical and health services.

On the other hand, when someone asks you for a date, respond as soon as you can. It is impolite to keep the other person waiting. He will want to make other plans. Remember the other person's feelings if you refuse a date. Be kind but honest about the reason you are refusing.

## Case Study: What Is the Appropriate Dating Etiquette?

Discuss the following situations and determine appropriate dating etiquette for each:

▶ Krissie and Matt have a date for the winter dance. The Saturday morning of the dance Matt wakes up with the flu.

▶ Mike asks Amanda at school on Monday to go to the movies on Friday night. Amanda tells Mike she will give him an answer later.

▶ Jessica is a senior in high school. Her boyfriend is in the military and can't get home for her senior prom. She really wants to go and is considering asking Adam.

**What should Matt do?**
**Is it right for Amanda to make Mike wait for an answer?**
**Should Jessica go to the prom with Adam when she has a boyfriend in the military?**

## Remaining Single

Quite often, people assume that everyone dates and that this is a natural pattern of development for everyone. We also assume that dating will eventually lead to love and marriage. Both of these assumptions do not apply to everyone. In today's society, the trend is to postpone marriage. Not all people want to date. Not all people who date want to marry. And the median age for a first marriage has increased to age 25 for women and 27 for men.

There are several reasons for not marrying—including social, legal, career goals, and personal independence. What do you think are some advantages of remaining single? What do you think are disadvantages of remaining single?

# Recognizing Love

Is it love or is it infatuation? What is "puppy love?" What is "romantic love?" How is it different from mature love? Poets, philosophers, and songwriters have been writing about love and trying to define love forever. Historically, love has been seen as an amusement, a distraction, or even a "sickness."

**Love** can be defined as a strong feeling of affection between two people. By learning the difference between love and **infatuation** (an intense feeling not based on reason), you will better understand your own feelings. "Puppy love" and "crushes" are other words for infatuation.

## Is It True Love?

| Love | Infatuation |
| --- | --- |
| Is a friendship that keeps growing | Is an overwhelming desire |
| Recognizes imperfections and accepts them | Ignores imperfections or tries to change the loved one |
| Trusts the loved one | Distrusts the loved one |
| Makes you a better person | Can cause regrets |

The concept of romantic love is very popular in America. Think about all the songs and phrases about love, such as "love at first sight," "falling in love," and "I can't live without him (or her)." **Romantic love** can be described as falling in love with an idea rather than with a real person. Unfortunately, this can lead to great disappointment. When you take off your "rose-colored glasses" you may see that the idea you fell in love with and the real person are nothing alike.

In **mature love**, which is a realistic sharing of a committed relationship, a person can maintain a sense of individuality and yet become part of a mutual relationship. Mature love includes friendship. In other words, you genuinely like the person as well as love him. Mature love also includes strong physical attraction, emotional attachment,

*How can you tell when you love someone enough to spend the rest of your life with him or her?*

## CAREER FACT

While pharmacists measure, package, and sell the medicines that doctors prescribe, they are becoming more involved in advising doctors and patients. One of the stresses of working in a pharmacy is the responsibility for the well-being of the patients; the slightest mistake, such as giving out the wrong medicine or dosage, could harm or kill a patient. Becoming a pharmacist requires graduating from a college of pharmacy, passing a state exam, and getting a license.

## WELLNESS

### Signs of Dating Abuse

Many teenagers are in dating relationships that are unhealthy or even dangerous. The following behaviors are warning signs of dating abuse:

▶ Excessive calling or texting to check up on a dating partner

▶ Repeatedly insulting or criticizing a dating partner

▶ Acting jealous or suspicious or making threats

▶ Pushing, shoving, or slapping

▶ Preventing a dating partner from spending time with family and friends

▶ Pressuring a dating partner into sexual activity

If you or someone you know is dating a person who is behaving this way, you need to tell a friend or trusted adult so that the abuse can stop. You also can contact the National Teen Dating Abuse Helpline on the Internet at www.loveisrespect.org or by calling 1-866-331-9474 or 1-866-331-8453 (TTY).

and the ability to confide in one another. Mature love requires that you learn how to communicate with a partner. You try to understand each other. Love then becomes what your partner and you make it.

## Case Study: Should This Couple Stay Together?

Amber and Kyle are in love and plan to marry in one year. Amber is a moody person. Kyle thinks that sometimes she understands him completely, and other times she seems so far away that he wonders if he knows her at all. Kyle is attached to Amber in so many ways, but he doesn't believe that she understands his problems and doesn't seem very interested in hearing about them. Amber just teases Kyle and says, "Just tell me you love me, and everything will be fine." When Kyle and Amber have disagreements, Amber has a way of working it out so the whole thing seems to be Kyle's fault. She can be quite sarcastic. It's getting so Kyle doesn't tell her what's on his mind anymore for fear of annoying her. The two of them still get along well together and have fun—as long as everything is okay. Kyle sometimes wishes that Amber were more sympathetic and supportive. He wants to talk all this out with her to see if he can make her understand what he needs from her. But he's afraid he will lose her if he starts complaining.

**Do you think Kyle and Amber love one another?**
**Do you think one shows more love than the other? Why or why not?**
**Do you think they can resolve their differences?**

**Understanding Key Concept**

1. What is the purpose of dating?
2. What are the stages of dating?
3. What are the differences between infatuation and love?

**Thinking Creatively**

What roles do families have in guiding young people as they begin to date?

Why does the term "puppy love" make some young people angry?

**Taking It a Step Further**

What messages do television, movies, and music videos give about dating? Are there any current television series that show teens socializing in groups rather than in paired (single) dating? What would dating be like if it matched the experiences portrayed in music videos?

# Section 14-2: Beginning Your Own Family

If you choose to have a family, you are in for a wonderful adventure. A family is one of life's most fulfilling experiences. It is also a challenge because of the demands it makes on every family member. When you choose to have a family, you accept several new roles: spouse, in-law, and potentially a parent. Your responsibilities increase as you accept those roles. If you choose to be a parent, it will be the most important career you will ever have.

## Creating a Successful Marriage

A successful marriage is always in the process of becoming. It develops day by day. To achieve a successful marriage, both people must make many adjustments and readjustments. Each person must be committed to helping make the other person happy. A successful marriage involves sacrifice by both individuals.

## How Can You Know When You're Ready for Marriage?

Getting ready for marriage is a slow process that starts long before you meet your future mate. Success in marriage is possible when you

▶ Understand yourself

▶ Understand your partner

**COMMUNITY**

Health Occupations Students of America (HOSA) is a career and technical student organization for students who are interested in medicine, nursing, dentistry, and other health-related careers. This organization focuses on helping students expand their knowledge of health care and develop their leadership, problem-solving, and social skills. Contact your local chapter or the Web site, www.hosa.org, for more information.

- Accept responsibility
- Demonstrate emotional maturity

Understanding yourself might sound quite simple, but remember that you are a very complex person. You have your own physical characteristics, thoughts, feelings, values and goals. Until you understand yourself, is it possible to understand another person in a close relationship?

Your future partner will also have his or her own **individuality** (the characteristics that distinguish one person from another). It is important to realize that this person is different from you. You must accept this person and his or her differences. Do you think you can change another person who does not want to change?

Accepting responsibility is a critical step in preparing for marriage and parenting. Responsibility is a broad category that includes such things as

- Financial responsibility (not only paying the bills on time but providing security for the family)

- Relationship responsibility (for example, taking care of your partner or children when they are sick)

- Home and household responsibility (keeping up your investment in your home and possessions)

- Educational and career responsibility (providing your family with security and opportunities for desired lifestyles)

Demonstrating emotional maturity involves coping with all of these responsibilities. Your relationships will depend on your total emotional development. The best way to understand your relationships is to understand yourself.

The number one task for any person hoping to improve his marriage is to increase self-esteem and emotional maturity. A marriage is only as well-adjusted as the two partners.

## Why Should a Couple Become Engaged?

We know that not all dating relationships lead to marriage. However, when couples do choose to marry, the final stage before marriage is called **engagement**. It is a testing period in which the couple evaluates the relationship and prepares for marriage. The engagement period serves many purposes, including the following:

- Planning the wedding
- Determining the role of religion in your married lives
- Getting acquainted with one another's families
- Planning for children
- Arranging your lives

- Managing money
- Getting to know each other's friends

**Wedding** planning is important, but it's not the most important part of the engagement. The wedding is only one party that will take up a very small part of your married life together. Enjoy the planning and the activities leading up to your marriage, but keep everything in perspective. Weddings can be very expensive. According to *Bride's Magazine*, it takes close to $19,000 to turn a dream wedding into a reality! Are you willing to spend that much money? Can your parents afford to pay those expenses? Are there other things you could spend the money on?

*Why is the engagement period important?*

## Healthy Marriages

According to the National Healthy Marriage Resource Center, the following factors are an important part of a healthy marriage:

- The couple is committed to staying together even when things are difficult. Both people are willing to make sacrifices for each other.
- Both people feel happy about the marriage most of the time.
- When the two people talk to each other, they are respectful and positive.
- The couple is able to resolve conflicts effectively.
- Neither person is ever violent or aggressive toward the other person.
- Both people are faithful to each other.
- The people are friends and enjoy being with each other.
- Both people trust each other. They are physically affectionate and care for each other emotionally.
- If the couple has children, both parents are focused on the children's well-being.
- Both people believe that marriage is permanent and that their relationship will last.

The following conditions present difficult challenges that can lead to divorce if they are not addressed appropriately:

- Addictions
- Anger
- Mental and physical illness
- Work issues
- Financial stress
- Infidelity

Counseling can often help couples work through these and other relationship challenges.

### CAREER FACT

Recreational therapists use activities and objects such as arts and crafts, animals, sports, games, dance, drama, music, and community outings to improve the physical, mental, and emotional health of their patients. Training for the occupation requires a bachelor's degree in either therapeutic recreation or recreation (with courses in therapeutic recreation).

About 75 percent of couples getting married choose to have a religious ceremony. If you share the same religion, planning the wedding ceremony will be much easier. Having different religious, ethnic, or economic backgrounds can create more difficulty in making wedding plans. You might want to consider religious counseling with your pastor, priest, or rabbi during your engagement period.

Marriage is said to be the joining of two families. "When you marry, you marry the family." Whether you agree with this statement or not, it is true. In-laws can be a great source of support, but not having a good relationship with them can create some serious problems for your marriage.

Time spent with your families will give you the opportunity to think about starting your own. You need to discuss whether you want to have children, and when and how many if you decide to have them. You will also want to talk about whether one parent will stay home with the children. Who will care for the children if both parents work? Resolving parenting issues before the marriage will help you understand each other's values and expectations.

The engagement period is the time to decide where you are going to live and make all the other decisions that go along with daily living. Go shopping with one another and discuss your likes and dislikes about food, home furnishings, and pets, for example. Look at and discuss your choices.

*How much money and time are you willing to spend on a wedding?*

*What issues face two people considering getting married?*

One of the greatest sources of conflict for married couples is money. Agreeing on money issues while you are engaged is very helpful. Shopping expeditions automatically bring up the subject of money management. This is a very important area of discussion during your engagement. You will need to work out a spending plan and discuss what is important to each of you. Look at your long-term goals and discuss how you plan to reach those goals.

No one is expected to give up his or her friends after marriage. However, marriage does change friendships. Because you are doing more as a couple, as you should, plans with friends require discussion with your future spouse. What if you don't like your fiancee's friends? You need to be honest with your fiancee as well as with yourself. What don't you like about the friends?

## Why Should You Have a Wedding?

The wedding provides a transition from single life to married life. You might choose to have a small, intimate wedding on an island in the Bahamas. You might want a large church wedding and reception with several hundred guests. Some couples choose to **elope** (run away and marry secretly). You will need to decide what is best for you as a couple and how much you want your families involved. Remember, however, that your parents do have the right to express opinions about your wedding plans if they are paying the expenses.

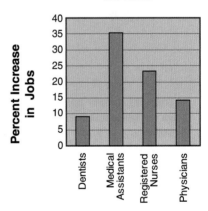

*What does this chart tell you about future opportunities in these careers?*

## Stages of Child Development

As children grow into adults, they go through many stages:

▶ **Babies (0–1 year old):** Babies are learning to focus their vision and understand language and are developing bonds of love and trust with their parents. Parents keep babies safe by using car seats, keeping small items away from babies to prevent choking, and taking them to the doctor for vaccinations. When you spend time with babies, try playing music, talking to them, showing them colorful or moving objects, and cuddling them.

▶ **Toddlers (1–3 years old):** Toddlers are more independent (and sometimes defiant) and mobile. They can follow simple commands and enjoy exploring new places and imitating people. Parents keep toddlers safe by blocking off stairways and other dangerous areas, locking up poisons, and never leaving them alone in a car or near water. To play with toddlers, try reading to them, taking them to a playground or park, and teaching them songs or nursery rhymes.

▶ **Preschoolers (3–5 years old):** Preschoolers are learning to dress themselves and can help with simple chores. They also are starting to play with children their own age. Parents keep their preschoolers safe by keeping them away from traffic, checking out playground equipment, and teaching them about strangers. Preschoolers enjoy riding tricycles, doing simple art projects, and listening to stories.

▶ **Grade schoolers (6–8 years old):** By this age, children know how to catch a ball and tie their shoes. They can read and do simple math. Parents keep their grade schoolers safe by making sure they wear bike helmets and other safety gear, teaching them how to swim, and locking up power tools and other dangerous equipment. When you spend time with children at this age, try teaching them a game, playing sports with them, and helping them with their homework.

▶ **Preadolescents (9–11 years old):** Friends are becoming more important to children at this age. They are more independent and may have some responsibility around the home, such as taking care of pets. Parents keep their preadolescents safe by making sure they wear seatbelts and knowing where they are and whom they are with at all times. Children at this age are interested in joining community groups and volunteering, learning crafts or playing instruments, and competing in sports.

As you move into your teenage years, what challenges do you face? What skills have you developed? How are you becoming more independent and responsible?

---

As you make your decisions, keep in mind that you want your wedding day to be one of the happiest, most memorable days of your married life. Wise decisions, careful planning, and making the day an expression of your mutual love will help to make it a joy, not a stressed-out disaster.

## What Makes a Marriage Successful?

Marriage requires major adjustments. It brings with it many duties and obligations. This transition is often a big step. The adjustments cover a broad range of topics, such as

▶ Who pays the bills or does the laundry?

▶ Who walks the dog or changes the cat litter box?

▶ Which way should the toilet paper unroll?

▶ What financial goals do you have? Do you want to own your own home? Do you want to start a college savings account for your children?

▶ What role should your parents and extended families play in your marriage, especially during holidays and celebrations?

### Word from the Wise

The kind of marriage you make depends upon the kind of person you are. If you are a happy, well-adjusted person, the chances are your marriage will be a happy one. If you have made adjustments so far with more satisfaction than distress, you are likely to make your marriage and family adjustments satisfactorily. If you are discontented and bitter about your lot in life, you will have to change before you can expect to live happily ever after.

Evelyn Duvall and Reuben Hill
—*When You Marry*

- Which is most important: the wife-husband relationship or parent-child relationship?

- How can you create a mutually satisfactory sexual relationship?

A successful marriage isn't like a game that has established rules. Learning each other's likes, dislikes, and desires takes time. Living with another person requires adjustments. Having problem-solving skills is very important for creating a successful marriage and managing a family. Additionally, understanding, commitment, and effective communication are essential.

## Case Study: Where Should You Go for Thanksgiving Dinner?

Your spouse's family is having Thanksgiving dinner with the entire extended family. At the same time, your family is also having Thanksgiving dinner, and your mother will be very disappointed if you are not there.

**What alternatives do you and your spouse have?**
**What are the advantages and disadvantages of each?**
**Which appears to be the best alternative? Why?**

## Preparing for Parenting

"And baby makes three!" How do you know when you are ready for children? The ideal situation is one in which both the husband and wife want children, are healthy enough for parenthood, and can financially support a family. There are both positive and negative reasons for having children. Can you list some? What effects do children have on a marriage?

Having a child is complicated and involves many factors including conceiving, dealing with pregnancy, getting through the childbirth, and adjusting to and caring for the new baby. Even when parents believe that they are completely prepared for a child, they still have fears and conflicting feelings. The transition from couple to parents causes emotional and physical adjustments.

*How does having a baby change a couple's life?*

Bringing that new baby home is exciting and frightening at the same time. If the baby cries, parents worry. If the baby doesn't cry, parents worry. A baby is extremely demanding. Parents will spend a great deal of their time focusing on the needs and demands of the new baby. All have to adjust to taking second place to the baby, which can create feelings of jealousy and insecurity for some. This means that couples' social lives have changed drastically. Careers are also affected: If one spouse chooses to stay at home while the other works, all kinds of questions and potential conflicts arise.

Even with all these problems, most parents agree that parenting is one of the most fulfilling experiences in their entire lifetimes. In a national survey, 90 percent of the parents surveyed said that they would have children again. The joys and happiness that children experience give parents the opportunity to see the world through their own children's eyes. Relationships with extended families strengthen as the couple's parents take on the role of grandparents. There certainly are both positives and negatives of parenthood.

## Overcoming Family Problems

Nearly every family will face problems at some point. What do you think are some problems families face today? The ways in which a family reacts to those difficult times is a reflection of its problem-solving skills, knowledge of resources available, commitment, and willingness to work together to find solutions.

One common family problem is caused by the availability of credit cards. They sometimes bring the temptation to overspend. Within a short time, a family can find itself in deep financial trouble. Rather than becoming angry with each other, members of a family should contact one of the many free financial counseling agencies for advice. However, be careful when choosing an agency. Some charge for their services and take advantage of their clients.

*How could calling a meeting help a family find solutions to problems?*

A family with emotional, mental, or medical struggles can find help through religious organizations, social service organizations, or community support groups. Quite often, national groups host Web sites that provide free information and give contact information for local groups.

## Section 14-2: Review

**Understanding Key Concepts**

1. What is the purpose of an engagement?
2. What can increase the possibility of a successful marriage?
3. How can a couple know that they are ready to have children?

**Thinking Creatively**

Describe a marriage that seems successful to you.

Given the fact that children require so much work and money, why do people continue to have them?

**Taking It a Step Further**

According to the U.S. government, what constitutes a family? Do people who live together without marriage have a family? Research the definition of marriage online.

# Section 14-3: Balancing Your Personal, Family, and Work Life

Many movies, sitcoms, and books present the problem of balancing personal, family, and work life. It is definitely a balancing act! Can you think of examples from movies or television?

Think about your own life and all the things you have to balance: school, homework, chores, extracurricular activities, and a part-time job (to mention just a few). Now, take your responsibilities times the number of people in your family. Does that give you a clearer picture of the balancing act your parents are performing? Some workplaces are more family-oriented than others. For example, some employers provide child day care facilities at or near the workplace or allow flexible work schedules to meet family needs. In addition to your parents' careers, they are trying to balance between family, extended family, friends, community and church or synagogue commitments, and some personal time for themselves.

Some tips that will help your parents and you balance your lives include the following:

> **Communicate.** It is important to share your thoughts with your family, friends, employer, and co-workers. By communicating, you will receive more support and understanding from those who love you and want you to be successful. Co-workers will be more supportive and helpful. Don't forget that communication involves more than just words. Make sure that your nonverbal messages help create a peaceful home.

> **Manage your time.** Time is the only resource that everyone receives in equal amounts. If you don't use it, you lose it. Time management is critical when you have several things to accomplish in a short period of time. Do two things at once when possible. Learn how to cut down on time-wasters. Focus on the task and don't get distracted. Time management strategies work well in a person's personal life and in a job.

> **Prioritize.** Setting priorities means deciding what is most important and doing it first or giving most of your attention to your goal or objective. Priorities can change depending on the situation. Think about your own priorities. List them in order of importance. Compare your list to a friend's. Are your lists similar or different?

> **Stay healthy.** Good health is one of the most important things you can have. Just ask someone who has health problems. Keeping your life in balance requires eating healthy foods, getting enough sleep, exercising, avoiding harmful substances, and controlling stress in your life.

## NETWORKING

Talk with your family members to determine the longest enduring marriage in the family. Then compare your findings with the rest of the class.

## COMMUNITY

Talk with several young mothers in your community about their greatest needs. Share their responses with other members of your class and look for a way to help meet the needs of the mothers.

*What responsibilities and pleasures does a family have?*

▶ **Take breaks.** With so much to do in our busy lives today, we all strive to be as organized as possible. But if you are trying to control every single minute of your life, you are missing out on the unexpected pleasures in life. "Stop and smell the roses" is a phrase you will hear often. What does this mean to you? Leisure time (time to do what you enjoy doing) is important to your health, both mental and physical.

## Section 14-3: Review

### Understanding Key Concepts

1. What are the responsibilities that many parents must balance?
2. What are five tips that can help a person maintain a balanced lifestyle?

### Thinking Creatively

What are the signs that a family is not living a balanced life?
What proves that our society does or does not value having a balanced life?

### Taking It a Step Further

Research a family-oriented workplace and identify advantages of working for such a company.

**Sally Russell**
**Director of Education Services**

I work for a firm that provides specialty nursing associations with conferences, executive directors, and other personnel. I am contracted out to those associations as their Director of Education. I work with committees that plan national conferences and other activities, and I write journal articles.

I graduated from Ball State University with a Bachelor of Science in Nursing and a Master of Arts in Nursing. I have passed certification exams, and am a Certified Medical Surgical Registered Nurse (CMSRN) and a Certified Program Planner (CPP).

When I was in high school, I wanted to be a nurse, a history teacher, or an English teacher. My first position after graduating from nursing school was as a staff nurse in a hospital. I managed the care of the clients assigned to me and supervised the non-licensed people in my patient units. After working there for five years, I moved to an entry-level teaching position at a school of nursing. These experiences were valuable for my work today.

I tend to bring work home frequently. That's why I set aside dates for visiting places such as Gettysburg and New York City. I have to schedule those times in order to make sure they happen. I read mysteries and books on history. I also play the piano, cook, and work in the flower gardens in my yard.

# Chapter Review and Activities

The following sections can help you review the contents of this chapter.

## Key Concepts

Following are the key concepts presented in the chapter.

▶ One of the best gifts you can give yourself is the gift of freedom and living on your own for a while.

▶ After you know yourself clearly, you might find that you want to develop meaningful relationships with other people by dating.

▶ Dating etiquette requires practice.

▶ By learning the difference between love and infatuation, you will better understand your own feelings.

▶ The engagement period serves many purposes, including wedding planning, determining the role of religion in your marriage, getting acquainted with one another's families and friends, and discussing many important life choices.

▶ To achieve a successful marriage, both partners must make many adjustments and readjustments and work toward making each other happy.

▶ When you choose to have a family, you accept several new roles and additional responsibilities.

### ROLE-PLAYING

**Scenario:** Two students will role play the parts of husband and wife, both of whom have full-time jobs. They have a three-year-old daughter who is sick and cannot go to the child care center. What are they going to do?

**Roles:** Husband and wife.

**Discussion:** How well did the couple communicate? Were their opinions and ideas realistic and reasonable? What other solutions do you see for their dilemma? What are the advantages and disadvantages of each solution? What would you do?

- Parenting will be the most important career you will ever have if you choose to accept it.

- To be prepared for parenting, the ideal situation is one in which both the husband and wife want children, are healthy, and can financially support a family.

- To balance your personal, family and work life, you must communicate, manage your time, prioritize, and stay healthy.

## Key Term Review

Complete the following activity to review your understanding of the key terms.

| | | |
|---|---|---|
| dating | individuality | romantic love |
| dating etiquette | infatuation | single dating |
| elope | love | wedding |
| engagement | mature love | |
| group dating | paired dating | |

You are a doctor volunteering at a clinic for unwed mothers. Young mothers-to-be frequently ask you how they can know the difference between infatuation and genuine love. Using at least 10 key terms, write a brochure that explains the purpose of dating and how to make the transition into a marriage.

## Comprehension Review

**1.** What are the purposes and stages of dating?

**2.** What are the differences between love and infatuation?

**3.** What purpose does an engagement fulfill?

**4.** What can increase the possibility of a successful marriage?

**5.** How can a couple know that they are ready to have children?

**6.** What responsibilities must many adults balance?

**7.** How can a person maintain a balanced lifestyle?

## School-to-Work

**Math:** Write down the steps you would take to solve this mathematical problem:

You are purchasing a new carpet for the living room. Its dimensions are 19 feet by 24 feet. Carpet comes in widths of 12 or 15 feet at $7.20 per square foot. Which width should you use and how much would just the carpet cost?

**Social Studies:** If you had to remain in your current community, on which street would you like to live? If you had to choose a location within your state but not in your community, where would you choose to live? If you had to choose a state other than the one in which you currently live, which city and state would you choose? Using Internet maps, print maps of each location.

**Writing:** Write a description of the type of person you want to marry. Include those factors that are most important to you: appearance, education, religion, values, goals, or personality.

**Science:** Use the Internet to find out how the heat packs in a first-aid kit work. Using images from the Web, write text that briefly explains the content of heat packs and how they work.

---

## Does This Job Interest You?

The following job is posted on the Internet. What education and experience are required? What requirements does this job have that most jobs do not have? What types of interests and skills should a person working in this position have? How could someone apply for the job? How could someone find out more about the job?

| FIND JOBS | POST RESUMES |
| --- | --- |

### Health Education Instructor

**Category:** Professional: Education/Training     **Position:** Full-time employment
**Department:** Health Education     **Location:** Modesto, California

### Description

Responsible for teaching prenatal classes to prospective parents, according to a standardized curriculum for topic area. Assesses needs of individuals and adapts class content to meet those needs. Model skills taught in class curriculum.

### Experience Required

Bachelor's degree in Health Education, Nursing or related field. Knowledge of the class topic area. Prior experience (minimum of one year, three years preferred) teaching classes in the topic area. Knowledge of adult learning theory and group process. Group facilitation skills.

### Compensation

$52,600–$63,700

### Contact

Healthful Beginnings
Modesto, California

**Apply Online**

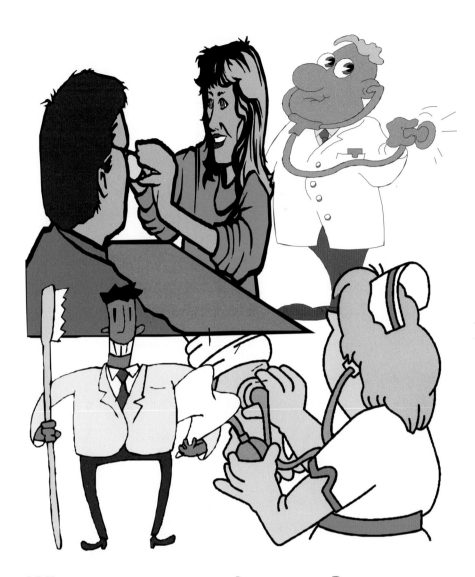

## What career appeals to you?

# Chapter 15

# Designing Your Tomorrow Today

## What You'll Learn

▶ Defining and evaluating your dreams

▶ Recording the goals required to make your dreams a reality

▶ Making a plan of action

▶ Evaluating your choices regularly

Who do you want to be when you are an independent adult? What kind of life do you want to have? The life you want will not fall into your lap; you have the responsibility to create it. How can you begin today to create the life you want tomorrow? The answers to these questions are inside you.

*I know of no more encouraging fact than the unquestioned ability of a man to elevate his life by conscious endeavor.*

—*Henry David Thoreau*

# Section 15-1: Define Your Dreams

The first step toward creating a lifestyle that will be satisfying for you is to describe everything you dream of being or having, what you want for your life today, and what you think you will want when you are an adult. The questions you need to answer are these:

▶ Who do you want to be?

▶ What do you want to do with your life?

▶ What do you want to own?

▶ Who do you want to have in your life?

Too often, people state their dreams for their life, but in the next breath say why they cannot achieve them. As you define your dreams, keep in mind these two thoughts:

▶ If you use brainstorming to list your dreams, you will come up with a broader range of possibilities. That is, write down any thoughts that come to you without evaluating them.

▶ Do not worry about whether you have all the resources you need to achieve your dreams—enough time, money, knowledge, self-confidence, love, and skill. You probably do have or can find those resources.

## Who Do You Want to Be?

Why should anyone ask, "Who do you want to be?" You are you. You cannot change that. Or can you? Although you cannot change certain physical features and characteristics of your personality, you can change many other facets of who you are.

You can strengthen your body through exercise. You can improve your appearance by learning more about personal hygiene or fashion. You can develop your mind through education. You can change your behavior or conquer bad habits through making different choices, seeing a counselor, or learning from others. Making changes is easier while you are still in school because you have many resources available to you. Most are free or nearly so.

*How important is it to have adults in your life who can help you make decisions?*

You will want to get advice from your parents and friends, for example. Talk to adults at work and in your community. Ask your teachers and guidance counselor questions. All these people can give you input on how they became who they are. The information they give you can help you decide who you want to be.

Learn to be comfortable with expressing your ideas and your needs. Doing so will make you more confident and understandable when talking about your future.

## What Do You Want to Do with Your Time?

How do you want to spend your days as an adult? Do you want to be married? Do you want to be a parent? Do you want to have a career? You need to explore how you feel about these questions even before you begin preparing for your future. Does that sentence sound confusing?

Think about this example. Would you order a year's supply of any of these foods before you knew whether you liked them: sushi (Japanese raw fish); seafood pizza with anchovies (small sardine-type fish); gyro sandwich (lamb meat); or caviar (very expensive sturgeon fish eggs)? If you buy the food and then discover that you do not like it, you have wasted your time and

*What is the benefit of approaching new experiences gradually?*

money—and you are probably still hungry! Trying new things is fun, but sometimes the best approach is to try them gradually.

This is also true when it comes to choosing and preparing for your career or lifestyle. You need to know whether you will like a career or lifestyle before you spend too much time, energy, or money on it. In your career, for example, what kind of work do you want to do each day? Do you want to work with people, machines, or paper? Do you want to be an **organizer** of information (to give order to it) or a **creator** (to bring something into existence)? Do you want to do the same tasks over and over or have a flexible schedule? Do you want to travel with your work or stay in one location? At the end of your day, do you want to be able to say "See what I did," or "See who I helped?" These are the "doing" questions that only you can answer about your future.

You begin determining how you want to spend your adult workdays while you are still in high school. The courses you select and the grades you earn lay the foundation for your postsecondary education.

In defining your dream, you also might want to describe the type of social life you will have as an adult. How much time will you want to spend with friends? What activities would you like to be involved in? Do you enjoy eating out, participating in or watching sports, attending concerts, or camping and hiking with friends?

## What Do You Want to Own?

Why should young people be thinking about what they want to own when they are adults? Thinking about what you want to own can help you determine the lifestyle you want. How?

Do you want to own a home in an urban or suburban area? Would you rather live in an apartment or condo (and not have to tend to a lawn or take care of the exterior of your home)? Would you rather live in a houseboat?

Do you want to rely on public transportation and save your money for other purposes, or do you want to own a vehicle? If you want a vehicle, what type would you enjoy driving?

If you want a house and a vehicle, you must find a way to pay for them. The career you choose should be one that enables you to earn enough money to buy and take care of your **possessions** (the items you own).

**Materialistic values** (an emphasis on goods and money) will be different for every person. What will satisfy you? **Nonmaterialistic values** (relationships and social causes) are equally important and also are directly related to your lifestyle. For example, if you value wealth (materialism), you might want a big house, a large boat, a new car, or all of the above. If you value

*Which of these would you choose?*

*No man is an island unto himself.*

—*John Donne*

relationships and social causes, you might want to live simply and use your extra money to help the needy.

Some of you might consider other values more important. You might believe that putting an emphasis on possessions is unimportant or overly **self-indulgent** (putting one's own wants and needs ahead of others). Be careful not to judge others. They must be free to choose a career that fits the lifestyle they desire.

## Who Do You Want to Have in Your Life?

What do you think the poet John Donne meant when he said that people are not islands? An important part of any life is the people in it. You have some choices about who is involved in your life. Of course, you do not have a choice about the family into which you were born, but you can choose your friends, roommates, spouse, and whether to have children.

*What type of people do you want to be with every day?*

When you choose a specific career, you also are choosing the type of people you are with every day. Let's say you are interested in education. If you choose a career as an elementary teacher, you will be working with children, their parents, and other educators. If you choose a career as a college professor, you will be working with adults—an entirely different group of people. The choice is yours.

Although there are times when you want to be alone, your relationships with other people (families, friends, and strangers) help shape your attitudes and beliefs. Relationships can expand your knowledge and determine your course in life. If you choose to have a relationship with a **significant other** (an important person in your life), or have a large circle of friends or extensive contacts with people at work, your life and its purposes will change with these relationships. Who do you want to have in your life?

## Case Study: What Tradeoffs Is Chantal Having to Make?

Chantal works for a large retail chain as a "secret shopper." She travels extensively, visiting stores in this chain to determine whether they are managed according to company policies. Chantal loves the travel. For example, during a three-week period, she may be in Kentucky, Texas, and Wisconsin. During the day, she is extremely busy—either posing as a shopper or working with the store's managers to help them improve. At night, however, she spends her time alone in hotels with very little to do and few personal contacts.

**Would you like Chantal's career?**

**Does it match your expected lifestyle?**

**What do you see as a tradeoff (the advantages and disadvantages) of this situation?**

*The most difficult thing in life is to know yourself.*

—*Thales*

# Section 15-2: Evaluate Your Dreams

After you define your dreams, go back and evaluate them by looking at whether your dreams reflect your values and how hard are you willing to work to achieve your dreams.

## Do Your Dreams Reflect Your Values?

When you evaluate your dreams of who you want to be today and who you want to become, think carefully about your values. Do you value having a healthy body? How important is an education to you? Do you value family, friends, and your community? What role do you want to play in society? How important is religion to you?

When you evaluate what you want to do with your time, make sure that your choices reflect your values. If you think helping people is important, find a career that gives you opportunities to do so. If you value music, make sure that you have a career that either involves music or leaves you with enough free time that you can pursue music as a hobby.

People either deliberately choose to purchase items because of their **personal values** (beliefs and standards of behavior that an individual accepts and follows) or because they want to have what everyone else has. Except for taxes and Social Security, you can spend your money the way you want. No law says that you have to have a great wardrobe, a television, a car, or a house. Compare what you dream of owning with what you personally think is important.

**CAREER FACT**

Protective service personnel are those who enforce military laws and regulations, provide emergency response to natural and human-made disasters, and maintain food standards in specialized units. Military police, for example, control traffic, prevent crime, and respond to emergencies.

# Occupations of Military Officers

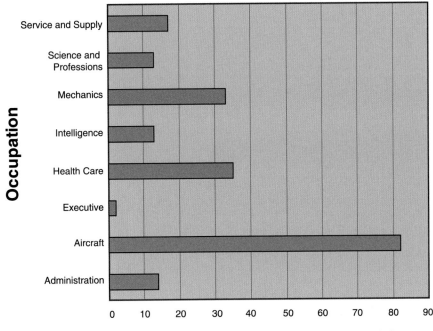

**Number of officers (in thousands)**

*Can you see yourself working for the U.S. military in any of these occupations?*

**ETHICS**

A snowstorm passed through, leaving six inches of snow everywhere. When you leave work, you can see that a customer's car is stuck, but you are very tired. You have to clean off your car before you can leave. What will you do?

Think carefully about the people you build into your life. They can help you become a better person, or they can create problems. If you find that a friendship is a negative factor in your life, you can choose to politely cool or end the relationship. However, you cannot walk away from some relationships so easily. A negative marriage relationship cannot be ended so easily, especially if you have children together. When you choose to have children, you are always their parent. In the role of a parent, you have many responsibilities. It's much better to choose not to have children than to end a relationship with them. Doing so creates guilt, anger, and suffering for everyone involved.

Thinking about your values will help you know yourself and your needs better. This will also help you determine what you want from a career.

*Do you plan to have children of your own?*

**Where Can You Go for Help?**

If you are struggling with any of the following, turn to someone for help.

▸ Often feeling sad and tearful

▸ Feeling that you have nothing to look forward to

▸ Feeling tired and bored with everything

▸ Preferring to be alone most of the time

▸ Blaming yourself for the bad things in your life

▸ Feeling as if you cannot do anything right

▸ Feeling grouchy and angry most of the time

▸ Skipping school or failing classes

▸ Thinking about running away

▸ Thinking about or actually hurting yourself

Find a friend or family member to talk with about your problems. See the counselor at school. Stop by a neighborhood mental health clinic. Life is too short to waste time being miserable.

*Never, never, never quit.*

*—Winston Churchill*

**CAREER FACT**

If you enjoy classes in history, math, or political science, you might want to consider a career in the military.

# Are You Willing to Work to Achieve Your Dreams?

After you make sure that your dreams align (match) with your values, you need to decide whether you are willing to work to achieve them. Some dreams require hard work, such as exercising regularly to run a marathon or studying to pass the bar exam to be a lawyer. Others require that you wait patiently, such as finding a publisher for a book that you wrote or developing a new type of flower. Are you willing to do whatever it takes to achieve your dreams? What are the keys to successfully achieving your dreams?

One of the keys has to be the willingness to take some risks. It's not easy to do this because with risks come failures, which are very difficult to deal with. On the other hand, where would our world be today if people had not been **risk-takers** (people willing to take risks)? Can you think of some examples of how we have benefited from others taking risks?

The second key is a **positive attitude** (a good feeling regarding people or things). Most employers agree that attitude separates good employees from bad ones. Your attitude definitely makes a difference. A favorite storybook for children is *The Little Engine That Could*. The line repeated over and over in it is "I think I can, I think I can, I think I can…" Negative thoughts will stop you dead in your tracks.

Working hard is the third key. Opportunities usually present themselves when you are willing to work hard. These include good attendance, punctuality, and reliability. To be successful, make decisions, accept responsibilities, and do your work to the best of your abilities.

*What can you do to make sure that you have a positive attitude?*

# Section 15-3: Develop a Plan That Will Make Your Dreams a Reality

You have tested your dream to see how well it reflects your values. You have decided whether you are willing to do whatever it takes to achieve your dream. Now you are ready to begin setting goals. Goals must be SMART: that is, they must be **S**pecific, **M**easurable, **A**ction-oriented, and **R**ealistic, and they must have a **T**ime limit.

If you dream of flying airplanes, for example, make it your goal to learn as much as you can about planes and explore a variety of experiences related to them—from engines to chassis to weather. Look for military service opportunities or postsecondary schools that offer courses in aviation. If you dream of designing clothing, set goals that will move you in that direction. The process for goal-setting is simple, but very important.

▸ **Identify your long-term goals.** List your long-term goals on paper. Committing yourself on paper gives you the confidence of making a decision. By listing and defining your long-term goals, you are more likely to reach them.

▸ **Divide your long-term goals into stepping-stone goals.** Stepping-stone goals will help you reach your ultimate goals. They will also allow you to adjust your plan or change it if you find out along the way that a change is necessary.

> **TECHNOLOGY**
>
> Technology may play a significant part in your long-term and short-term goals. Maybe you want to create a Web site about a cause that's important to you or make your band's music available on the Internet. In this case, your short-term goals will probably involve researching technical information or learning how to use special software or equipment. By working toward and achieving technological goals, you are likely to build skills that will help you in your future career.

*One of the most important principles of success is developing the habit of going the extra mile.*

*—Napoleon Hill*

**NETWORKING**

Find someone who seems to have the type of life you want to have. Interview that person and compare his goals with yours.

*If you can dream it, you can do it.*

—*Walt Disney*

▶ **Make a plan of action.** Your plan of action will guide you in reaching your goal. It will include how much education and training you will need, how much money you will need, and how you will get the money. Your plan of action will include dates and times to achieve stepping-stone goals as well as your ultimate long-term goals.

▶ **Evaluate your choices regularly.** Change is a part of life. Sometimes you will choose these changes. Sometimes these changes will happen even when you do not choose them. You might choose to change your major in college because you discovered a better educational opportunity, or you might choose to move to a different part of the country where you have more career opportunities. Other times, just when you believe you have everything under control and life is going the way you planned, along comes the unexpected. These transitional opportunities in your life will certainly make it interesting. How well you deal with them will determine your satisfaction with your life and career. It is your responsibility to evaluate your choices regularly throughout your entire lifetime.

*What goals do you have for your life?*

# Case Study: What Decisions Must Dana Make?

Dana's aunt and uncle live near the coast. During her annual summer visits to their home, she discovered that she loves being on the ocean and finds all sorts of boats fascinating. However, she lives in the Midwest and rarely gets an opportunity to be near a body of water or boat. Should Dana focus her goals on a career that involves water or just settle for something more convenient, such as applying for training in her mom's occupation as a medical assistant?

**If you were Dana, what would you do?**

**What long-term goals would you set?**

**What stepping-stone goals would you set?**

**What are possible risks Dana might face with either career choice?**

## Section 15-3: Review

### Understanding Key Concepts

1. Goals must be SMART. What do these letters represent?
2. What is the purpose of listing your long-term goals on paper?

### Thinking Creatively

What is an advantage of listing your long-term goals on paper?

Why are stepping-stone goals important for reaching your ultimate career goals?

### Taking It a Step Further

Look at goals you have set for yourself in the past. Have they been effective? Have you or circumstances around you changed since you set them? Write a description of who you are, what you want today, and where you want to be in 5, 10, and 15 years. Then create goals that will lead you to those results.

### Colin Powell
### Former Secretary of State

Colin Powell, the son of Jamaican immigrants, was raised in the South Bronx. He attended public school in New York City and the City College of New York (CCNY), earning a bachelor's degree in geology. While in college, Powell participated in Reserve Officers' Training Corps (ROTC). Because of that training, he entered the Army as an Army second lieutenant after he graduated from college. Later he earned a Master of Business Administration degree from George Washington University.

Powell was a battalion commander in Korea and fought in the Vietnam War. He also commanded the 2nd Brigade, 101st Airborne Division (Air Assault) and V Corps, United States Army, Europe. He served as the Commander-in-Chief, Forces Command, headquartered at Fort McPherson, Georgia. General Powell served as the 12th Chairman of the Joint Chiefs of Staff, Department of Defense, from October 1, 1989, to September 30, 1993, under both President George Bush and President Bill Clinton. He retired from the U.S. Army in 1993. In January 2001, President George W. Bush selected General Powell to be his Secretary of State. Powell was the first African-American to hold this high office in the United States government.

In addition to his governmental role, Powell is chairman of America's Promise, an organization that challenges Americans to invest in America's young people, making them a national priority. He is also a member of the Board of Trustees of Howard University and of the Board of Directors of the United Negro College Fund. He is also involved in other service organizations.

General Powell has won many U.S. military awards, including the Defense Distinguished Service Medal, the Bronze Star medal, and the Purple Heart. He has also received the Presidential Medal of Freedom, the Congressional Gold Medal, and an honorary knighthood (Knight Commander of the Bath) from the Queen of England. One of Powell's hobbies is working on old cars, especially fixing old Volvos. In a speech at the 2003 Job Shadow Day Program at the State Department, Colin Powell gave this advice:

> If you're going to be successful in life, hard work never ends. If you're going to be successful in life, homework never ends.

> I go home every night with two huge briefcases—briefcases full of homework. I've got briefing books, I've got things I've got to worry about for the next day, I've got speeches I have to look at that I have to deliver the next day with the whole world watching, waiting for me to goof. I've got all kinds of things I have to do, and I've got to do my homework every day. And I don't have to explain the next day why I didn't do my homework to the teacher. I've got to explain it to the President of the United States. And the President does not like it when you have not done your homework.

> And so hard work is a part of life. Preparation is a part of life—whether you're preparing for tomorrow as Secretary of State or whether you're preparing for tomorrow to go to school and do well on a test. Hard work requires discipline. You are at that stage in your life where you have to develop those habits of self-discipline—doing what you are supposed to do when you are supposed to do it, listening to instructions, reading constantly to gather in information, analyzing it, making right judgments, not being influenced by people in the wrong way, setting your own course, knowing right from wrong, knowing that right is going to take you to a bright future and wrong takes you nowhere.

You're at the age now where those habits have to become ingrained. You have to start disciplining yourself. You have to start doing what is required because you know it's required, not because your teacher or your mom or your dad or someone else is beating on you to do it.

You will find that if you develop those habits now—habits of discipline and hard work and homework and not being afraid of what the future has for you tomorrow—those habits become ingrained. And people notice that you are that kind of a person, someone who can be relied upon. And even at this early stage in your life, you begin to develop something called a reputation. You become someone who people look at and say, "I can count on him." "I can count on her." "I know that she does what she says she's going to do." "I know that that person has character."

This is the time when you learn how to fail. Failure is a part of life. Young people sometimes find failure difficult to take. You know, "Why did this happen to me? Why did I fail that test? Why is it that I had a problem with this friend at school?"

This is the time to understand that failure is a part of life. It never goes away. And what each of you as young people have to learn is how to deal with it. And the simple solution that I've found to deal with something going wrong, a failure, is to find out what you did wrong—not what someone else did wrong, not what someone did to you, "What did I do wrong that caused this failure?" And then learn from that. Examine it. Fix yourself. Prove yourself. And then roll up that failure in a little ball, throw it over your shoulder, and never think about it again. You cannot change yesterday—there is nothing you can do about yesterday. The only thing you can do is your best today and to get ready for tomorrow.

## Occupations of Enlisted Personnel

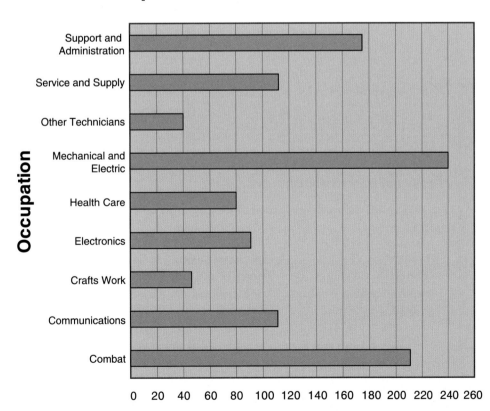

*Can you see yourself working for the U.S. military in any of these occupations?*

# Chapter Review and Activities

The following section can help you review the contents of this chapter.

## Key Concepts

Following are the key concepts presented in the chapter.

▶ The first step toward creating a lifestyle is to describe everything you dream of being or having, what you want for your life today, and when you are an adult.

▶ You can change many facets of who you are.

▶ Trying new things is fun, but sometimes the best choice is to try them gradually before you spend too much time, energy, or money.

▶ Thinking about what you want to own can help you determine the lifestyle you want.

▶ When you choose a specific career, you also are choosing the type of people you are with every day.

▶ After you define your dreams, go back and evaluate them.

▶ Think carefully about your values while you are evaluating your dreams.

▶ The keys to successfully achieving your dreams include taking risks, being positive, and working hard.

▶ Develop a plan that will make your dreams a reality.

## Key Term Review

Complete the following activity to review your understanding of the key terms.

| | | |
|---|---|---|
| creator | personal values | self-indulgent |
| materialistic values | positive attitude | significant other |
| nonmaterialistic values | possessions | tradeoff |
| organizer | risk-takers | |

Using the key terms, write a paragraph describing your values and explaining why you would or would not be willing to take risks.

## Comprehension Review

Answer the following questions to review your understanding of the key concepts in the chapter.

1. What four questions can help you define your dreams?

2. Why is it best to try new things a little at a time?

3. How can thinking about what you want to own help you determine the lifestyle you want?

4. Why do you need to think carefully about your values?

5. What is the purpose of listing your long-term goals on paper?

## School-to-Work

**Math:** Write the steps that you would take to solve the following mathematical problem and find the answer.

> You are working as an assistant manager of a clothing store and going to college for an accounting degree when the manager of the store calls you into her office and tells you that the district managers want to offer you a management position. Taking the job would mean that you would have to drop out of college. The salary they are offering you is $45,000 per year. That looks pretty good when compared to the $18,000 per year that you are making now. You know that the average income for an accountant is $65,000 per year, but tuition and books cost $8,000 per year, and you still have three more years to finish before you get your degree. Which option would give you more money over a 20-year span?

**Social Studies:** Enter the key term "utopian communities" into a search engine such as Google. Select one utopian community and write a paragraph about whether it is possible to have a perfect life.

**Writing:** Write a description (of at least five sentences) of a typical day in your life as an adult employee in the career that interests you the most right now.

**Science:** Using the Internet, find out what NASA's Earth Science division of the Science Mission Directorate is researching and create a poster or Power-Point presentation that summarizes your findings.

## Does This Job Interest You?

The following job is posted on the Internet. What education and experience are required? What requirement does this job have that most jobs do not have? What types of interests and skills should a person working in this position have? How could someone apply for the job? How could someone find out more about the job?

**FIND JOBS**   **POST RESUMES**

### Emergency Management Officer

Employer: U.S. Army

### Responsibilities

Emergency management officers in the military perform some or all of the following duties: organize emergency teams for quick responses to disaster situations; research ways to respond to possible disaster situations; conduct training programs for specialized disaster response teams; develop joint disaster response plans with local, state, and federal agencies; obtain supplies, equipment, and protective gear; develop warning systems and safe shelters; and direct disaster control centers.

### Helpful Attributes

Helpful fields of study include physical and environmental sciences, engineering, law enforcement, and business or public administration. Helpful attributes include ability to express ideas clearly and concisely, ability to remain calm in stressful situations, and an interest in developing detailed plans. A four-year college degree is normally required to enter this occupation.

### Training Provided

Job training consists of two to nine weeks of classroom instruction. Training length varies depending on specialty. Course content typically includes disaster planning; procedures for nuclear, biological, and chemical decontamination; effects of radiation; and procedures for nuclear accident teams.

Contact your nearest recruitment office if you are interested in learning more about serving your country as an emergency management officer.

**Apply Online**

**What career appeals to you?**

# Building Skills for the 21st Century

This section contains extra information about some of the topics covered in this book. Use it to help you as you work toward achieving your educational and career goals.

## Math Skills

Chapter 2, "Discovering Who You Are," presented the SCANS skills, which are the skills that the U.S. Department of Labor says are important to have in order to achieve success at work. One of the basic skills is working with numbers or math skills. Math skills include the ability to

▶ Perform basic computations including whole numbers and fractions

▶ Estimate mathematic results without a calculator

▶ Organize information with tables and graphs

▶ Choose from a variety of mathematical techniques to deal with practical problems

Chapter 12, "Managing Your Money," described everyday activities that require math skills, such as figuring out your taxes, balancing a checking account, managing credit cards and loans, and establishing a budget. Chapter 13, "Becoming a Responsible Consumer," also covered math-related topics such as choosing insurance, buying a car, and spending wisely on food and clothing.

### Connecting Math Skills to Careers

Almost all jobs require at least some understanding of basic mathematics. Some jobs, particularly those in science, engineering, and computers, require a deeper level of math skills. There are four levels of math skills: general, practical, applied, and advanced or theoretical.

People with general mathematics skills can add, subtract, multiply, and divide numbers. The following jobs require this level of math skills:

| | | |
|---|---|---|
| Accounting clerks | Plasterers | Shipping clerks |
| Bricklayers | Private investigators | Stock clerks |
| Drywall workers | Roofers | Taxi drivers |
| Medical assistants | Secretaries | Teacher aides |

Practical math skills include knowledge of algebra and geometry in addition to general math skills. Practical math skills are necessary in the following jobs:

| | | |
|---|---|---|
| Air traffic controllers | Jewelers | Nutritionists |
| Broadcast technicians | Landscape architects | Photographers |
| Carpenters | Machinists | Purchasers |
| Electricians | Mechanics | Welders |

People with applied math skills understand mathematical concepts and can apply them to their work. These skills include knowledge of statistics and trigonometry. The following jobs require these skills:

| | | |
|---|---|---|
| Accountants | Dentists | Legislators |
| Chiropractors | Drafters | Pilots |
| Computer programmers | Farmers | Surveyors |
| Construction contractors | General managers | Urban planners |

People with advanced or theoretical math skills understand more-complex math concepts such as calculus and linear algebra. The following jobs require advanced math skills:

| | | |
|---|---|---|
| Astronomers | Economists | Meteorologists |
| Actuaries | Engineers | Oceanographers |
| Computer scientists | Medical scientists | Statisticians |

## Improving Math Skills

To gain skill in working with numbers, you can

▸ Take courses in algebra and geometry. Algebra helps you with basic equations, and geometry helps you to measure and calculate the shapes of objects.

▸ Take classes to learn to use computer software that helps you calculate formulas, such as spreadsheet programs.

▸ Take courses in accounting to learn how to work with calculations concerning money.

▸ Keep a record of your own expenses and work up a monthly budget.

▸ Join a club or activity where math is involved, such as a club for people who work on electronics projects. Or serve as treasurer for a club to gain practice in managing budgets.

▸ Keep track of a particular stock's value on the stock market using the Internet. Create a graph showing the stock's highs and lows over a six-month period.

## Communication Skills

Chapter 6, "Developing Fundamental Workplace Skills," gave an overview of the four essential communication skills that play a role in nearly every job: speaking, listening, writing, and reading.

Speaking involves the ability to

▸ Organize ideas and speak clearly and effectively

▸ Use a style of speaking that fits your audience

▸ Understand and respond to listener feedback

Listening includes the ability to

▸ Pay attention to and understand spoken words and other sounds

▸ Notice and understand the meaning of a speaker's body language and tone of voice

▶ Respond to the speaker appropriately

Writing includes the ability to

▶ Communicate thoughts and information in writing

▶ Record information completely and accurately

▶ Use appropriate language, style, organization, and format

▶ Include supporting documentation

▶ Check, edit, and revise written material for correctness

The skill of reading includes the ability to

▶ Identify relevant facts

▶ Locate information

▶ Find meanings of words

▶ Judge accuracy of information

▶ Use a computer to find information

## Connecting Communication Skills to Careers

Although communication skills are a necessary part of every job, the level of communication skills that is required varies depending on the job. People with a basic level of communication skills can interact with others and follow simple oral and written instructions. High school English classes are helpful in developing this level of skill. Basic communication skills are required in these jobs:

| | | |
|---|---|---|
| Bank tellers | Dispatchers | Office clerks |
| Bus drivers | Flight attendants | Preschool teachers |
| Cashiers | Funeral directors | Proofreaders |
| Chauffeurs | Hotel desk clerks | Receptionists |
| Child care workers | Mail carriers | Ticket agents |
| Court reporters | Nursing aides | Visual artists |

People with intermediate communication skills can accurately give and follow instructions, persuade others, and write in an organized and grammatically correct manner. Both high school and college English classes are helpful in developing these skills. The following jobs require intermediate communication skills:

| | | |
|---|---|---|
| Architects | Financial managers | Paralegals |
| Building inspectors | Hotel managers | Pharmacists |
| Designers | Insurance agents | Physical therapists |
| Detectives | Licensed practical nurses | Real estate agents |

People with advanced communication skills have strong abilities in speaking and writing. To develop this level of skill, you should take college-level English courses. These jobs require advanced communication skills:

| | | |
|---|---|---|
| Actors | Editors | Podiatrists |
| Agricultural scientists | Geologists | Psychologists |
| Announcers | Lawyers | Reporters |
| Biologists | Librarians | Social workers |
| Chemists | Marketing managers | Teachers |
| Directors | Newscasters | Veterinarians |
| Doctors | Optometrists | Writers |

## Improving Communication Skills

There are several things you can do to improve your communication skills. Chapter 6 provided some tips on how to become a better speaker; this section provides tips on listening, writing, and reading.

Listening well is an important job skill, particularly when you are dealing with customers. To improve your listening skills, you can

▶ Take courses in speech or drama to practice speaking and listening to others speak.

▶ Listen closely in your classes and learn how to take good notes to help you remember important points.

▶ Learn another language. Listening to somebody speaking in another language can help you pay attention because your mind is actively engaged in translating each word.

▶ Listen to talk radio, audio books, or podcasts and focus on what's being said.

▶ Join a debating club or book discussion group.

▶ If you have trouble listening, every once in a while repeat back to the speaker what you think he or she has just said in your own words.

▶ Try to give the speaker an appropriate response. Nothing sends a clearer message that you're not listening than to respond to what's been said with an inappropriate comment.

▶ Let people finish what they are saying before responding.

▶ Ask questions when you don't understand what's being said.

▶ Avoid thinking about your own reply to what's being said and instead pay attention to the speaker.

▶ Notice nonverbal clues such as tone of voice or body language when somebody speaks to you. These clues can help you understand what the person is saying. Make sure you give such clues back to the speaker to let him or her know you're listening.

The best way to improve your writing is to take high school English classes to learn the basics of using language, such as vocabulary, spelling, composition, and grammar. In these classes, you will practice using this knowledge to craft sentences and paragraphs, which become the building blocks of essays, term papers, and reports. Research skills, such as how to find information in the library or online and how to conduct interviews, are also an important part of becoming a good writer.

Take the opportunity to practice writing outside of class as well. For example, you can keep a daily journal of your thoughts and activities or write letters and e-mail messages to your friends or family who are far away.

Use your writing skills to support your interests or issues that are important to you by writing letters to the editor when you want to comment on a local issue or posting to online discussion groups in your areas of interest. If writing is something you enjoy, volunteer to write for your school yearbook, newspaper, or Web site.

Whenever you write something, keep these guidelines in mind:

▶ Create an outline to help you organize information logically in your writing.

▶ Take the time to review and revise your work and check for details like spelling and grammar. Use your computer spell checker function to catch spelling errors.

▶ Focus on getting your message across in a concise, clear way. Keep a dictionary handy to make sure you've used the correct word. Don't be afraid to cut out extra words and phrases.

▶ Have somebody else read what you've written to see whether it's clear. If you do a lot of writing, join a writer's group and get feedback from other writers about your writing.

Many of the projects or assignments you do every day involve reading in some form or other. Once you read information, you often have to use it to make a decision, build something, find your way to a location, and more. Just about every job in the world involves the skill of reading. As with writing, high school English classes will help you improve your reading skills by giving you the opportunity to analyze and discuss all types of writing, including poetry, short stories, novels, and nonfiction.

The best way to improve your reading skills is to read as much as you can outside of school. Read a variety of things, such as newspapers, Web sites, and novels. In particular, read material that relates to the careers that interest you so that you can learn the concepts and vocabulary that are important in that industry.

As you read, try these strategies to get the most out of the material:

▶ Identify the most important information. Look for topic sentences or main characters. Write an outline of the key points to get better at identifying relevant facts and help you remember the material.

▶ Look up words you don't understand in the dictionary.

▶ Ask questions of others if you don't understand something you read. Discussing what you read with others can help you notice things that you may have overlooked.

▶ Evaluate the information you read. Is it accurate and true? Draw conclusions from what you read. Did the material change your opinion about something or provide the information you wanted?

# Personal Skills

You may not think of being responsible or acting confidently as job skills, but the truth is that these personal qualities are a key factor in being successful in a career and in other areas of your life. The SCANS list in Chapter 2 listed several personal qualities that employers have identified as being important:

▶ Responsibility

▶ Self-management

▶ Self-esteem

▶ Integrity and honesty

▶ Sociability

Just like math or reading, these personal qualities are skills that can be developed. Chapter 1, "Mapping Your Path to Success," discussed how to develop self-management skills. The following sections provide some ideas that you can use to develop the rest of the skills today.

# Becoming Responsible

Responsible people are admired by others. They often become leaders. Recognition, awards, and higher pay can come with responsibility. On the other hand, people who are irresponsible are not trusted. Employers are unlikely to promote people they cannot depend on. They will not give responsibility to those who can't handle it. If you are irresponsible, your work will never be very challenging or rewarding.

Being responsible includes the ability to

▶ Work hard to reach a goal

▶ Set high standards in order to achieve excellence

▶ Pay attention to details and concentrate on a task

▶ Show up on time

▶ Be enthusiastic and optimistic while working on tasks

Start taking responsibility by doing the following:

▶ Complete all of your assignments by the due date. Double-check your work before you hand it in to make sure that it is complete and shows your best work. Try to exceed your teacher's expectations.

▶ Take on more responsibility at home by taking care of a pet, for example, or babysitting for a younger sibling. Show your parents that you are responsible by completing assigned chores willingly and without needing to be reminded.

▶ Run for a position in student government or volunteer to head a committee in a club or group that you belong to. Part of being a good leader is accepting responsibility for the group and project you are in charge of. When you take on a task, be sure that you can commit the time, energy, and enthusiasm required to get the job done.

▶ Set high goals for yourself in school and in your extracurricular activities. Whether you are at soccer practice or in a piano lesson, concentrate on doing your personal best.

When you are responsible, you follow through on promises, admit when you make mistakes, and never blame others for your actions. Keep in mind that the best benefit of responsibility is feeling good about the fact that people can count on you.

# Having Self-Esteem

Having self-esteem means that you have respect for yourself and understand your own value. Self-esteem doesn't mean that you think you are better than others. The trick to having self-esteem is to have a realistic view of your own abilities. People with strong self-esteem often have a positive view towards others as well because they are not threatened by the success of others. This skill is particularly helpful when you are facing a job interview.

The various aspects to having self-esteem include

▶ Maintaining a positive view of yourself

▶ Demonstrating knowledge of your skills and abilities

▶ Being aware of the impact you have on others

▶ Knowing how to deal with your emotions

Self-esteem is something you can develop over time through your education and other activities:

▶ Take classes in your area of interest so that you can have confidence in your abilities when you enter the job market.

▶ Approach challenging assignments with confidence. Usually the worst thing that can happen if you fail isn't all that bad, so don't dwell on the negative but on the opportunity for success and growth.

▶ Test your skills in a competition. Practicing for and participating in a competition are good ways to get a clear view of what your strengths are.

▶ Volunteer your skills. Are you good at math? Offer to tutor younger kids who are struggling with that subject. Do you like to build things? Sign up to help with a local Habitat for Humanity project. Using your skills to help someone else will help you to feel good about yourself.

▶ Spend time with your friends. Good friends like you for who you are, and they are happy for you when you do well. They know just what to say when you are feeling bad about yourself, and they can put you in your place if you start thinking too much of yourself. Remember that people who make you participate in self-destructive behavior or feel bad about yourself are not your friends.

## Being Sociable

The Networking features throughout this textbook provide activities that you can do to make connections with people in order to find out more about the world of work or even get a job. In order to be successful at networking, you must be sociable.

Being sociable includes the ability to

▶ Show friendliness and politeness in a group

▶ Adapt to a variety of social settings

▶ Respond appropriately to social situations

In most jobs people have to interact with others, whether with their boss, their co-workers, or customers. Employers appreciate sociable people because these people know how to get along with others. In some jobs, such as sales or customer support, being able to connect with other people is part of the job description. In other jobs, sociability just helps them get along with the people they deal with on a daily basis.

People who aren't sociable may do fine in jobs where they work on their own most of the time. Still, some degree of sociability helps any employee to make and maintain healthy relationships with others. Sociable people typically are well-liked and don't get into fights with co-workers. They tend to be good communicators because they aren't nervous about speaking with others.

Sociable employees need to be careful not to take up too much of their work time socializing. After all, they must be able to complete their work. But when the situation is appropriate to socializing, the ability to do so can make a sale, earn a customer, or keep the morale of the office high.

To be more sociable, you can

▶ Take classes where you work closely with others. Performing arts classes such as band, choir, or acting provide the opportunity to work with larger groups. In science classes, you can work on experiments with a lab partner.

▶ Look at issues and events from a different person's point of view. While studying history, think about historical events from different points of view. Reading literature can also help you understand the feelings of others.

- Join a club or participate in a team sport to learn how to function in groups.

- Make an effort to meet new people. Take the time to talk to them and learn about their interests and their backgrounds.

- Host a party. A party is a fun way to practice your manners and interact with your favorite people. Remember that the best hosts are good at making all the party guests feel comfortable.

## Being Honest

Society views honesty as an important value. Honesty involves telling the truth as well as not performing dishonest acts such as stealing from others. Honesty and integrity often go hand in hand. Integrity means that you stick to a set of values. For example, if you believe that being late for work is wrong because you are cheating your employer, and so you are never late, you show integrity.

Being honest and having integrity include the ability to

- Recognize when a choice breaks with society's values

- Act in a way that matches your values

- Understand the impact of dishonest actions on yourself, others, and your organization

- Choose the ethical course of action

Employers often state that honesty is the most important factor in hiring an employee. Employers have to trust employees to be honest with them about how they spend their time on the job, how they use the company equipment, and whether they take company supplies for their own use. Employees who are caught being dishonest are typically fired immediately.

Employers have to be able to trust their employees to handle information ethically and act in an honest way. For example, employees who take customer orders have access to credit card numbers and checking account numbers, and they are expected to keep that information safe and private. One dishonest employee could take that information and steal from a customer, which could leave the employer open to legal action.

You are expected to be honest in your work life in many large and small ways. Big acts of dishonesty, such as stealing from your employer, increase the employer's costs. But smaller acts of dishonesty affect employers as well. For example, if you call in sick when you are feeling well in order to get a day off, the rest of the employees end up having more work to do.

Being honest on the job is difficult. You have to consider not only your actions, but also the actions of those who work with you. Not saying anything about somebody else's dishonesty may hurt your employer, but for some of us reporting on someone else's bad behavior feels wrong, too. That's why it's important that you develop your own set of values so you have the tools to face difficult ethical decisions throughout your life.

## Science Skills

The School to Work section at the end of every chapter in this book contains a science-related activity. Why is science emphasized in a book about careers and living skills? The answer is that the study of science develops the reasoning, information, technology, and systems skills that employers want.

By studying science, you learn how the universe works. You learn how to observe, classify, measure, predict, interpret, and communicate data. You also develop the ability to think logically and solve problems. The skills and knowledge that come from studying science are important in many occupations.

# Connecting Science Skills to Careers

Hundreds of thousands of scientists are employed in the United States, but millions of workers use science on the job. For example, mechanics use scientific procedures when repairing or testing equipment. Physical therapists use biology and physics to rehabilitate patients. Journalists use scientific knowledge when writing about technology, health, or the environment. And scientific problem-solving skills are necessary for most computer occupations.

Science courses are also important if you want an advanced education. College admissions officers often favor individuals who have taken science classes. Many colleges require at least two years of high school science courses, regardless of your intended major. If you want to be admitted into scientific and technical programs, you will probably need three or four years of high school science.

There are three main levels of science skills: practical, applied, and advanced. People with a practical knowledge of science are familiar with the basic principles of biology, chemistry, or physics and have completed high school–level classes in these subjects. The following jobs require the practical application of science skills:

| | | |
|---|---|---|
| Cosmetologists | Funeral directors | Pharmacy technicians |
| Chefs | Heating and air-conditioning technicians | Plumbers |
| Dental assistants | Landscapers | Prepress workers |
| Electricians | Mechanics | Tool-and-die makers |
| Farm managers | Medical assistants | Urban planners |
| Firefighters | Nursing aides | Vending machine repairers |
| Fishers | Pest controllers | Welders |

People with applied science skills understand scientific principles and can apply them to their work. They have some postsecondary science training. The following jobs require applied science skills:

| | | |
|---|---|---|
| Aircraft mechanics | Dental hygienists | Opticians |
| Broadcast technicians | Dietitians | Photographers |
| Building inspectors | Drafters | Physical therapists |
| Cardiovascular technologists | Emergency medical technicians | Psychologists |
| College professors | Nurses | Recreational therapists |
| Construction managers | Occupational therapists | Surveyors |

People with advanced science skills have a thorough knowledge of scientific principles. They have at least a bachelor's degree with a number of college science courses. However, many jobs that require advanced science skills also require a master's or doctoral degree. The following jobs require advanced science skills:

| | | |
|---|---|---|
| Architects | Doctors | Meteorologists |
| Chemists | Engineers | Optometrists |
| Chiropractors | Forensic scientists | Pharmacists |
| Computer systems analysts | Foresters | Physicists |
| Dentists | Geologists | Veterinarians |

## Improving Science Skills

Careers in science require orderly thinking, systematic work habits, and perseverance. If you are a student who is interested in scientific and technical careers, you should take as many science classes in high school as possible. Basic courses in earth science, biology, chemistry, and physics will form a solid foundation for further study. A strong background in mathematics is also important for those who want to pursue scientific, engineering, and technology-related careers.

Here are some other ways that you can boost your science skills:

▶ Participate in a science fair. Science fairs require you to interpret the information you gather from the experiments you perform. You then have to create a display that presents the details of your experiment in a clear and appealing way. You may also have to verbally present your data and conclusions to several judges.

▶ With the career that interests you in mind, search the Internet to see what kinds of software programs a person in that job might use. Determine to learn a couple of those programs this year.

▶ Learn to use a new piece of technology you have access to. Read the manual to learn about the various features and potential problems you might encounter.

▶ Try a hobby that uses machinery in some way. For example, you can make yourself some pants on a sewing machine or create your own movies on a digital video recorder. Use kitchen appliances to prepare dinner for your family or a drill to make some shelves for your room. When you understand how one machine works, you can often generalize that information to other machines. Before you touch any of these machines, however, have an adult show you how to operate them and explain the safety rules you need to follow to protect yourself.

# Resources Skills

Resources skills are one of the workplace competencies mentioned in the SCANS skills list in Chapter 2. These skills could also be known as managing skills because they involve managing workplace resources. Two of the most important resources are time and money.

## Managing Time

Managing time often means juggling several types of tasks and deadlines. You have to make the right decisions about what to do first and what you can put off. Sometimes this means deciding what tasks you can skip entirely.

Managing time includes the ability to

▶ Select relevant, goal-related activities

▶ Rank activities in order of importance

▶ Allocate time to activities

▶ Understand, prepare, and follow schedules

Chapter 6 provides some time management strategies; here are some additional ones to consider:

▶ Take courses in mathematics to help you learn how to calculate things, such as the amount of time you have available for various tasks or the percentage of your workday to allocate to certain tasks.

- Set long-term goals and calculate how much time you have to make them happen. For example, if you want to learn a piece of music for a concert three months from now, how much time do you have to practice every day to become perfect?

- Use technology to help you manage your time. Computer programs such as Microsoft Outlook include a calendar function that allows you to enter tasks so you can see at a glance what activities are coming up. In addition, handheld devices—everything from cell phones to personal digital assistants—often include scheduling programs to keep you on time when you're on the go. If you want to use a more low-tech method, buy a day planner or wall calendar.

## Managing Money

Chapter 12 and Chapter 13 cover personal finance issues such as banking, handling loans and credit, buying insurance, and finding the best deals on food and clothing. These financial skills are not only useful in your personal life, but they are useful in your professional life as well. Many jobs involve managing how money is earned or spent, and employees, particularly those in management positions, are often judged on their ability to control costs and increase profits.

Managing money can involve several abilities, including making forecasts, keeping records, and evaluating changes in a budget. Look for opportunities in your education and activities to develop this skill:

- Take courses in mathematics and accounting to learn how to make financial calculations.

- Learn to use computer spreadsheet programs, such as Excel or Quicken. You can use spreadsheets to create budgets or financial statements.

- Take business courses to learn about standard business financial statements and money management techniques.

- Set up a monthly budget for yourself. For one month, record all the money you get and exactly how you spent it. Use that information as a model for your budget.

- Volunteer to help track the finances for a club or organization you belong to.

- Practice performing calculations on your calculator or computer.

- Try to save some money every month, and track what you've saved.

## Interpersonal Skills

The term *interpersonal* refers to the relationships between people. The U.S. Department of Labor identified six important interpersonal skills that every worker should develop:

- Working with a team
- Leading
- Teaching
- Negotiating
- Serving customers
- Working with diversity

The following sections discuss each of these skills in more detail.

## Working with a Team

A team is any group of people that comes together to accomplish something. For example, a basketball team works together to win games. Working on a team involves getting along with other people, as well as doing your share of the work. You have to be able to communicate with other people and work through differences in order to achieve the goal. As Chapter 6 describes, certain skills and traits help teams and certain behaviors harm teams.

Working on a team includes the ability to

▶ Contribute ideas and effort

▶ Encourage team members

▶ Do your share of the work

▶ Resolve differences

In the workplace, many projects require teams of people to be successful. That's because a variety of talents and experience are needed to accomplish many tasks. For this reason, the ability to work well as a member of a team is useful in many jobs.

Employers often refer to the ability to work well as a member of a team as being a "team player." Team players always do their part and work for the good of the team, not just themselves. Team players respect the other members of the team and know that each team member has something to contribute. They feel a sense of responsibility that goes beyond the piece of the project they are assigned. They communicate with the other team members to make sure everyone is working toward the goal. Teams that include good team players tend to achieve their goals, so their employers are therefore more successful.

Experience in dealing with people is one of the best ways to get better at working with them. Take advantage of any opportunities you have to work as part of a team and keep these guidelines in mind:

▶ Know what tasks you are responsible for; do them well and complete them on time.

▶ Do whatever you can to help the team accomplish its goal.

▶ Speak up when you see a problem, but make sure you can also offer a solution.

▶ Motivate your team by providing encouragement and having a positive attitude.

## Teaching

All of us are teachers in some way. Maybe you helped your younger brother learn how to tie his shoelaces, or perhaps you taught your friends a song. In the working world, you will be asked to teach others frequently, whether you hold a formal teaching position or you simply help a new employee to learn the ropes. When you teach someone, you communicate information in a way that the person understands.

When you teach someone, follow these guidelines:

▶ Present information in a logical order.

▶ Repeat important information several times. Repetition helps people retain information.

▶ Ask the person you're teaching to repeat what you've said in his or her own words to show that he or she has understood your meaning.

▶ Encourage questions. Questions are a great way to clarify what's being said and receive additional information.

A great way to improve your teaching skills is to volunteer to share your knowledge in some way. Perhaps you could tutor younger kids in basic math or reading skills or help older people learn how to use a computer.

## Serving Customers

In most careers, you deal with customers. Sometimes those customers are people who buy your company's product or service. In other cases, your customers are the people inside your company whom you help; for example, you might help other employees understand their insurance benefits. Customers usually are what keep a business going, so being able to serve them well is an important skill for everybody to have, from the mail clerk to the company president.

A good way to develop customer service skills is to work at a retail store. Whenever you work with customers, remember these tips:

▶ Be polite and friendly, even if you're rushed.

▶ Do your best to fulfill the customer's expectations. If you can't, explain why and offer some other option to make it up to him or her.

▶ Show that you understand the customer's point of view.

▶ Admit when a situation is frustrating for the customer and work hard to make things right.

## Leading

Chapter 6 explains the difference between controlled and shared leadership and why leadership skills are so important to develop. Leading is more than just being in charge. Leadership involves the ability to communicate your ideas or passion to others, to provide a vision, and to motivate people to act. A leader often takes a group in a new, bold direction, challenging the way things are in a responsible way. Whether you are leading an entire country or a person assigned to work on a project with you, you need this same basic set of leadership skills.

Leading includes the ability to

▶ Communicate thoughts, feelings, and ideas

▶ Provide your vision of a goal

▶ Encourage, persuade, and motivate people or groups

▶ Responsibly challenge existing procedures or authority

Leaders make things happen. They have solid ideas about how to improve their organizations and have the confidence and people skills to convince others to go along with their ideas. Strong leaders can attract other talented employees by creating a positive, productive work environment where employees feel valued. In contrast, managers with poor leadership skills can cause good employees to leave organizations by making the employees feel disrespected, underappreciated, or overworked. If investors or customers feel a leader is taking a company in a bad direction, they might stop doing business with that company.

Leaders are responsible for the success or failure of the groups they lead. When leaders make big changes, they risk losing their jobs if the changes turn out badly. But with this risk and responsibility comes the possibility of great rewards. Leaders often earn more money than other workers and take pride in knowing that they help shape the organizations they work for.

## Negotiating

Chapter 6 defines negotiating as looking at all the options and then discussing the benefits and drawbacks of each to arrive at the settlement of a matter. People who are skilled in negotiating are very helpful in the workplace. They find ways for people to compromise or come up with a solution that works for everybody.

Negotiating includes the ability to

- Identify common goals
- Clearly present your position
- Understand the other person's position
- Examine possible options
- Make compromises

To improve your negotiating skills, try the following:

- Take a speech class to learn persuasive speaking. In language arts, focus on learning to write persuasively.

- When you learn about treaties and other important political agreements in history class, think about the negotiation that was necessary. What were the goals of the people involved? Was the compromise a success?

- Negotiate with your parents. Your goal might be a bigger allowance, a pet, or a party. Think about what your parents' concerns might be and have facts ready to answer them. Also, have options in mind so that you can work out a compromise. For example, they might agree to a sleepover with a few friends instead of a big party. Remember to remain calm; whining and yelling are not the best way to negotiate. You might be surprised at your results!

- Practice negotiating prices at a garage sale or swap meet. Before you start talking, have a price in mind. (Look on the Internet to figure out what a reasonable price is.) Be prepared to walk away if the person you are dealing with doesn't come close to the price you want.

## Working with Diversity

The Diversity features throughout this book present situations of people who have to find a way to work well together even though they may feel or behave differently from each other. Chapter 10, "Understanding Workplace Issues," explains the issues involved when people of different genders, ages, abilities, races, or religious groups work together.

Cultural diversity in many workplaces is a reality; learning and benefiting from it is better than being frustrated by it. Diversity on the job can make for a more interesting workplace. Different perspectives on a problem can result in a more creative solution.

On the other hand, culture clashes can make communication difficult and keep people from reaching their goals. Some people make the mistake of assuming that everybody thinks like they do instead of asking others how they usually approach things. People need to reach out to others to overcome differences that are interfering with working together successfully. For example, if somebody does something that bothers you, ask that person why he or she does that. Understanding this may help you get comfortable with their style. Be willing to explain why you do things a certain way and make sure others are comfortable with you.

The best way to work with different people is to

- Avoid making assumptions about people
- Work to improve communication and increase understanding
- Focus on common goals instead of different ways of working

You can improve the way you handle diversity by doing the following:

- Study another language. The way other cultures speak is sometimes a clue to how they think.

- In social studies class, learn as much as you can about other cultures. Start by learning the basics of world geography and reading about major current world events.

*This bonus content was adapted from* Young Person's Career Skills Handbook *and* Exploring Careers, *both by JIST Publishing.*

# Glossary

## A

**Ability**   How well you perform certain tasks.

**Accredited**   Ruling that a school has met certain minimum standards in the United States.

**Active listening**   Listening, watching, and paying attention to what someone says so that you can understand the spoken and unspoken message.

**Addictive**   Creating an uncontrollable need for a substance or activity.

**Advancement**   Getting more responsibility and authority.

**Americans with Disabilities Act (ADA)**   A federal law that protects the rights of employees who have disabilities.

**Annual percentage rate (APR)**   The cost of credit that you pay on a yearly basis.

**Apprenticeship**   A type of training in which a person learns a trade while working for an employer.

**Aptitudes**   The part of your personality that involves your being able to naturally perform certain tasks.

**Assessment**   A form, either paper or electronic, that measures progress or qualities.

**Associate degree**   A two-year degree.

**Attitude**   The part of your personality that is the way you look at life and act toward others.

**Authoritarian**   The style of decision making in which someone makes the decision without consulting the people who will be affected by the decision.

**Authority**   The person or organization in charge.

**Automated teller machine (ATM)**   A banking machine that gives you 24-hour access to banking services.

**Automatic deposit**   A service in which the employer deposits each paycheck directly into an employee's bank account or accounts.

## B

**Bachelor's degree**   A four-year degree.

**Background checks**   Investigations of past and present information about you from former employers, schools, and the police.

**Bankruptcy**   A process in which people or businesses state that they cannot pay their debts. Their property is sometimes then given to their creditors.

**Basic training**   The first few weeks of military training (officially called Initial-Entry Training and informally called "Boot Camp").

**Beneficiary**   The person receiving the benefits, usually the policyholder. In the case of the death of the policyholder, the money will go to another beneficiary, usually a parent, spouse, or child.

**Benefits**   The money paid by insurance for a loss.

**Birth certificate**   An official document issued when a baby is born by the Department of Health in the county and state where the baby is born.

**Body language**   The messages people send through the way they move their bodies.

**Bounced check**   A check that is rejected by the bank because the account does not have enough money in it.

**Brainstorming**   Thinking of as many ideas as you can and sharing them to come up with the best solution.

## C

**Calculated risk**   Analyzing possible outcomes before making a decision.

**Capitalism**    The economic system in which individuals and private businesses are free to organize and operate without government control.

**Career**    A person's life work, which requires planning, preparation, interest, and time.

**Career and Technical Education** (CTE schools) Schools that prepare students for the job market by teaching very specific skills.

**Career cluster**    A group of occupations having related interests.

**Career shadowing**    Taking a day or less to watch and ask questions of a person who works in a career you find interesting.

**Certificate of Deposit (CD)**    A type of saving that pays a higher rate of interest to customers than a savings account pays. You deposit a larger amount of money and leave it in the bank for a longer period of time. The bank will charge you if you withdraw the money out early.

**Certificate program**    Training that typically requires completing several months to two years of classes.

**Character**    The part of your personality that reflects the principles that guide your choices.

**Check register**    A little booklet of pages of blank columns and rows for recording the date, check number or type of withdrawal, the name you wrote in the Pay to the Order of line or source of the deposits, the amount of each withdrawal, and any deposits.

**Checking account**    A bank account in which you store your money and then write checks or use a debit card to make payments. The bank usually charges a small fee for each use.

**Checking account balance**    Money you have in your checking account.

**Civic responsibility**    Responding to the rights, privileges, laws, and policies of your community in an informed, committed, and positive way.

**Claim**    A request that the insurance company pay for a loss.

**Classified ads**    The newspaper section of advertisements that includes job openings.

**Cold contact**    Contacting a person you don't know.

**Communication**    Sending, receiving, and understanding messages.

**Communication style**    The way you give and receive information from others.

**Compensation**    Money or services received to make up for a loss or to pay for work completed.

**Competency**    Being able to complete a task correctly.

**Competition**    When people or businesses try to do better than each other.

**Competitors**    Companies trying to get business from the same customer.

**Complex**    Involving more than one factor.

**Compromising**    Making mutual concessions to, or giving in on, parts of team members' ideas to create a solution everyone accepts.

**Con**    Negative, or against.

**Concise**    Short and to the point.

**Conflict resolution**    Solving problems between opposing forces.

**Conflicts of interest**    When a company or government official gets personal gain from official business.

**Consequences**    Results.

**Conservative**    Not taking many risks.

**Conspicuous consumption**    Buying products and services to impress others.

**Consumer counseling service**    A service that gives advice to people who do not manage money well.

**Consumers**    People who spend money to buy goods and services.

**Contact person**    The person you need to speak to.

**Controlled leadership**    Forcing other people to follow your instructions.

**Convicted**    Found guilty by law.

**Cooperative education**    A school program that gives high school students opportunities to go to school and work for pay at the same time, typically spending part of the day at school and part of the day on the job.

**Co-payment**   The set portion of the total cost that you pay.

**Co-signing**   Signing a legal contract that states that an adult will be financially responsible for your loan or credit card debt if you don't pay on time.

**Cosmetology**   The art of styling hair, applying makeup, and grooming nails.

**Cost-of-living pay increase**   A raise in pay given to workers to keep up with rising costs of daily life.

**Cover letter**   A letter that introduces your resume and asks for an interview.

**Co-workers**   The people who work with you.

**Creator**   A person who brings something into existence.

**Credit**   Borrowing money.

**Credit report**   A report that shows how much money a person owes and how regularly he pays his debts.

**Creditor**   A company or person who loans money to others.

**Culture**   The way a group of people live.

# D

**Data**   Information, words, facts, numbers, or statistics.

**Dating**   When two people spend time together getting to know each other romantically.

**Dating etiquette**   The skills you need and rules or manners to follow when you are taking on the role of a date.

**Deadline**   A date or time when a project, report, or assignment must be finished.

**Debit card**   A card that lets you withdraw the money for a purchase from your bank account without writing a check.

**Debt consolidation**   Asking a nonprofit organization to arrange lower payments and interest rates with your creditors.

**Debtor**   Someone who owes money.

**Decision making**   The process of choosing among options.

**Deductible**   The portion of the loss that an insurance policy requires you to pay.

**Deduction**   Money taken out of a paycheck.

**Deflation**   A period of time in which people cannot find work and prices drop.

**Delegating tasks**   Asking others to do part or all of a project or tasks.

**Demand**   When people want goods or services.

**Democracy**   The form of government in which the citizens give power to leaders whom they choose.

**Destination**   A goal, an ending place.

**Dialect**   The accepted vocabulary, grammar, and pronunciation of an area or group in society.

**Diet**   The food and drink a person takes into the body.

**Diploma program**   A series of classes that require completing several months to two years of classes. (Also called *certificate program.*)

**Discrepancy**   The difference between the way things are and the way things need to be.

**Discrimination**   Treating a person or a group differently or unfairly because of race, gender, age, culture, and so on.

**Distance learning**   Classes that you complete on the Internet.

**Diversity**   The presence of people of different race, gender, age, and so on.

**Down payment**   A beginning payment that is a certain percentage of the total cost of an item.

# E

**Early withdrawal penalty**   A fee for taking money out of an account early.

**Economic recession**   A period of economic decline when demand for work is low or even stops.

**Economic system**   The way a society produces, sells, and uses goods and services.

**Efficiently**   Not wasting anything.

**Elope**   To run away and marry secretly.

**Employment application**   A form that requests information about you, your education, and your work experience.

**Employment tests**   Examinations that you must pass in order to get a job. They can be either paper-and-pencil or computerized tests.

**Engagement**   A period in which the couple evaluates the relationship and prepares for marriage.

**Enlist**   To join a branch of the military.

**Enthusiastically**   Eagerly and with interest.

**Entrepreneur**   Someone who owns and operates his or her own business.

**Entrepreneurship**   Creating your own job.

**Entry-level job**   A "stepping stone" or a beginning job that will take you on a path to your ultimate career.

**Environment**   Your surroundings.

**Environmental Protection Agency (EPA)**   A U.S. government agency that enforces laws and regulations that protect the environment.

**Ethics**   The code of values of a person, organization, or society; what you believe is acceptable or unacceptable.

**Etiquette**   Treating people and behaving in ways that society says are correct. (Also called *manners*.)

**Evaluation**   Determining how good something is or how well a person did.

## F

**Fair Labor Standards Act (FLSA)**   Laws passed to protect workers in the United States.

**Fatalistic**   A style of problem solving in which a person believes that fate controls all decisions.

**Feedback**   Performance evaluations.

**Felony**   A serious criminal offense such as murder or burglary.

**Finance charges**   The extra dollar amount paid by a borrower for using the money.

**First impression**   The way you come across to people when you first meet them. Comes from your appearance, actions, speech, and body language.

**Fixed expenses**   Bills you pay on a regular basis, such as every week, month, or year.

**Flexibility**   Your willingness to change or adapt.

**Flexible expenses**   Expenses that can vary and are not the same every week or month.

**Flextime**   An arrangement in which employees set their schedules to fit their lives.

**Food Guide Pyramid**   A suggestion of the amounts of each food group that a person needs to eat daily in order to be healthy.

**Foreclosure**   A process in which a mortgage company takes the property away from the owners because they have not been paying for the loan.

**Formal feedback**   Learning how well you did through a grade on a paper, a report card, or a review at work.

**Formal research**   Using books, databases, or other sources of information as tools to investigate facts.

**Free enterprise system**   The system in which individuals and private businesses are free to organize and operate without government control. (Also called *capitalism*.)

**Fringe benefits**   The extras that a company provides in addition to wages.

**Front line for the interviewer**   The first person you meet who is evaluating your behavior.

## G

**Gender**   Being male or female.

**Generate**   To think of or come up with something new.

**Generic brands**   Brands of goods that have no trademark.

**Glass ceilings**   Barriers to promotions or advancements to positions that offer higher pay and more responsibilities.

**Global**   Relating to the entire world.

**Globalization**   The concept that the entire world is connected economically, politically, and culturally.

**Goals**   Plans you want to accomplish or promises to yourself.

**Goods**   Products that can be produced.

**Graduate degree**   An advanced degree from a college or university.

**Grid**   A chart for recording information.

**Gross income**   The total amount of money earned before any taxes or other fees are taken out of the paycheck.

**Group dating**   Going out with several people to an activity.

# H

**Hands-on experiences**   Actually spending time in work environments.

**Heredity**   Traits that are passed down through a family.

**Hobby**   Something you enjoy and do regularly during free time.

**Homeowner's insurance**   Insurance that protects your house and its contents.

**House brands**   Private-label goods that are frequently packed for stores by the same companies that package nationally advertised brands.

**Hygiene**   Keeping your body clean.

# I

**Implications**   The possible results of a decision.

**Impulse buying**   Buying things without thinking about the consequences.

**Impulsive**   Acting on a fleeting feeling.

**Income taxes**   Money paid to support government services at local, state, and federal levels.

**Indentured**   The condition of having a legal contract between an employer and an employee that says that the employee will work for the employer for about seven years to learn a trade.

**Independent living**   Being able to take care of oneself financially, emotionally, and physically without the help of others.

**Individuality**   The characteristics that distinguish one person from another.

**Infatuation**   An intense liking not based on reason.

**Inflation**   A time when prices and people's spending rise.

**Informal feedback**   Having others let you know how well you did through the words they say or notes they write.

**Informal research**   Learning about careers through a casual and friendly approach.

**Ingenuity**   Cleverness.

**Initiative**   Doing what needs to be done without being told.

**Installment credit**   A loan that is paid back in regular scheduled payments.

**Insufficient funds**   Not having enough money in the bank to pay for a check that has been written.

**Insurance**   Paying a company in advance to help you cover the costs when problems such as ill health, fire, or accidents occur.

**Interdisciplinary Cooperative Education (I.C.E.)**   A school program in which students receive credits, grades, and a salary for working in a career-related field as part of their daily class schedule.

**Interest**   A charge for borrowing money or a payment the bank makes to you for storing your money there.

**Internship**   Working in an industry through a school program (usually when you are in college) to gain skills and experience, usually without pay.

**Interview**   Meeting with applicants for jobs to find the person who best meets the needs of the company. Also just asking someone questions.

**Intuitive**   A type of problem solving in which the person uses an inner guidance based on a calm awareness of the right choice rather than facts or fleeting feelings.

**Inventory**   A list of items owned or goods a store has on hand to sell.

**I-statements**   Telling others what you think or feel without blaming anyone.

## J-K

**JIST Card**   A small card that contains information employers need to know about a person.

**Job**   Work a person does for pay.

**Job applicant**   A person looking for a job.

**Job interview**   A meeting between an employer and a person seeking a job.

**Job leads**   Information about a business or company that is hiring workers.

## L

**Landlord**   The owner of an apartment.

**Leadership**   To guide others.

**Learning style**   The way(s) you learn.

**Lease**   An agreement between the owner of a property and a person who pays money to use it.

**Leisure time**   Time that you can spend however you choose.

**Letter of inquiry**   A letter asking for an application or more information.

**Life insurance**   Insurance that provides money to the people you choose to receive it when you die.

**Lifelong learner**   Someone who believes that education and training will never be finished.

**Lifestyle**   A way of life, including a person's location, type of work, daily schedule, friendships, and so on.

**Liquidation of assets**   Selling the items that you own.

**Long-term goals**   Goals that will take a long time and several steps to meet.

**Loss leaders**   Items priced at or below cost.

**Love**   A strong feeling of affection between two people.

## M

**Master's degree or doctoral degree**   Degrees earned after earning a four-year bachelor's degree.

**Materialistic values**   Wanting to own things that money can buy.

**Mature love**   A realistic sharing of a committed relationship.

**Mentor**   An advisor and role model.

**Merit pay increase**   Pay increase that rewards an employee who has performed at an exceptional level.

**Misdemeanor**   A less-serious offense such as theft.

**Monopolies**   Businesses that have no competition.

**Mortgage**   Money borrowed to pay for a house.

**Motivation**   A reason for doing what you choose to do.

## N

**NA**   Used on an application to stand for "not applicable" or "does not apply."

**Negotiable**   Able to be arranged through discussion and bargaining.

**Negotiating**   Looking at all the options and then discussing the benefits and drawbacks of each to arrive at the settlement of a matter.

**Networking**   Asking people for help or gathering information about a need you have.

**Non-essentials**   Items that are not needed.

**Nonmaterialistic values**   Believing that relationships and social causes are more important than things.

**Nonverbal behavior**   What a person does rather than what he or she says.

**Nonverbal communication**   Using facial expressions and body positions to show feelings.

**Note-taker**   The type of interviewer who takes notes throughout the interview.

**Nutrients**   Chemicals in the body that strengthen it.

## O

**O*NET**   A government-sponsored database that collects information from workers about their jobs.

**Objectively**   Without being influenced by personal feelings.

**Observe**   To follow rules or to watch someone.

**Occupational Outlook Handbook**   The database and printed book of information the U.S. Department of Labor collects about the country's workforce.

**Occupational Safety and Health Act (OSHA)**
A federal law that established a government agency to set standards and policies for the safety of workplaces.

**Online services**   Services banks provide so that you can manage your money from your computer.

**Onsite**   At the place of the business.

**Ophthalmologist**   An eye doctor.

**Organizational values**   Attitudes and ethics that each organization establishes for its behavior and decision making.

**Organizer of information**   The person whose work involves arranging information.

**Oriented**   Knowing where you are in relation to everything else.

# P

**Paired dating**   Dating one exclusive partner.

**Pareto** (pä re' to) **Principle**   A decision-making tool that can help you decide where to begin when you have several tasks or problems.

**Part-time work**   Working less than 40 hours per week.

**Passive**   Not taking action.

**Password**   A secret code required to use something.

**Performance appraisal**   A written evaluation of job performance.

**Personal**   Private, for one person.

**Personal road map**   A plan you make early in your high school career so that you can reach your goals for the future.

**Personal transition**   An important change in your personal or work life.

**Personal values**   Beliefs and standards of behavior that an individual accepts and follows.

**Personality**   The psychological and behavioral characteristics that make you different from everyone else.

**Personnel department**   The department within a company that oversees issues involving the employees, such as hiring, firing, and paying salaries and wages.

**Philosophy**   Beliefs about yourself and others as well as career goals.

**Policies**   Rules, or ways of acting. Also, contracts stating that an insurance company will pay you for loss of health or property.

**Policyholder**   A person who has bought insurance.

**Portfolio**   A collection of samples of your work.

**Positive attitude**   A good outlook regarding people or things.

**Possessions**   The items you own.

**Postsecondary**   After high school.

**Prejudiced**   Holding negative opinions of a person or group of people that are based on beliefs and stereotypes rather than facts.

**Premiums**   The payments a policyholder makes to the insurance company.

**Price fixing**   An agreement between businesses to set the price of products.

**Principal**   The amount of money borrowed.

**Principles**   What you believe is acceptable or unacceptable.

**Prioritizing**   Ranking a list of items according to importance.

**Private employment agency**   An organization that helps people find jobs but charges a fee for the service.

**Pro**   Positive, or in favor of something.

**Probationary period**   A trial period of work.

**Problem solving**   Realizing that something is wrong and finding solutions.

**Procedures**   Ways of doing things.

**Professional level**   High-level careers that require earning a particular degree.

**Profit**   The money that's left after the company pays its expenses.

**Projected outlook**   The prediction of future jobs and number of job openings expected.

**Public employment agency**   An organization that helps people find jobs without charging them for the service.

**Punctuality**   Being on time.

# Q

**Quality**   How good something is.

**Quantity**   How much of something.

**Questioner**   The type of interviewer who just asks questions.

# R

**Realistic**   A form of problem solving that considers the feelings, values, advantages, and disadvantages of a situation.

**Receptionist**   The person who greets visitors as they walk into an office or building.

**Recessions**   Times when the economy is suffering and people quit spending money.

**References**   The names of and contact information for people who will recommend you for employment.

**Referrals**   Recommendations made by current employees.

**Renter's insurance**   Insurance that protects your personal belongings when you rent a place to live.

**Responsibility**   Accepting blame or praise.

**Resume**   A summary of information about a person: the contact information, education, skills, activities, and recognitions you've received.

**Risk**   Hazard or danger.

**Risk-takers**   People willing to take risks.

**Roles**   The behaviors others expect of you because of your positions.

**Romantic love**   The type of love based on feelings of happiness.

# S

**Safe deposit box**   A locked box for storing valuable items at a bank.

**Salary**   Payment for work performed.

**Savings account**   An account that pays you a small amount of money (or *interest)* for keeping your money in the bank.

**Scanning**   Looking through printed material to find specific information.

**Screens**   Looks over applications or resumes to decide which people to interview.

**Security deposit**   Money a landlord requires when you rent a property; it is to be used to pay for any damages that may occur while you live there. (Also called *damage deposit.)*

**Self-conscious**   Feeling awkward about your appearance, speech, or actions.

**Self-concept**   How you see yourself.

**Self-directed job search**   Looking for jobs on your own.

**Self-esteem**   How you feel about yourself.

**Self-indulgent**   Putting one's own wants and needs ahead of others'.

**Self-management**   Taking good care of yourself.

**Service learning**   Doing community service as part of a classroom assignment.

**Services**   Doing work for people.

**Sex-role stereotypes**   Roles assigned to people or beliefs about people based on gender, not personal interests or skills.

**Sexual harassment**   Unwelcome sexual advances, requests for sexual favors, and other verbal or physical conduct of a sexual nature.

**Shared leadership**   A form of guiding others that gives everyone a chance to have a say in the way things are being done.

**Shift**   A scheduled period of time for working, such as 8 a.m. to 5 p.m.

**Shift manager** The person who manages people working together at the same time.

**Significant other** An important person in your life, probably someone you are dating.

**Single dating** Dating several different people instead of dating just one person.

**Skills** Abilities to successfully complete tasks; knowledge of how to do tasks.

**Skimming** A way of reading to get a quick impression of printed materials.

**Small business** An independently owned and operated business.

**SMART** A way to remember the parts every goal should have: Specific, Measurable, Achievable, Realistic, and a Time limit.

**Social Security Act** A government law that created a program for paying taxes to the government so that when you retire or become disabled, you, your spouse, and your dependent children receive monthly benefits based on your reported earnings. Also, your survivors can collect benefits if you die.

**Special-interest groups** People with particular concerns.

**Spending plan** A plan for saving and spending your income. (Also called a *budget*.)

**Standards of conduct** Established guidelines for how to behave.

**Stepping-stone goals** Short-term goals.

**Stereotyping** Judging other people because of their appearance, age, gender, or race.

**Strategies** Planning tools.

**Supply** The quantity of goods or services available.

## T

**Tact** Style or grace.

**Talker** An interviewer who does all the talking.

**Teamwork** Working together in an efficient way to solve problems and reach goals.

**Teleconferencing** Meeting by electronic means.

**Temperament** The way a person usually acts, feels, and thinks.

**Template** A form to use as a guide.

**Temporary work** An arrangement to work full-time or part-time for only a few weeks or months.

**Tenant** The person paying rent.

**Text messaging** Using your phone to type and send a message.

**Textiles** Cloth or fabric used to make clothes.

**Time management** The way you spend your time.

**Transcript** The record of your grades.

**Transfer credits** Having course credits earned at one school applied toward a degree at another school.

**Transferable skills** Skills you can use in many different jobs.

**Transit number** The numeric code for your bank.

**Transitions** Planned and unplanned changes in your life.

**Trend** The general direction the economy is going.

## U

**Unemployed** Not having a job.

**Union** A group of workers who form an organization to protect their interests and require members to pay dues.

**Unit prices** The cost of one standard measure of a product, such as its cost per ounce.

**United States Office of Personnel Management (OPM)** The human resources office for the federal government.

## V

**Values** Beliefs about what is important to you.

**Verbal communication** Using words to give information to others.

**Voice inflection** The tone of your voice.

**Volunteering** Working for an organization without payment.

## W-Z

**Wage discrimination**   Unequal pay for equal work.

**Wages**   The money paid to employees for work.

**Warm contact**   Getting help from people you know.

**Warranties**   Guarantees from companies that they will replace or repair defective products.

**Wedding**   A marriage ceremony.

**Well-groomed**   The quality of being clean and neatly dressed.

**Whistle blowing**   Reporting unethical behavior to authorities.

**White Pages**   A telephone book that lists names, home addresses, and phone numbers alphabetically by last names.

**Windfall**   An unexpected gift, usually money.

**Win-win solution**   A way of dealing with a problem that is fair and beneficial for everyone.

**Work environment**   The surroundings at a job.

**Work ethic**   Being willing to work hard and do a job well.

**Work permit**   A license that allows students to work.

**Workers' compensation laws**   Federal laws that provide money or services to workers who are injured on the job.

**World-wise view**   Realizing that the people of the world have many different customs and ways of living.

**Yellow Pages**   A telephone book that lists businesses' names, addresses, and phone numbers.

# Index

biomedical engineering careers, 38, 47
birth certificate, 181
BlackBerrys, 139, 150
blogging, 112
bloodborne infections, preventing transmission of, 214
body art, 193
body language, 128–129, 197
boilermakers, 102, 122–123, 132–133
bonuses, 262
book binding careers, 169
bookkeepers, 193, 198
boot camp. *See* basic training
borrowing money, 271–273. *See also* credit
bounced checks, 266–267
brainstorming, 57, 132
breaks, right to, 101
brickmasons, 122, 126, 133
*Bride's Magazine*, 333
Buddhist economy, 247
budget. *See* spending plan
bus drivers, 148, 152, 155
business careers, 59, 193, 204, 206
business colleges. *See* CTE schools
business owners, 243
business plans, 247
Business Professionals of America, 206
buying
    clothing, 311–314
    food, 309–311
    versus renting, 293–297
    vehicles, 300–301

# C

CAD (computer-aided design), 299
calculated risk, 247
capitalism, 241
car insurance, 305–306
career and technical student organizations
    Business Professionals of America, 206
    DECA, 221
    Family, Career, and Community Leaders of America (FCCLA), 249
    Future Business Leaders of America–Phi Beta Lambda, 315
    Health Occupations Students of America (HOSA), 331
    National FFA Organization (FFA), 53

SkillsUSA, 103
Technology Student Association, 46
career clusters, 76–77
career exploration, 71–85
    formal research, 76–79
    hands-on experiences, 82–84
    informal research, 75
    Internet research, 80–82
    jobs versus careers, 73–74
    recording information, 84
Career Game Show, 92–93
career outlook, 93. *See also* projected outlook
career plans, 92–110
    education levels, 99–106
    goal definition, 97–98
    lifestyle exploration, 93–97
    steps for, 107–110
career shadowing, 80, 82
career spotlights
    Architect, 44
    Auto Repair Facility President, 111
    Construction Company Owner, 138
    Director of Education Services, 342
    Executive Producer, 19
    Family and Consumer Sciences Education, 282
    Funeral Director, 315
    Locomotive Engineer, 161
    Research Scientist, 183
    Room Leader, 231
    Secretary of State, 360–361
    Small Business Owner, 255
    Superior Court Judge, 86
    Tax Preparer, 205
    Waters Area Manager, 65
career values, 41
career videos, 82
CareerBuilder.com, 154
careers, 3, 73
    in acting, 13
    advancement, taking on extra responsibility, 225
    in advertising and marketing, 223
    in agricultural work, 53, 58
    in appliance repair, 103
    in arts, entertainment, media, 5
    in automotive services, 100
    in business detail, 193, 204, 206
    in computer science, 34, 42
    in construction, mining, drilling, 122
    in cooking, 254
    in dentistry, 326

    in education and social services, 265, 277
    education levels, 79
    in engineering, 27, 34, 38
    English requirement, 100–101
    in environmental engineering, 43
    evaluating, 93–98
    in finance, 34
    in general management and support, 292, 294
    in health services management, 300
    in heating and air conditioning, 102
    in industrial production, 169, 174
    in industrial production management, 170
    in law, law enforcement, public safety, 73, 78
    in math, 27, 34
    math requirement, 100–101
    in mechanics, installation, repairing, 93
    in medical and health services, 325, 327
    in medical research, infection-control programs, bioterrorism, 37
    in military service, 350–353, 362
    in music, 6
    in oceanography, 39
    in personal services, 242, 246
    in physics, 34
    in plants and animals, 53
    in retail sales, 220
    in sales and marketing, 215, 218, 228
    in science, 27
    selecting, 33
    in social work, 275
    in software engineering, 44
    in sports, 14
    statistics on changes, 15
    in transportation, 148, 160
    in water transportation, 158
    in welding, 175
    in woodworking, 180
    versus jobs, 73–74
carpenters, 102, 122, 132–133
case studies
    aptitude, 35
    attitude, 199
    brainstorming, 132
    budget, 277
    car buying, 301
    career options, 107

kissing on both cheeks, 84
loudness, 268
personality differences, 31
punctuality, 192
question-asking, 171
refusing payment, 123
SCANS skills, 38
snobby co-workers, 94
speaking foreign language, 8
workplace issues, 219–223
doctor appointments, importance of, 309
doctoral degrees, 105
doctors, 325, 332, 335
documentation when applying for jobs, 180–182
Donne, John, 352
door-to-door salespeople, 228
down payments, 272
drafting careers, 108
drama careers, 12
dreams. *See also* goals
defining, 348–354
evaluating, 354–357
as reflection of values, 354–355
setting goals to achieve, 357–359
"what do you want to do with your time?", 349–351
"what do you want to own?", 351–352
"who do you want to be?", 348–349
"who do you want to have in your life?", 352–353
working to achieve, 356
dressing for job interviews, 193
drilling careers, 122
drug tests, 179–180, 214
drywallers, 122, 133
Duvall, Evelyn, 336

# E

e-mail etiquette, 232
e-mail monitoring, 245
early withdrawal penalty, 269
earnings. *See* salary
eating healthy, 308
eBay, 318
economic recession, 101
economic systems, 240
American economic system, 240–247
Buddhist economy, 247
global economy, 248–249

socialist economy, 247
subsistence economy, 247
Edmunds (researching vehicles), 300
education. *See also* teachers
careers in, 265, 277, 342
issues concerning, 252
education levels, 79
descriptions of, 99–106
evaluating careers, 94
salary, 96
unemployment rate, 95
efficiently, 136, 241
electives, 100
electrical engineering careers, 38
electrical repairers, 93, 108
electricians, 122, 129, 133
electronic employment applications, 177
elementary education careers, 265
elevator installation and repair, 131
eligibility interviewers, 206
eloping, 335
emergency management officer, 364
emergency medical technicians, 73, 85
emotional maturity, readiness for marriage, 332
empathy, 131
employee guidelines handbook versus student handbook, 11
employee performance evaluations, 8
employees. *See also* workplace issues
Internet and e-mail monitoring, 245
learning opportunities in entry-level jobs, 216–218
performance evaluations, 223–224
responsibility for safety, 213–215
taking on extra responsibility, 225
employer pension plans, 280
employers
contacting potential employers, 157–161
employee monitoring, 245
identifying, 151–156
reasons for not hiring someone, 202
skills sought by, 121
what you can offer to, 146–147
employment agencies, identifying employers, 155–156
employment applications, 174
credit applications, compared to, 271
filling out, 174–179
leasing applications, compared to, 294

employment outlook, 80. *See also* projected outlook
employment tests, 179
ending job interviews, 198–199
endorsing checks, 267
Enelow, Wendy S., 171
engagements, 332–335
engineering careers, 27, 34, 38
English careers, 12, 85, 100–101
enlisted personnel, 352, 361
enlisting, 103
entertainment careers, 5
enthusiastically, 198
entrepreneurship, 84, 246–247
career facts, 181
spotlight on a career, 111, 138, 255, 315
entry-level jobs, 73, 76, 216
learning opportunities in, 216–218
environment, 26
discovering yourself, 27
environmental engineering, 38, 43, 47
environmental issues, 252–253
environmental scientists, 47
EPA (Environmental Protection Agency), 212, 252
Equal Credit Opportunity Act, 274
ethics, 30, 218. *See also* character
company-owned materials, 15, 83
compassion, 355
courage, 293
customer rudeness, handling, 198
in genetics, 47
honesty, 267
integrity, 56
patience, 326
problem solving, 56
reliability, 32
reporting criminal activity, 217
respect, 96
taking initiative, 251
trustworthiness, 171
work ethics, 218–219
ethnic, 27
ethnic diversity, statistics, 219
evaluating, 6
evaluations
after job interviews, 201
poor evaluations, response to, 9
poor work performance, 226–227
response to, 7–8
role of, 7
of work performance, 223–224
executive chefs, 254

executive producers, 19
executives, 292, 298, 304
exercise, importance of, 296, 308
expanded grid method of problem
  solving, 60
expectations, balancing, 77
expenses versus income, 278
experiential learning style, 32
exploratory interviews, 75

# F

Facebook, 33
facial expressions. *See* nonverbal
  communication
factory management careers, 169
FAFSA (Free Application for Federal
  Student Aid), 104
Fair and Accurate Credit Transactions
  Act of 2003, 274
Fair Credit Billing Act, 318
Fair Credit Reporting Act, 274
Fair Labor Standards Act (FLSA), 182,
  234
fairness, 131
  credit for sales, 147
family
  close family ties, 219
  starting, 331–339
Family, Career, and Community
  Leaders of America (FCCLA), 249
  case study, 13
  study tips, 18
family life, balancing with personal
  and work life, 340–341
family problems, overcoming, 338–339
family-oriented workplaces,
  researching, 341
farming careers, 15, 58–60
Farr, Michael, 8, 146, 150
  contacting potential employers, 157
  skills for success, identifying, 36
Fasano, Crisanta, 183
fastest-growing occupations, 95
fatalistic problem-solving style, 53
FCCLA. *See* Family, Career, and
  Community Leaders of America
federal government, responsibilities of,
  250
federal taxes, 254
feedback, 7
  on resume, 182
felonies, 177
FFA, 52

FICA (Social Security), 263
finance careers, 34
finance charges, 270
financial advice careers, 208, 228, 265
financial aid, 104
financial institutions
  researching, 270
  selecting, 264–266
firefighters, 73, 85
firewalls, 283
first impressions, 193
fishers, 53, 59
fitness workers, 251
fixed expenses, 276
flexibility, 107, 132
flexible expenses, 276
flextime, 97
flight attendance careers, 242
flooring installers and finishers, 122,
  133
FLSA (Fair Labor Standards Act), 182
followthrough
  after job interviews, 200–201
  contacting potential employers, 160
  filling out job applications, 178
food, buying, 309–311
Food Guide Pyramid, 308
food services careers, 242, 254
foreclosure, 296
foreign languages
  careers in, 12
  speaking, 8
foresters, 15, 53, 59–60
formal feedback, 7
formal research, 76–79
foundation skills (SCANS skills), 38
Fowkes, Charlotte, 246
franchises, 248
Free Application for Federal Student
  Aid (FAFSA), 104
free enterprise system, 241
free stuff advertising technique, 291
friendship
  case study, 15
  changes after marriage, 335
  negative, 355
fringe benefits, 148
front line, 194
funeral directors, 292, 298, 315
furnishings for your home, 298–299
future and money management,
  279–280
Future Business Leaders of America–
  Phi Beta Lambda, 315

# G

Gardner, Howard (learning style), 32
GED tests and certificate, 100
gender, 27
gender discrimination, 57, 221
  women's salaries versus men's
    salaries, 222, 266
general internists, 332
general management and support
  careers, 292, 294
generating, 57
generic brands, 310
genetics, ethics in, 47
geological oceanographers, 39
glass ceilings, 221
glaziers, 130
glittering generalities advertising
  techniques, 290
global communication, 5
global competition, 15
global economy, 248–249
globalization, 248
goals, 41. *See also* dreams; long-term
  goals; short-term goals
  defining for career plans, 97–98
  long-term versus short-term, 41–42
  selecting, 56–57
  selecting who to date, 324
  setting, 357–359
  SMART goals, 19, 357
Golden Rule (conflict resolution), 229
good citizenship, 245
goods, 241–242
Goodwill, 313
Google, 58
government accountants, 306
government careers, 85
grades, importance of, 101
graduate degrees, 105
grants, 104
Gray, John, 323
Greenleaf, Robert K., 135
grids, 59
groceries, buying, 309–311
gross pay, 262
group activities, isolation from, 125
group dating, 323
*Guide for Occupational Exploration
  (GOE)*, 82
  career clusters, 77
gynecologists, 332

# H

hair styling careers, 242
hands-on experiences, career exploration, 82–84
harassment. *See* sexual harassment
harmful behavior for teamwork, 133
Hawkins, Grant, 86
hazardous waste removers, 102, 122, 132–133
hazards at work, 234
HBV (hepatitis B virus), preventing transmission of, 214
head cooks, 254
health and safety issues in the workplace, 212–216
health care workers, 214
health careers, 85
health insurance, 306–307
Health Maintenance Organizations (HMOs), 306
Health Occupations Students of America (HOSA), 331
health services careers, 298, 300
healthy living, 307–311
    balanced life, 340
heating and air-conditioning technicians, 93, 102, 108
help-wanted ads. *See* classified ads
hepatitis B virus (HBV), preventing transmission of, 214
heredity, 26
hidden fears advertising technique, 290
high school diplomas, 100–101
high school education careers, 265, 278
Hill, Reuben, 336
hiring practices, 202
hiring relatives, 122
HIV (human immunodeficiency virus), preventing transmission of, 214
HMOs (Health Maintenance Organizations), 306
hobbies, 33
home health aides, 95
homeowner's insurance, 304–305
homosexuality
    discrimination based on, 351
    kissing on both cheeks, 84
honesty, 56, 132, 267
    dating, 327
    SCANS skills, 38
HOSA (Health Occupations Students of America), 331
house brands, 310

housing options, 292–299
    furnishings for your home, 298–299
    renting versus buying, 293–297
    roommates, 297–298
human immunodeficiency virus (HIV), preventing transmission of, 214
human resources managers, 292, 298, 302
humor advertising technique, 290
Hurst, Mike, 111
hygiene, 309

# I

I-statements, 230
ICE (Interdisciplinary Cooperative Education), 83
*Identify Your Skills for School, Work, and Life*, 8
identity theft, 283
illegal job interview questions, 195
Imboden, Karen, 65
implications, 59
impulse buying, 277, 310
impulsive problem-solving style, 53
in-laws, 334
in-person visits, contacting potential employers, 158–159
income taxes, 254, 263
income versus expenses, 278
indentured, 101
independent living skills, 289
    buying clothing, 311–314
    consumer awareness, 290–292
    healthy living, 307–311
    housing options, 292–299
    insurance, 303–307
    transportation options, 299–303
individual retirement accounts (IRAs), 280
individuality, 332
industrial arts careers, 108, 133
industrial machinery mechanics, 102
industrial production careers, 169–170, 174
infatuation, 329
infection-control programs careers, 37
inflation, 244
influencing others, 126
informal feedback, 7
informal research, 75
information skills (SCANS skills), 38
information technology jobs, 55

informational interviews, 75
    role-playing, 86
ingenuity, 246
initiative, 217
inspections of rental property, 295
inspectors, 122, 133
installation careers, 93
installment credit, 272
instant messaging, 130
insufficient funds. *See* NSF (non-sufficient funds)
insurance, 303–307
    automobile, 305–306
    health, 306–307
    homeowner's, 304–305
    life, 307
    renter's, 305
integrity, 56, 132
Interdisciplinary Cooperative Education (ICE), 83
interest, 265
    on borrowed money, 270
    on savings accounts, 268
interest inventories, 43
interests, 32–34
    selecting who to date, 325
internal auditors, 306
Internet advertising techniques, 291
Internet search activities, 9, 16, 40, 47, 85, 106, 110, 135, 156, 195, 249, 303, 307, 339, 363
Internet search tips, 58
Internet usage monitoring, 245
internships, 83
interpersonal skills (SCANS skills), 38
interviewers, 206
interviewing supervisors, 182
interviews, 146. *See also* job interviews
    discrimination in, 207
    information interviews, 86
    leadership interview, 137
    personality and career choice, 98
    problem-solving styles, 54
introspective intelligence, 32
intuitive problem-solving style, 53
inventory of personal property, 305
investigative reporting, 19
investors, 243
iPhones, 139
IRAs (individual retirement accounts), 280
isolation, responding to, 125

## O

obeying laws, as civic responsibility, 250
objectively, 52
observing, 11
obstetricians, 332
occupational outlook, 80. *See also* projected outlook
*Occupational Outlook Handbook (OOH),* 80, 82
Occupational Safety and Health Administration (OSHA) Act, 213
oceanography careers, 39
office management careers, 193
officers (military), 352
    occupations of, 355
    training for, 362
on-the-job competency
    assumptions about others, 297
    attendance, 148
    attitude, 100
    customer service, 224, 328
    effective leadership, 252
    influencing others, 126
    organizing tasks, 54
    personal phone calls, 359
    responding to others' promotions, 77
    self-management, 16
    teaching co-workers, 269
    transferable skills, 43
    using co-worker's computer, 194
    work attire, 172
on-the-job training, 101
O*NET database, 80, 82
online colleges and universities, 106
online employment applications, 177
online resume tips, 169
online services, 266
online shopping, 318
onsite, 178
*OOH (Occupational Outlook Handbook),* 80, 82
operating expenses, 276
OPM (United States Office of Personnel Management), 155
order delays and customer service, 328
organizational values, 218
organizers, 350
organizing job searches, 150–151. *See also* prioritizing
orientation to new situations, 10–14
oriented, 5
orthodontists, 325

OSHA (Occupational Safety and Health Administration) Act, 213
outcome-directed thinking, 56
overtime, 262
ownership, "what do you want to own?", 351–352

## P

painters, 122, 133
paired dating, 323
paralegals, 73, 83, 85
parenthood, 355
    child development, 336
    discussing before marriage, 334
    preparations for, 337–338
Pareto Principle, 58–59
part-time work, 82
partnerships, 243
passbook savings, 269
Passive (interviewer type), 196
passive communication style, 34–35
passwords, 267
path to success. *See* skills for success
patience
    customer service, 326
    money management, 278
patriotism advertising technique, 290
pay raises
    cost-of-living pay increase, 223
    merit pay increase, 224
paychecks, 262–264
    automatic deposit, 268–269
paying for college, 104
paying taxes as civic responsibility, 254
payment, refusing, 123
payment requirements on job applications, 177
PayPal, 318
PDAs (personal digital assistants), 139, 150
pediatricians, levels of education, 79
pension plans, 280
people's demands and world-wise view, 15
performance appraisals, 223. *See also* evaluations
persistence (quote), 246
personal and home care aides, 95, 242, 248, 251
personal appearance workers, 253
personal digital assistants (PDAs), 139, 150
personal financial advisors, 95
personal interests. *See* interests

personal life, balancing with family and work life, 340–341
personal property inventory, 305
personal qualities (SCANS skills), 38
personal road map, 98
personal savings for retirement, 280
personal services careers, 242, 246
personal transitions, 10–14
    new school transitions, 63
personal values, 354
personality, 26
    aptitudes, 30
    career choice, 98
    character, 30–31
    communication style, 34–35
    discovering yourself, 29–35
    interests, 32–34
    learning style, 32
    Myers-Briggs Type Indicator, 29
    problem-solving, 52–54
    selecting who to date, 325
    self-concept, 34
    self-esteem, 34
    temperament, 30
personality clashes, 31
petroleum engineering careers, 38
Pew Internet and American Life Project, 112
pharmacists, 325, 330
philosophy, 172
phishing, 283
phone conversations, 123–124
physical characteristics, discovering yourself, 26–27
physical education careers, 59
physical oceanographers, 39
physical therapist assistants, 95
physical therapists, 325
physician assistants, 95
physicians. *See* doctors
physics careers, 34
piercings, 193
pilots, 148, 155, 164
pipe fitters, 128
pipe layers, 128
plain folks advertising technique, 290
plan of action (goals), 358
plans. *See also* career plans, creating
    in problem-solving process, 62
    for success, 16–17
plant managers, 318
plants, careers involving, 53
plumbers, 102, 122, 128, 132–133
police officers, 73, 85
policies, 5, 10–11

resources skills (SCANS skills), 38
respect, 96, 132
responsibility, 6
    accepting, 12–13
    balancing, 340–341
    citizenship responsibilities, 245, 250–255
    evaluating careers, 94
    job searches, 148
    readiness for marriage, 332
    SCANS skills, 38
    system for tracking responsibilities, 16–17
    taking on extra responsibility, 225
    wedding planning, 336
    for yourself, 224
responsible consumers. *See* consumer awareness
resumes, 168
    e-mail, 169
    feedback on, 182
    formatting, 169
    online, 169
    writing, 168–170
retail sales careers, 215, 220, 231
retirement plans, 279–280
rights
    of debtors, 274
    when filling out job applications, 177
risk, 61, 247
risk taking, 356
    in decision making, 61–62
role-playing, 255
    applying for jobs, 176
    balancing responsibilities, 342
    career counseling, 362
    career plans, creating, 110
    clothing budget, 280
    communication, 139
    crime, 252
    day care center interview, 229
    information interviews, 86
    job interview, 204
    marketing clothing, 314
    product availability, 64
    study skills, 20
    telephone conversations, 162
    values, 39
roles, 4
romantic love, 329
roofers, 122, 127, 133
room design, 299
roommates, 297–298

Roscka, John, 315
routines for overcoming disorganization, 18
rude customers, handling, 198
rules. *See* company policies
Russell, Sally, 342

## S

Saddam Hussein, authoritarian problem-solving style, 53
safe deposit boxes, 269
safe driving, 302
safety issues in the workplace, 212–216, 234
SAG (Screen Actors Guild), 13
salary, 96
    accepting job offer, 203
    education levels, 96
    evaluating careers, 96
    women's salaries versus men's salaries, 222, 266
salary requirements on job applications, 177
sales careers, 215, 218, 221, 225, 228
sales credit, 147
sales taxes, 254
Salvation Army, 313
savings account, 265
    opening, 264–266
    usage, 268
savings bonds, 269
savings plans, 269
scanning, 128
SCANS (Secretary's Commission on Achieving Necessary Skills), 37–38
    Internet research, 40
scholarships, 104
school skills versus job skills, 9
schools, selecting, 108–110
science assignments
    age of rocks and fossils, 285
    animal body language, 141
    biomechanics, 317
    Earth Science mission, 363
    EPA (Environmental Protection Agency), 233
    ethics in genetics, 47
    global warming, 207
    high-definition television, 113
    Mars exploration, 164
    neuroscience research, 21
    NIEHS scientists, 88

    pyrotechnic devices, 185
    scientific method, 67
    simple machines, 257
science careers, 27, 58, 183
scientific method, 63
Screen Actors Guild (SAG), 13
screens, 155
second-hand stores, buying clothing, 313
secretaries, 201
Secretary's Commission on Achieving Necessary Skills. *See* SCANS
secure Web sites, 318
securities sales agents, 228
security deposits, 293
security guards, 73
Selective Service, registering for, 104
self-concept, 34
self-directed job search, 153–155
self-esteem, 30, 34–35
    SCANS skills, 38
self-indulgent, 352
self-management, 5
    developing, 6–9
    Internet research, 9
    orientation to new situations, 10–14
    SCANS skills, 38
    school skills versus job skills, 9
self-management skills, 36–37
selflessness, 132
servant-leadership, 135
service learning, 83
services, 241–242
sex-role stereotypes, 220
sexual harassment, 219, 221–222
sexual preference, discrimination based on, 351
shadowing leaders, 137
Shakespeare, William, 25
shared leadership, 134
shareholders, 243
short-term goals, 41–42
    in career planning, 108
significant others, 353
silversmithing careers, 169, 181
single dating, 323
single life, 328–329
single-purpose credit cards, 273
skills, 5
    versus aptitudes, 36
    evaluating careers, 96
    needed for teamwork, 132
    sought by employers, 121

technology and world-wise view, 14–15

technology skills (SCANS skills), 38

Technology Student Association, 46

teleconferencing, 124

telemarketing careers, 215, 228

telephone book, identifying employers, 153–154

telephone conversations, 123–124
    contacting potential employers, 157–158
    rules for, 158

Telephone Game, 120

tellers. *See* bank tellers

temperament, 30

templates, 151

temporary work, 82

tenants, 296

testimonial advertising technique, 290

tests
    drug tests, 179–180, 214
    employment tests, 179

text messaging, 124

textiles, 248

texting, 124

thank-you notes
    contacting potential employers, 160
    sending after job interviews, 200–201

theatre arts assistant professor, 286

things, 93

thinking skills (SCANS skills), 38

thought patterns, men versus women, 329

time management, 119, 136–138
    balanced life, 340
    fulfilling your dreams, 349–351
    SCANS skills, 38
    technology, 139

timeline, problem-solving styles, 54

tool setting careers, 169

tracking
    activities/responsibilities, 16–17
    spending, 276–277

trade schools. *See* CTE schools

tradeoffs, 353

traditional learning style, 32

traffic technicians (O*NET database summary), 81

training. *See* education levels

training managers, 292

transcripts, 172

translators, 15

transferable skills, 36–37

transfering, 105

transit (ABA) number, 266

transitions. *See* personal transitions

transmission of bloodborne infections, preventing, 214

transportation careers, 148, 160

transportation options, 299–303
    buying a vehicle, 300–301
    maintaining a vehicle, 301–302

traveling to job interviews, 194

trends, 244

troubleshooting (SCANS skills), 38

truck drivers, 148, 155

trustworthiness, 171

Truth in Lending Act, 274

tuition, 104

## U

unadvertised job openings, 153

unemployment rate and education levels, 95

uninsured motorist insurance, 306

unions, 203

unit prices, 310

universal precautions, 214

universities, 104–106
    admissions requirements for, 109

U.S. Department of Health, 308

U.S. Department of Labor, 212
    Web site, 80

U.S. Office of Personnel Management (OPM), 155

U.S. savings bonds, 269

## V

values, 40–41
    dreams as reflection of, 354–355
    evaluating careers, 96
    money values, 281
    selecting who to date, 324

Vault, 154

vehicles
    buying, 300–301
    maintaining, 301–302

verbal communication, 121
    active listening, 125–126
    during job interview, 198
    reading, 127–128
    speaking, 121–125
    writing, 126–127

verbal intelligence, 32

veterans appreciation party, 359

veterinarians, 15, 60, 95

veterinary technologists and technicians, 95

video activities, 13

video interviews, 154

video games, careers using, 33

video resumes, 154

visiting in person, contacting potential employers, 158–159

visualizing (SCANS skills), 38

vocational school instructors, 272

vocational schools. *See* CTE schools

voice inflection, 122

voice mail messages, 124–125

volunteering, 83
    career spotlight, 111
    community activity, 82
    Internet research, 85

voting as civic responsibility, 250–251

## W

W-2 tax forms, 264

W-4 tax forms, 263

wage discrimination, 221

wage requirements on job applications, 177

wages, 148
    calculating, 262
    of electricians, 129
    job searches, 148

Waldron, Eileen, 19

want ads. *See* classified ads

wants versus needs, 279

warm contacts, 152

warranties, 278

water transportation careers, 148, 158

Web sites, U.S. Department of Labor, 80

webcams, 154

weddings, 333, 335–336

welding careers, 169, 175, 178

well-groomed, 193

wellness
    attitude, 192
    balance, 77
    benefits of exercise, 296
    change, 54
    dating abuse, 330
    disorganization, 18
    feeling left out, 125
    getting help, 356
    good citizenship, 245
    healthy relationships, 336
    ongoing stress, 27

responsibility for self, 224
self-acceptance, 97
self-concept, 151
self-esteem, 35
worrying, 176, 288
"what do you want to do with your time?", 349–351
"what do you want to own?", 351–352
*When You Marry*, 336
whistle blowing, 218
White Pages, 153
"who do you want to be?", 348–349
"who do you want to have in your life?", 352–353
Wild, Peggy, 282
win-win solution, 130
windfalls, 281
women's salaries versus men's salaries, 222, 266
women's thinking versus men's thinking, 329
woodworking careers, 169, 178, 180
word-processing activities, 13, 65
work assignments, helping with, 124
work attire, 172
work environment, 84, 96
work ethics, 218–219
work life, balancing with personal and family life, 340–341
work permits, 181–182
work responsibilities (accepting job offer), 202

work-study programs, 104
Workers' Compensation, 212
working hours, 97, 148, 202
workplace competencies (SCANS skills), 38
workplace issues
    accepting criticism, 227
    conflict resolution, 228–230
    diversity, 219–223
    ethics, 218–219
    extra responsibilities, 225
    health and safety, 212–216
    learning opportunities in entry-level jobs, 216–218
    performance evaluations, 223–224
    problem solving, 226–230
workplace skills, 119
    communication, 120–129
    leadership, 134–135
    teamwork, 130–134
    time management, 136–138
world-wise view, 5–6
    obtaining, 14–16
worrying, 176, 268
Wright brothers, 246
writing, 126–127
    contacting potential employers, 159–160
    cover letters, 171–172
    resumes, 168–170

writing assignments
    budget, 317
    career research, 88
    co-workers and workplace issues, 141
    cover letter and resume, 185
    "day in the life" description, 363
    electronic banking, 285
    letter of application, 164
    letter to Senator or Representative, 257
    personal traits for marriage, 344
    personality description, 47
    problem solving, 67
    sexual harassment, 233
    skills for success, 21
    thank-you notes, 207
    volunteering, 113
writing skills (SCANS skills), 38

# X–Z

Yahoo! Messenger, 130
Yellow Pages, 153
*Young Person's Guide to Getting & Keeping a Good Job*, 146, 150
yourself, taking care of, 224
YouTube, 154
zookeepers, 65. *See also* animal caretakers
zoology careers, 59